The Politics

Why was the Eurozone crisis so diffi   a manner in which some countries bore a much larger share of the pain than other countries? Why did no country leave the Eurozone rather than implement unprecedented austerity? Who supported and opposed the different policy options in the crisis domestically, and how did the distributive struggles among these groups shape crisis politics?

Building on macro-level statistical data, original survey data from interest groups, and qualitative comparative case studies, this book argues and shows that the answers to these questions revolve around distributive struggles about how the costs of the Eurozone crisis should be divided among countries, and within countries, among different socioeconomic groups. Together with divergent but strongly held ideas about the 'right way' to conduct economic policy and asymmetries in the distribution of power among actors, severe distributive concerns of important actors lie at the root of the difficulties of resolving the Eurozone crisis as well as the difficulties to substantially reform EMU. The book provides new insights into the politics of the Eurozone crisis by emphasizing three perspectives that have received scant attention in existing research: a comparative perspective on the Eurozone crisis by systematically comparing it to previous financial crises, an analysis of the whole range of policy options, including the ones not chosen, and a unified framework that examines crisis politics not just in deficit-debtor, but also in surplus-creditor countries.

The Politics of Bad Options

Why the Eurozone's Problems Have Been So Hard to Resolve

STEFANIE WALTER, ARI RAY, AND NILS REDEKER

Great Clarendon Street, Oxford, OX2 6DP,
United Kingdom

Oxford University Press is a department of the University of Oxford.
It furthers the University's objective of excellence in research, scholarship,
and education by publishing worldwide. Oxford is a registered trade mark of
Oxford University Press in the UK and in certain other countries

© Stefanie Walter, Ari Ray, and Nils Redeker 2020
© Chapter 2: Raphael Reinke, Stefanie Walter, Ari Ray, and Nils Redeker 2020
© Chapter 5: Raphael Reinke, Nils Redeker, Stefanie Walter, and Ari Ray 2020

The moral rights of the authors have been asserted

First Edition published in 2020

Impression: 1

All rights reserved. No part of this publication may be reproduced, stored in
a retrieval system, or transmitted, in any form or by any means, without the
prior permission in writing of Oxford University Press, or as expressly permitted
by law, by licence or under terms agreed with the appropriate reprographics
rights organization. Enquiries concerning reproduction outside the scope of the
above should be sent to the Rights Department, Oxford University Press, at the
address above

You must not circulate this work in any other form
and you must impose this same condition on any acquirer

Published in the United States of America by Oxford University Press
198 Madison Avenue, New York, NY 10016, United States of America

British Library Cataloguing in Publication Data

Data available

Library of Congress Control Number: 2020945882

ISBN 978-0-19-885701-3 (hbk.)
978-0-19-885702-0 (pbk.)

DOI: 10.1093/oso/9780198857013.001.0001

Printed and bound in Great Britain by
Clays Ltd, Elcograf S.p.A.

Links to third party websites are provided by Oxford in good faith and
for information only. Oxford disclaims any responsibility for the materials
contained in any third party website referenced in this work.

To

Jörn, Nils and Lukas
Toton, Khoka, Reeju and Dadu Bhai
Uschi and Winni

Acknowledgments

The Eurozone crisis has been the most severe economic and financial crisis in the European Union's history. It has shaken Europe's economy to the core, brought the monetary union to the brink of collapse and left the continent economically and politically vulnerable until today. It created severe political conflicts both among the member states of the common currency and within the societies of these member states, and helped pave the way for the rise of Eurosceptic parties across the EU. The crisis proved very difficult to resolve, and some of the underlying problems in the Eurozone that contributed to the outbreak of the crisis remain unresolved to this day.

This book argues and shows that distributive struggles about how the costs of the Eurozone crisis should be divided among countries, and among organized interest groups and voters within countries, made crisis resolution so difficult. Together with divergent but strongly held ideas about the "right way" to conduct economic policy and asymmetries in the distribution of power among actors, severe distributive concerns of important actors lie at the root of the difficulties of resolving the Eurozone crisis as well as the difficulties to substantially reform European Monetary Union (EMU). As is so often the case, the core problem hindering a swift and easy solution of the crisis was politics. Building on a vast amount of macro-level statistics, original survey data, and case studies, the book sheds new light on the history of the crisis and provides crucial lessons for the way forward.

Despite the crisis' importance, it is legitimate to wonder whether we need yet another book on the Eurozone crisis. Our answer is that our book complements the many insightful existing studies in three ways. First, our book puts the Eurozone crisis in a comparative perspective, both in theoretical and empirical terms. It provides a theoretical framework for this endeavor and is the first major study to quantitatively examine the Eurozone crisis in comparison to earlier crises and episodes of sustained current account surpluses. By teasing out the particularities of the Eurozone crisis, the book thus situates the Eurozone crisis in the context of other financial crises that required balance-of-payment adjustment and the problem of global imbalances more generally. On this basis, we can identify in what respects the Eurozone crisis is similar to other crises, and in which respects the Eurozone crisis is unique.

Second, our book examines the political dynamics and key policy decisions that shaped the management of the Euro crisis with a focus on the whole range of policy options, including the ones not chosen, and the trade-offs these policy options entail. This approach means taking seriously the whole range of—often bad—options and not considering policy choices in isolation, but rather in the context of the—often difficult—trade-offs they pose. For this purpose, the book presents original and detailed survey data from about 700 European interest groups on these issues. It uses this data to perform a fine-grained analysis of interest groups' preferences on a large range of policies that explores in detail how vulnerable domestic economic and social interest groups in the Eurozone were to different crisis strategies, which types of policies they preferred, and how they assessed the difficult trade-offs that the crisis presented them with. Our book thus contributes to our understanding of the crisis by underlining the importance of considering policy alternatives, actors' vulnerabilities to each of these (often bad) options, and the trade-offs they entail: The unusual trajectory of the Eurozone crisis becomes less puzzling if we consider that for the deficit-debtor countries, the alternatives to unprecedented austerity was Eurozone breakup and possibly default, an outcome that most actors opposed even more.

Third, our book provides an encompassing and unified framework for analyzing crisis politics not just in deficit-debtor, but also in surplus-creditor countries, which shows that the distributive struggles surrounding the politics of the Eurozone crisis in surplus and deficit countries are distinct, yet they also revolve around common themes and are intricately linked. This allows for a better understanding of the interdependencies and dynamics of crisis politics in the Eurozone.

Overall, the book thus provides new insights into the political dynamics and constraints underlying some of the key policy decisions that shaped the management of the Euro crisis by providing a comparative analysis, new data, and insights into surplus country politics based on a unified theoretical framework. The datasets used in the book, particularly the survey data on interest group preferences, will moreover provide a rich resource for anyone interested in European politics, interest groups, and political economy.

Our book is a collaborative piece of work that presents the main findings from Stefanie Walter's research project on "Distributional conflicts and the politics of adjustment in the Eurozone crisis," generously funded by the Swiss National Science Foundation (grant number 100017_156574). The book is co-authored by Stefanie Walter, the project's principle investigator, and two members of the project team, Ari Ray and Nils Redeker, who not only made important contributions to the research project, but also wrote their doctoral dissertations in the context of the project. Stefanie developed the book's theoretical framework, and was heavily involved both in designing the research strategies for all parts of the project and in writing and editing the chapters of this book. Ari's research focus has been on crisis politics in deficit countries, and she is the main author of Chapters 3 and 4. Nils has predominantly worked on surplus countries and is the main author of Chapters 5 and 6, as well as co-author of Chapter 4. A fourth member of the project team, Raphael Reinke, has co-authored the two macro-level analyses in this book (Chapters 2 and 5), but opted out of being a co-author after his new job outside academia left him little time for the book.

Writing this book would not have been possible without the support of many people. Raphael Reinke was a great mentor for Ari and Nils, coordinated much of the early work on the project, and provided much feedback on their dissertation and chapter ideas. Rafaela Catena, Clint Claessens, Anastasios Gkiokas, Benjamin Kilchherr, Céline Neuenschwander, Reto Mitteregger, Lisa Rogenmoser, and Alex Roth provided excellent research assistance over the years. At various stages of the project, we have benefitted from comments and questions by Klaus Armingeon, Lucio Baccaro, Daniel Bischof, Björn Bremer, Loriana Crasnic, Adam Dean, Hanno Degner, Donato Di Carlo, Fabio Franchino, Jeff Frieden, Juliet Johnson, Lukas Haffert, Silja Häusermann, Eve Hübscher, Martin Höpner, Valentin Lang, David Leblang, Alexis Lubow, Hannes Malmberg, Jonas Markgraf, Michael Marsh (who also supported our book project by sharing his data), Gemma Mateo, Nadja Mosimann, Stefan Müller, Clara Neupert-Wentz, Tabea Palmtag, Amy Pond, Jonas Pontusson, Tobias Rommel, Tal Sadeh, Thomas Sattler, Lena Schaffer, Waltraud Schelkle, Sebastian Schneider, Tomasz Siczek, David Soskice, Wolfgang Streeck, Kathleen Thelen, Denise Traber, and David Woodruff.

We also received valuable feedback from many participants at conferences and workshops at which we presented parts of the book manuscript: The 2015 APSA annual meeting in San Francisco, the 2016 meetings of the DVPW in Heidelberg, the European Graduate Network in Budapest, and the ISA in Atlanta, the 2016 SNIS conference on "Political and Economic Inequality: Concepts, Causes, and Consequences," the 2017 annual meetings of SPSA in Sankt Gallen and the MPSA in Chicago, the 2017 CUSO PhD workshop on "Comparative Capitalisms" in Nyon, the 2017 CIS Graduate Workshop in Castasegna, the 2017 International Relations Seminar at Harvard University, the 2017 EMUChoices workshop in Rome, the 2018 "One Crisis, many Perspectives: Understanding the Politics of the Eurozone Crisis" Workshop, the 2019 Dreiländertagung in Zurich, and the 2019 Institute of European Politics meeting in Berlin. The audiences at presentations of the full book manuscript at the Max Planck Institute for the study of societies in Cologne and the London School of Economics additionally provided valuable feedback.

Our editor at Oxford University Press, Dominic Byatt, has patiently accompanied the writing process and has been positive about and supportive of the project from the start. Two anonymous reviewers made many helpful suggestions based on a careful reading of our work, which significantly strengthened this manuscript. We are particularly indebted to the many interviewees who agreed to patiently answer our questions, share their insights into the actual working of crisis politics, and in doing so provided us with a much more detailed understanding of the distributive conflicts and considerations shaping the Eurozone crisis.

Stefanie Walter thanks her colleagues at the Institute of Political Science for providing a stimulating, challenging and always friendly and supportive research environment. Silja Häusermann in particular has been a source of encouragement, input, and advice from the start. Special thanks go to my IPE and CPE colleagues for inspiration, heated debates, and insights into Eurozone crisis politics. Mark Copelovitch, Jeff Frieden, and I co-organized an early workshop on the euro crisis, from which our co-edited special issue on "The Political Economy of the Eurozone Crisis" in *Comparative Political Studies* emerged. The discussions surrounding these projects have broadened my understanding of the crisis, crisis politics, and the politics of adjustment. Jeff and I co-authored two additional pieces on Eurozone crisis politics. One of them, a piece in the *Annual Review of Political Science* summarizes some of the core ideas presented in this book, and I thank Jeff for allowing us to reuse some of the materials covered in this review in this book's introduction. As always, co-authoring with Jeff has been a great pleasure, not just because of his sharp observations and probing questions, his insistence on getting it right, but also because we share a certain sense of humor (also, Jeff has been the first co-author to introduce me to underground archeological catacombs in Rome, but that is another story). Lila Ziegler, Neli Razzaghinejad, and Sarah Shepard deserve many thanks for helping me to navigate the organizational challenges involved in writing such a book. The staff at Kafi Schnaps, especially Jenny, Isabel, Luca, and Peter, deserve great thanks for making my "second office" such a welcoming, productive, and happy place, where I can get my writing done best. Most importantly, I would like to thank my family. Without their love, patience, and support, I would not be where I am today. My husband Jörn has not only been willing to discuss Eurozone and financial crisis issues with me for the last decade, but has also patiently endured my reports on the many detours, dead ends, and little triumphs that such a project entails. I am incredibly grateful to him for being there for me. My sons Nils and Lukas don't really care about the Eurozone crisis, but remind me every day of what really counts in life. They are the greatest gift of all.

Ari Ray thanks her friends and colleagues in Zurich, Florence and beyond. I worked on this book throughout my doctoral studies, during which I was fortunate to benefit from the help and advice of many people. I am deeply grateful for the time they took to support me in my academic endeavors. In particular, my work improved substantially from discussions in Zurich with Lukas Haffert, Julian Garritzmann, Tobias Rommel, and Lukas Stötzer. And Chandreyee Namhata and Su Yun Woo were quick to make me cups of chai during those inevitable moments when progress sooner felt remote. Both Anastasios Gkiokas and Alex Roth provided us with excellent research assistance, by doing everything from editing surveys and collecting data, to real-time translation during interviews undertaken in Athens and Madrid: I fondly recall a number of funny moments from those trips. I am also deeply indebted to Mike Tomz, who invited me to spend nine wonderful months at Stanford. During my time there, I exchanged so many ideas with inquisitive and motivated people. I particularly enjoyed talks with Nathan Lee, Hannes Malmberg, William Marble, and Clara Neupert-Wentz. I undertook the final stages of writing in Italy, surrounded by a number of supportive and inspiring colleagues at the European University Institute in Florence. I am particularly happy to have found such great confidantes there in Lola Avril, Meira Gold, and Lachlan McNamee—and a great mentor in Elias Dinas. Lastly, the biggest debts of gratitude I owe to my brilliant parents, who enabled me to become the inquisitive person that I am today. And to my baby brother Aniket, the kindest sibling one could ever have.

Nils Redeker thanks his peers and colleagues at the Institute for Political Science. Large parts of my contributions to this book are based on two chapters of my dissertation and I could not have wished for a more supportive, inspiring, open, and motivating academic home to work on them during the last years. In particular, I want to thank Tabea Palmtag, Raphael Reinke, and Tobias Rommel, for the myriad ways in which they supported my chapters and the impressive patience with which they endured my daily trips for advice into their offices, especially in the beginning of this project. Special thanks also go to Lukas Haffert for sharing my interest in surpluses of any kind. Lukas' countless comments, questions, and suggestions have substantially improved Chapters 6 and 7 of this book. I am especially grateful to Silja Häusermann and Jeff Frieden who both served on my dissertation committee. Silja has greatly supported and encouraged me along the way and I was extremely lucky to have had her supervising my work on this book. Jeff kindly invited me to do some of the research linked to my chapters at Harvard and his eye-opening comments and passion to get to the bottom of things will remain a lasting source of inspiration. Jeff's flexibility and unmatched physical stamina also were a main reason for why I was able to defend my dissertation on time despite some self-inflicted administrative bumps along the road (but that too is another story). I also want to thank Alex Roth for his outstanding research assistance in the collection of our survey data. The stoic friendliness with which he was able to charm interest group representatives into filling out our questionnaire in three different languages is one of the main reasons we had data to work with. Most importantly, I want to thank my parents. Without their encouragement I would not have started the dissertation that led to my chapters in this book and without their steadfast support, optimism, belief in me and alarmingly strong reviewer competencies, I probably would not have finished it. My last and most wholehearted thanks go to Charlotte. I could not have happily worked on this book without her support, humor and friendship and I am deeply grateful for her ability to know better than I do when to take me seriously and when not to.

Table of Contents

List of Figures   xvii
List of Tables   xxi

1. Introduction: Bad Options and Difficult Choices in the Eurozone Crisis   1
   - A Short Primer on the Eurozone Crisis   4
   - The Unequal Distribution of Crisis-Resolution Costs   12
   - Bad Options, Difficult Choices   17
   - The Argument in Brief   22
   - Plan of the Book   27
     - Putting the Eurozone Crisis in Context: Country-Level Vulnerability Profiles   27
     - Interest Group Vulnerability Profile and Crisis Resolution Preferences   28
     - Crisis Politics   29
   - Conclusion   31

2. Putting the Eurozone Crisis Experience in Perspective   33
   - The Argument: Vulnerability Profiles and Crisis Responses   36
     - Weighing Bad Options: The Potential Costs of External and Internal Adjustment   38
     - The Relative Costs of Adjustment: Vulnerability Profiles and Policy Responses   41
   - Research Design   43
     - Sample Selection: Identifying Balance-of-Payment Crises   43
     - Operationalization: Vulnerability Profiles   45
   - How is the Euro Crisis Different? Putting the Eurozone Crisis in Context   50
   - The 1992 EMS Crisis and the Eurozone Crisis   53
   - The 1997 Asian Financial Crisis and the Eurozone Crisis   55
   - Eastern European Responses to the 2008/9 Global Financial Crisis and the Eurozone Crisis   57
   - Crisis Dynamics: Changing Vulnerabilities in the Eurozone Crisis   59
   - Conclusion   61
   - Appendix   62

3. Distributive Conflict and Interest Group Preferences in Deficit Countries   66
   - Interest Groups and Deficit Country Policymaking   68
   - Group-Specific Adjustment Preferences in Eurozone Deficit Countries   71

Interest Group Vulnerability to External Adjustment	71
Interest Group Vulnerability to Internal Adjustment	72
Group-Specific Vulnerability Profiles and Preferred Crisis Resolution Strategies	74
Research Design	76
Case Selection	77
Interest Group Survey: Sampling and Design	77
Structure of the Analysis	79
Policy-Specific Preferences on Eurozone Crisis Management	80
Preferences about Overall Crisis Management Strategies	80
External Adjustment Policies	81
Internal Adjustment Policies	83
Financing Policies	88
Vulnerability Profiles and Preferred Eurozone Crisis Management Strategies	90
Vulnerability Profiles of Deficit Country Interest Groups	90
Vulnerability Profiles and Evaluations of Crisis Strategies	93
Choosing Among Bad Options: Preferred Crisis Management Strategies in Trade-Off Situations	96
Vulnerability Profiles and Preferred Adjustment Strategies	99
Conclusion: From Adjustment Preferences to Adjustment Policies	102
Appendix	104
4. Crisis Politics in Deficit Countries	**108**
Ireland in Crisis	111
Policies and Conflict Lines Surrounding External Adjustment in Ireland	114
Policies and Conflict Lines Surrounding Internal Adjustment in Ireland	115
Policies and Conflict Lines Surrounding Financing in Ireland	120
Crisis Politics in Ireland: Conclusion	122
Spain in Crisis	122
Policies and Conflict Lines Surrounding External Adjustment in Spain	125
Policies and Conflict Lines Surrounding Internal Adjustment in Spain	126
Policies and Conflict Lines Surrounding Financing in Spain	130
Crisis Politics in Spain: Conclusion	132
Greece in Crisis	132
Policies and Conflict Lines Surrounding External Adjustment in Greece	135
Policies and Conflict Lines Surrounding Internal Adjustment in Greece	137
Policies and Conflict Lines Surrounding Financing in Greece	143
Crisis Politics in Greece: Conclusion	147
Conclusion	147
Appendix	149

5. Surplus Country Vulnerability to Rebalancing:
   A Comparative Analysis ... 150
   Introduction ... 150
   Surplus Country Preferences and National Interests in the
     Eurozone Crisis ... 154
   Vulnerability Profiles—Concept and Argument ... 155
   Weighing Bad Options: Vulnerabilities to External and
     Internal Adjustment ... 158
   Research Design ... 159
     Sample Selection: Identifying Surplus Countries during
       Balance-of-Payments Crises ... 160
     Operationalization: Vulnerability Profiles ... 161
   Creating the Cost Indexes Using PCA ... 164
   Vulnerability Profiles of Surplus Countries in the Eurozone Crisis ... 167
   Vulnerability Profiles of Non-Eurozone Surplus Countries
     during the Eurozone Crisis ... 169
   Vulnerability Profiles of Surplus Countries in the 1992/3 EMS Crisis ... 170
   Conclusion ... 171

6. Distributive Conflict and Interest Group Preferences in
   Surplus Countries ... 172
   Domestic Trade-Offs, Vulnerability Profiles, and Adjustment
     in Surplus Countries ... 175
   Research Design: Studying Interest Group Preferences in Surplus
     Countries ... 179
   Policy-Specific Preferences on Eurozone Crisis Management ... 182
     External Adjustment Preferences ... 185
     Internal Adjustment Preferences ... 187
     Financing Preferences ... 190
   Material Interests and Policy Preferences ... 190
   Policy Salience ... 195
   Trade-Offs and Difficult Choices between External Adjustment,
     Internal Adjustment, and Financing ... 197
   Vulnerability Profiles and Preferred Crisis Responses ... 200
   Conclusion ... 204

7. Crisis Politics in Surplus Countries: Caught between
   Voter Pressure and Interest Group Stalemate ... 206
   Voter Preferences about How to Resolve the Eurozone Crisis ... 208
     External Adjustment: Surplus Country Voters and a Breakup
       of the Eurozone ... 209
     Internal Adjustment: Public Opinion on Domestic Rebalancing ... 212
     Financing: Public Opinion on Financial Transfers to Deficit States ... 214

Diverging Preferences: Public Opinion and Interest Group
  Preferences in the Euro Crisis ... 216
Voters, Interest Groups, and Eurozone Crisis Politics in
  Surplus Countries ... 217
Eurozone Crisis Politics in Germany, Austria, and the Netherlands ... 221
Not an Option: External Adjustment ... 223
The Vocal Politics of Financing in Surplus Countries ... 225
Context Matters: The Politics of Internal Adjustment ... 229
  Germany ... 229
  Austria ... 234
  The Netherlands ... 237
  Internal Adjustment in Eurozone Surplus Countries ... 240
Conclusion ... 241
Appendix ... 242

8. Conclusion ... 244
Three New Perspectives on the Eurozone Crisis ... 245
  What's So Special? Analyzing the Eurozone Crisis in a
    Comparative Perspective ... 245
  Examining the Road not Traveled: Policy Alternatives
    and Trade-Offs ... 246
  Looking at Both Sides of the Coin: Crisis Politics in Both
    Deficit-Debtor and Surplus-Creditor Countries ... 249
The Politics of Bad Options in European Crisis Management ... 250
  Research Design ... 251
  Eurozone Crisis Bargaining between Deficit-Debtor and
    Surplus-Creditor States ... 253
Policy Implications and Avenues for Future Research ... 256
Appendix ... 259

Bibliography ... 261
Index ... 295

List of Figures

1.1	Eurozone current account imbalances before and after the outbreak of the Eurozone crisis	5
1.2a	Creditor country bank claims on deficit countries	8
1.2b	Creditor country bank claims on Greece	9
1.3a	Varieties of adjustment. Deficit and surplus countries in the Eurozone crisis: Fiscal reform	14
1.3b	Varieties of adjustment. Deficit and surplus countries in the Eurozone crisis: Current account	15
1.4	Crisis cost for selected Eurozone countries	15
1.5	Classification of vulnerability profiles and preferred policy response	24
2.1	Vulnerability profiles and expected crisis responses	41
2.2	Vulnerability profiles of the Eurozone crisis countries and all other crisis episodes	51
2.3	Vulnerability profiles in the 1992 EMS and the Eurozone crises	54
2.4	Vulnerability profiles in the Asian financial and the Eurozone crises	56
2.5	Eastern European states in 2008 and the Eurozone crisis	58
2.6	Current accounts and vulnerability profiles of Eurozone crisis countries, 2007–14	60
3.1	Vulnerability profiles and preferred crisis responses	75
3.2	Aggregate interest group characteristics per country: population vs. respondent sample	79
3.3	Evaluations of different crisis strategies in Ireland, Spain, and Greece	81
3.4	Interest group evaluations of different Eurozone break-up scenarios	83
3.5	Interest group evaluations of different austerity measures	86
3.6	Interest group evaluations of different structural reform proposals	87
3.7	Interest group evaluations of different financing measures	89
3.8	Distribution of vulnerability profiles in Ireland, Spain, and Greece	92
3.9	Results of OLS regression models on absolute adjustment strategy preferences	94
3.10	Choice between customized internal and external adjustment packages	96
3.11	Choices between external and internal adjustment packages	97
3.12	Group vulnerability profiles and preferred adjustment strategies	99
3.13	Vulnerability profiles and preferred adjustment strategy	101

A3.1	Results of OLS regression models on absolute financing policy preferences	105
4.1	A timeline of crisis-time governments in Ireland, Spain, and Greece	110
4.2	A timeline of government bond interest rate differentials and key events in the Irish crisis (2007–16)	113
4.3	Irish vs. EMU country average public support for the euro, 2005–16	115
4.4	Irish voter attitudes toward level of spending across policy areas	117
4.5	Public support of sovereign bailouts and defaults in Ireland (2011)	121
4.6	A timeline of government bond interest rate differentials and key events in the Spanish crisis	124
4.7	Spanish public opinion on euro vs. returning to national currency	125
4.8	Spanish voter attitudes toward level of spending across policy areas	128
4.9	A timeline of government bond interest rate differentials and key events in the Greek crisis (2007–16)	134
4.10	Greek public opinion on euro vs. returning to national currency	136
4.11	Greek voter attitudes toward level of spending across policy areas	139
4.12	Public support of sovereign bailouts and defaults in Greece (Nov. 2012–Feb. 2013)	145
5.1	Countries with periods of sustained current account surpluses (defined as a surplus of more than 3% of GDP which is sustained for at least 3 years) since 1980	151
5.2	Vulnerability profiles and crisis response for surplus countries	157
5.3	Vulnerability profiles of the Eurozone surplus countries compared to other episodes with sustained current account surpluses	165
5.4	Vulnerability profiles of the European surplus countries at the outset of the Eurozone crisis	166
5.5	Vulnerability profiles in the 1992 EMS and the Eurozone crises	166
6.1	Policy-specific vulnerability profiles to internal adjustment	177
6.2	Net international investment positions and average growth rates for Eurozone surplus countries	180
6.3	Average policy evaluations for the three possible crisis strategies	185
6.4	Interest group evaluations of different Eurozone breakup scenarios	186
6.5	Interest group evaluations of internal adjustment policies	188
6.6	Interest group evaluations of different forms of financing	191
6.7	Effect of the interest groups' material exposure on their policy evaluations	194
6.8a	Share of indifferent policy positions by crisis strategy	195
6.8b	Salience of different crisis resolution strategies	196
6.9	Customized construction of choice set for the three different crisis strategies	198

6.10	Choice between most-preferred (left) and least-preferred (right) crisis strategies	199
6.11	Vulnerability profiles for highest-ranked (left) and lowest-ranked (right) policies	201
6.12	Predicted probabilities of choosing internal adjustment and financing at different levels of vulnerability toward internal adjustment	204
7.1	Overall evaluation of the euro between 2013 and 2015	209
7.2	Should crisis countries remain in the Eurozone? Responses from Germany	211
7.3	Public opinion on various forms of internal adjustment in Germany	212
7.4	Public opinion on various forms of internal adjustment in Austria	213
7.5	Public opinion on various forms of internal adjustment in the Netherlands	213
7.6	Public opinion on financing	215
7.7a	Macroeconomic developments in Germany	230
7.7b	Salience of economic issues for German voters	230
7.8a	Macroeconomic developments in Austria	235
7.8b	Salience of economic issues for Austrian voters	235
7.9a	Macroeconomic developments in the Netherlands	238
7.9b	Salience of economic issues for Dutch voters	238
8.1	Negotiation positions of Eurozone countries on adjustment issues, by countries' average pre-crisis current account balance	254
8.2	Negotiation positions of Eurozone countries on financing issues, by countries' average pre-crisis current account balance	255

List of Tables

1.1	Policy options to resolve balance of payments imbalances	18
2.1	Indicators measuring the national vulnerabilities to internal and external adjustment	46
2.2	PCA results for deficit countries	49
A2.1	Crisis episodes identified using the EMP index	62
3.1	External adjustment scenarios in the Eurozone	82
3.2	Internal adjustment policies in Eurozone deficit countries	84
3.3	Financing policies in Eurozone deficit countries	89
3.4	Survey items used to operationalize interest group vulnerability profiles	91
A3.1	OLS regression results—absolute preferences toward adjustment strategies	104
A3.2	OLS regression results—absolute preferences toward financing policies	106
A3.3	Logit regressions on relative adjustment preferences: likelihood of preferring Eurozone exit (1) to an internal adjustment package (0)	107
A4.1	List of interview partners	149
5.1	Indicator operationalization for surplus countries	162
5.2	PCA results for surplus countries	164
6.1	Policy options by crisis strategy	183
6.2	Probit regression—vulnerabilities and likelihood of choosing adjustment strategies	203
7.1	Voter and interest group preferences on crisis strategies	217
A7.I	List of interview partners	242
8.1	Eurozone country bargaining positions on policy issues regarding adjustment	252
8.2	Eurozone country bargaining positions on policy issues regarding financing	252
A8.1	Other Eurozone crisis policy issues	259

1
Introduction
Bad Options and Difficult Choices in the Eurozone Crisis

The Eurozone crisis began in late 2009. It followed in the wake of the global financial crisis and quickly developed into one of the most serious economic and political crises in the history of the European Union (EU). Nonetheless, after a decade of unsuccessful attempts to resolve the fundamental structural and institutional issues that underlie the Eurozone's problems, a long-term reform that addresses these problems remains elusive (Mody 2018). Although no country so far has seriously entertained the idea of leaving the Eurozone, the monetary union's problems are far from resolved. The dominant approach has been to force the countries hit hardest by the Eurozone crisis to implement unprecedented austerity. These policies have resulted in a huge loss in confidence in national governments (Foster and Frieden 2017; Kriesi 2012), the EU (Hobolt 2015; Hobolt and de Vries 2016a), and democracy more generally (Armingeon and Guthmann 2014; Cramme and Hobolt 2014; Streeck and Schäfer 2013), and they have helped pave the way for the rise of Eurosceptic parties across the Eurozone (Bellucci et al. 2012; Kriesi and Pappas 2015; Usherwood and Startin 2013). Despite these fundamental challenges, no consensus about how to fundamentally reform the monetary union has emerged (for a review, see Sadeh 2018). Although the EU has of late been battling with other crises as well, the unresolved problems of the Eurozone remain the Union's Achilles' heel.

The inability or unwillingness of Eurozone governments to change course in their attempts to resolve the Eurozone's problems is particularly puzzling because the European approach to resolving the crisis has been very unusual. The Eurozone crisis is in its essence both a classic debt and balance-of-payments (BOP) crisis, caused by huge imbalances in capital and trade flows (Baldwin et al. 2015; Lane 2013; Wihlborg et al. 2010). Such crises are costly: Debts have to be repaid or written off to address the debt problem, and macroeconomic policies have to be adjusted to prevent a further build-up of debts in the future. This means that not just the problem of the stock of debts has to be resolved, but also the flow problem, because debts owed to foreign actors usually accumulate in the wake of an extended period of current account deficits which by definition also imply a capital account deficit (both are contained as mirror images in the balance of payments). Countries with current account deficits thus not only import more goods and services than they export, but also experience net capital inflows. Debtor countries therefore need to reduce not just the accumulated debts but also their current account deficit; they do so by implementing austerity and other measures to reduce spending, repay their debts, reduce imports, and stimulate exports. These adjustments become necessary irrespective of whether the crisis was predominantly caused by financial flows or by flows of goods and services.

In contrast, creditor countries are often characterized by current account and capital account surpluses,[1] which means that they export more goods and capital than they import and therefore build up financial claims in the deficit countries. These countries can contribute to crisis-resolution costs by agreeing to restructure or even write-off debts and by creating new export opportunities for debtor countries via a boost in domestic demand in their own economies (Frieden 2015b). Usually, debtor and creditor countries share these crisis resolution costs, even though the weaker bargaining position of debtor countries means that they usually pay a larger share of these costs (Dyson 2014; Eichengreen 1991).

In contrast with other debt and BOP crises, the political conflicts about sharing the burden of crisis resolution in the Eurozone crisis have played themselves out in unusual ways. Although the crisis happened in the context of a close economic and political union, whose members are highly interdependent, the amount of burden sharing has been surprisingly small. One set of countries, mostly the creditor countries and those states with large current account surpluses, has been exceptionally successful in shifting most of the crisis resolution burden onto the debtor states mired in crisis. While debtor states were forced to implement austerity measures and structural reforms that were almost unprecedented in scale, surplus countries did not significantly adjust their economic policies. When compared with other financial crises, it is particularly unusual that surplus countries agreed only to minimal debt relief and debt restructuring in the debtor countries, limited to Greece and Cyprus (Zettelmeyer 2018). And although there has been more institutional reform at the European level than one would have thought possible at the outset of the crisis, these reforms neither resolved the Eurozone's fundamental problems nor fostered a more equal distribution of crisis-resolution costs among Eurozone member states (Jones et al. 2016). Instead, creditor countries undersigned huge bailout programs combined with strong conditionality that pushed the crisis countries into deep recessions. This put the burden of crisis resolution almost entirely on the shoulders the debtor states, who implemented austerity packages on a scale unprecedented in Europe (Perez and Matsaganis 2018).

---

[1] Because current account and capital account surpluses and deficits are two sides of the same coin, the convention is to refer only to the current account, even though current account adjustments always implicate changes in the capital account as well.

The costs of crisis resolution in the Eurozone crisis were, thus, borne almost exclusively by indebted deficit countries, whereas the creditor-surplus states did little to share the burden (Copelovitch et al. 2016; Frieden 2015b; Frieden and Walter 2017).[2] This is an unusual outcome, especially since it happened in the unique setting of the European Economic and Monetary Union (EMU), which involves a wide range of economic and political relations among members of a single market and a common currency (Mabbett and Schelkle 2015). Such a setting usually facilitates cooperation (Keohane 1984). One would also expect more burden-sharing because a lasting resolution of the Eurozone crisis is central to the stabilization of the monetary union and, thus, to the future of European integration.[3]

Our book sets out to explain the unusual European crisis experience by examining the politics surrounding the choice of crisis strategies in both debtor-deficit and creditor-surplus countries. Although it is well understood that the structural diversity of the Eurozone is an important cause of the crisis and a major obstacle to its resolution (Hall 2012; Moravcsik 2012; Scharpf 2013; Streeck and Elsässer 2016), what is less well understood is how these structural constraints translate into politics, and particularly, how they affect the political will on the part of policymakers to find a viable long-term solution to the ongoing crisis. Who supports and who opposes different policy options domestically? How do distributive struggles among interest groups and voters, and distributive conflicts both within countries and between countries, shape crisis politics?

This book answers these questions by investigating how the structural characteristics of a diverse set of Eurozone economies have affected the interests of important societal and political actors and how these interests, in turn, have shaped Eurozone crisis management. It argues that as in all debt and balance-of-payment crises, distributive concerns—both within countries and among countries—have shaped the politics of Eurozone crisis resolution.[4] At the international level, creditor countries with current account surpluses have fought with debtor countries with current account deficits over who should implement the policies necessary to reduce the current and capital account imbalances and who should take responsibility for the accumulated debts. Within deficit-debtor and surplus-creditor countries, interest groups and voters have fought to shift the costs of crisis resolution away from themselves. Such contexts make crisis resolution difficult for policymakers, especially if crisis-resolution preferences vary widely. Swift and substantial policy adjustment is easiest when politically influential interest groups clearly favor one type of crisis-resolution strategy. In contrast, in

---

[2] For a discussion of the burden-sharing that did occur, see Schelkle (2017).
[3] There is also a normative argument that can be made for more solidarity (Viehoff 2018).
[4] See, for example, Eichengreen (1996), Frieden (1991a), Nelson (1990), Pepinsky (2009), Simmons (1994), Walter (2013b).

contexts where significant parts of society are vulnerable to any type of reform, crisis politics becomes contentious and much more difficult to resolve.

A better understanding of Eurozone crisis politics thus requires a systematic comprehension of the policy options available to policymakers during the crisis as well as the trade-offs and costs associated with each of these alternative options; and it involves an analysis of how politically influential actors evaluate these policy options on that basis. Our book focuses on the three broad strategies that can be pursued in order to resolve the imbalances underlying much of the Eurozone's problems: Internal adjustment, external adjustment, and financing (such as bailouts or debt relief). It examines the vulnerabilities of deficit-debtor and surplus-creditor country economies to each of these strategies on the macro level and on the level of interest groups, and zooms in on the difficult policy trade-offs that these options entail. Our analyses suggest that surplus-creditor country governments faced strong domestic incentives to push most of the adjustment burden onto deficit countries and to provide external financing in the form of bailout packages to deficit-debtor countries in return. Since deficit-debtor countries mired in crisis were in a weaker position to push adjustment costs onto surplus-creditor countries, they ultimately accepted this crisis-resolution approach. Distributional conflicts in the crisis countries, therefore, revolved mostly around how the cost of adjustment was to be distributed among different societal groups.

Overall, the book explores why the Eurozone crisis proved so difficult to resolve, why adjustment burdens were distributed so unevenly, and why despite all this, no country left the Eurozone during the crisis. As such, it presents a theoretical framework and an analysis that applies broadly to financial crises which require macroeconomic adjustment.

A Short Primer on the Eurozone Crisis

In essence, the Eurozone crisis is a classic combination of a debt and balance-of-payments crisis (Atoyan et al. 2013; Baldwin et al. 2015; Gibson et al. 2014; Higgins and Klitgaard 2014).[5] Countries in the Eurozone borrowed heavily, largely to finance current consumption, as financial institutions in the rest of Europe were eager to lend (Fuller 2018). Capital and goods flowed out of countries with current and capital account surpluses into those countries with current and capital account deficits. In the process, the Eurozone developed large current account imbalances (Iversen and Soskice 2018; Johnston 2016; Johnston et al. 2014). Figure 1.1 shows just how much the current accounts of Eurozone member

---

[5] As discussed above, the two are intimately related: a country running a current account deficit is accumulating debts. This is why countries as diverse as Mexico in 1994, South Korea in 1997, and Lithuania in 2008 experienced both debt and BOP crises.

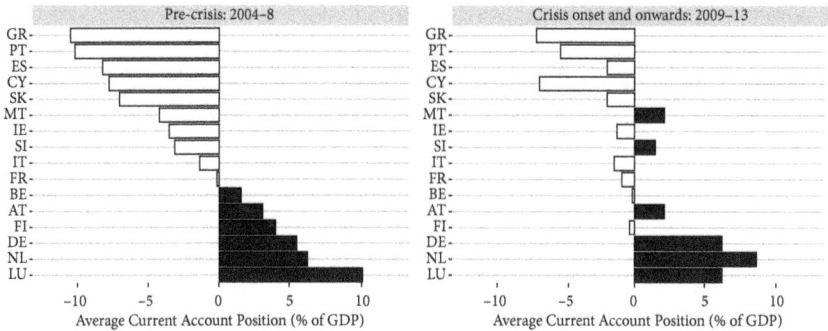

Figure 1.1 Eurozone current account imbalances before and after the outbreak of the Eurozone crisis
Source: Authors' own calculations, based on data from the IMF (2016a).

states diverged: Whereas Greece and Portugal recorded an average current account deficit of more than 10 percent of their GDP per year during the five years leading up to the crisis, Germany and the Netherlands recorded current account surpluses that exceeded 5 percent of their GDP over the same period (IMF 2016a). These surplus countries exported more goods and services than they imported, yet they were simultaneously characterized by considerable capital outflows.[6] The resulting financial flows directed savings from surplus economies into mortgage and construction bubbles in deficit states and, at least partly, financed the build-up of substantial debts in the peripheral Eurozone economies by making credit widely available for these countries (Thompson 2016). In some countries, these debts were concentrated in the private sector (e.g., in Irish banks, firms, and households), in others in the public sector (e.g., in Greece), and in some (e.g., in Portugal), the foreign capital flowed into both the private and public sector (Blyth 2013; Sandbu 2017). Despite these different paths, the capital and current account imbalances produced significant risks both financially and for the real economy (Fuller 2018; Lane and Milesi-Ferretti 2011; Pérez 2019).

This macroeconomic divergence was amplified by three features unique to the Eurozone (Copelovitch et al. 2016). First, because the EMU-wide "no bailout commitment" was not credible, financial markets widely expected that a Eurozone country in financial distress would be bailed out by the other member states. As a result, all member states across the Eurozone could borrow at rates roughly equivalent to those charged to Germany (Chang and Leblond 2015; Ghosh et al. 2013). This made borrowing very cheap. Both private and, to a lesser

---

[6] There is an academic debate about whether the current account drives the capital account, or vice versa, which remains unresolved (Caballero and Krishnamurthy 2009; Claessens et al. 2010; Yan 2007). The most plausible theory is that both dynamics occur simultaneously and usually reinforce each other (Obstfeld and Rogoff 2009). Irrespective of how one classifies the cause of a crisis, however, once the crisis erupts, current account adjustment often becomes a core issue for crisis management.

extent, public actors borrowed heavily, fueling a strong economic expansion and an increase in unit labor costs (Hopkin 2015). Between 2003 and 2007, the Irish economy grew on average by 5.3 percent per year, the Greek economy expanded by 4.1 percent per year, and Spain's economy grew at an average rate of 3.6 percent (calculations are based on Feenstra et al. 2015). Similar to the run-up to many other financial crises (Reinhart and Rogoff 2010), this expansion first grew into a boom and then into a bubble, in which booming housing markets, strong increases in domestic consumption, and concomitant increases in imports were financed by significant capital inflows.[7] Both borrowers and lenders thus contributed to creating a situation that was vulnerable to a sudden stop in capital inflows. When the global financial crisis suddenly halted capital inflows, this resulted in both BOP and debt problems and created the need for adjustment and/or debt relief.

A second feature was the lack of fiscal policy coordination, which meant that Eurozone governments had little incentive to adjust their fiscal policies to counteract the growing imbalances (Baerg and Hallerberg 2016). Research suggests, for example, that the consequences of the crisis would have been much less severe if deficit had followed more conservative fiscal policies during the boom (Martin and Philippon 2017). Yet the political incentives to do this were small. That said, it is important to note that this was not a crisis of government over-borrowing. It was not the countries with the highest debt-to-GDP ratios that were hit hardest by the crisis (Johnston et al. 2014; Wihlborg et al. 2010).

Finally, the weak fragmented nature of financial regulation coupled with the creation of a single market in financial services in the Eurozone created possibilities for regulatory arbitrage, which financial institutions readily exploited. At the same time it did not create any incentives for national regulators to internalize the potential systemic effects of the rapidly increasing financial flows between countries (Jones et al. 2016). The institutional setup of the Eurozone institutions remained incomplete and would soon prove inadequate in dealing with the challenges of the crisis. All these developments attest to the difficulties of managing risks in a confederation of structurally diverse states bound together by an economic but not a political union (Hall 2012; Matthijs and Blyth 2015; Moravcsik 2012).

As a result of these developments, on the eve of the crisis, many financial institutions in the Eurozone's northern member states were exposed to both public and private debt from the periphery. At the same time, the financial, corporate, and/or public sector in the deficit countries were highly indebted to the North (Fuller 2018; Lane 2012), which is why the Eurozone crisis has been identified as a crisis of systemic over-lending by European banks (Matthijs and Blyth 2015). As in many other banking crises before the European one

---

[7] For a detailed discussion of the causes of the Eurozone crisis, see, for example, Baldwin et al. (2015).

(Copelovitch and Singer 2020; Jorda et al. 2010), massive capital inflows preceded the outbreak of this crisis.

The shock waves caused by the global financial crisis that started in 2007 then served as a trigger and catalyst for these European imbalances to erupt into a major debt and balance-of-payment crisis: the Eurozone crisis (Aizenman, Hutchison, and Lothian 2013; Lane 2012). Lending dried up, leading to a "sudden stop" of capital inflow (Merler and Pisani-Ferry 2012; Milesi-Ferretti and Tille 2011), and the heavily indebted borrowers found themselves unable to service their debts. What was initially predominantly a banking crisis quickly developed into a sovereign debt crisis. Because most foreign capital had flown into countries' private sectors in the boom years, at its outset the crisis was mainly one of private loans to private borrowers (Blyth 2013; Sandbu 2017).[8] Only when private banks approached illiquidity and insolvency did governments come to their rescue to prevent a financial meltdown. In the process of these massive banking crises, governments assumed many of the bad debts of their banks, which turned a private debt crisis into a sovereign debt crisis (Mabbett and Schelkle 2015).

However, the growing public debt increased the country's sovereign credit risk, which further weakened the financial system and, thus, created a negative bank-sovereign "doom" loop (Acharya et al. 2014). Markets panicked and risk premia surged, especially in those Eurozone countries with the largest current account deficits who saw their premiums spike (Baldwin and Giavazzi 2015: 20; Johnston et al. 2014). Governments in deficit countries suddenly faced a large debt burden, a deteriorating financial situation, and a collapse of domestic demand. In the face of these problems, financial markets panicked and risk premia on sovereign debt soared, further deteriorating the financial situation of governments in crisis countries. Unable to cover their continuing payments deficits by exporting or by borrowing additional funds, these governments were suddenly faced with a very real risk of sovereign default, which loomed large over several Eurozone countries and an emerging balance-of-payments crisis (Quaglia and Royo 2015). At the same time, surplus country creditors saw their investments in the Eurozone's periphery increasingly at risk.

The first country to face an imminent risk of sovereign default was Greece.[9] In late 2009, the Greek government revealed that its budget deficit was much higher than it had reported previously. The financial markets reacted immediately, and Greek borrowing costs soared. Soon, the Greek government had to ask for outside help. Although there was widespread agreement that a breakup of the Eurozone was to be avoided at all costs, it took protracted deliberations and negotiations

---

[8] This is why government deficits prior to the crisis do not predict the severity with which the countries were hit by the crisis (Johnston et al. 2014).
[9] We only present a brief overview of the Eurozone crisis here. For a more detailed account of the trajectory of the crisis see, for example, Copelovitch et al. (2016) or Mody (2018).

before European governments approved a financial assistance program in May 2010. In the context of this program, Eurozone member states together with the International Monetary Fund (IMF) would provide Greece with financial assistance on the condition of fiscal austerity and structural reforms. But this did not end the crisis. Rather, it spread quickly, and Ireland and Portugal, where huge credit booms had also turned into busts, equally had to ask for financial help. Both countries received bailouts—Ireland in November 2010 and Portugal in May 2011—under the auspices of the Troika, a tripartite committee formed by the European Commission, the European Central Bank (ECB), and the IMF. Again, these bailouts were granted under the condition that the countries implemented far-reaching austerity measures and structural reforms. As a result, unemployment surged, poverty spread, and most people in deficit countries saw their incomes fall (Dølvik and Martin 2014).

In the meantime, financial institutions in the creditor countries—which were still weakened from the 2007–9 global financial storm—used the time bought by the bailouts to deleverage. Figure 1.2a shows how quickly and how pervasively these banks reduced their exposure to crisis-country debt, which, at the same time, reduced the risk that a sovereign default in the Eurozone periphery would seriously threaten the stability of banks in the creditor states. Three years into the crisis, creditor country banks had reduced their claims on the main crisis countries by about half. Figure 1.2b shows that by the time Greece received a second bailout package in March 2012, the exposure of German, Dutch, French, and Belgian banks to a Greek default or a debt restructuring had dramatically decreased. Although this second bailout package for the first time included a significant debt write-down, a so-called haircut, for private creditors and wealthy bank depositors, the effect on surplus country investors was, thus, limited

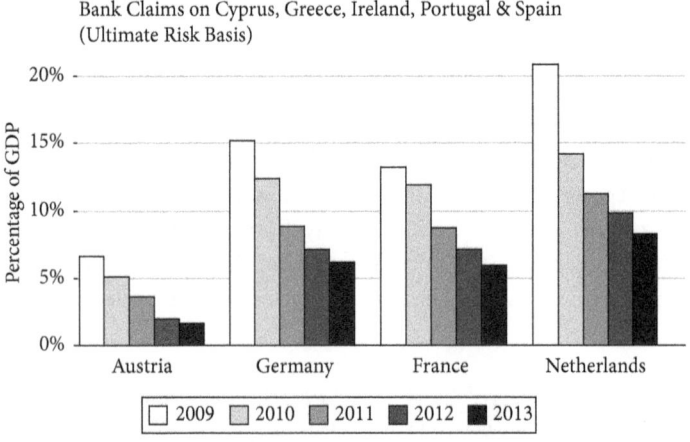

Figure 1.2a Creditor country bank claims on deficit countries

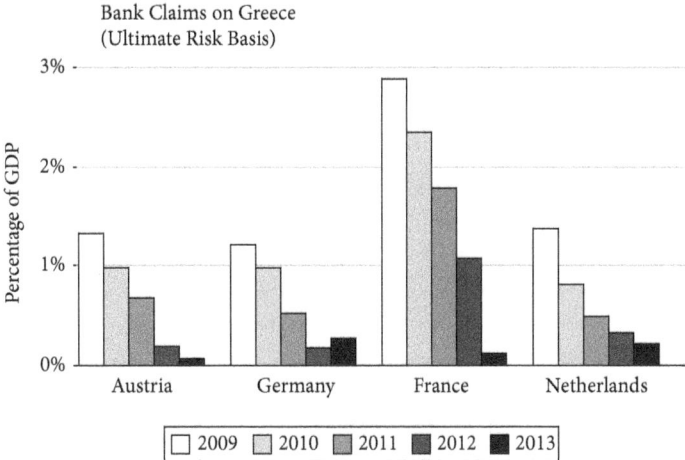

Figure 1.2b Creditor country bank claims on Greece
Source: Authors' own calculations, based on data from the Bank of International Settlements (2016).

(Zettelmeyer, Trebesch, and Gulati 2013). Spain also received financial assistance in June 2012 and Cyprus in March 2013. The Cypriot bailout package was unusual in that it also included a haircut, especially on wealthy (and mostly Russian) depositors.

In effect, the bailouts made it possible for surplus country governments to support their domestic banks indirectly via a bailout of a Eurozone debtor state (Ardagna and Caselli 2014; Mody 2018; Thompson 2015). Although this allowed surplus country governments to avoid a second round of banking crises and costly bailouts at home, this was not how they framed the international bailouts in the public debate, most likely because bank bailouts, whether direct or indirect, were deeply unpopular among the public (Goerres and Walter 2016; Thompson 2015). Moreover, they would have had to acknowledge that this strategy allowed creditor country banks to offload their exposure to creditor country taxpayers and socialize the potential losses from investments gone bad (Blyth 2013). Rather, surplus country policymakers engaged in a narrative of "northern saints and southern sinners" (Matthijs and McNamara 2015), in which the bailout packages were presented as acts of "solidarity" and necessary evils designed to protect the European project (Degner and Leuffen 2016; Wendler 2014). These arguments generally resonated with the public (Bechtel et al. 2014). Nonetheless, surplus country taxpayers were not particularly positive about the bailouts, and crisis politics became contentious in these countries even though surplus country governments tried to time and design the bailouts in a manner that would not alienate their voters too much (Christina Schneider and Slantchev 2018). In January 2012, 61 percent of German respondents in a large survey reported that they were against bailout payments for over-indebted EU countries (Bechtel et al. 2014). In November 2011, 60 percent of Dutch voters thought that their government should stop lending money to Eurozone countries in crisis, and another survey found that 64 percent opposed the creation of a rescue fund for crisis countries at the European level (Die Presse 2011; Maurice-De-Hond 2011b).

In addition to the bailout packages, European policymakers also worked to address the crisis at the European level. The Eurozone governments created the European Financial Stability Facility (EFSF), later replaced by the European Stability Mechanism (ESM), a permanent international financing institution with a mandate and funds to provide assistance to member states in financial distress. They adopted "six-pack" and later the "two-pack" reforms intended to strengthen the Stability and Growth Pact and to introduce greater macroeconomic and fiscal surveillance in an effort to improve compliance with the Pact's rules. In March 2012, all European leaders, except those from the UK and the Czech Republic, signed the "fiscal compact," a treaty designed to force member state governments to balance their budgets over the business cycle. In June 2012, Eurozone leaders also endorsed the idea of a banking union, in which Eurozone banks would operate under a set of common rules, with a single supervisory authority and a single resolution mechanism for bank failures. This idea has, however, since been implemented only with much delays and in an incomplete manner, as attempts to establish a European deposit insurance scheme have been derailed (Gros and Schoenmaker 2014; Howarth and Quaglia 2014, 2018).

The negotiations on how to address the crisis and on how to try to prevent future crises were difficult from the start. Although Eurozone governments agreed from the start that any form of a Eurozone breakup was not an option, they agreed on little else. The core divide between Eurozone governments in all these negotiations was between current-account surplus-running creditor states and deficit states with large current account deficits (Armingeon and Cranmer 2017b; Tarlea et al. 2019). For example, different proposals for new financing schemes, from Eurobonds (e.g., De Grauwe and Moesen 2009) over a European deposit insurance scheme (Donnelly 2018; Howarth and Quaglia 2018) to a European unemployment insurance scheme (Claeys et al. 2014), have faced the problem that they are unpopular in both surplus states—because they would likely foot the bill—and deficit countries—because this would likely reduce their national sovereignty in economic policymaking. A large-scale study of intergovernmental negotiations on forty-seven Eurozone-related issues between 2010 and 2015 found a fundamental divide between these states (Wasserfallen and Lehner 2018), with conflicts between the two couched mainly along the fiscal transfers vs. fiscal discipline divide. Surplus countries generally supported reforms that would require more fiscal discipline, whereas deficit countries were in favor of designing European-level schemes in ways that would result in fiscal transfers. States leveraged both their bargaining power and (often self-serving) ideas to support their preferred positions (Blyth 2013; Bulmer 2014; Dyson 2010, 2017; Howarth and Quaglia 2015; Matthijs and McNamara 2015; Moschella 2017; Schimmelfennig 2015).

Considering the politicization of the issues and the loss of popular trust in the EU, the institutional reforms on the European level went further than many predicted and are seen by some as a major leap in integration (Börzel and Risse 2018; Schimmelfennig 2018). More often than not, however, these European-level solutions did not address the fundamental Eurozone problems (Copelovitch et al., 2016; Jones et al. 2016; Matthijs and Blyth 2015; McNamara 2015; Mody 2018).

This left the ECB as the principal Eurozone economic institution to manage the crisis at the European level. It took quite aggressive measures designed to provide relief to deficit countries and banks, including a substantial bond-buying program to shore up financial markets as well as a monetary policy to push interest rates into negative territory. However, these policies also embroiled the ECB in political controversy. Many in northern Europe criticized the central bank for its expansionary monetary policy and unconventional measures, whereas for many in peripheral Europe, it did not do enough to alleviate the impact of the crisis.

It was also the ECB who managed to mark a turning point of the crisis: In July 2012, ECB president Mario Draghi famously stated that the ECB stood ready to do "whatever it takes to preserve the euro," as the bank unveiled a new bond-purchasing program, called "Outright Monetary Transactions" (OMT). This statement calmed financial markets. The crisis returned briefly—albeit vigorously—to the center of European politics in July 2015 when difficult negotiations between the new populist left Greek government and the Troika culminated in a referendum about Greece's bailout package that pushed Greece to the brink of Eurozone exit. After Greece received a third bailout package, however, the Eurozone crisis slowly calmed down.

While financial market volatility has subsided, many of the underlying problems that fueled the outbreak of the Eurozone crisis remain unresolved (Mody 2018). The euro still binds together a highly diverse set of countries within a uniform monetary framework. Some progress has been made, for example with the establishment of the ESM or the single supervisory mechanism, but other institutional reforms, such as the new the single resolution mechanism, remain inadequate (Jones et al. 2016). Proposals that aim at more risk-sharing among Eurozone economies (such as Eurobonds or a pan-European unemployment scheme) have so far not gone anywhere.

The severe consequences of the crisis also linger. Unemployment rates are still high in many crisis countries, and rather than lower, the current account surpluses of countries such as Germany or the Netherlands are now higher than before the crisis. Moreover, the political ramifications of the crisis have been enormous (Hernández and Kriesi 2016; Kriesi and Pappas 2015; Kurer et al. 2018; Della Porta 2015; Streeck and Schäfer 2013). The austerity measures and structural reforms in the crisis states were difficult to implement and politically costly. One government fell after another. In the deficit countries, voters' support for democracy (Armingeon and Guthmann 2014; Armingeon et al. 2016), their trust in national governments (Foster and Frieden 2017), and their general satisfaction with the EU reached unprecedented lows (Guiso et al. 2016; De Vries 2018). The crisis also fueled support for Eurosceptic parties in both surplus and deficit states and especially among those voters hit hardest by the crisis (Hobolt and de Vries 2016b). And although support for the euro remained remarkably high in all Eurozone countries throughout the crisis (Hobolt and Wratil 2015; Roth et al. 2016), populist support for leaving the Eurozone or dissolving it altogether gained significant momentum (Heinen et al. 2015, Jurado et al. 2020). Explicit support for dissolving the monetary union has been most pronounced in the surplus countries: The Dutch PVV, the German AfD, the French Front National, and the Austrian FPÖ have all at times called for a controlled dissolution of the Eurozone, with the True Finns in Finland taking a critical but more cautious position. There has also been a strong push for a referendum on the euro in Italy and by some fringe parties in Greece[10]—even though most parties, including some influential populist parties, such as Spain's Podemos and Greece's SYRIZA, support staying in the Eurozone.

This development shows that the Eurozone crisis has had consequences that extend far beyond the economy and continue to shape and challenge European politics. The jitters of financial markets caused by the 2018 Italian elections or the 2020 COVID-19 pandemic demonstrate that the Eurozone crisis may come back to haunt the EU in the not too distant future. Ultimately, the underlying causes of the crisis have not been resolved, and the political consequences of the crisis still linger. As a result, the narrative that "the crisis is over" seems misguided. While the short-term panic has subsided, serious questions remain about the future of the monetary union itself. A better understanding about why it has proven so difficult to resolve the Eurozone crisis is, therefore, urgently needed.

The Unequal Distribution of Crisis-Resolution Costs

In all debt and balance-of-payments crises, governments and societies disagree heavily about the question of who should bear the costs of dealing with the accumulated debts and the costs of rebalancing the current accounts. The Eurozone crisis was no exception (Dyson 2014; Eichengreen 1992; Frieden 2015b; Hall 2014; Simmons 1994; Walter 2013a; Woodruff 2016). In the ensuing conflicts about crisis resolution, both sides have bargaining chips: Creditor states

---

[10] The communist KKE party and the SYRIZA-spinoff Popular Unity party have proposed leaving the Eurozone.

can threaten to shut errant debtors out of credit markets and to block future access to credit, but debtors can threaten to stop payment, especially if default in one country is likely to cause panic to spread into financial markets more widely. Although deficit-debtor states tend to be in a structurally weaker bargaining position, most crises are resolved with both sides making some compromises about how to share the crisis resolution costs (Dooley et al. 2004; Frieden 2015b; Kaufmann 1969; Mabbett and Schelkle 2015).

Nonetheless, debt and BOP crises are characterized by difficult trade-offs and bitter disputes surrounding questions such as: Should debtor countries repay the outstanding debt or should creditor countries grant debt relief? Should current account imbalances be resolved by deficit states cutting back on domestic consumption and increasing their exports or by surplus states boosting their domestic demand? Should adjustment instead work via the exchange rate, which in a monetary union like the Eurozone boils down to the question of whether that union should be broken up? To what extent should surplus countries support deficit countries by providing funds to finance the current account deficit?

Not surprisingly, then, the questions of who should adjust and of how the adjustment burden should be distributed were front and center in Eurozone crisis politics as well (Frieden and Walter 2017; Moschella 2017). What makes the Eurozone crisis unusual in comparison to other crises, however, is that relatively little burden sharing occurred. While some risk sharing took place, although most of this occurred in the form of "solidarity by stealth" (Schelkle 2017): After initial hesitations, the ECB engaged in an expansionary monetary policy of a scale that had been unthinkable only a few years before. It provided emergency liquidity assistance to troubled banks in crisis countries, and ECB president Mario Draghi promised to do everything necessary to preserve the euro. Moreover, some debt restructuring occurred in Greece and Cyprus. Yet overall, especially considering the extent of the crisis, little debt relief was granted for the countries hit hardest by the Eurozone crisis, such as Ireland, Portugal, and Spain. Moreover, deficit countries were required to undertake substantial fiscal and structural reforms designed to address their chronic balance-of-payments problems (Hall 2012; Heins and de la Porte 2015). As a result, the burden of adjustment in the Eurozone crisis has been almost exclusively put on the shoulders of the deficit countries (Matthijs and Blyth 2015).[11] The silence on calls for adjustment in surplus countries, in contrast, was often "deafening" (Featherstone 2011).

---

[11] There are a number of reasons why the principal burden of adjustment to the Eurozone crisis fell upon the debtors' shoulders (Frieden and Walter 2017). For one, the threat of being cut off from the tightly integrated European financial markets loomed large for the crisis countries and gave creditor countries considerable bargaining leverage. Moreover, surplus countries also invoked the requirements of broader EU and Eurozone membership, implying, sometimes stating, that something less than full repayment could result in expulsion from the Eurozone or the EU. Whether the threat of expulsion was

Figures 1.3a and 1.3b show two examples of just how much surplus and deficit states differed in their contribution to crisis resolution. Figure 1.3a looks at changes in statutory tax rates in surplus and deficit states during the first five years of the Eurozone crisis. It shows that all deficit states increased taxes during that period in line with their general policy of austerity. Tax reform in surplus states, in contrast, was much more limited or, in fact, non-existent. Rather than lowering taxes in an effort to boost domestic demand, these countries did very little to adjust their fiscal policies, and Austria even increased taxes. It therefore comes as no surprise that the surplus countries maintained or even increased their current account surpluses throughout the crisis (Figure 1.3b). In contrast, the deficit states implemented major current account adjustment during the same period. Over the course of the crisis, all deficit states significantly reduced their current account deficits, with most even turning their deficits into surpluses.

The effect of this unequal distribution of the adjustment burden between deficit and creditor states on economic growth and employment prospects in these countries has been harsh. Figure 1.4 illustrates how unequally the costs of the adjustment have been spread across Eurozone countries and how different Eurozone countries have fared throughout the crisis, and traces their economic

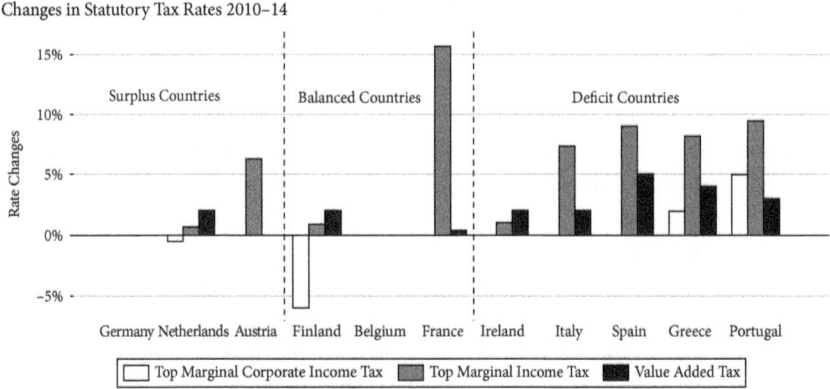

Figure 1.3a Varieties of adjustment. Deficit and surplus countries in the Eurozone crisis: Fiscal reform

real and legal or not, many in the debtor countries were reluctant to press the issue, for fear that it might affect their economic relations with the rest of the Eurozone or that it might cause the fickle financial markets to turn against them. In addition, Eurozone creditors used their political influence over the International Monetary Fund to force the IMF to ignore the Fund's own rules, which would have required substantial debt restructuring (Copelovitch and Enderlein 2016; IEO 2016; Mody 2018). Finally, emphasizing ordo-liberal ideas, creditor countries have been successful in framing the crisis in ways that suggest that deficit countries caused, and hence should resolve, the crisis (Blyth 2013; Matthijs and McNamara 2015).

Development of Net Current Accounts 2008–13

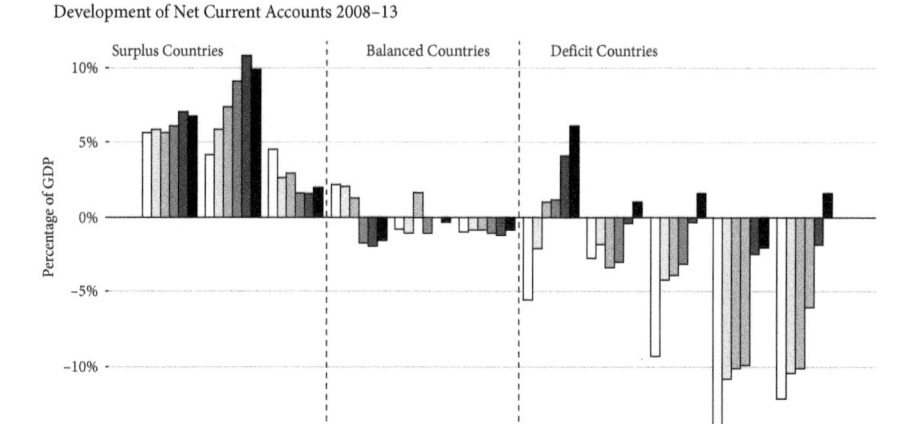

Figure 1.3b Varieties of adjustment. Deficit and surplus countries in the Eurozone crisis: Current account

Sources: Authors' own calculations, based on tax data from OECD (2016c) and current account data from IMF (2016a).

Changes in GDP and Unemployment 2007–13

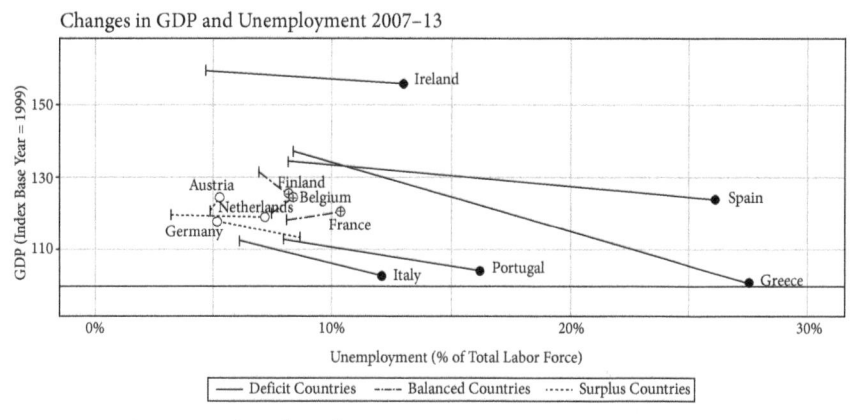

Figure 1.4 Crisis cost for selected Eurozone countries

Note: Short vertical lines indicate 2007 values. Dots indicate 2013 values.

Source: World Bank (2016a, 2016b); see also Frieden and Walter (2017): Figure 2.

development between 2007 (noted by the line) and 2013 (noted by the dot). The large increases on the horizontal axis show that the five main Eurozone debtor-deficit countries—Ireland, Italy, Portugal, and, especially, Spain and Greece—witnessed massive increases in unemployment over the course of the crisis. GDP decreased significantly in all five debtor states, and GDP fell back to the levels of when the Eurozone was first founded in three of these countries (the respective 1999 levels are represented by the value of 100). In contrast, the economic costs of the crisis were much smaller or even nonexistent in the surplus states, such as Germany, Austria, and the Netherlands. Over the same period of unprecedented contraction in Greece, for example, the German economy grew and unemployment fell. Overall, the European response to the crisis achieved the one common goal all Eurozone policymakers agreed upon: preventing the breakup of the monetary union. But the price to achieve this goal varied among the Eurozone members, as it was paid predominantly by the crisis countries.

Yet to say that the costs of the crisis have been predominantly borne by deficit states does not mean that everyone in deficit states was equally hurt by the crisis. Instead, the impact of the crisis has varied considerably among social and economic groups in these countries. For example, unemployment has hit young people, men, and the less educated the hardest (Gutiérrez 2014). Youth unemployment tripled in Ireland between 2007 and 2012, and between 2012 and 2014, more than half of economically active people under the age of 25 in Greece and Spain were without work.[12] Likewise, relative poverty rates for young people went up in Italy, Portugal, and especially in Spain and Greece, while at the same time they declined considerably for the elderly. Interestingly, inequality has only increased in some countries (most notably, Greece), whereas crisis policies seem to have had no impact on equality in other countries, or even an inequality-decreasing impact in some (Matsaganis and Leventi 2014). Both crisis-related policies and the overall impact of the economic crisis in deficit states have, thus, differed in how they have affected different socioeconomic groups (Avram, Figari, Leventi, Levy, Navicke, Matsaganis, Militaru, Paulus, Rastringina, et al. 2013).

More generally, deficit states were relatively quick to adopt austerity measures, whereas structural reforms were implemented more hesitantly. Given that the latter were often aimed at stripping privileges from politically influential groups, they were often implemented only under considerable external pressure, and even then, compliance has been spotty. Similarly, banks and other financial market participants have largely socialized their losses, rolling them over to taxpayers (Blyth 2013). As discussed above, debtor-country governments ended up assuming many of the bad debts of their banks, and thus converted private debt into sovereign debt. Entrenched insider-outsider structures (Bentolila et al. 2012), strong resistance by vested interests (Featherstone 2015), and clientelistic politics (Afonso et al. 2015) have generally protected politically influential groups. As in earlier crises, governments have often shielded their own voter base from the crisis consequences as much as possible (Walter 2016).

---

[12] Eurostat (2016): http://ec.europa.eu/eurostat/web/lfs/data/database.

The impact of the crisis among social and economic groups has also varied in surplus states. One of the most important distributive questions was how to deal with deficit country debts: Should surplus countries allow the deficit states to default and restructure their debts, thus requiring their own financial systems to absorb the costs of the crisis? Or should the costs of the crisis be transferred onto surplus country taxpayers by way of providing public funds to the debtor countries that would allow them to continue servicing their debts to financial institutions in the North? Surplus country governments generally opted for the latter option. For example, of the €215.9 billion in taxpayer loans provided to Greece in the first two bailout packages, only about 5 percent actually ended up in the Greek state budget. The rest was used to finance old debts and interest rate payments to private banks, a lot of which were located in surplus countries (Rocholl and Stahmer 2016; Thompson 2015).

Bad Options, Difficult Choices

Why did deficit countries accept to implement unprecedented levels of austerity during the crisis? Why did surplus countries put together huge bailout packages but not allow any meaningful debt relief? Why did they not adjust their policies to share some of the crisis-resolution cost? Why has it been so difficult to find common ground on the European level for sustainable EMU reform? And why, despite of all this, did no country leave the Eurozone?

To understand the unusual choices policymakers took to respond to the Eurozone crisis, it is important to understand the range of options available to them. As discussed above, the principal options in a debt crisis revolve around how to deal with accumulated bad debts. Do debtor countries repay the outstanding debt, or do creditor countries grant debt restructuring, hence providing some relief to debtor countries? However, this only resolves the stock problem of accumulated debts, not the flow problem of growing debt levels. Because the Eurozone crisis is, at its root, both a debt and a balance-of-payment crisis (Baldwin et al. 2015; Baldwin and Giavazzi 2015; Johnston et al. 2014; Wihlborg et al. 2010), solving the underlying problems of the Eurozone in a sustainable manner requires more far-reaching economic adjustments designed to address the flow problem of continuing current account imbalances that fueled the debt problems in the first place.

Several options exist for resolving balance-of-payments imbalances (Algieri and Bracke 2011; Broz et al. 2016; Frieden and Walter 2017; Walter 2013a). In contrast to the conventional narrative that the solution for such problems lies with deficit countries—who have to cut back domestic consumption and increase their competitiveness in order to reduce imports and boost exports of goods and services as well as capital—both deficit *and* surplus countries can contribute to the policy adjustment necessary for rebalancing (Willett and Chiu 2012).[13] A so-called internal adjustment of domestic economic policies can be achieved by deflating prices in deficit countries and by boosting domestic demand in surplus countries. Adjustment can also occur externally through the adjustment of exchange rates. Finally, current account imbalances can be made more sustainable if surplus states cover deficit states' financing needs. Table 1.1 summarizes these different policy options that deficit and surplus countries have to resolve current account imbalances as well as their implications for the Eurozone.

Although these options differ in their implications for deficit and surplus countries, they all have significant downsides. These downsides form the basis for the distributional conflicts surrounding the resolution of balance-of-payment crises. Whenever current account adjustment is required to solve a crisis, regardless of whether the crisis was predominantly caused by financial flows or by flows of goods and services, policymakers face trade-offs and difficult choices with regard to these options.

The first option for rebalancing the current account is *external adjustment*. This strategy involves a change of the nominal exchange rate, which for Eurozone members means that the Eurozone would have to be broken up in some sort of way. Deficit countries adjust externally by devaluing their exchange rate, making domestic products more competitive internationally. As expenditure is switched away from the consumption of internationally tradable goods and toward the

Table 1.1 Policy options to resolve balance of payments imbalances

	EXTERNAL ADJUSTMENT	INTERNAL ADJUSTMENT	FINANCING
DEFICIT COUNTRY	Exchange-rate devaluation	Austerity and structural reforms	Cover funding gap through external funding
SURPLUS COUNTRY	Exchange-rate appreciation	Inflation and reforms aimed at boosting domestic demand	Provide financing for deficit countries with BOP problems
IMPLICATION FOR THE EUROZONE	Eurozone breakup	Convergence of deficit and surplus countries	Permanent financing structures (e.g., fiscal federalism, automatic stabilizers)

Source: Frieden and Walter (2017: Table 1).

[13] Note that our distinction between surplus and deficit countries is based on whether they exhibit a current account surplus or deficit during the buildup and outbreak of a given crisis. In the short run this is relevant for crisis management, and the dynamics and relevant trade-offs will be different across deficit and surplus countries. This does not mean that surplus and deficit countries are so different that countries are structurally either always deficit or surplus countries. Rather, countries' current accounts can change from a deficit to a surplus and vice versa (see Figure 1.1 and Manger and Sattler 2019).

production and export of such goods, the current account rebalances. Because this means that less capital is needed to finance the current account deficit, capital inflows decrease and the capital account deficit equally shrinks. This adjustment strategy can benefit the export-oriented sector, but it hurts other groups because it also leads to a reduction of purchasing power, increased exchange-rate volatility, and rising debt service on foreign-currency denominated loans (Frieden 1991b, 2015a; Steinberg and Walter 2013; Walter 2008, 2013a). In addition, external adjustment is often associated with higher rates of inflation, and it creates contagion risks for states with similar problems. For surplus countries, external adjustment implies an exchange-rate revaluation, which makes domestic products more expensive relative to foreign products, thereby increasing imports and reducing exports, as well as capital outflows. Many of the effects of external adjustment in surplus countries mirror the effects in deficit countries: Currency appreciation hurts the export-oriented sector, whereas domestic consumers and holders of foreign-currency-denominated debt benefit. At the same time, holders of assets denominated in foreign currencies lose out. Exiting a fixed exchange-rate regime such as a monetary union creates significant additional costs for both surplus and deficit states, however. Not only does it create significant volatility, but breaking up a monetary union also leads to a loss of credibility that is likely to have long-lasting negative effects. By demonstrating the possibility of exit, it is particularly likely to encourage speculation, which in turn is likely to extend to other member states of the currency union (Chang and Leblond 2015). The resulting contagion effects are expected to have negative consequences both in surplus and deficit countries. External adjustment is thus a particularly costly policy option in a currency union such as EMU.

It is important to understand that this does not mean that external adjustment is impossible—after all, it was discussed as a serious policy option in Greece in 2015 and euro exit was a pledge in French presidential candidate Marine Le Pen's 2017 election campaign. But it does mean that external adjustment is a much more costly policy strategy for members of a currency union than for countries with other forms of exchange rate regimes.

The second possible adjustment strategy is *internal adjustment*, in which relative prices are adjusted through domestic fiscal and monetary policy changes and structural reforms. In deficit countries, the aim is to engineer an "internal devaluation" that deflates domestic prices through productivity gains and a reduction in domestic demand. This makes domestic products more competitive, reduces demand for imports and foreign capital, and increases exports. Because this adjustment strategy requires austerity policies such as public spending cuts, tax increases, and structural reforms (e.g., measures designed to increase labor market flexibility or policies aimed at increasing competitiveness), it is typically associated with higher unemployment, lower wages, asset price deflation, and recession in deficit countries. Implementing such policies is politically difficult

(Barta 2018). For surplus countries, internal adjustment implies policies and reforms that increase relative prices—for example, a loose monetary policy or reforms stimulating domestic demand, such as increasing public investments, cutting taxes, or increasing the minimum wage. These policies increase the price of domestic relative to foreign prices, which lowers exports and increases imports as well as domestic consumption.

Both the external and the internal adjustment strategy aim at the long-term resolution of current account imbalances. Policymakers also have a third option, however, which is to simply *finance* the current account deficit and not adjust. Deficit countries can do this by using their foreign currency reserves or procuring external funding from international actors or other countries.[14] Surplus countries, who tend to be the creditors of deficit countries, are often willing to support such funding—either bilaterally or through international organizations such as the IMF—because it not only reduces the risk that a deficit country defaults on its debt, but also allows surplus countries to forgo adjustment at home. But the financing strategy has an important downside: It does not resolve the underlying structural problems and often even aggravates them. Thus, this approach carries the risk that eventual adjustment will have to be more extensive than if it had been implemented early on (Frankel and Wei 2004; Walter and Willett 2012). To avoid such a situation, official foreign funds, such as those given by the IMF, are usually only provided under strict conditionality which forces the recipient country to implement adjustment.[15] For surplus countries, the main drawback of the financing option is that they have to provide the necessary funds in a setting where it is unclear when or whether the recipient will pay back those funds.

What does this mean for the politics of the Eurozone crisis? Because the crisis occurred within a currency union, some policy options would play out differently in this context than in the context of regular BOP crises. Most importantly, in a monetary union, external adjustment implies a breakup of the union, in this case the Eurozone. Although declared as highly unlikely by many observers (Eichengreen 2010b), historical evidence shows that currency unions can and do break up (Cohen 1993). Different variants of such a breakup are thinkable—from the exit of a single country to the formation of two or more currency blocs or the introduction of parallel currencies (e.g., Brown 2012; Crafts 2014; Kawalec and Pytlarczyk 2013; Watts et al. 2014). But whatever its form, external adjustment would mean that the Eurozone would cease to exist in its current configuration. This would carry huge costs for everyone involved, with consequences ranging

---

[14] This explains why deficit countries are typically in a worse bargaining position about the burden sharing of adjustment than surplus countries. Reserve sales are often not enough to stop the crisis (Walter and Willett 2012).

[15] Though both the extent of these conditions (Copelovitch 2010; Dreher and Vaubel 2004) and the compliance with conditionality vary significantly (Stone 2008).

from widespread defaults, bank runs, and massive economic turmoil in the European economy.

For this reason, the external adjustment path was quickly ruled out by virtually all Eurozone policymakers who worried that, as Angela Merkel put it in a famous speech, a failure of the euro would lead to a failure of Europe.[16] In contrast, internal adjustment was seen as a desirable outcome because it would ultimately lead to a convergence of Eurozone economies. From its start, many observers have doubted the feasibility of a currency union in the European context because it clearly does not constitute an optimum currency area, with heterogeneous member states that are subject to asymmetric vulnerability to shocks, a lack of labor mobility, and an absence of sufficient fiscal stabilizers (Bayoumi and Eichengreen 1992; Hall and Franzese 1998; Johnston 2016).[17] Internal adjustment, especially when undertaken not just in terms of fiscal policy but through structural reforms of labor and product markets, is designed to let Eurozone economies converge more closely to one another. The idea is that this would not only serve to solve the short-term pressures of the Eurozone crisis but also lead to more long-term stability in the Eurozone. The political reality, however, has put the onus of achieving such adjustment squarely on the shoulders of the deficit countries, whereas surplus countries have done little to adjust their economic policies, let alone their economic growth models (Hall 2014; Matthijs 2016b; Willett and Chiu 2012).

Finally, a long-term financing of European current account imbalances would require the creation of a set of institutions designed to facilitate the permanent transfer of funds from surplus to deficit states—such as a fiscal union, a banking union, and/or the establishment of a larger, more permanent transfer mechanism to replace the European Stability Mechanism. Many economists have called for such structures (e.g., De Grauwe 2013a; Lane 2012; Pisani-Ferry 2012), yet political progress toward establishing such long-term financing structures has been limited.

Overall, this discussion shows that crises that require balance-of-payments adjustment, such as the Eurozone crisis, confront policymakers with a list of unattractive options. The general approach taken in the Eurozone crisis has been one of internal adjustment in debtor states, coupled with temporary financing (bailout packages) and expansionary monetary policy implemented by the ECB. Large bailout programs were set up, but crisis countries were forced to implement austerity and structural reforms in return, and no major debt relief was granted. Deficit countries largely accepted surplus countries' refusal to grant debt

---

[16] https://www.bundestag.de/dokumente/textarchiv/2010/29826227_kw20_de_stabilisierungs mechanismus/201760.
[17] Based on the criteria set forth in the canonical studies by Kenen (1969), McKinnon (1963), and Mundell (1961).

relief as well as their insistence that deficit countries should mostly shoulder the burden of internal adjustment alone, even though this resulted in deep recessions and record levels of unemployment in the deficit countries, whereas creditor countries were much less affected by the crisis.

The Argument in Brief

This book argues that distributive concerns are important for understanding not only Eurozone crisis politics but also the ongoing difficulties to substantially reform EMU. Distributive concerns, both within countries and among countries, always influence the politics of resolving debt and balance-of-payment crises. Research on the politics of past balance-of-payment crises—such as the breakdown of the gold standard (Eichengreen 1992; Simmons 1994), the Latin American Debt Crisis (Frieden 1991a; Nelson 1990), or the Asian Financial Crisis (Pepinsky 2009; Walter 2008, 2013a)—emphasizes the important role that distributive struggles played in these crises. At the international level, countries with current account surpluses and deficits fight over who should implement the policies necessary to reduce the current account imbalances and who should take responsibility for the accumulated debts (Willett and Chiu 2012).[18] Within countries, firms, interest groups, and voters fight to shift the costs of crisis resolution away from themselves (e.g., Alesina and Drazen 1991; Fernandez and Rodrik 1991; Gourevitch 1986). Much research on the Eurozone crisis has zoomed in on these struggles in deficit countries, which have been at the center of the crisis (e.g., Afonso et al. 2015; Armingeon and Baccaro 2012b; Culpepper and Regan 2014; Fernández-Albertos and Kuo 2016; Kurer et al. 2018; Picot and Tassinari 2017). However, because both deficit and surplus countries can contribute to resolving the crisis, it is important to also analyze crisis politics in surplus countries and how the distributive struggles and concerns within these countries have shaped their response to the Eurozone crisis. We argue that the distributive struggles surrounding the politics of the Eurozone crisis in surplus and deficit countries are distinct but related, and that they should be analyzed in a unified framework.

This book, therefore, analyzes the distributive struggles shaping Eurozone crisis politics in a comprehensive manner, which gives equal attention to crisis politics in deficit and surplus countries and considers all available options, including those that were not chosen. As we have seen, balance-of-payments crises confront policymakers with a list of unattractive, bad options. Different socioeconomic

---

[18] Our analysis focuses on Eurozone member states and their domestic politics. Others have emphasized the role of international (such as the IMF) and supranational institutions (such as the European Commission or the ECB), who also pursued their own agendas during the Eurozone crisis (Copelovitch and Enderlein 2016; Lütz and Hilgers 2018; Lütz et al. 2019a; Moschella 2016).

groups, and, at the aggregate level, different societies, differ in the extent to which they are vulnerable to each of these options. We argue that these vulnerabilities—and the trade-offs they present for individuals, interest groups, and national governments—strongly influence the politics of balance-of-payment adjustment in the wake of a financial crisis both within countries and at the international level. The puzzle of why deficit countries agreed to unprecedented austerity, which has taken such a heavy toll on their economies, becomes less puzzling, for example, if one considers that the alternatives available to them were Eurozone exit and/or unilateral debt default, both costly and highly undesirable outcomes. Likewise, many have puzzled over the reluctance of surplus countries to boost domestic demand at home. We argue, and show, that this decision is less puzzling if one considers that such a rebalancing was unpopular domestically and that surplus countries had a viable alternative: Bailouts with strict conditionality.

Confronted with a serious BOP crisis such as the Eurozone crisis, voters, interest groups, and national policymakers vary in their preferred crisis response, since the two main strategies for rebalancing the current account, external and internal adjustment, vary in how costly they are for each of these actors. If one adjustment path (say Eurozone exit) clearly imposes more costs than the alternative (say internal adjustment), then the latter alternative will clearly be preferred. Oftentimes, however, both adjustment paths will be costly, and it is in those instances when preferences will be less clear, when the politics of crisis resolution will become more difficult, and when financing turns into an increasingly attractive third alternative. These are also the instances when attempts to eschew the burden of adjustment (by pushing it on other states) will be most pronounced. Eurozone crisis politics, thus, cannot be understood without considering the trade-offs and costs associated with each of the three main alternative options: Internal adjustment, external adjustment, and financing (including debt relief).

The preferred choice of crisis-resolution strategy, then, depends on the potential costs that external adjustment would impose on an actor, relative to the potential costs of internal adjustment. In short, crisis-resolution preferences are informed by an actor's "vulnerability profile" (Walter 2008, 2013a, 2016) in both deficit and surplus countries. Figure 1.5 presents a stylized overview of the four ideal-type vulnerability profiles that voters, interest groups, and, in the aggregate, societies can exhibit, as well as the preferred policy response associated with each of these profiles.

This classification suggests that there are four types of vulnerability profiles. Actors with a vulnerability profile I are predominantly vulnerable to internal adjustment—austerity in deficit countries and an expansion of domestic demand in surplus countries—and they are, therefore, more likely to prefer resolving the crisis through external adjustment. Actors with a vulnerability profile III also have a clear-cut preference, that is, internal adjustment, because they are much more vulnerable to external adjustment—devaluation in deficit countries and

Figure 1.5

A two-dimensional classification diagram with:
- Y-axis: **Vulnerability to Internal Adjustment** (Deficit countries: austerity and structural reforms; Surplus countries: policies that boost domestic demand), ranging from low to high
- X-axis: **Vulnerability to External Adjustment** (Deficit countries: euro exit and exchange-rate devaluation; Surplus countries: euro exit and exchange-rate revaluation), ranging from low to high

Four quadrants:

I (high internal, low external): Only vulnerable to internal adjustment — *External adjustment*

II (high internal, high external): Vulnerable to internal and external adjustment ("misery corner") — *Financing / Delayed + mixed adjustment*

III (low internal, high external): Only vulnerable to external adjustment — *Internal adjustment*

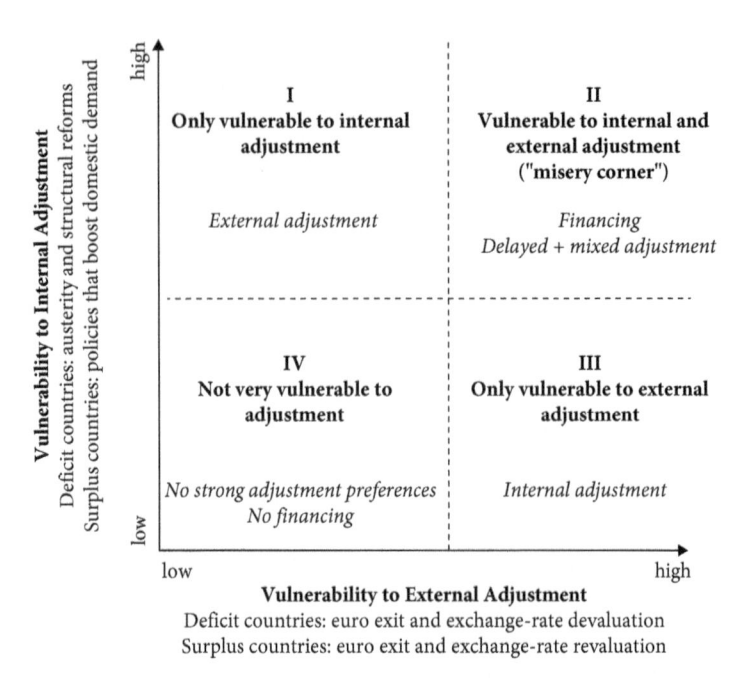

IV (low internal, low external): Not very vulnerable to adjustment — *No strong adjustment preferences / No financing*

Figure 1.5 Classification of vulnerability profiles and preferred policy response

---

revaluation in surplus countries—than to internal adjustment. When the costs of one adjustment strategy clearly outweigh the costs of the alternative (vulnerability profiles I and III), the choice is thus relatively straightforward: Quick implementation of the less costly adjustment strategy.

Voters, interest groups, and policymakers face a much more difficult situation when both internal and external adjustment are costly (vulnerability profile II). Actors who find themselves in this "misery corner" would ideally prefer no adjustment; they are, therefore, most amenable toward addressing the current account imbalance through financing. Finally, actors for whom the costs of both internal and external adjustment are low (vulnerability profile IV) are unlikely to have strong preferences about the type of adjustment strategy, although they are likely to be opposed to the financing option because this would stand in the way of a crisis resolution in deficit countries or would likely come at the expense of taxpayers in the surplus countries. Because these scenarios do not result in a clear preference for one adjustment strategy, crisis politics in settings with vulnerability profiles II and IV will be more amenable to preference shaping. This offers domestic and international political elites an opportunity to shape policymaking and societal preferences about crisis management and their preferences and ideas. In these instances, moreover, ideology is likely to take a more prominent role in guiding policymaking. As such, our explanation complements existing accounts that highlight the importance of ideas for crisis politics both in the Eurozone crisis (e.g., Carstensen and Schmidt 2018; Matthijs 2016a; Matthijs and McNamara 2015) and beyond (e.g., Blyth 2013; Chwieroth 2009; McNamara 1998; Morrison 2016).

The vulnerability profile is a useful heuristic for analyzing Eurozone crisis politics because it sheds light on the distributive concerns regarding the trade-offs between different policy options in both deficit and surplus countries. First, it can be used to examine which crisis responses countries opt for overall. Countries for which one type of adjustment strategy is significantly more costly than another have strong incentives to implement the less costly strategy in a swift and decisive manner. Countries more vulnerable to austerity and structural reforms than external adjustment (vulnerability profile I) are more likely to respond with a swift devaluation of the exchange rate without much financing. Finding an example of a Eurozone country with this vulnerability profile is difficult because all Eurozone member states are highly vulnerable to a Eurozone breakup, but such vulnerability profiles have not been unusual in past BOP crises. Likewise, countries with a vulnerability profile in quadrant III also are more likely to clearly opt for one type of adjustment over the other; in this case, governments will opt for internal adjustment and exchange-rate stability. In terms of financing, countries with both vulnerability profiles I and III should show little enthusiasm for long-term, low-conditionality financing facilities such as Eurobonds, but they should be more open to financing measures that smooth rather than avoid adjustment in economic policies.

The situation is more difficult in countries that are vulnerable to any type of adjustment (the "misery profile" II). Here, any adjustment is unpopular and politically difficult to implement. Given the country's high exposure to both domestic reforms and Eurozone exit, these countries should be more intent to receive (deficit countries) or be more willing to grant (surplus countries) different forms of financing instead. In the process, deficit countries should try to keep the conditions attached to the external funds to a minimal level, favoring Eurobonds and debt haircuts for international investors over bailouts. Surplus countries with this vulnerability profile should push for high-conditionality types of financing that transfer the burden of adjustment onto the deficit countries in exchange for foreign funds.

Second, vulnerability profiles help us understand who supports and who opposes different policy options domestically. Vulnerability profiles can be conceptualized for individuals, interest groups, and societies overall. Individuals matter for crisis politics as voters. Interest groups represent larger segments of society: Business and employer associations represent certain types of firms and economic sectors, trade unions represent certain types of workers, and groups such as taxpayer associations or pro-poor groups represent certain groups of individuals. These groups are more likely to have a direct voice in the policy-making process and are, therefore, important for shaping overall crisis politics.

We argue that individuals and interest groups also form their policy preferences on the basis of their vulnerability profiles. For example, deficit country homeowners who have mortgaged their home in euros but have very secure employment are highly vulnerable to an exit from the Eurozone, but they are much less exposed to internal adjustment than to external adjustment. Voters and interest groups with such clear-cut vulnerability profiles (I and III) are likely to share a strong preference for the type of adjustment to which they are not very vulnerable. Moreover, they should see financing predominantly as a means to smooth adjustment. Interest groups whose members are very vulnerable to both internal and external adjustment (vulnerability profile II) are in a more difficult situation. For them, any adjustment in micro- and macroeconomic policies will be painful, which is why these groups would likely oppose any significant policy reforms. Surplus country interest groups in this category are most interested to make sure that adjustment is undertaken elsewhere, but they are most willing to support deficit countries' efforts in this direction through bailout packages. Deficit country interest groups in this category are in a more difficult situation, but they are also expected to most favor receiving financing support from abroad. Given that these interest groups have much to lose from an adjustment of policies, the expectation is that they will be very vocal and combative in the political process.

Finally, examining vulnerability profiles can shed light on why crisis politics are more contested in some countries than in others. Political conflict is likely to be particularly high in countries with a vulnerability profile II. Such a vulnerability profile arises either when politically influential groups are very vulnerable to both internal and external adjustment, or when politically important groups vulnerable to internal adjustment are equally prevalent as groups vulnerable to external adjustment. In such a setting, any type of adjustment will inevitably hurt at least one set of domestic interests. Especially in deficit countries in this category, crisis politics should be characterized by political turmoil, low levels of political stability, divisions within governments, and debates about the appropriate policy response to the crisis. Since deficit countries cannot easily push adjustment costs onto surplus countries, these distributional conflicts tend to revolve around how the cost of adjustment is to be distributed among different societal groups. But surplus countries with this vulnerability profile should also experience elevated levels of contestation, centered mostly around struggles over how financing should be provided to deficit countries in an effort to avoid adjustment in their own economies. In contrast, in countries exhibiting any of the other three vulnerability profiles, crisis politics will be less conflictual, especially when the country's aggregate vulnerability profile also reflects the vulnerability profile of the country's politically most influential interest groups. Crisis politics in these countries should be characterized by lower levels of opposition and a less tumultuous political environment than in countries where policymakers impose significant costs on influential groups.

Taken together, answering these three questions provides us with a solid understanding of the distributive struggles that have led to the unequal burden sharing in the Eurozone crisis and the continued difficulties to achieve meaningful EMU reform.

Plan of the Book

Our book examines why the Eurozone crisis was so difficult to resolve and argues that distributive conflicts both among and within Eurozone countries lay at the core of these difficulties. It explores the importance of considering trade-offs and alternative options for both deficit countries (Part II) and surplus countries (Part III). For each of these sets of countries, the book explores how vulnerabilities to different crisis-resolution options shaped crisis politics both on the country level and among interest groups and voters within countries.

Putting the Eurozone Crisis in Context: Country-Level Vulnerability Profiles

Each set of analyses begins with an analysis of country-level vulnerability profiles. This sets the stage by putting the Eurozone crisis in comparative perspective. Rather than treating the Eurozone crisis as a *sui generis* event, as much existing work has done, these chapters (Chapters 2 and 5) explore the similarities and differences between the Eurozone crisis and earlier well-known financial crises, such as the 1992 Crisis of the European Monetary System (EMS) or the 1997 Asian Financial Crisis. Chapter 2 focuses on deficit countries and lays out in detail the trade-offs that crises requiring balance of payments adjustment create for deficit country policymakers. It argues that the relative costs of external vs. internal adjustment will shape crisis politics, including the willingness of these countries to accept harsh conditionality in return for external financial support. The chapter develops measures to compare national vulnerabilities to internal and external adjustment and analyzes the crisis responses for a sample of 142 crisis episodes that occurred in a sample of 122 countries between 1990 and 2014. Our analysis shows that the vulnerability profile is a useful tool for analyzing crisis responses across a wide variety of BOP crises. It also demonstrates that the Eurozone crisis is unusual because all crisis countries were located in the "misery corner": Deficit country vulnerabilities to both internal and external adjustments were exceptionally high, and vulnerabilities increased frequently over the course of the crisis. In such a setting, quick and decisive crisis solutions are hard to find.

Likewise, the second part of the book (Chapter 5) identifies and examines 272 episodes of substantial current account surpluses for the same set of countries during the same time period and compares country-level vulnerability profiles in those episodes to those of the five Eurozone surplus countries. Contrasting the Eurozone experience with the same countries' experience in the 1992 EMS crisis, for example, shows that European surplus countries exhibited a much higher vulnerability to both types of adjustment at the outset of the Eurozone crisis. They were very vulnerable to the breakup of the Eurozone, but they also shared high levels of vulnerability toward internal adjustment. Our analyses also show that whereas all Eurozone surplus countries were located in the "misery corner" during the Eurozone crisis, other European surplus countries such as Switzerland or Sweden were not confronted with such a difficult vulnerability profile. Chapter 5, thus, provides evidence for why surplus countries had an interest in making financing the main crisis response and in pushing the adjustment burden onto deficit countries, and why they were able to form a unified coalition in negotiations at the European level.

Overall, the country-level analyses show that the Eurozone crisis shares many features of previous debt and balance-of-payment crises, but is also distinct in that societies in both deficit and surplus countries exhibited an unusually high vulnerability to both internal and external adjustments—a vulnerability profile in the "misery corner" that makes crisis resolution politically difficult. The Eurozone's predicament is, thus, unusual because its setting within a monetary union significantly increases the costs of external adjustment. Moreover, the rigid nature of many European economies makes internal adjustment costly, and the high level of interdependence between Eurozone economies increases the costs associated with a debt default.

Interest Group Vulnerability Profile and Crisis Resolution Preferences

The book then moves to the interest group level and explores in much detail how domestic economic and social interest groups viewed their vulnerabilities to the crisis, which types of policies they preferred, and how they assessed the difficult trade-offs that the crisis presented them with. Focusing on the role of economic interest groups as important intermediaries in the political process, we argue that interest group vulnerability profiles influence their preferences regarding crisis resolution. A growing literature emphasizes the importance of societal interests, varieties of capitalism, and growth models in shaping the politics of the Eurozone crisis (Armingeon and Baccaro 2012a; Frieden 2015a; Hall 2014; Moravcsik 2012; Schimmelfennig 2015; Tarlea et al. 2019). Much of this literature builds on assumptions about the preferences of core economic interests, but treats these preferences largely as a "black box" (Baccaro and Pontusson 2016: 200–1). Our book contributes to this debate by "looking into the box": It presents the results of a broad, systematic and theoretically guided original data collection effort on interest group vulnerabilities and preferences regarding Eurozone crisis management based on original survey data from 716 interest groups in both deficit and surplus countries, that allows us to empirically validate many of these assumptions.

Chapter 3 focuses on interest groups in deficit countries and explores why policymakers in crisis countries implemented unprecedented austerity and painful structural reforms, even though public opposition to these measures was considerable. Empirically, the chapter leverages data collected through surveys among 359 interest groups in Spain, Greece, and Ireland. The data show that although a vast majority of interest groups in deficit countries viewed internal adjustment negatively, they still preferred it to a breakup of the Eurozone, especially when pressed to choose. Nonetheless, interest groups varied considerably in their assessment of specific internal, external, and financing policies. Overall, we find that despite some variation in vulnerability profiles and the large variation in the evaluation of specific crisis policies, most groups valued avoiding a Eurozone breakup more than avoiding austerity, a finding that explains why deficit country governments could implement this strategy.

Whereas much scholarly attention has focused on deficit countries, much less is known about the politics of adjustment in surplus countries, especially beyond Germany. Chapter 6, therefore, examines interest group preferences in three surplus countries: Germany, Austria, and the Netherlands. It explores to what extent the reluctance among surplus countries to engage in internal adjustment—that is, policies aimed at boosting domestic demand—can be explained by pressure from special interests. We present original survey data collected from 357 socioeconomic interest groups in the three surplus countries. Our analysis shows that as in deficit countries, vulnerability profiles played an important role in informing preferences about different crisis strategies and political strategies. Our key finding is that surplus country interest groups are not against internal adjustment in principle. In fact, general support for expansionary economic policies among interest groups in all the three countries was surprisingly high. However, domestic actors disagreed about which specific policies should be implemented to achieve this goal. Together with a broad consensus to avoid a breakup of the Eurozone (though some variants, such as a Greek exit, were viewed as less detrimental), this polarization turned financing into the politically most attractive strategy. The persistent surplus country resistance against internal adjustment thus seems rooted, at least partly, in distributive struggles about the design of possible adjustment policies among interest groups.

Crisis Politics

Policymakers need to balance the demands from special interest groups with those from their voters. The third set of analyses in the book, therefore, looks at how interest group preferences influenced the politics of Eurozone crisis management in each of the three deficit and surplus countries, and how they interacted with the preferences and ideas of other domestic and international actors.

In deficit countries (Chapter 4), the analysis centers on how the preferences of interest groups shaped the design and contentiousness of crisis policies, and how external actors influenced crisis responses. For this, we draw on a combination of primary and secondary sources including newspaper coverage, voter public opinion data, interest group position papers, and sovereign bailout documentation, as well as original qualitative evidence from seventeen in-depth interviews with national interest group representatives in Ireland, Spain, and Greece. We find that there was a large consensus among both interest groups as well as voters across all three countries that external adjustment—that is, unilateral euro exit— should be avoided at all costs. This left financing and internal adjustment as the only options, and significant conflicts flared up in all three countries about how the costs associated with internal adjustment (and to a lesser extent financing) should be distributed. Within the confines set by the Troika, which effectively narrowed down the range of options available to deficit countries, interest groups pushed for reforms to which they were least vulnerable: Business interests, for example, generally supported adopting comprehensive spending-based consolidation measures and labor market reform. Conversely, labor unions and social policy groups actively supported policies that would entail stronger burden-sharing between firms and workers. Overall, internal adjustment policies adopted across all three cases generally reflected the preferences of employer associations more than those of workers but, especially in Spain and Greece, this was associated with considerable political upheaval.

For the surplus countries (Chapter 7), the analysis focuses on the puzzle that although bailouts were a politically expedient option in light of the distributive struggles among surplus-country interest groups, the surplus-country governments remained hesitant toward bailouts and alternative financing measures, such as debt relief or the introduction of Eurobonds, and tied the provision of any financial support to strict and strong conditionality. Leveraging public opinion data, qualitative evidence and information gathered in thirty interviews with policymakers, we show that popular resistance against interstate financing constrained governments' appetite for more generous financing approaches. Whereas surplus-country voters generally supported the goal of safeguarding the Eurozone, most remained skeptical about the provision of financing. This broad-based skepticism, together with the high salience of the issue, provided few electoral incentives for policymakers to consider more far-reaching financing alternatives. Being caught in between interest groups blocking internal adjustment and voters opposing generous interstate financing, governments thus opted for the path of least resistance—piecemeal financing combined with high conditionality. Overall, our analysis shows that given the broad opposition of both voters and interest groups, external adjustment never became a politically viable option for surplus countries. Vocal and clear opposition from voters in all three countries blocked the route toward more encompassing financing approaches. Finally, more accommodating economic policies were pursued only in Austria. In that country the salience of the state of the domestic economy made expansionary policies electorally expedient and led the government to force economic interest groups to accept domestic reforms.

This final set of analyses once more demonstrates the importance of jointly analyzing the (un)popularity of all possible crisis-resolution alternatives, including those not chosen by policymakers. It provides insights into how the distributive concerns of voters, special interest groups and policymakers interacted with ideas, economic constraints, and international political pressure to shape the unusual crisis response to the Eurozone crisis.

The final chapter (Chapter 8) concludes by discussing the insights that these three perspectives have yielded and summarizes the book's main findings in the process. Because the bulk of our analyses have focused on domestic distributive struggles, the conclusion then turns to the question to what extent our approach is useful for understanding the distributive struggles on the European level as well. For this purpose, we examine how surplus and deficit states positioned themselves with regard to the core EMU-related issues and reforms that were discussed in the European Council during the Eurozone crisis (Wasserfallen et al. 2019). Our analysis shows that on policy issues related to questions of adjustment and financing, deficit and surplus countries aligned in opposing camps. Moreover, creditor-surplus countries managed to secure policy decisions in line with their preferences on almost all adjustment-related policy issues, which meant that deficit countries had to carry the bulk of the adjustment burden. In contrast, they showed more willingness to compromise on issues related to financing. We conclude with a discussion of the policy implications of our findings and an agenda for future research.

Conclusion

Overall, this book contributes to our understanding of the Eurozone crisis and the politics of crisis management more generally. First, it puts the Eurozone crisis in a comparative perspective, both in theoretical and empirical terms. Acknowledging that the Eurozone crisis is neither a normal recession nor a *sui generis* event, allows us to draw on the rich set of theoretical approaches and empirical investigations of past crises to tease out the similarities and differences of the Eurozone crisis. Empirically, this book is the first major study to quantitatively examine the Eurozone crisis in comparison to earlier crises. As such, it situates the Eurozone crisis in the context of other financial crises that required balance-of-payment adjustment and the problem of global imbalances more generally.

Second, the book considers both deficit and surplus countries, whereas the majority of studies of the Eurozone crisis (and financial crises more generally) have focused exclusively on crisis politics in the deficit and debtor countries. Although surplus countries have been instrumental in shaping the European crisis-resolution framework, little research so far exists on their interests and domestic political constraints, especially when it comes to surplus countries beyond Germany. Our book is one of the first to present such an analysis in a systematic manner. The book provides an encompassing and unified framework, which shows that the distributive struggles surrounding the politics of the Eurozone crisis in surplus and deficit countries are distinct, yet they also revolve around common themes and are intricately linked. This allows us to better explore the interdependencies and dynamics of crisis politics in the Eurozone.

Finally, the book presents the results of a large data-collection effort on interest group vulnerabilities and policy preferences in six Eurozone economies. This data allow us to test both our argument and competing explanations in much greater detail, but they will also serve as an important resource for future scholars. The data and replication packages for all analyses presented in the book can be found online.[19] In sum, our book generates an encompassing picture of the distributional politics of the Eurozone crisis and a better understanding of the constraints under which policymakers have operated in their attempts to solve the crisis.

More generally, the book argues and shows that it matters whether policy options are considered in isolation or in the context of trade-offs. As such, the book contributes to the wider emerging literature in political economy that highlights the importance of trade-offs in social and economic policymaking (Busemeyer and Garritzmann 2017; Emmenegger et al. 2018; Häusermann et al. 2018; Jacobs 2011). These trade-offs are ubiquitous and confront political actors with difficult decisions, but they also create space for creative options in the design of policies. Our book demonstrates that some policy choices that seem puzzling at first can be much more readily understood once the alternatives are considered.

---

[19] The data used in this book are available for download and replication at the FORS data archive (https://forsbase.unil.ch/project/my-study-overview/16230/).

2
Putting the Eurozone Crisis Experience in Perspective

Raphael Reinke, Stefanie Walter, Ari Ray, and Nils Redeker

The Eurozone crisis has been a watershed of European politics, with vast economic, social, and political ramifications in all countries of the Eurozone.[1] While these political ramifications go far beyond those countries most hit by the crisis, those countries that were running large current account deficits before the crisis were hardest hit in economic and social terms. The paths into the crisis varied across deficit countries (Jones 2015; Wihlborg et al. 2010), but they all responded in a similar way. When market pressure became too strong, Greece, Ireland, Portugal, Spain, and Cyprus all obtained external funding to overcome short-term funding shortfalls and resorted to austerity. Although this move allowed them to remain in the Eurozone and to avoid defaulting on their sovereign debt, accepting assistance also forced them to implement far-reaching fiscal and structural reforms. Austerity, increasing poverty and unemployment, as well as disillusionment with politics have been the result. In the post-crisis period, these countries increased their primary balances by more than 7 percent of potential GDP, to a large extent, by cutting public expenditures (OECD 2016a). Another commonality among the Eurozone countries was that none resorted to another usual crisis response: Devaluing the currency, also known as "external adjustment."

Scholars and pundits have emphasized that both the trajectory and the depth of the crisis in the Eurozone's periphery is unusual (Frieden and Walter 2017; De Grauwe 2013b; Mody 2018). One reason is that their situation was *un*usual—they did not have national currencies. Monetary policy is set at the European level, and devaluing the currency unilaterally would have required exiting the Eurozone and reintroducing the drachma, escudo, peseta or the Irish pound. Because exiting the currency union is complex and implies an array of negative consequences, many observers dismiss the notion that exit was an option and see the crisis of the Eurozone as being entirely unique (Armingeon and Baccaro 2012b). The fact that the crisis played out in the context of a monetary union—with a supranational central bank and some, albeit limited, common risk-sharing mechanisms

---

[1] The views expressed in this text are those of the authors and do not necessarily represent those of the Swiss National Bank.

The Politics of Bad Options: Why the Eurozone's Problems Have Been So Hard to Resolve. Raphael Reinke, Stefanie Walter, Ari Ray, and Nils Redeker, Oxford University Press (2020). © Raphael Reinke, Stefanie Walter, Ari Ray, and Nils Redeker.
DOI: 10.1093/oso/9780198857013.001.0001

(Schelkle 2017)—does, indeed, present a very special case. Most studies of policymaking in the Eurozone crisis consequently only focus on Eurozone countries.[2] They examine how crisis management differed among Eurozone economies (Bermeo and Pontusson 2012; Dølvik and Martin 2015; Heins and de la Porte 2015) or how Eurozone countries positioned themselves and bargained with each other about how to resolve the crisis (Armingeon and Cranmer 2017b; Lundgren et al. 2018; Tarlea et al. 2019).

Although these studies provide important insights into the details of the Eurozone crisis, treating the Eurozone crisis as a *sui generis* event comes at a price: By treating the Eurozone crisis as unique, scholars forgo the opportunity to examine exactly *how* the Eurozone crisis is distinct from other crises. Only by comparing the Eurozone crisis to other crises can we draw conclusions both about the nature of the crisis and how the responses to it differed from previous crises.

This chapter engages in such a comparative enterprise. It builds on the growing consensus among economists that the Eurozone crisis was a classic balance-of-payments (BOP) and debt crisis that was triggered by a sudden stop of capital inflows into countries that were running large current account deficits and were thus heavily dependent on foreign capital (Baldwin et al. 2015). It also examines *whether*, *how*, and *why* the policy responses to this crisis differed from responses to similar crises. Our perspective thus does not deny the special characteristics of the Eurozone crisis, but aims to uncover what is particular about this crisis and which characteristics it shares with others. Indeed, our analysis shows that although the Eurozone crisis is special in some important dimensions, it also shares many commonalities with earlier balance-of-payment crises.

Analyzing the policy response to the Eurozone crisis in the broader context of balance-of-payment crises forces us to think more systematically about the typical responses to such crises, including those paths not chosen in the Eurozone crisis: Substantial debt restructuring and external adjustment, that is, devaluing the crisis country's currency (Broz et al. 2016; Forbes and Klein 2015). When the Eurozone crisis occurred, many policymakers, such as Angela Merkel, famously argued that a failure of the euro was not possible because it would spell the failure of Europe.[3] Even academics, such as Barry Eichengreen, argued that a unilateral exit from or even a dissolution of the Eurozone would be associated with such prohibitively high costs that it would hardly be a viable option and, therefore, very unlikely to occur (Eichengreen 2010b; Eichengreen et al. 2013). History tells us, however, that currency unions can fail, that countries do in fact exit such unions, and that

---

[2] A broad range of work combines the study of the global financial crisis and the Eurozone crisis (Bermeo and Pontusson 2012; Lütz and Hilgers 2018; Pepinsky 2012; Walter 2016), but once again, there is little comparative attention to the broader universe of cases.

[3] https://www.bundestag.de/dokumente/textarchiv/2010/29826227_kw20_de_stabilisierungs mechanismus/201760.

such unions sometimes break up altogether (Cohen 1993; Rose 2007). While a departure from a currency union certainly involves high costs, an exit from the Eurozone is thus not impossible.[4] Rather than assuming that a break-up of the Eurozone was not a policy option, it is thus important to understand why this option was not exercised. This is especially true in a context where the alternative—severe austerity—not only caused severe recessions, but also had very adverse political consequences for the governments who chose to address the crisis with an internal rather than an external adjustment strategy (Bosco and Verney 2012, 2016; Freire et al. 2014; Morlino and Quaranta 2016).

This chapter explores this puzzle by comparing the Eurozone crisis to a large set of earlier balance-of-payments crises in an analysis centered on the policy trade-offs politicians face in such crises. Countries differ considerably in how they respond to balance-of-payments (BOP) crises. Some countries opt to depreciate their exchange rates (such as Italy and Spain in the 1992 European Monetary System (EMS) crisis or Indonesia during the 1997 Asian financial crisis), while others implement painful domestic reforms instead (such as the Baltic states during the 2008/9 global financial crisis). Yet others combine exchange-rate depreciation with internal reforms (such as Thailand and South Korea in the 1997 Asian financial crisis). Through an impressive array of case studies spanning BOP crises in different eras, different continents and across different political regimes, existing research has shown that distributive considerations and the difficult choices they create are an important determinant of national-level crisis management (Eichengreen 1992; Frieden 1991a; Gourevitch 1986; Pepinsky 2009; Simmons 1994; Walter 2013a; Walter and Willett 2012). These qualitative studies highlight the costs associated with different policy options for policymakers in times of financial crises, and show in much detail how the trade-offs associated with different configurations of these potential costs led to variation in national policy response to such crises. Although this research gives us a lot of case-by-case evidence on the importance of distributive considerations for national-level crisis management, quantitative studies on the distributional trade-offs inherent in crisis management for a larger set of countries are rare.[5]

This chapter therefore develops a comparative framework that allows us to quantitatively study the distributional trade-offs inherent in crisis management of a large set of crises, including the Eurozone crisis. Following the central theme of this book, it builds on the concept of vulnerability profiles (Walter 2013a) that

---

[4] Some legal (Estella 2015) and economic scholarship (Bagnai et al. 2017) has explored this possibility.

[5] Existing quantitative studies of BOP crisis management focus only on the distributive struggles associated with certain policy options, such as external adjustment (Kraay 2003; Leblang 2003; Sattler and Walter 2010; Walter 2009). This approach neglects the wider picture of how the respective net costs relate to each other and sum up across different policy options. For exceptions, see (Algieri and Bracke 2011; Broz et al. 2016).

allows us to analyze the costs of one set of policy options (external adjustment) *relative* to the costs of the main policy alternative (internal adjustment). National vulnerability profiles shed light on the trade-offs crisis country policymakers face when they have to choose between different policy options, thus allowing us to examine which crisis responses countries opt for overall. Empirically, this chapter develops comparative measures for national vulnerabilities to external and internal adjustment and analyzes the crisis responses for a sample of 142 crisis episodes between 1990 and 2014.

This chapter explores the similarities and differences between the Eurozone crisis and earlier well-known financial crises, such as the 1992 EMS crisis or the 1997 Asian financial crisis. It investigates how the Eurozone experience relates to the crisis responses more generally, whether membership in a monetary union dictates internal adjustment—or whether other factors were at play—and how vulnerabilities in the Eurozone crisis evolved over time. Our analysis shows that, in line with our theoretical framework, national vulnerability profiles shape countries' crisis resolutions, and the Eurozone crisis is no exception. High costs of external adjustment increase the likelihood of internal adjustment and reduce the likelihood of external adjustment, especially when the costs of the alternative are small. However, the analysis also shows that the Eurozone crisis is unusual in that deficit country vulnerabilities to both internal and external adjustment were exceptionally high. In such a setting, quick and decisive crisis solutions are hard to find. The predominant response in the Eurozone—internal adjustment coupled with external financing—is, however, not at all unusual for countries who are confronted with such a vulnerability profile. When seen from a distance, the responses to the Eurozone crisis thus become less puzzling and reflect the specific trade-offs that Eurozone policymakers faced.

The Argument: Vulnerability Profiles and Crisis Responses

We posit that the Eurozone crisis need be compared to other balance-of-payment crises and that the explanations for these crises also help us to better understand the policy response in the Eurozone. Balance-of-payments crises have been a recurring feature of the international economy and are often associated with other crises, most notably debt, banking, and currency crises (Kaminsky and Reinhart 1999). Countries hit by such crises share the same core problems: They are investing more than they are saving, consuming more than they are producing, and usually importing more than they are exporting, all of which is reflected in a current account deficit. During good times preceding the crisis, investment, consumption, and imports are encouraged and financed by the inflow of foreign capital. But large capital inflows often also lead to real appreciation, strong increases in aggregate demand, rising debt levels and credit bubbles, and declines in labor productivity, relative to other countries (Cardarelli et al. 2009). When these capital inflows dry up, the country experiences what is called "balance-of-payments pressure," often in the form of speculative pressure on the exchange rate. Faced with a large, unsustainable outflow of funds, countries essentially run out of foreign currency to repay investors and creditors. Often this comes in the form of a "sudden stop", an abrupt change after a period of high inflows of capital (Calvo 1998). The Eurozone crisis was no exception (Merler and Pisani-Ferry 2012).

In these cases, a substantial adjustment of economic policies aimed at realigning foreign and domestic prices is usually needed. Adjustment can be achieved in two ways (Algieri and Bracke 2011; Walter 2013b; Webb 1991): First, a reduction in relative prices can result from a depreciation or devaluation of the nominal exchange rate, a strategy called *external adjustment* (also known as price-based adjustment). By lowering the value of the domestic currency, external adjustment makes domestic products more competitive and raises the price of imports, so that domestic expenditure is switched away from the consumption of internationally tradable goods and toward the production and export of such goods. In the context of the Eurozone crisis, this strategy implies a break-up of the monetary union and a devaluation of the re-introduced crisis countries' currencies. Alternatively, rebalancing the current account can be achieved through macroeconomic austerity and structural reforms. This strategy is called *internal adjustment*, also known as internal devaluation or quantity-based adjustment. Austerity reduces domestic demand, which leads to a compression of imports, and is usually associated with an economic downturn that leads to lower wages or job losses. Structural reforms are implemented to increase productivity and to lower production costs, thus increasing the competitiveness of domestic products. These strategies can also be (and frequently are) combined, resulting in a mixed adjustment strategy that contains elements of both external and internal adjustment. Countries may hold off on either adjustment strategy, but to achieve this delay, they require savings or other financial assistance to afford the outflow of capital. Such assistance is often provided by the International Monetary Fund (IMF) and other sources, especially when exchange-market pressures are large and threaten to affect international financial stability. However, these external funds are usually only provided under strict conditionality that requires recipient countries to implement reforms in return for access to foreign funds.[6] As a result, external and internal adjustment are the basic options in balance-of-payments crises. They were also the basic options in the Eurozone crisis.

---

[6] One goal is to avoid a delay in necessary adjustment, through which the underlying problems deteriorate further and necessitate much more extensive adjustment later on when the funds run out (Bird and Willett 2008).

Weighing Bad Options: The Potential Costs of External and Internal Adjustment

Much political economy research on how policymakers manage balance-of-payment crises suggests that domestic political considerations are key in explaining governments' responses to speculative pressure (Amri and Willett 2017; Broz et al. 2016; Frieden 1991a, 2015b; Leblang 2003; Pepinsky 2009; Sattler and Walter 2009, 2010; Simmons 1994; Stallings 1992; Walter 2013a). For example, upcoming elections tend to delay devaluations (Stein and Streb 2004; Walter 2009). Political considerations are often related to the distributive effects of different policy alternatives. Policymakers' choices are influenced by how economically costly alternative policy options are likely to be, who will be most hurt by and who will benefit from different policy alternatives, and how these economic costs and benefits will translate into political costs and benefits. In short, when faced with balance-of-payments problems, they consider the specific positive and negative consequences of both available adjustment strategies for important socioeconomic and political groups as well the national economy as a whole, comparing the overall costs associated with each adjustment strategy. They then choose the option that is associated with the lowest economic and political costs.

External adjustment—a significant devaluation or depreciation of the exchange rate—has both positive and negative consequences (Frieden 2014; Steinberg 2015). On the upside, a depreciated currency makes a country's goods, services and assets cheaper abroad. This drop in relative prices makes investments in the domestic economy more attractive for international investors and improves the current account by boosting exports and lowering imports. These beneficial effects are biggest for countries that rely heavily on international trade, although the extent of this effect is influenced by a number of additional characteristics, such as the level of the exchange-rate pass-through on product prices (Frieden 2002; Kinderman 2008b), producers' reliance on imported goods (Helleiner 2005), the level of corporate indebtedness (Walter 2008), or the structure of the domestic banking system (Grittersová 2019). Overall, external adjustment tends to be beneficial for countries with large tradables sectors (Frieden 1991b, 2014; Steinberg 2015).

But external adjustment also has a number of downsides. It reduces purchasing power, which hurts consumers and firms that rely heavily on imported goods (Frieden 2014). Increasing import prices is particularly costly for countries that cannot easily substitute their imports. Substitution is usually very costly, and sometimes prohibitively so, for raw materials and highly specialized products, such as pharmaceuticals. The potential costs of external adjustment are also high for countries whose government, businesses, or households hold high levels of external debt, especially foreign-currency denominated debt (Walter 2008, 2013a; Woodruff 2005). Devaluation raises the debt burden in these countries, which lowers the profitability of both private and public debtors, thereby increasing their risk of bankruptcy. All this is particularly problematic, as the negative effects of a devaluation are likely to materialize more quickly than export performance improves (Willett 1998).

The costs of devaluation tend to be larger in countries with fixed exchange-rate regimes than in countries with intermediate or floating exchange-rate regimes, with regard to both economic costs and countries' reputations (Barro and Gordon 1983; McKinnon and Pill 1999; Willett 2007). Devaluation, therefore, also tends to carry particularly large political costs in fixed exchange-rate regimes (Blomberg et al. 2005; Cooper 1971). This is even more true for members of a currency union, because external adjustment requires them to abandon the common currency and to (re)introduce a national currency. Such reforms create an array of significant costs. They not only require crisis countries to produce the necessary infrastructure for such a move, such as introducing new coins and bills or establishing a payments system for the new national currency, but also pose significant challenges for the transition period. Such a move requires temporary measures to facilitate the transition from the common to the national currency, such as the rewriting of financial contracts, the introduction of capital controls, and negotiations about the currency in which debt denominated in the common currency will be repaid (Amiel and Hyppolite 2016; Bagnai et al. 2017; Estella 2015). Such a process generates high degrees of uncertainty, which itself is damaging. Exiting a common currency such as the Euro is thus a rather radical step with costs above and beyond the mere effects of currency devaluation. It should be noted, however, that this move is not unprecedented: History contains multiple instances of countries leaving currency unions (Cohen 1993; Rose 2007).

In sum, external adjustment is likely to be more costly the smaller the tradables sector in a country is and the more strongly it relies on imports that cannot easily be substituted. It is also likely costlier the higher its level of net external debt (especially foreign-currency denominated debt), and if the country follows a fixed exchange-rate regime—especially when it does not even have a national currency.

The main policy alternative to external adjustment is *internal adjustment* of the domestic economy via austerity and structural reforms. The goal of this adjustment strategy, like that for external adjustment, is to reduce imports, boost exports, and make the domestic economy more attractive for investments. The strategy entails pursuing these goals, however, without changing the nominal value of the currency and, therefore, keeps the relative values of investments and debt in foreign currency. Rather, lower public spending, higher taxes, a tight monetary policy, and a lower public wage bill are used to depress domestic demand for imported goods and to lower domestic relative prices. These efforts are combined with structural reforms, which aim at increasing international competitiveness, for example, by overcoming market inefficiencies, such as monopolistic structures.

Although these measures increase a country's international competitiveness and allow it to generate the resources to repay outstanding debts, internal adjustment tends to come with significant negative side-effects: Austerity policies tend to depress growth and are, therefore, typically associated with higher unemployment, lower wages, asset price deflation, and recession. All of these tend to be politically costly for incumbent policymakers, as the large literature on economic voting has shown (Duch 2007; Lewis-Beck and Stegmaier 2000).[7] Cutting public employment, pensions, and other benefits is never well received—and they are all the more unpopular when economic growth is already slow and unemployment high—but implementing these policies is especially difficult when the country is already in recession or faces high unemployment (Bartels and Bermeo 2013; Boeri et al. 2001). Some reforms, like reducing job protection, may stimulate the economy in good times but have a negative effect during economic slumps (Banerji et al. 2017). In addition, fiscal cuts tend to be more devastating when households have saved only a small part of their income, because low savings constrain the ability of households to compensate for lower wages and benefits by shifting expenditures from saving to consumption. Moreover, the costs of internal adjustment increase when the need to cut public spending is intensified by an accompanying debt crisis. In this case, a government not only needs to balance the current account deficit, but must also reverse fiscal deficits and lower its debt to a sustainable level. The costs of austerity are thus likely to be particularly high when the country has had difficulties pursuing fiscally conservative policies in the past, as evidenced by large public deficits and public debt (Alesina and Drazen 1991; Roubini and Sachs 1989). Structural reforms, such as labor or product market reforms, range from lowering the cost of hiring and dismissing regular workers and improving collective bargaining frameworks to deregulating retail trade and professional services or reducing barriers to market entry for producers. Although they generally increase employment, output, and competitiveness, in the long run they can have serious negative short-run effects (de Almeida and Balasundharam 2018; Duval and Furceri 2018). The costs of reforming product and labor markets are, therefore, not so much economic as they are genuinely political: Such reforms often generate political conflict—particularly when existing structures are well entrenched and supported by powerful interests who have much to lose from reforms and liberalization (Alesina and Drazen 1991; Haggard and Webb 1994; Pierson 1996; Steinberg 2017). In this case, structural reforms are likely to prompt strong opposition and high political costs.

Overall, this suggests that internal adjustment is particularly costly for deficit countries when their macroeconomic situation is poor to begin with, when unemployment is high, when debt burdens and fiscal deficits are high, when households have little leeway in savings to compensate for the adverse

---

[7] Internal adjustment also takes place much more slowly than external adjustment.

The Relative Costs of Adjustment: Vulnerability Profiles and Policy Responses

The costs of both external and internal adjustment vary across countries and across time. When faced with balance-of-payments problems, policymakers therefore evaluate the potential economic and political costs associated with each of these adjustment strategies. That is, they consider the specific positive and negative consequences of each of these strategies for important socioeconomic and political groups and the national economy as a whole, and then compare the overall costs associated with each of the possible adjustment strategies. Finally, they choose the option that is associated with the lowest economic and political costs.

This choice can be best understood by considering the potential costs of external adjustment *relative* to the potential costs associated with internal adjustment in a country at the time of crisis. The combination of these costs is reflected in a country's *vulnerability profile* (Walter 2008, 2013a, 2016). Figure 2.1 displays the grid introduced in Chapter 1 (see Figure 1.5), from which countries' vulnerability profiles can be identified based on their positions in the grid. The horizontal axis denotes the costs that external adjustment would inflict on the country, whereas the vertical axis denotes the potential costs associated with internal adjustment.

	I Only vulnerable to internal adjustment	II Vulnerable to internal and external adjustment ("misery corner")
high	• External adjustment	• Delay • Mixed adjustment • Extensive financing
low	IV Not very vulnerable to adjustment • No clear predictions on policy response	III Only vulnerable to external adjustment • Internal adjustment,

Vulnerability to Internal Adjustment (austerity and structural reforms)

Vulnerability to External Adjustment
(exchange rate devaluation, Eurozone: euro exit)

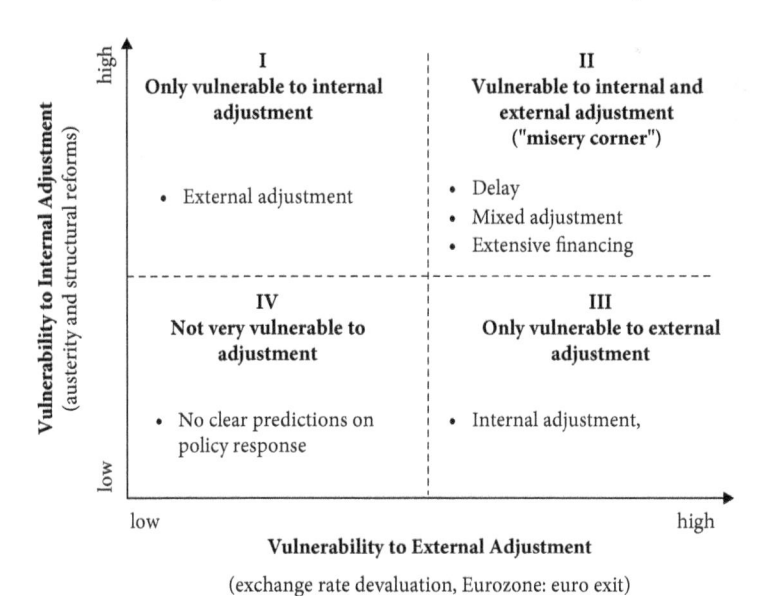

Figure 2.1 Vulnerability profiles and expected crisis responses

There are four idea-type vulnerability profiles that influence policymakers' responses to balance-of-payments crises. As discussed in Chapter 1, countries with vulnerability profiles I or III face a context in which one adjustment path clearly imposes more costs than the alternative. Countries exhibiting these vulnerability profiles are therefore likely to swiftly pursue the less costly alternative. Countries with vulnerability profile I, for whom austerity and structural reforms would be very costly but an exchange-rate depreciation would not, are likely to devalue their currencies quickly when faced with speculative pressure. Italy in 1992, for instance, found itself in such a position: Devaluing the overvalued lira was comparatively less costly than defending the fixed exchange rate by increasing interest rates in the short term and lowering wages and prices in the medium term. As a result, Italy was one of the first countries to opt for devaluation during the 1992 EMS crisis.

Countries with vulnerability profile III face high potential costs associated with external adjustment, but only low to medium costs from internal adjustment. These countries are likely to respond to BOP crises with painful domestic reforms while keeping their exchange rates unchanged. An example of a country with such a vulnerability profile is Estonia, which was hit hard by the global financial crisis in 2008. A heavy reliance on imported goods, large debts in foreign currency, and a strong, geopolitically motivated desire to join the euro meant that depreciation would have been very costly. In contrast, Estonia's healthy fiscal position and relatively flexible economic structures reduced the costs of internal adjustment for the country. In line with our expectations, Estonia opted for significant internal reforms while leaving untouched its fixed exchange-rate regime, a currency board with the euro.

In contrast, for countries with vulnerability profile II, both types of adjustment strategies are likely to impose high potential economic, social, and political costs. For countries in this "misery corner," crisis politics will be fraught with political conflict and delay. Given that they can only choose between bad options, policymakers are likely to try to avoid adjustment altogether, for example, by using their foreign-currency reserves to finance the deficit. When adjustment eventually can no longer be avoided, these countries are likely to mix adjustment strategies by combining exchange-rate devaluation, austerity policies, and structural reforms—although implementation will often occur only halfheartedly. The Argentinian currency crisis that took place at the turn of the millennium represents an archetypical instance of a country attempting to adjust while displaying this vulnerability profile. The country had fixed its exchange rate to the US dollar for almost a decade in a currency board arrangement. While initially a big success—the introduction of the currency board contained inflation and led to a resurgence in growth—the fixed exchange rate also induced a growing overvaluation of the Argentine peso that reduced Argentine competitiveness and resulted in a growing current account deficit. The arrangement ultimately stifled growth, growing unemployment and growing dollar-denominated debt. This made

Argentina vulnerable to internal adjustment—the country was experiencing economic problems to begin with, and also had deeply entrenched structural problems that were hard to resolve. But the high level of foreign-currency denominated debt also made external adjustment very costly. As a result, the Argentine crisis response was characterized by much delay and ultimately, in 2001, a default on and restructuring of its sovereign debt. Argentina thus sought to reduce the level of necessary adjustment by reducing its debt burden through default.

Finally, responding to BOP pressures is easiest for countries with vulnerability profile IV. Policymakers in these countries tend to have a lot of leeway in choosing their response, because neither option is overly costly. Their responses are likely to vary widely, may include a mix of both internal and external adjustment strategies, and are often not very salient and controversial.

The remainder of this chapter uses this framework to analyze countries' vulnerability profiles for a large set of crisis episodes and the policy responses that policymakers chose in response to these crises.

Research Design

To better understand how countries, including those in the Eurozone, respond to balance-of-payments crises, we develop a quantitative measure of countries' vulnerability profiles that allows us to compare the Eurozone countries to a wide range of other balance-of-payments crises. To this end, we identify crisis episodes, construct indices of countries' vulnerabilities to external and internal adjustment, and then use these indices to determine countries' vulnerability profiles for each crisis period. We then analyze and compare the vulnerability profiles of the Eurozone crisis countries to national vulnerability profiles in the 1992 EMS crisis, the 2008 global financial crisis in Eastern Europe, and the 1997 Asian financial crisis. In a final step, we examine how the vulnerability profiles of the Eurozone crisis countries evolved throughout the Eurozone crisis.

Sample Selection: Identifying Balance-of-Payment Crises

The goal of our analysis is to examine national vulnerability profiles for a large set of balance-of-payment crises in 122 developed and emerging economies between 1990 and 2014.[8] To identify crisis episodes, we follow the standard approach of measuring exchange market pressure (EMP) as exceptional movements in

---

[8] Data for non-OECD countries start in 1995. Because of data availability problems, we exclude microstates, least-developed countries (LDCs) and countries without reliable data (Cuba, Libya, Iraq, and North Korea).

exchange rates and international reserves (e.g., Chiu and Willett 2009; Eichengreen 2003; Eichengreen et al. 1996; Leblang 2002). This approach acknowledges that balance-of-payment crises tend to be associated with speculative pressure on the exchange rate, which is reflected in a devaluation of the currency and/or sales of a country's international reserves. Instances of high exchange market pressure are not necessarily full-blown crises. With enough reserves, for instance, a country can absorb the capital outflow, preventing a deep crisis. The advantage of identifying crisis episodes in this manner is that the EMP index includes all episodes of speculative pressure, irrespective of how the crisis was resolved. This is crucial for our analysis, because we are interested in examining the choice between different types of resolution strategies—external and internal adjustment.

We calculate exchange market pressure using a country's nominal effective exchange rate against the country's changes in international reserves (each with a quarterly frequency).[9] For the Eurozone countries, we additionally consider countries' changes in their *Target2* balances in the Eurozone's payment system Target2, which functions as an alternative to foreign reserve sales. This approach is in line with the view that rapidly increasing Target2 balances are symptoms of a balance-of-payment crisis akin to capital outflows during capital account reversals (Cecchetti et al. 2012). We use Target2 balances to identify instances where adjustment is needed, but refrain from making assumptions about the cause of this need, given that there is considerable debate about the meaning of variation in Target2 balances (Bindseil and König 2012). Changes in exchange rates, reserves, and Target2 balances are weighted by their standard deviation to avoid one variable from swamping out the other (e.g. Leblang 2002, 76ff).[10]

Crisis episodes are defined as those years in which the EMP index exceeds the average EMP value by more than one-and-a-half standard deviations.[11] We only consider the first year the EMP index indicates a period of elevated pressure within a three-year crisis period to avoid double-counting longer crises (Frankel and Rose 1996). Because the scope of our argument includes countries with current account deficits, we also limit our sample to those countries whose current account on average exhibited a deficit in the two years prior to the crisis. Using this methodology, we identify many well-known crisis episodes, such as the Mexican peso crisis of 1994/5, or the Argentine debt crisis of 2001/2.

---

[9] When the nominal effective exchange rate is not available, we use the nominal exchange rate against the dollar. This applies to forty-one countries.
[10] Accordingly, the EMP index is calculated as $MP_{j,t} = \frac{\Delta e_{j,t}}{\sigma_{\Delta e_j}} - \frac{\Delta r_{j,t}}{\sigma_{\Delta r_j}}$, and for Eurozone members as $EMP_{j,t} = \frac{\Delta e_{j,t}}{\sigma_{\Delta e_j}} - \frac{\Delta r_{j,t}}{\sigma_{\Delta r_j}} - \frac{\Delta T_{j,t}}{\sigma_{\Delta T_j}}$.
[11] We calculate the standard deviations for each variable based on the values between the 1st and 99th percentiles so as to lessen the impact of outliers on the calculation of the EMP threshold.

A complete list of the 142 crisis episodes can be found in the appendix at the end of this chapter (Table A2.1).

Operationalization: Vulnerability Profiles

We have argued that policy responses to speculative pressure are shaped by countries' vulnerability profiles, that is, the potential cost of external adjustment relative to the potential cost of internal adjustment. To operationalize national vulnerability profiles quantitatively, we generate two indices that combine different variables that capture the potential costs of external and internal adjustment. For external adjustment these variables include, for example, purchasing power effects and the costs associated with exiting a fixed exchange-rate regime. For internal adjustment, these capture measurements of the overall state of the domestic economy, the government's fiscal room to maneuver and the rigidity of economic structures.[12] The relevant variables are identified based on the theoretical considerations discussed above and represent the costs that would materialize if a country chose to pursue the respective strategies. We use principal component analysis (PCA) to combine each set of variables into a vulnerability measure for internal and external adjustment, respectively. We once more restrict our analysis to deficit countries and base this analysis on data for all country-years in which a country exhibits a current account deficit of at least 2 percent, irrespective of whether it experienced a crisis or not. After determining a country's vulnerability to external and internal adjustments, we then construct the national vulnerability profile as a combination of these two dimensions.

Existing work suggests that the potential costs of external adjustment for deficit countries grow larger the less a country relies on trade and the more it relies on imports that cannot easily be substituted. It also suggests that external vulnerability increases with higher level of net external debt (especially foreign-currency denominated debt), and if the country has a fixed exchange-rate regime. We measure these dimensions of external adjustment costs as follows (the exact data sources and definitions are shown in Table 2.1.

- *Competitiveness effects.* Because depreciation increases the competitiveness of domestically produced exports and import-competing products, the cost of external adjustment is likely to be lower in countries with a large tradables sector and higher in countries with a large nontradables sector (Frieden 1991b, 2014). To capture this dimension, we use the relative size of the

---

[12] To address the problem of missing values in our data (King et al. 2001), we use multiple imputation, as described in Honaker, King, and Blackwell (2011), and use the Amelia II package in the software R. We calculate the means from eleven imputations (Lall 2016).

Table 2.1 Indicators measuring the national vulnerabilities to internal and external adjustment

Vulnerability dimension	Variable	Operationalization and Sources
External adjustment		
Competitiveness	Tradables sector	Value added of the agricultural sector (ISIC divisions 1–5) and of the manufacturing sectors (ISIC divisions 15–37) in percent of GDP. Source: World Development Indicators, World Bank
Purchasing power	High-tech imports	Value of imports from high-technology sectors (i.e., aerospace, computers, pharmacy, scientific instruments, machinery, chemistry and armament (see Hatzichronoglou 1997, 9) in percent of GDP. Source: STAN database, OECD
Balance-sheet effects	External debt	Gross external debt position as percent of GDP. Source: Quarterly External Debt Statistics SDDS database, World Bank
Exchange-rate Regime	Fixed exchange-rate regime	Dummy variable, coded one for currency unions (no separate legal tender), currency boards, pre-announced pegs or bands that are at most +/− 2 percent, and zero otherwise. Source: Ilzetzki, Reinhart, and Rogoff (2017)
Internal adjustment		
Economic conditions	Unemployment	Unemployment, total, in percent of total labor force minus the national mean of the sample period. Source: World Bank: World Development Indicators
Fiscal conditions	Government deficit	Cash deficit (or surplus) is revenue (including grants) minus expense, minus net acquisition of nonfinancial assets, in percent of GDP. Source: World Bank: World Development Indicators
	Government debt	Government debt in percent of GDP. Source: World Bank and IMF Historical Debt Database.
Households	Domestic savings	Gross domestic savings are calculated as GDP less final consumption expenditure, in percent of GDP. Source: World Development Indicators, World Bank.
Economic structures	Regulatory quality	Regulatory quality captures perceptions of the ability of the government to formulate and implement sound policies and regulations that permit and promote private sector development. Source: Worldwide Governance Indicators, World Bank.
	Union density	Union density rate, net union membership as a proportion of wage and salary earners in employment. Sources: ILO, OECD, ICTWSS Database.

tradables sector, covering especially the agricultural, mining, and manufacturing sectors, measured as value added in percent of GDP.[13]
- *Purchasing power effects.* External adjustment is costly because it reduces the purchasing power of domestic consumers. Measuring this effect is difficult, because consumers tend to change their consumption patterns when import prices rise (Engel 1993). We proxy the purchasing power loss by focusing on imports of a product group for which few domestic alternatives tend to exist—high-technology products. In the short run, it is difficult for a country to substitute for high-technology products, because their production requires specific and long-term investments in physical and human capital. With limited viable substitutes for these products, consumers thus feel the purchasing power effect directly, and this effect increases the more a country relies on high-technology imports as a percentage of GDP.
- *Balance-sheet effects.* Devaluations significantly increase the debt burden for debt denominated in foreign currency (Eichengreen et al. 2005; Galindo et al. 2003). The more widespread foreign-currency debt is among households and firms, the more costly external adjustment becomes (Walter 2013a). Because data on the prevalence of foreign-currency denominated debt do not exist for large parts of our sample, we proxy for these balance-sheet effects by including the gross external debt position as a percentage of GDP.
- *Costs associated with leaving a fixed exchange rate regime.* The costs of external adjustment are particularly high in countries with a fixed exchange-rate regime, since market actors do not expect a devaluation of the currency and because a devaluation then badly damages a government's credibility (Blomberg et al. 2005; Sattler and Walter 2010; Stein and Streb 2004; Willett 2007). We use Ilzetzki, Reinhart, and Rogoff's (2017) coarse classification of de facto exchange-rate regimes. The category of fixed exchange-rate regimes covers countries with no separate legal tender, currency boards, pre-announced pegs, or bands that allow fluctuations of at most +/−2 percent.[14] This operationalization represents a conservative approach to coding currency unions. Currency unions, such as the Eurozone crisis are coded in the same way as pegged exchange-rate systems, such as the EMS. We choose this conservative coding to avoid assigning Eurozone members a high vulnerability to external adjustment by construction. Our index is thus likely to underestimate the external vulnerability of the Eurozone countries, because we would like to examine to what extent other factors than simply the cost of exiting the Euro may have influenced Eurozone members' decision calculus.

---

[13] ISIC Rev. 3 divisions 1 to 5 (agricultural sector) and 15 to 37 (manufacturing sectors).
[14] For "freely falling" exchange rates (category 14 in the fine classification), we use the coding of the last preceding categorization in order to assess the effect of the country's original exchange-rate regime.

Vulnerability to internal adjustment also varies across countries and time. It is higher when the macro-economic situation of a country is poor and unemployment high, when the state is ridden by fiscal problems—such as a high debt burden and a large deficit—or when regulation protects insiders. More specifically, we include in the construction of our index the following dimensions that measure countries' vulnerability to internal adjustment.

- *State of the domestic economy.* Internal adjustment slows the economy and creates more unemployment in the short and medium term (Eichengreen 1992; Simmons 1994). This prospect is never politically appealing, but it is particularly hard when the economy is in a dire state to begin with and many people are already unemployed (Singer and Gélineau 2012; Soroka 2006). Because threats to employment are particularly relevant to voters, and unemployment is very salient politically, we use the *unemployment rate* adjusted by subtracting the long-term national average to represent the level of existing economic distress.
- *Fiscal room to maneuver.* We measure the obstacles to fiscal consolidation with the government's *budget deficit* and *government debt*. The budget deficit indicates whether a country generally experiences difficulties implementing fiscal restraint, and the interest payments capture the overall debt burden. We use the average value of the fiscal deficit as a percentage of GDP over the previous three years and government debt in percent of GDP as measures of governments' fiscal room to maneuver—the higher the deficit and interest payments, the less room a government has, increasing the country's vulnerability to internal adjustment.
- *Household Savings.* Fiscal consolidation distresses households more when they have saved only small parts of their incomes. Low savings rates restrict the extent to which households can compensate lower wages and benefits. We measure savings with gross domestic savings in percent of GDP.
- *Rigidity of economic structures and organized interests.* Internal reforms are difficult when existing economic structures are deeply entrenched and interests well organized. We measure these rigidities with the World Bank's regulatory quality indicator. Regulatory quality captures experts' perceptions of the government's ability to formulate and implement sound policies and regulations that promote private sector development. We proxy organized interests with trade union density. Particularly for internal reforms, trade unions are the key interest groups.

To combine the different aspects of adjustment vulnerabilities into one overall measure of vulnerability to external and internal adjustment, respectively, we employ principal component analysis (PCA) (Jolliffe 2011). PCA is a method that reduces the information contained in several variables by calculating

Table 2.2 PCA results for deficit countries

External Adjustment	Loadings	Internal Adjustment	Loadings
Exchange-rate regime	−0.55	Unemployment	0.48
Tradables	−0.68	Budget deficit	0.43
External debt	0.45	Government debt	0.49
High-tech imports	0.25	Domestic savings	−0.49
		Regulatory quality	−0.21
		Union density	0.23
Proportion explained	0.35		0.29

"components" that capture as much variation from the original variables as possible, taking into account the correlation between these variables. Each principal component can be interpreted as a common underlying dimension of the original data. We conduct two separate PCAs for each set of variables representing the costs of external and internal adjustment, respectively. Following Walter (2016), we then take the first principal component of each set of variables as a measure of a country's vulnerability to external and internal adjustment.

Table 2.2 presents the results of the principal component analysis for external and internal adjustment, respectively. The estimated PCA loadings for the variables point in their theoretically expected directions. For instance, a more flexible exchange rate regime and a larger tradables sector reduce vulnerability to external adjustment, while higher levels of external debt increase it. Likewise, higher unemployment raises vulnerability to internal adjustment, while a better and more flexible regulatory environment lowers this type of vulnerability. Given that the directions of estimated weights are intuitively plausible, we are confident that the aggregated index captures what we intend to measure conceptually. The first components explain about one-third of the overall sample variation, and (with the exception of high-tech imports and union density) the loadings are substantially important for all variables.

In the last step, we combine our measures for adjustment vulnerabilities to construct a country's vulnerability profile, as depicted in Figure 2.2. This allows us to place each country during each crisis episode onto a vulnerability grid, denoted by vulnerability to internal adjustment on the vertical axis and vulnerability to external adjustment the horizontal axis of the grid. Countries in the top half of the space are particularly vulnerable to internal adjustment. Conversely, countries more to the right-hand side of the space are particularly vulnerable to external adjustment. To place each episode in one of the four quadrants, we drew lines at the sample means for internal and external adjustment vulnerabilities, respectively. Because the indices are constructed with PCA, the means always take the value of zero. This does not mean that the costs are zero, but zero represents the average cost of external/internal adjustment, with negative values representing lower and positive values representing higher costs of external/internal adjustment. As a result, the vulnerability profiles are constructed as relative measures and represent the vulnerability profiles of a given episode, relative to all other crisis episodes in the sample. The lines are thus best seen as indicative rather than sharp, categorical separations. Based on the country's location in one of the four quadrants, we can then infer the country's vulnerability profile.

How is the Euro Crisis Different? Putting the Eurozone Crisis in Context

The unusual trajectory of the Eurozone crisis can best be understood by putting the crisis in a comparative context and analyzing whether, how, and why the policy responses to this crisis differed from responses to similar crises in the past. Our analysis begins, therefore, with a comparison of national vulnerability profiles from all crisis episodes in our sample. We then examine in more detail the vulnerability profiles and policy responses for a set of well-known BOP crises and compare them to the Eurozone crisis. This comparison demonstrates that the Eurozone crisis is indeed unusual, because virtually all Eurozone crisis countries were located in the "misery corner," where any type of adjustment is painful. Viewed from this angle, the vehemence of the crisis, the political difficulties of resolving it, and the severe societal repercussions of the crisis become less puzzling.

Figure 2.2 uses the vulnerability indices for internal and external adjustment to locate countries' vulnerability profiles in the two-dimensional vulnerability space for each crisis episode in our sample. Crisis episodes located in the different quadrants exhibit different vulnerability profiles: Countries in the upper left-hand corner (quadrant I) are much more vulnerable to internal adjustment than external adjustment, whereas the opposite holds in the lower right-hand corner (quadrant III), where countries that are more vulnerable to external than to internal adjustment are located. Countries in the lower left-hand corner are less vulnerable to both internal and external adjustment than the average crisis country. And those in the upper right-hand corner find themselves in the "misery corner" and exhibit higher-than-average levels of vulnerability to both internal and external adjustment.

Figure 2.2 shows that there is considerable variation in the distribution of vulnerability profiles of the 142 crisis episodes in our sample. It plots all crisis episodes in gray, highlighting the Eurozone crisis countries in black. Using this classification, 35 percent of countries experiencing a crisis were only vulnerable to internal adjustment (quadrant I), whereas 22 percent were only vulnerable to external adjustment (located in quadrant III). A minority of 15 percent of crisis

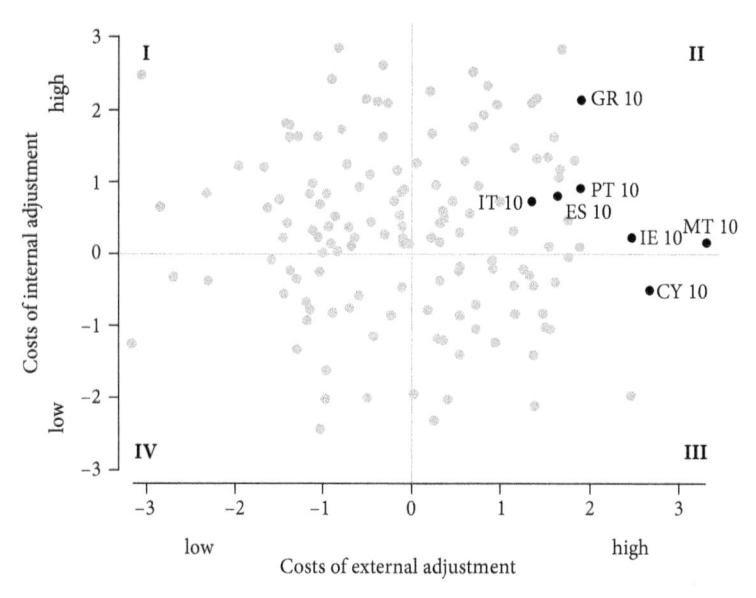

Figure 2.2 Vulnerability profiles of the Eurozone crisis countries and all other crisis episodes

episodes is located in quadrant IV, indicating that their vulnerability to both types of adjustment is lower than average. Finally, 28 percent of countries experiencing exchange-market pressure found themselves in the "misery corner" and were vulnerable to both internal and external adjustment (quadrant II).

How does the Eurozone crisis compare to this universe of BOP crises? Figure 2.2 shows that at the outset of the Eurozone crisis in 2010, virtually all Eurozone countries (denoted in black) were located in the misery corner. Among them, all episodes display exceptionally high levels of vulnerability to external adjustment and all cases, except Cyprus, also exhibit above-average levels of vulnerability to internal adjustment. The Eurozone's crisis countries thus confronted a situation in which any policy adjustment was going to be economically and socially painful and, therefore, politically difficult. Adjusting internally by curbing domestic demand, lowering wages, increasing taxes, and implementing structural reforms was difficult for these countries. But it was also costly to devalue, because their debt burden would have increased (or they would have been forced to default) and consumers' purchasing power would have been diminished. Our analyses also suggest that these negative effects usually offset the benefits of devaluation for the tradables sector.

Overall, by comparing the Eurozone crisis to other crisis episodes our analysis shows that the Eurozone crisis is not completely distinct, but is indeed highly unusual because virtually all crisis countries exhibited a high vulnerability to internal and external adjustment. Given this vulnerability profile in the "misery corner," it is not surprising that crisis resolution in the Eurozone has been protracted and difficult politically to resolve, painful, and associated with huge bailouts.

Our analysis also reveals some interesting variation among the Eurozone crisis countries. The country that stands out most clearly is Greece, because it exhibits unusually high levels of vulnerability to both internal and external adjustment even by Eurozone crisis standards. Given this vulnerability profile, it is not surprising that the implementation of internal adjustment was incredibly protracted and difficult in this country, leading to heavily instable government coalitions, mass-strikes, and even outright violence (Dinas and Rori 2013; Pitsoulis and Schwuchow 2016; Rüdig and Karyotis 2014; Vasilopoulou et al. 2014). Moreover, Greece's vulnerability to internal adjustment is significantly higher than for all the other Eurozone crisis countries. This may explain why Greece is the only Eurozone country for which exiting the monetary union during the Eurozone crisis became a distinct possibility.

A second set of countries consists of Ireland, Malta, and Cyprus. These countries exhibited exceptionally high levels of vulnerability to external adjustment, but were less vulnerable to internal adjustment than the other Eurozone countries. Implementing internal reforms is easier in such a setting, and it is therefore not surprising that Ireland is the country that acted most swiftly when the crisis hit (Brazys and Regan 2017; Whelan 2014). Nonetheless, adjustment was not easy either, and incentives were high to delay adjustment as long as possible. For example, Cyprus only began to substantially reform in mid 2012, when it became obvious that the country would likely have to accept a European bailout (Michaelides 2014). What is clear, however, is that societal conflicts about crisis management and the distribution of the crisis costs were more contained in these countries than in other peripheral Eurozone member states (O'Connor 2017; Pappas and O'Malley 2014; Vogiatzoglou 2017).

Finally, a third set of countries consists of Italy, Spain, and Portugal. These countries exhibited similar levels of vulnerability to external adjustment as Greece, but were somewhat were less vulnerable to internal adjustment than Greece. Although the crisis experience in these countries was less extreme than in Greece, and although they did implement domestic reforms, they also faced immense political difficulties and domestic opposition toward domestic reforms. Portugal began implementing austerity reforms—such as across-the-board cuts to pensions and comprehensive privatization schemes in 2010—as public finances and market confidence deteriorated, and accepted a bailout package in April 2011 (Afonso et al. 2015). Spain managed to secure the international funds needed to recapitalize its ailing banking sector without a formal bailout program, but nonetheless had to implement austerity policies, such as increasing VAT and income tax rates and freezing pensions, as well as significant labor market reforms (Cioffi and Dubin 2016; Fernández-Albertos and Kuo 2016). Italy is the only peripheral country that did not receive a bailout package, although the European Central Bank (ECB) devised several policies that were at least partly designed to support the country (Quaglia and Royo 2015; Sacchi 2015). Nonetheless, Italy's high level of vulnerability to both internal adjustment and the absence of conditionality rendered it difficult for the Italian government to enact substantive internal adjustment reforms.

This brief discussion suggests that the vulnerability profile is a useful heuristic for comparing the Eurozone crisis to other crisis episodes and for examining differences among the crisis trajectories of Eurozone countries. We next extend this comparative analysis and use this heuristic to compare the Eurozone crisis to a set of well-known major crises of the past decades: The EMS crisis in the early 1990s in Europe, the global financial crisis in Eastern Europe in 2008, and the 1997/8 Asian financial crisis. These crises include European countries before and after the introduction of the euro, advanced and emerging economies, and different crisis responses. As such, they capture important variations that allow us to examine in more detail the commonalities and differences between the euro crisis and these earlier crises.

The 1992 EMS Crisis and the Eurozone Crisis

We start with a comparison between the Eurozone crisis and the 1992 crisis of the European Monetary System (EMS). Both crises partly involved a similar set of countries before (EMS crisis) and after they had joined the euro (Eurozone crisis) and, therefore, allow us to trace how their vulnerabilities changed between these two crises.

The European Monetary System was a system of pegged-but-adjustable exchange rates that several European states had created after the collapse of the Bretton Woods system in 1971.[15] It was set in a context of increasing economic and monetary integration that had culminated in the agreement to create the Single Market in 1986, along with plans for a common currency among European countries. In the EMS system, European exchange rates were pegged to the German deutschmark, forcing European central banks to mimic German monetary policy decisions. This turned into a problem when German reunification fueled domestic demand and inflation, a development that the German Bundesbank sought to limit with higher interest rates. While this tightening of monetary policy may have been appropriate for the German economy, it was not aligned with the recessionary economic context in other European economies. This made these countries vulnerable to speculative attacks (Eichengreen 1996).

---

[15] For an overview of the EMS crisis, see, for example, Eichengreen (1996) or Höpner and Spielau (2018).

54 THE POLITICS OF BAD OPTIONS

The EMS crisis of 1992–3 began when Denmark rejected the Maastricht Treaty in June 1992, and confidence in further monetary integration waned. International markets began to exert pressure, especially on the pegged European currencies. The first to experience speculative pressure was the Finnish markka. In September of 1992, speculative pressure drove the Italian lira and British sterling from the Exchange Rate Mechanism (ERM). Sweden (not officially a member of the EMS but pegged to the European Currency Unit (ECU)) gave up its peg in November 1992, and Ireland, Spain, and Portugal devalued their currencies in early 1993. By the summer, when market participants turned their attention to France, the fate of the EMS and of Europe's monetary unification project hung in the balance. European policymakers eventually agreed to widen the fluctuation band in ERM to 15 percent in the summer of 1993.

Does the vulnerability profile approach help us to understand the trajectory of the EMS crisis and its similarities and differences from the Eurozone crisis? Figure 2.3 plots the vulnerability profiles of the EMS crisis and the Eurozone crisis countries. The graph highlights two key differences between the vulnerabilities in the two crises. For one, in the 1990s, countries' vulnerabilities to external adjustment were also high, but much lower than during the Eurozone crisis. This is not simply a measurement feature because of the EMU countries' membership in a monetary union (it is only one aspect in our coding of external adjustment vulnerability), but reflects that monetary integration indirectly increased countries' exposure to exchange-rate adjustment by facilitating cross-border financial flows and growing external debt. Nonetheless, the elevated vulnerability to

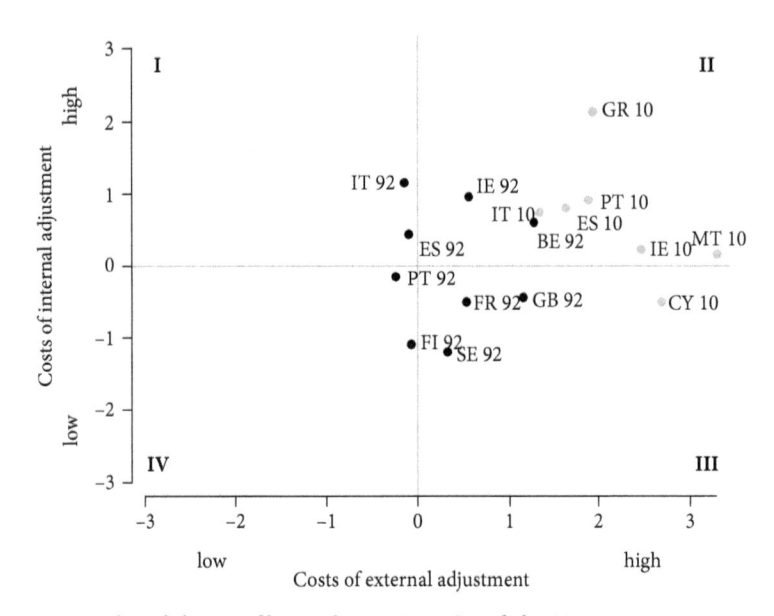

Figure 2.3 Vulnerability profiles in the 1992 EMS and the Eurozone crises

external adjustment in many crisis countries explains why several European governments initially tried hard to avoid a devaluation of their currencies, why they eventually allowed their currencies to adjust downward, and why devaluation was politically costly once it had eventually occurred. In Britain, for example, the pound's devaluation and exit from ERM led to a huge loss in government popularity (Bernhard and Leblang 2006). Others, however, such as Finnish and Italian policymakers, were much quicker to allow their currencies to devalue, which is not surprising given that their vulnerability to external adjustment was considerably lower.

Second, during the EMS crisis, countries were, on average, less vulnerable to internal adjustment than during the Eurozone crisis. In response, national central banks raised interest rates to defend the value of the currencies and tried to assuage markets by selling foreign reserves. The most extreme case was the Swedish Riksbank, which raised marginal overnight lending rates to 500 percent in September 1992 and spent a staggering amount of reserves in an effort to defend the krona (Eichengreen 1996: 174). But policymakers nonetheless feared the adverse effect of high interest rates on their economies, and therefore were reluctant to follow through with tight monetary policies over an extended period of time (Obstfeld and Rogoff 1995). As a result, most countries eventually gave up their pegs to the deutschmark and devalued their currencies. This move is surprising for those countries with an elevated vulnerability to external adjustment—and especially for the UK, for which one would have predicted a much higher willingness to defend the pound based on its vulnerability profile.

The 1997 Asian Financial Crisis and the Eurozone Crisis

A second set of crisis episodes that can provide an insightful comparison to the Eurozone crisis is the 1997/8 Asian financial crisis. Throughout the region, growth had turned into a bubble, credit had boomed (especially in the private sector), and current account deficits had grown, making a number of Asian economies vulnerable to crisis (Willett et al. 2005). The crisis itself started in Thailand, which, after months of speculative pressure against the Thai baht, devalued the currency in the summer of 1997.[16] Speculative pressure then quickly spread across the region, especially South Korea, Indonesia, Malaysia, and the Philippines. Thailand, South Korea, and Indonesia received IMF programs and were required to both devalue their currencies and to implement significant internal adjustment measures. The devaluations of the Indonesian rupiah and the Philippine peso were

---

[16] For an encompassing but entertaining account of the Asian financial crisis, see Blustein (2001).

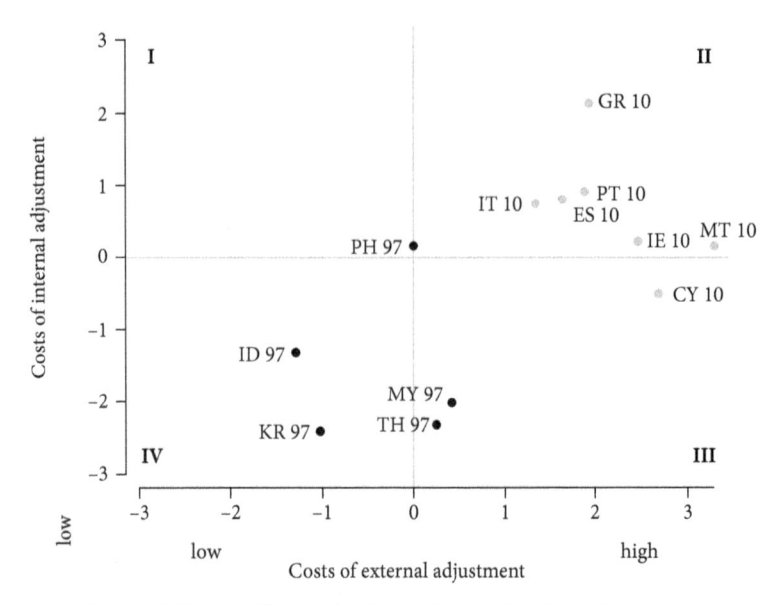

Figure 2.4 Vulnerability profiles in the Asian financial and the Eurozone crises

particularly dramatic, and the crisis led to the downfall of President Suharto's authoritarian regime in Indonesia (Pepinsky 2009).

Figure 2.4 plots the vulnerability profiles of the core crisis countries in the Asian financial crisis (in black) and compares them to national vulnerability profiles in the Eurozone crisis (in gray). The graph suggests that the Asian countries exhibited a significantly lower level of vulnerability to both external and internal adjustment. For example, Indonesia, the country whose currency devalued most drastically—losing up to 85 percent of its value—is also the country that exhibits the lowest vulnerability to external adjustment among all the crisis countries. In contrast, Malaysia is the country with the highest level of vulnerability to internal adjustment and also the country that refused to adjust internally, instead implementing capital controls to stem the outflow of capital from the country (Pepinsky 2009).

Given the severe economic, social, and political fallout from the crisis (Agénor et al. 2006; Haggard 2000), classifying the countries of the Asian financial crisis as being in the "lucky" corner seems questionable, however. Our measure of vulnerability profiles suggests that even some of the hardest hit Asian crisis countries—South Korea and Indonesia—were located in quadrant IV, exhibiting low vulnerability to both internal and external adjustment. This points to a shortcoming of our measure, the fact that data availability problems make it difficult to measure some important dimensions of vulnerability to external and internal adjustment for a large number of countries and a longer period of time. For example, we lack data on two aspects that were of particular importance in the Asian financial crisis:

The prevalence of foreign-currency denominated debt as an important determinant of a country's vulnerability to external adjustment, and the exposure of the domestic economy to a monetary tightening (Walter 2008, 2013a; Woodruff 2005). Measures—such as the percentage of non-performing loans, the level of foreign-currency borrowing, or the level of indebtedness of domestic economic actors—are generally not available for a larger sample of countries and a longer time period. But the analysis in Figure 2.4 shows that ignoring these issues risks severely underestimating the potential costs of internal and external adjustment for crisis countries.

Eastern European Responses to the 2008/9 Global Financial Crisis and the Eurozone Crisis

We conclude this section by comparing the Eurozone crisis to the crises that swept through eight new EU member states in Central and Eastern Europe in the wake of the 2008/9 global financial crisis. These countries had boomed in the years following EU accession in the mid 2000s. The boom was accompanied, however, by large inflows of foreign funds, corresponding current account deficits, and a fast accumulation of foreign debt (Kattel and Raudla 2013). When the collapse of Lehman Brothers sent shock waves around the world in the fall of 2008, the region was hit particularly hard (EBRD 2010), and all eight countries faced balance-of-payments pressures. As EU members, these countries operated in a framework that is similar to those of Eurozone countries, in many respects. But as EU countries outside the Eurozone, these countries were much less constrained in their choice between internal and external adjustment than the countries in the Eurozone. As such, they provide an instructive comparison to countries' Eurozone crisis experiences.

Figure 2.5 plots the vulnerability profiles of eight Eastern and Central European crisis countries (in black) and the Eurozone crisis countries (in gray). The countries vary considerably in their vulnerabilities. While four countries (the Baltic states and Bulgaria) are located in quadrant III—indicating that their vulnerability to external adjustment far exceeded their vulnerability to internal adjustment—one country (Hungary) is located in the "misery corner" (quadrant II). Romania and the Czech Republic are located in quadrant IV, indicating a low vulnerability to either kind of adjustment, and Poland is more vulnerable to internal adjustment than external adjustment.

These vulnerability profiles align quite well with the countries' actual crisis responses (Walter 2016). Bulgaria, Estonia, Latvia, and Lithuania implemented significant internal adjustment, an approach that plunged these countries into deep recessions, but allowed them to retain their close pegs or even currency boards with the euro throughout the crisis. Despite drastic public expenditure and

58   THE POLITICS OF BAD OPTIONS

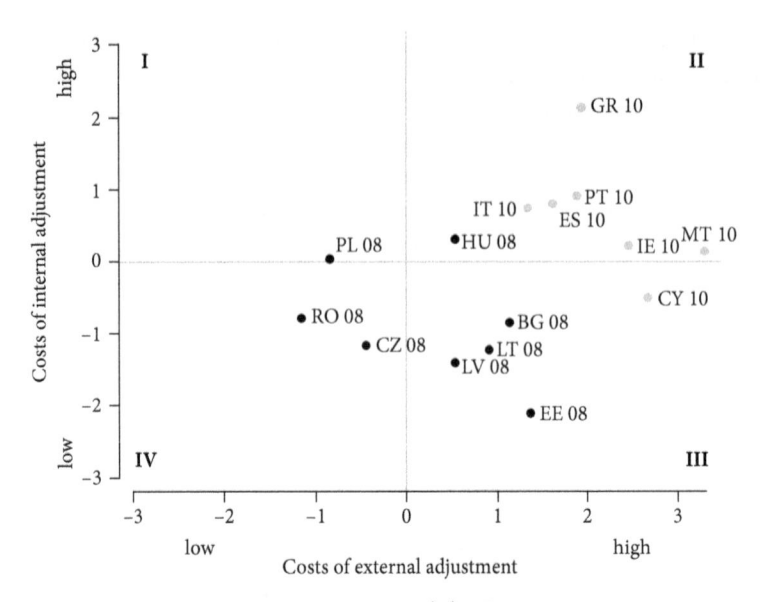

Figure 2.5 Eastern European states in 2008 and the Eurozone crisis

public sector wage cuts (Kattel and Raudla 2013), this strategy enjoyed wide popular support (Groenendijk and Jaansoo 2015), which is not surprising considering that the vulnerability profile suggests that an external adjustment would have been even more costly. In contrast, crisis resolution was much more difficult and contentious in Hungary and Romania, where adjustment measures included elements of both internal reforms and exchange-rate devaluation. When their currencies came under pressure in 2008, both national central banks raised interest rates and intervened in the foreign exchange market to counter this pressure. But when the pressure accelerated, both countries sought financial help from the IMF and the EU. Hungary concluded a US$25 billion package with the IMF, the EU, and others in October 2008, and Romania followed with a US$27 billion package in March 2009. In return for these funds, both countries agreed to pursue substantial fiscal consolidation and structural reforms. The crisis trajectory was painful in both countries: Unemployment and bankruptcies increased, wages declined, and real GDP fell by almost 7 percent in 2009. The political difficulties are fully in line with Hungary's vulnerability profile, but more surprising in light of Romania's profile. Finally, Poland and, to a lesser extent, the Czech Republic let their exchange rates depreciate immediately when their currencies came under pressure in the late summer of 2008, and initially even pursued expansionary fiscal and monetary policies rather than austerity policies. In both countries, the crisis response was relatively uncontroversial, politically speaking, in line with a low vulnerability to external adjustment.

Especially, the Baltic crisis experience is instructive for understanding the crisis response in the Eurozone. It demonstrates that it is not necessary for a country to be in a monetary union to pursue the difficult strategy of internal adjustment. Rather, the sufficiently high potential costs of external adjustment make it increasingly unattractive for policymakers. In the Baltics, several aspects combined to make countries very vulnerable to external adjustment. For one, the countries feared that devaluation would jeopardize their prospects of joining the Eurozone, thus limiting their integration into the European Union, which also mattered to the Baltic states for geopolitical reasons. A second reason was economic: The vast majority of private borrowing in the Baltics and, to a lesser extent in Bulgaria, was denominated in foreign currency, mostly in euros. This made devaluing very risky and costly, and thus significantly increased these countries' vulnerabilities to internal adjustment. With a vulnerability profile, such as that of the Baltic countries, the choice to adjust internally is attractive even without a currency union's additional constraints.

Crisis Dynamics: Changing Vulnerabilities in the Eurozone Crisis

So far, our analysis has focused on comparing countries' vulnerability profiles across different crisis episodes. For this purpose, we have focused on the vulnerability profile that a country exhibits at the outset of a crisis. However, countries' vulnerabilities to external and internal adjustment are not static but can change over time. The vulnerability profile heuristic not only allows us to examine cross-crisis variation, but also enables us to explore these dynamic changes in national vulnerability profiles over time. Such an analysis can then help to explain how countries' crisis policies and adjustment choices change over time.

We briefly illustrate this point by plotting the trajectories of national vulnerability profiles for six major Eurozone crisis countries. Figure 2.6 shows how countries' vulnerability profiles changed from 2007 to 2014. To give some context, the graphs plot both the development of countries' current account (left), with negative values denoting a current account deficit and positive values a current account surplus. The left-hand panels thus indicate to what extent countries are resolving their current account problems through adjustment. They also demonstrate that in the Eurozone crisis, countries adjusted at different speeds. The right-hand panels depict the development of each country's vulnerability profile throughout the same period.

While a detailed analysis of the trajectories is beyond the scope of this chapter, three things stand out from Figure 2.6. First, as we have seen above, all crisis countries started out with high vulnerabilities to external adjustment and moderate to high vulnerabilities to internal adjustment. Yet all of them moved into the

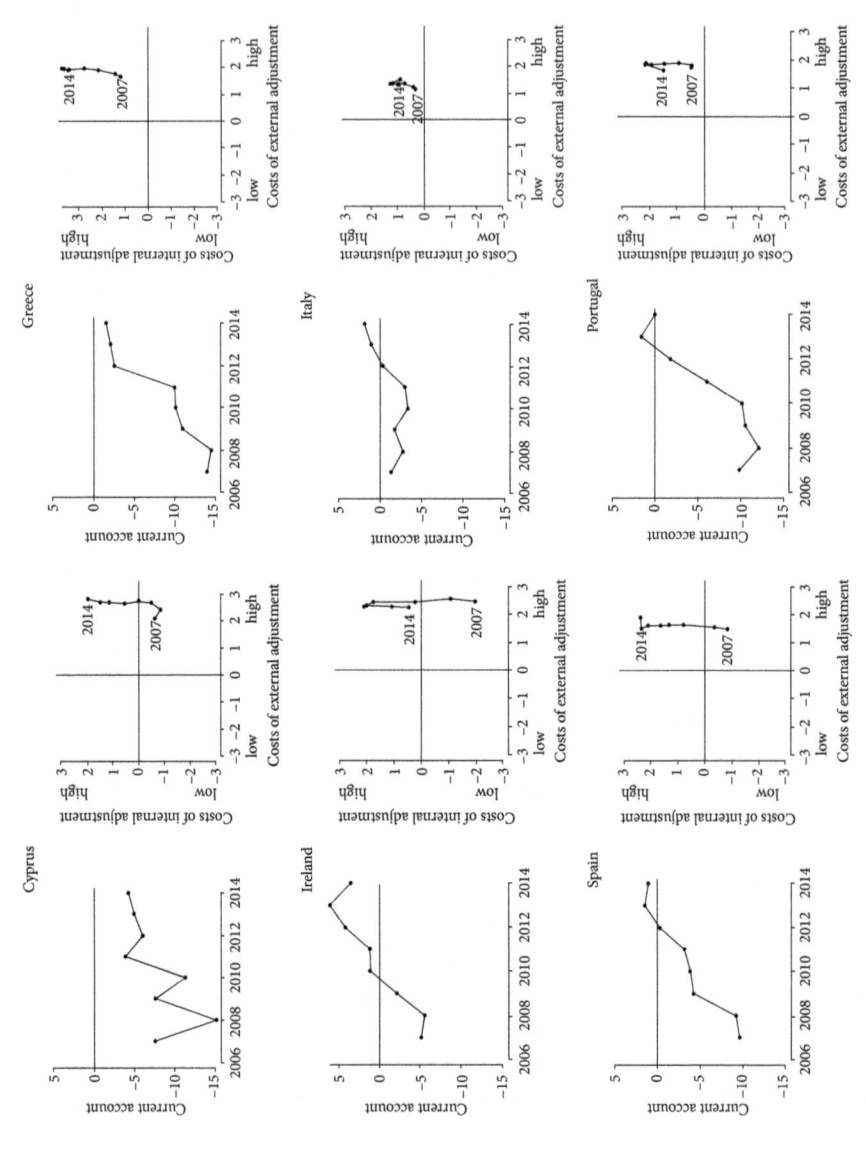

Figure 2.6 Current accounts and vulnerability profiles of Eurozone crisis countries, 2007–14

"misery corner" of quadrant II as the crisis progressed, suggesting that crisis politics became increasingly difficult as the crisis continued. This increase came from mounting public debt and a worsening macroeconomic situation (measured as unemployment), both in cases of countries that adjusted rapidly to the crisis, such as Ireland and Portugal (Reis 2015; Whelan 2014), and also in countries that delayed taking action, such as Cyprus and Greece (Dinas and Rori 2013; Michaelides 2014). Second, this deterioration suggests that adjustment became increasingly difficult throughout the crisis, creating political incentives to delay adjustment as long as possible (Walter and Willett 2012). Third, some countries adjusted faster than others, and a turnaround in the current account was generally associated with a decrease in vulnerabilities, especially with regard to internal adjustment. Thus, while an unfavorable vulnerability profile creates incentives to delay adjustment, biting the acid apple lessens the political difficulties when actually implementing adjustment in the medium term.

Conclusion

With the introduction of the euro, the countries participating in the European Economic and Monetary Union entered a unique arrangement. The monetary union fostered economic integration and facilitated cross-border flows of goods, services, and capital. But by adopting a common currency, the member states were no longer able to set independent interest rates for their domestic economies, to adjust national exchange rates, and were not prepared to have the ECB act as a lender of last resort to address Eurozone-wide systemic problems (De Grauwe 2013b). Membership in the common currency led to huge imbalances among Eurozone members that made the deficit countries vulnerable to BOP crises. It also shaped and constrained member states' options of how to respond to the Eurozone crisis that engulfed these countries just after the euro had celebrated its tenth birthday.

The analyses in this chapter have shown that despite all of these unique circumstances, it is valuable not to view the Eurozone crisis as an entirely different "beast," but to compare it to other balance-of-payments crises. Completing such an exercise, our analysis showed that the Eurozone crisis shares many features of previous debt and balance-of-payments crises. However, it was unusual in that societies in deficit countries exhibited an unusually high vulnerability not just with regard to external adjustment, but also with regard to internal adjustment. Such a vulnerability profile in the misery corner makes crisis resolution politically difficult. These high costs help explain why these countries had considerably higher difficulties implementing domestic reforms than for example the Baltic countries, who responded much more quickly and efficiently when they faced a similar crisis in 2008. In contrast, in the Eurozone, crisis politics was often characterized by political conflicts and delay.

Our analysis has also underscored the importance of jointly considering the different options available to policymakers to resolve a crisis, including the ones that were not chosen. Eurozone crisis politics can best be understood by considering the trade-offs and costs associated with each of the three main alternative options—internal adjustment, external adjustment, and financing (including debt relief). Many observers have puzzled over why deficit countries agreed to unprecedented austerity that has taken such a heavy toll on their economies. Our analysis indicates that for one, even though internal adjustment was likely to be costly to crisis country governments in general, external adjustment was likely to have been even more unpopular. Second, external financial support was an option for the crisis countries, even though it came with the condition to implement austerity. Finally, internal adjustment can be tailored much more to spare certain groups in society and to hurt others than external adjustment, which means that governments can try to buy support from influential groups by designing internal adjustment in line with their preferences.

This suggests, however, that the potential for domestic distributive conflict is high. If domestic interests diverge in how they evaluate different variants of internal adjustment, they are likely to fight to shift the costs of crisis resolution away from themselves. In what follows, we examine these domestic distributive struggles in Eurozone countries in more detail. The next chapter focuses on interest group preferences, especially on the question how they evaluate the different options available to policymakers during a BOP crisis and the trade-offs they pose. Chapter 4 then presents a more detailed case study in how the distributional struggles surrounding Eurozone crisis resolution shaped deficit country crisis politics and policies.

Appendix

Table A2.1 Crisis episodes identified using the EMP index

Albania	1997
Albania	2008
Azerbaijan	2001
Argentina	2002
Argentina	2014
Australia	2008
Austria	1999
Armenia	2009
Bosnia and Herzegovina	2005
Bosnia and Herzegovina	2008
Brazil	1999

Brazil	2002
Belize	2000
Bulgaria	2000
Bulgaria	2004
Bulgaria	2008
Bulgaria	2013
Belarus	1997
Belarus	2006
Cape Verde	1996
Cape Verde	2000
Cape Verde	2008
Sri Lanka	2009
Chile	1995
Colombia	2008
Congo	2008
Costa Rica	2008
Croatia	2004
Croatia	2008
Cyprus	1999
Cyprus	2004
Cyprus	2010
Czech Republic	2005
Czech Republic	2008
Dominican Republic	2002
Estonia	2001
Estonia	2005
Estonia	2008
Fiji	1998
Fiji	2001
Fiji	2005
Fiji	2008
Finland	1991
Finland	2013
France	2008
Georgia	1998
Georgia	2008
Ghana	1999
Ghana	2006
Greece	1991
Greece	2001
Greece	2008
Guyana	1997
Guyana	2005
Honduras	2011
Hungary	2003
Hungary	2008
Iceland	1991
Iceland	2012
India	2008
Indonesia	1997
Ireland	2008
Italy	1992

Continued

Table A2.1 *Continued*

Italy	2008
Jamaica	2003
Jamaica	2009
Kazakhstan	1999
Kazakhstan	2005
Jordan	1998
Jordan	2008
Kenya	2008
South Korea	1997
Kyrgyz Republic	1998
Kyrgyz Republic	2008
Kyrgyz Republic	2011
Lebanon	2005
Lebanon	2011
Latvia	2008
Latvia	2012
Lithuania	2008
Lithuania	2013
Malaysia	1997
Maldives	2001
Malta	1995
Malta	2000
Malta	2004
Mauritius	2008
Mexico	1995
Mexico	2008
Mongolia	2002
Mongolia	2012
Moldova	1998
Moldova	2009
Montenegro	2008
Oman	2000
New Zealand	2008
Nigeria	1999
Pakistan	1995
Pakistan	2008
Papua New Guinea	1998
Papua New Guinea	2013
Peru	1999
Philippines	1997
Poland	2008
Portugal	1999
Portugal	2008
Romania	1997
Romania	2008
Romania	2014
Slovak Republic	2005
Slovak Republic	2008
Vietnam	2008
Slovenia	2007
South Africa	1996

South Africa	2001
South Africa	2008
Spain	1991
Spain	1999
Spain	2008
Spain	2012
Swaziland	1995
Swaziland	2000
Swaziland	2008
Sweden	1992
Tajikistan	2007
Tajikistan	2014
Thailand	1997
Tunisia	2008
Turkey	1991
Turkey	2001
Turkey	2008
Ukraine	1998
Ukraine	2008
Ukraine	2014
Macedonia	1997
Macedonia	2008
United Kingdom	1992
United Kingdom	2008
Uruguay	2002
Uruguay	2008
Serbia	2008
Serbia	2012

3
Distributive Conflict and Interest Group Preferences in Deficit Countries

Health care cuts, lower pensions and slashed public sector employment all featured during the Eurozone crisis as deficit states were forced to implement harsh policy reforms aimed at achieving internal adjustment (Blyth 2013; Bojar et al. 2019; Kriesi et al. 2019; Monastiriotis et al. 2013). However, public opposition to governments' plans to implement austerity and structural reforms was considerable, and public discontent grew during the crisis (Armingeon et al. 2016). Citizens mobilized in public demonstrations (Kriesi et al. 2019; Kurer et al. 2018; Della Porta 2015) and economic strikes (Genovese et al. 2016; Rüdig and Karyotis 2014), and displayed their dissatisfaction at the voting booth, where populist, anti-austerity parties became increasingly successful (Hernández and Kriesi 2016; Hobolt and Tilley 2016). As in many other balance-of-payments crises (Eichengreen 1992; Haggard 1985; Simmons 1997), internal adjustment thus proved politically difficult to realize.

Why did policymakers in crisis countries nonetheless implement unprecedented austerity and painful structural reforms? Chapter 2 showed that deficit countries exhibited an unusually high vulnerability to both internal and external adjustment—a vulnerability profile that makes crisis resolution politically difficult. Why did, ultimately, none of them opt for external adjustment; that is, an exit from the Eurozone? How did governments decide which specific reforms to implement? And why did some governments achieve internal adjustment more quickly and in a less politically contentious way than others?

To answer these questions, this chapter and Chapter 4 concentrate on deficit country crisis politics and examine in more detail the distributive struggles surrounding domestic policymaking during the crisis. In these countries, the struggles centered on the question of who would bear the brunt of crisis costs: Consumers, taxpayers, investors, government employees, pensioners, the unemployed, the export sector, the non-tradable sector, and so on.

A growing literature emphasizes that societal interests were important in shaping the politics of the Eurozone crisis (Armingeon and Baccaro 2012a; Frieden 2014; Frieden and Walter 2017; Hall 2014; Moravcsik 2012; Schimmelfennig 2015). To study how these societal interests mattered for Eurozone crisis politics in deficit countries, this chapter begins with an analysis of the preferences of a wide array of organized socioeconomic interest groups. Such interest groups tend to represent large numbers of voters and/or firms, and lobby on economic and regulatory policies (Giger and Klüver 2016). As such, they often serve as strategic intermediaries between constituents and policymakers during economic crises. For one, organized interests are better placed than politicians to assess the economic impact of policy decisions on subsets of the domestic electorate (Mansbridge 1992). Interest groups therefore play an important role in providing information that helps policymakers assess the distributional effects of different policy options (Halpin and Fraussen 2017; Woll 2007). This is particularly true during times of crisis, when uncertainty is high and time constraints are strong (Gourevitch 1986).

Second, policymakers often rely on interest group cooperation to ensure the effective implementation of broadly unpopular reforms (Avdagic 2010; Baccaro and Sang-Hoon 2007; Baccaro and Simoni 2008). Interest groups can provide cues to the public of whether or not the enactment of a reform represents a necessary course of action (Dür 2019; Kim and Margalit 2016). Moreover, these groups can overcome collective action problems to mobilize support or opposition toward these policies (Dür and Mateo 2013a). Unsurprisingly, interest groups thus tend to be politically influential during economic crises (Alesina and Drazen 1991; Drazen 2000; Rodrik 1996; Sturzenegger and Tommasi 1998; Walter 2008). The Eurozone crisis has been no exception (Afonso et al. 2015; Armingeon and Baccaro 2012b; Culpepper and Regan 2014; Picot and Tassinari 2017; Regalia and Regini 2018).

Against the backdrop of this general consensus that organized interest groups play a key role in shaping crisis-time policymaking, both in deficit countries more broadly, as well as in Eurozone crisis countries more specifically, the scarcity of systematic empirical analyses of the actual policy preferences of interest groups in crisis contexts is notable. To address this lacuna, this chapter presents and analyzes original survey data from over 300 interest groups in Ireland, Spain, and Greece. As discussed in Chapter 2, these country cases were similar in many respects. They were all Eurozone members that suffered from substantial financial crises and were highly vulnerable toward both internal and external adjustment during their respective crisis years.

Making use of the theoretical framework guiding this book, this chapter explores in much detail how domestic economic and social interest groups viewed their vulnerabilities to the crisis, which types of policies they preferred, and how they assessed the difficult trade-offs the crisis presented them with. We argue that interest groups varied in their vulnerabilities to the policy strategies available to policymakers during the crisis: *External adjustment* (i.e., Eurozone exit), *internal adjustment* (austerity and structural reform), and/or *financing* (external funding of the current account deficit). These strategies present interest groups with difficult trade-offs, which then inform their overall assessments about the relative desirability of different reform strategies.

Our analyses show that interest groups varied considerably in their assessment of specific internal, external, and financing policies in a way that reflected their economic vulnerabilities. Groups that were vulnerable to a specific adjustment strategy were also more likely to dislike it. For example, social policy groups were significantly more likely to assess austerity measures and structural reforms negatively than did business groups.

A core contribution of our analysis is its focus on trade-offs and the relative costs of different, possible crisis policies. Although we find, for example, that interest groups that were predominantly vulnerable to austerity tended to prefer a Eurozone exit, those vulnerable to any type of adjustment tended ultimately to favor internal adjustment over an exit. Especially when pressed to choose, many groups valued remaining in the Eurozone more strongly than avoiding austerity. To the extent that a majority of groups falls in the cross-pressured category, this made it easier for deficit country governments to implement this strategy. Our analysis thus provides an explanation of why no crisis country left the Eurozone, although a strong majority of interest groups in Eurozone deficit states disapproved of austerity measures; in the end, they still preferred austerity to leaving the common currency.

Because different policy strategies can be implemented through different sets of policies, we also explore interest groups' assessment of specific policies, with a particular focus on internal adjustment, where the range of policy options is particularly large. These analyses of interest groups' policy-specific preferences suggest that internal adjustment was further facilitated by the fact that policymakers have some room to tailor austerity policies and structural reforms to the liking of influential interest groups. Tailoring reform packages to these policy-specific preferences thus allows policymakers to moderate domestic opposition to internal adjustment.

This chapter starts out by discussing existing work on distributional conflict and the politics of adjustment in the Eurozone periphery. It then explains the research design, and presents descriptive statistics of interest group adjustment preferences and vulnerabilities. In a next step, we analyze statistically interest group adjustment preferences by means of regression analyses. This part is divided into looking at, in turn, both the absolute preferences of groups, that is, their preferences absent the salience of an external vs. internal adjustment trade-off, as well as the relative preferences of interest groups, where groups are obliged to make hard choices between the two adjustment strategies. The final discussion summarizes our findings and concludes.

Interest Groups and Deficit Country Policymaking

What explains the willingness of Eurozone periphery governments to implement far-reaching austerity and structural reforms? Existing accounts can be broadly classified into two streams that emphasize, in turn, the international or the domestic drivers of internal adjustment.

One set of explanations sees internal adjustment as the result of international pressure that forced deficit countries to accept harsh austerity and structural reform. Some authors argue that this pressure originated mainly from the Eurozone creditor and surplus countries, either because it was to their economic advantage (Frieden 2015b; Frieden and Walter 2017; Schimmelfennig 2014; Steinberg and Vermeiren 2015), or because they wanted to avoid unpopular and electorally costly short-run costs (Aizenman 2015; Baldwin and Giavazzi 2015; Schneider and Slantchev 2018), or because of their strong ordoliberal ideologies (Blyth 2013; Enderlein and Verdun 2009; Matthijs and McNamara 2015). Further narratives emphasize the role of other external actors, such as the European Central Bank (ECB) or the European Commission (Kranke and Luetz 2014), or fiscally conservative technocrats (Blyth 2013; Helgadóttir 2016) who were able to impose their preferences on crisis-afflicted countries. These accounts often assume implicitly that domestic interests in crisis countries uniformly disliked internal adjustment policies, which suggests that internal adjustment arises because it is externally imposed on crisis countries (e.g., Blyth 2013; Mody 2018).

However, there is also considerable evidence that the policies demanded by international institutions are often supported by at least some domestic interests. After all, the distributional effects of different forms of adjustment harm some interests more than others, thus leading to divergences in attitudes towards adjustment (e.g., Frieden 2014; Haggard and Kaufman 1992; Simmons 1997; Walter 2008, 2013a). This suggests that preferences about the specific make-up of policy packages designed to combat a crisis is likely to vary among domestic interests, some of whom are more politically influential than others. Not surprisingly, research on International Monetary Fund (IMF) conditionality, for example, has shown that reform demands are often in line with the preferences of the government and select domestic interests (Caraway et al. 2012; Dhonte 1997; Drazen 2002; Dreher 2009; Mussa and Savastano 1999). An IMF program can thus provide a government with the opportunity to scapegoat external actors because the pain of unpopular policies favored it and its domestic support coalition (Bird and Willett 2004; Vreeland 1999).

In light of these considerations, a second strand of research therefore argues that, even during crises, policy design is (also) a function of the coalitions domestic governments can build among voter and producer groups (Afonso et al. 2015; Armingeon and Baccaro 2012b; Fernández-Albertos and Kuo 2016; Frieden 2015b; Walter 2016). Given that the shape and availability of these coalitions varies, as does the strength of societal interests opposed to reform, the ease with which governments are able to implement internal adjustment measures also varies. For the Eurozone crisis, this suggests that despite external pressures, crisis politics in deficit states were also driven by domestic considerations (Frieden and Walter 2017; Hall 2018a).[1] This is in line with case study evidence from the crisis. For example, Cioffi and Dubin (2016) argue that internal adjustment measures in Spain enacted by the conservative Rajoy government allowed the cabinet to accommodate producer interests, while simultaneously suppressing the domestic labor movement, a key constituency of its left-wing opposition. Similarly, research suggests that austerity in Ireland has been driven mainly by the close ties between successive Irish governments and employer associations, often representing foreign firms (Brazys and Regan 2017; Culpepper and Regan 2014). More generally, both crisis-related policies and the overall impact of the economic crisis in deficit states have differed in how they have affected different socioeconomic groups (Avram, Figari, Leventi, Levy, Navicke, Matsaganis, Militaru, Paulus, Rastrigina, et al. 2013). Whereas the costs of the crisis have been large, especially for the most vulnerable groups in society, the political clout of banks and other financial market actors (Blyth 2013), insider–outsider structures (Bentolila et al. 2012), the strong resistance of vested interests (Featherstone 2015), and clientelist politics (Afonso et al. 2015) have generally protected politically influential groups.

These accounts serve to highlight that attitudes toward internal adjustment are not homogeneously negative in countries suffering from crisis. Some groups may strongly support certain policies designed to achieve internal adjustment, and these preferences often influence policymaking. At the same time, entrenched interest group opposition makes it difficult and politically costly for the government to enact austerity measures and structural reforms, as evidenced in Greece (Afonso et al. 2015; Featherstone 2011; Pappas and O'Malley 2014), in Italy (Culpepper 2014; Regalia and Regini 2018), and to a lesser extent in Portugal (Costa 2012). Because influential interest groups tend to be more successful in shaping policy decisions, more vulnerable and politically less influential groups tend to pay the highest price of adjustment. In the Eurozone crisis, for example, the young have been hit hardest by the crisis. Youth unemployment tripled in Ireland between 2007 and 2012, and between 2012 and 2014 more than half of economically active people under 25 in Greece and Spain were without work.[2] More generally, unemployment has risen most among the young, men, and less educated people (Gutiérrez 2014).

Understanding crisis politics in deficit countries thus requires an in-depth understanding of the interplay between external pressures, the preferences of domestic interests, and the political strength of these interests. We therefore begin our analysis with a detailed exploration of domestic preferences regarding

---

[1] Some scholars have also emphasized the role of constrained opportunity sets and unintended consequences as the main explanatory variables for crisis resolution outcomes (Aizenman 2015; Mény 2014). From this perspective, austerity in deficit countries results from EMU policymakers' attempts to 'muddle through' the crisis (Mény 2014).

[2] Eurostat (2016): http://ec.europa.eu/eurostat/web/lfs/data/database.

different policy options in the Eurozone crisis, a situation in which external pressure was large.

Group-Specific Adjustment Preferences in Eurozone Deficit Countries

We argue that interest group-specific vulnerability profiles shape the adjustment preferences of domestic interest groups. This means that interest group preferences about possible crisis responses are driven by the potential costs of external adjustment for an interest group, relative to the potential interest group-specific costs of internal adjustment. Interest groups' vulnerabilities to an adjustment strategy vary not just by interest group, however, but also by how exactly the strategy is implemented. This is particularly true of internal adjustment, where structural reforms and austerity can be implemented in a myriad of ways. Analyzing vulnerability profiles of interest groups thus requires paying much more attention than at the country-level to how interest group characteristics affect their vulnerabilities to different *policies* associated with each adjustment strategy. In addition, it is important to distinguish between interest groups' *absolute* and *relative adjustment preferences*. Absolute preferences denote interest groups' general support or opposition to a given crisis policy or adjustment strategy. But because crises are complex situations in which not implementing one adjustment strategy means that another form of crisis resolution will have to be implemented (and vice versa), it is important to consider the trade-offs and opportunity costs each policy and strategy entails for each interest group. We take these opportunity costs into consideration by analyzing their relative adjustment preferences, which is how societal interests rank adjustment strategies against each other. This distinction is key when governments are confronted with bad, but necessary, options, as is often the case in a crisis: When all policies are disliked in absolute terms, relative preferences tell us which policies can most readily be implemented from among this choice set.

Interest Group Vulnerability to External Adjustment

One option for countries confronted with balance-of-payments pressures is external adjustment, that is a devaluation of the nominal exchange rate. This strategy is most commonly resorted to via a unilateral devaluation of the domestic currency. But particularly within currency unions, external adjustment can also come about in other ways. For instance, a crisis-afflicted deficit country such as Greece could, in 2011, have left the Eurozone and lowered the value of its national currency, but a surplus country such as Germany could also have chosen to abandon the euro; either scenario would have led to a de facto nominal exchange rate-devaluation in Greece.

Regardless of the exact policy that leads to external adjustment per se, the strategy makes domestic products more competitive internationally and increases the cost of imports. As a result, exports increase, imports decrease, and the current account rebalances. This tends to benefit the tradable sector, but hurts consumers and the non-tradable sector, whose purchasing power is reduced (Broz and Frieden 2001; Frieden 1991b; Steinberg 2015; Steinberg and Walter 2013) as well as holders of foreign currency-denominated debt (Cleeland Knight 2010; Walter 2008, 2013a). However, external adjustment does not affect only the level of the exchange rate, but also its stability. The volatility induced by external adjustment tends to affect the tradable sector most negatively because of the transaction costs it produces (Broz and Frieden 2001; Frieden 1991b, 2014). The risks to exchange-rate stability are particularly pronounced for Eurozone economies, where an external adjustment strategy implies an exit from, or a breakup of, the European monetary union. In addition to increased volatility, a Eurozone exit would potentially also be detrimental to those who owe euro-denominated debt abroad, because it is not clear whether such debt would have to be repaid in a (devalued) national currency, or in (appreciated) euros (Allen et al. 2011). This problem also raises significantly the risk that a euro exit would be accompanied by many defaults, including sovereign defaults. The more an interest group's members rely, either directly or indirectly, on foreign investment capital (Culpepper and Regan 2014) and foreign demand (Frieden 1991b, 2014), the more we expect them to oppose external adjustment. And, by extension, the more strongly that these groups concentrate in a given crisis country, the more likely it becomes that the country will formulate a clear position against external adjustment.

Interest Group Vulnerability to Internal Adjustment

Interest groups also vary in their vulnerability to internal adjustment (Eichengreen 1992; Simmons 1997; Walter 2013a). Overall, internal adjustment is painful because it implies austerity (brought about by higher interest rates, public spending cuts, and tax increases) and structural reforms (such as labor market reforms or policies aimed at increasing competitiveness), both of which usually lead to higher unemployment, lower wages, asset price deflation, and recession in the short run. Internal adjustment tends to harm workers and those groups who rely predominantly on the domestic economy or income from the state, such as producers of non-tradable goods and services, state-financed services, or the unemployed.

However, because internal adjustment can be carried out in a far greater variety of ways than external adjustment, it is more susceptible to particularistic interests and political conflict over specific policy design than external adjustment. Most policies that can be implemented to achieve internal adjustment hurt some interest groups more than others. Public spending cuts, such as lower public transfers and wages, for example, aim directly at reducing labor costs, which decreases domestic purchasing power. This reduces domestic demand significantly, generating costs for consumers and those active in non-tradable sectors that depend on the national economy, while benefitting export-oriented interests as labor costs effectively decline (Frieden 1991b, 2014; Simmons 1997). Cuts to public investment disproportionally hurt sectors reliant on government contract work (Bulfone and Afonso 2019), while cuts to social and unemployment benefits generally harm low income groups, and occupational groups that rely strongly on atypical work contracts (Burgoon and Dekker 2010; Hacker et al. 2013). Pension cuts generate losses for older people, while cuts in public education hurt the young (Busemeyer et al. 2009). On the revenue side, VAT increases come at high costs for producer groups oriented toward the domestic market (Haffert 2018; Haffert and Schultz 2019), whereas exporting interests are affected to a much lesser extent because this type of consumption tax does not have an effect on foreign customers. And increases to personal income taxes and capital taxes negatively affect (richer) individuals (Ganghof 2006; Kato 2003), whereas corporate tax increases the burden for firms.

Vulnerability to structural reforms, such as efforts to privatize state-owned enterprises or to deregulate product and labor markets, is equally group- and policy-specific: Privatization schemes can harm workers in privatized enterprises significantly, as this process often results in wage cuts and/or job losses (Peters 2012). Product market liberalization aimed at reducing price markups sustained by mono- or oligopolistic competition in specific markets can have strong negative effects on producers who have so far been protected by heavy regulations. At the same time, consumers are likely to benefit from more competition, lower prices and greater product variety. Finally, labor market deregulation aims at increasing labor market flexibility. These reforms are likely to benefit employers and workers with atypical contracts, at the expense of labor market "insiders," that is, workers in permanent positions subject to high levels of employment and income protection (Rueda 2006, 2014; Schwander and Hausermann 2013).

This discussion demonstrates two things. First, on average and in absolute terms, internal adjustment tends to harm most interest groups. However, the discussion highlights that interest groups' vulnerability to internal adjustment is strongly contingent on the specific policies chosen to implement this adjustment strategy. Interest groups can thus be highly exposed to one type of internal adjustment, but much less vulnerable to another form of internal adjustment. Opposition and support for internal adjustment is thus likely to vary considerably according to concrete policy proposals. The more vulnerable an interest group is to a specific policy proposal on the table, the more opposed it is likely to be to it, and vice versa. This also implies that although a group may be opposed to both policies in absolute terms, it is still likely to favor the policy to which it is less vulnerable.

Group-Specific Vulnerability Profiles and Preferred Crisis Resolution Strategies

In situations in which an economy faces balance-of-payments (BOP) pressure, macroeconomic adjustment is almost always a painful. Not surprisingly, it tends to be heavily disliked by most interest groups. However, we have seen that this dislike is likely to vary by adjustment strategy, by interest group, and by specific policy package. Moreover, as we have discussed throughout this book, preferences about different adjustment strategies do not form in isolation, but reflect factors such as opportunity costs and strategy alternatives.[3] When BOP pressures are strong, for example, "doing nothing" is no longer an option. The government must then either secure funding from abroad to cover its current account deficit (the financing strategy), or will be forced to adjust (either internally or externally). This is where interest groups' relative adjustment preferences come into play.

We argue that the type of approach interest groups favor in this situation depends on their vulnerability profile (Figure 3.1). For those groups that are much more vulnerable to one adjustment strategy than the alternative (profiles I and III), the choice is easy and clear: Interest groups that are vulnerable to internal adjustment, but much less vulnerable to external adjustment (vulnerability profile I), are more likely to prefer resolving the crisis through external adjustment, even if this implies an exit from the Eurozone. Likewise, interest groups that are much more vulnerable to a euro exit than austerity and structural reforms (vulnerability profile III) also have a clear-cut preference, in this case for internal adjustment.

However, when interest groups are not significantly more vulnerable to either external *or* internal adjustment but exhibit mixed vulnerabilities, their preferences are no longer clear-cut. This is not so much a problem for interest groups for which the costs of both internal and external adjustment are low (vulnerability profile IV). These groups are likely to favor a swift resolution of the crisis but are unlikely to systematically oppose one type of adjustment over another. Interest groups face a much more difficult situation when they find themselves in a situation where both the internal and external adjustment policies on the table

---

[3] For broader discussions of how trade-offs between policies affect policy preferences, see, for example, Bremer and Bürgisser 2019, Busemeyer and Garritzmann 2017, Gallego and Marx 2017, or Häusermann et al. 2018.

DISTRIBUTIVE CONFLICT 75

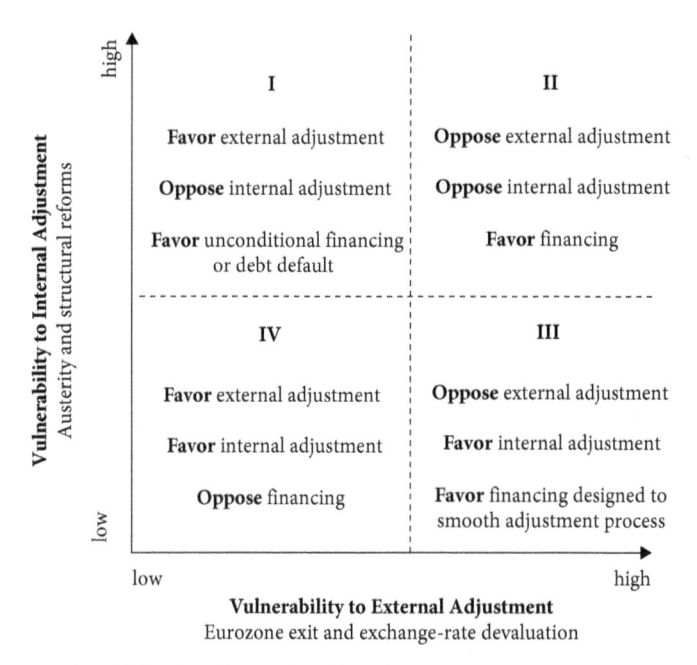

Figure 3.1 Vulnerability profiles and preferred crisis responses

Quadrant I (high vulnerability to internal adjustment, low vulnerability to external adjustment):
- **Favor** external adjustment
- **Oppose** internal adjustment
- **Favor** unconditional financing or debt default

Quadrant II (high vulnerability to internal adjustment, high vulnerability to external adjustment):
- **Oppose** external adjustment
- **Oppose** internal adjustment
- **Favor** financing

Quadrant IV (low vulnerability to internal adjustment, low vulnerability to external adjustment):
- **Favor** external adjustment
- **Favor** internal adjustment
- **Oppose** financing

Quadrant III (low vulnerability to internal adjustment, high vulnerability to external adjustment):
- **Oppose** external adjustment
- **Favor** internal adjustment
- **Favor** financing designed to smooth adjustment process

Y-axis: **Vulnerability to Internal Adjustment** — Austerity and structural reforms (low to high)
X-axis: **Vulnerability to External Adjustment** — Eurozone exit and exchange-rate devaluation (low to high)

are likely to be very costly for the group. We therefore expect that interest groups that find themselves in this "misery corner" (vulnerability profile II) prefer as little adjustment as possible.

Interest groups' vulnerability profiles not only influence which adjustment strategy they prefer, however, but also their stance on financing. Financing comes about as countries run down their foreign currency reserves or procure external funds from abroad; for example, in the form of fiscal transfers, debt forgiveness, or in the form of attaining emergency loans. Because financing allows deficit countries to carry on without any adjustment, however, it does not often resolve the underlying structural problems and can often even aggravate them (Frankel and Wei 2004; Walter and Willett 2012). Official foreign funds are therefore usually provided only on the condition that the recipient country actually adjusts its policies. As a result, financing usually comes with strings attached, and interest groups will vary in how they evaluate the overall attractiveness of financing, based on how vulnerable they are to the conditionality attached to such funds.

Once again, interest groups' preferences on financing and the specific forms of financing is likely to vary by vulnerability profile: Profile I interest groups that favor external adjustment are also likely to favor any kind of financing that allows the country to avoid internal adjustment. In contrast, profile II interest groups that want to avoid external adjustment at all costs are likely to be most accepting of financing that helps the country to adjust internally. These interest groups should be most accepting of conditionality, especially if the financing and conditionality attached to it are designed in a way that allows the country to avoid external adjustment in a sustainable manner. Financing is unlikely to be a very salient issue for profile III interest groups, especially when it allows for adjustment, but they are unlikely to support financing that prolongs the time it takes for countries to resolve the crisis. For interest groups in the "misery corner," in contrast, financing that allows putting off any adjustment is an attractive short-term strategy (Frieden and Walter 2017; Walter 2016). This is particularly true for types of financing that come with few conditions, because this allows the government to address the country's current account imbalance without significant external and internal adjustment. But to the extent that financing reduces or smoothens the domestic adjustment burden, these interest groups are also likely to support conditional financing.

Overall, interest groups' policy preferences thus depend on their group-specific vulnerability profile. Yet, as the discussion has shown above, these vulnerability profiles are policy specific. Interest groups can exhibit a very high vulnerability to some forms of internal adjustment, but a low vulnerability to others. Groups' vulnerability profiles thus vary with the specific reform packages proposed. Moreover, what matters ultimately for the politics of adjustment are not interest groups' absolute evaluations of policy options, but rather their *relative* adjustment preferences; that is, their preferred adjustment policy relative to other available policies within that adjustment strategy, the alternative adjustment strategy, and financing. As is frequently the case in policymaking (Bremer and Bürgisser 2019; Busemeyer and Garritzmann 2017; Gallego and Marx 2017; Häusermann et al. 2018), trade-offs are thus likely to dominate crisis policymaking. In the end, crises are usually resolved by adopting an adjustment strategy that is the most preferred among bad options.

Research Design

In the remaining part of this chapter, we explore empirically the implications of our theoretical framework on interest groups' adjustment preferences on crisis resolution strategies in Eurozone deficit countries. For this purpose, we use a quantitative approach that draws on original online survey data of interest group attitudes within three crisis afflicted Eurozone member states (Ireland, Spain, and Greece). The analysis examines interest group preferences of both specific adjustment policies and broader adjustment strategies, as well as absolute and relative preferences.

Case Selection

We study interest group preferences in three major Eurozone crisis countries: Ireland, Spain, and Greece. We chose these countries because all of them experienced deep crises in the context of the Eurozone crisis; all found themselves with a national vulnerability profile in the "misery corner," as shown in Chapter 2, and all received some external financial support during the crisis. Yet, despite these commonalities, these countries also differ in important ways. Even though they all found themselves vulnerable to both internal and external adjustment at the onset of the crisis in 2010, the levels of vulnerability varied, especially with regard to internal adjustment. While Greece exhibits one of the highest levels of vulnerability to internal adjustment in our sample, Ireland's vulnerability to internal adjustment was closer to the average, and Spain found itself between those extremes. Chapter 2 also showed that their crisis trajectories varied noticeably. Spain and Greece became increasingly vulnerable to austerity and structural reform throughout the crisis, whereas Ireland turned this trend around after a relatively short period of time. Moreover, the three cases also exhibit significant macro-level institutional variation, which affected the way the crisis played out politically in these countries, as Chapter 4 will show. Finally, crisis politics also varied considerably in these countries and proved much more contentious in Greece—pushing the country to the brink of Eurozone exit—less so in Spain, and considerably less contentious in Ireland (Genovese et al. 2016; Kriesi and Häusermann 2019).

Our expectation is that, despite this variation, we should find similar patterns of interest group preferences in all three countries that are related to groups' vulnerability profiles. Moreover, since Chapter 2 showed limited variation in the three countries' overall vulnerability to external adjustment, but considerable variation with regard to internal adjustment, we expect few country differences for the former, and more differences for internal adjustment and, to a lesser extent, financing.

Interest Group Survey: Sampling and Design

We designed and conducted original online surveys of interest groups in each of our selected country cases. Because we are primarily interested in socioeconomic interest groups, we limited our analysis to groups that engage with domestic economic or social policy issues. These were business and professional associations, trade unions and different types of social policy groups, such as charity groups, anti-poverty groups and consumer associations.

We first identified the country-specific populations of organized interest groups, and then contacted each of these groups (this is the established approach in interest group research; see for example Dür and Mateo (2016) and Klüver (2013)). In Ireland, we contacted 433 organizations, identified mainly from the 2016 edition of an annual directory published by the Irish Institute of Public Administration (IIPA 2015).[4] In Spain, we identified 1,897 interest groups based on entries in two government directories, of which 295 were social policy groups.[5,6] In Greece, no register or overall database of interest groups was available at time of data collection. We therefore identified the relevant interest group population by looking up national, sectoral, regional and/or occupational factions among the country's main umbrella-level business associations, labor unions and chambers of commerce, such as the Federation of Greek Industries (SEV), the General Confederation of Greek Workers (GSEE), and the Civil Servants' Confederation (ADEDY). We also included approximately 30 sectoral business associations and trade unions that regularly bargain for wages separately from the main umbrella organizations as well as 94 social policy groups that were listed in online NGO directories. Overall, this resulted in a list of 476 Greek interest groups.

We contacted one leader in each individual interest group (i.e., a CEO, general secretary, or senior economic policy advisor) via email during the late spring and summer of 2017. In addition, we dispatched four rounds of email reminders and completed one round of follow-up phone calls to Irish and Greek groups, as well as to a selection of the 50 largest interest groups in Spain. Our final response rates vary between 17 percent (78 interest groups in Ireland), 16 percent (77 interest groups in Greece) and 11 percent (204 interest groups in Spain), which is on the lower end of the response rates recorded by interest group surveys.[7] To check for major sources of bias, we therefore compared some known characteristics of each interest group population, such as interest group types and sectoral affiliations, to the characteristics of the three samples. The results, displayed in Figure 3.2,

---

[4] For a near-identical methodology, see Dür and Mateo (2010, 2016). We refrained from using the lobbying register of the Irish parliament, as it was newly opened when we created our list (June 2016) and therefore heavily incomplete. The sample was controlled to make sure that all sectoral factions of the main labor and employer umbrella organizations, Irish Business and Employers' Confederation (IBEC) and the Irish Congress of Trade Unions (ICTU) were included.

[5] The government directories are the Spanish Ministry of Employment and Social Affairs (which lists a total of 5,702 organizations) and the register of civil society organizations provided by the Spanish Ministry of Foreign Affairs (2,075 organizations). We excluded inactive groups (proxied by whether they no longer maintained an active website or social media presence (Twitter or Facebook)), environmental groups, and groups lobbying solely on issues pertaining to foreign aid and development.

[6] The high number of interest groups in Spain can be attributed to the country's highly fractionalized interest group system, with multiple peak federations and a large number of region-specific groups.

[7] Scholars distributing low complexity interest group surveys have success in improving response rates to between 20% and 40%, particularly via mixed-mode surveys (Marchetti 2015). That said, response rates decline dramatically among small populations that are frequently approached by scholars and institutions to participate in surveys. In the aftermath of the euro crisis, we uncovered that this was a particularly strong problem among interest groups in Eurozone crisis countries.

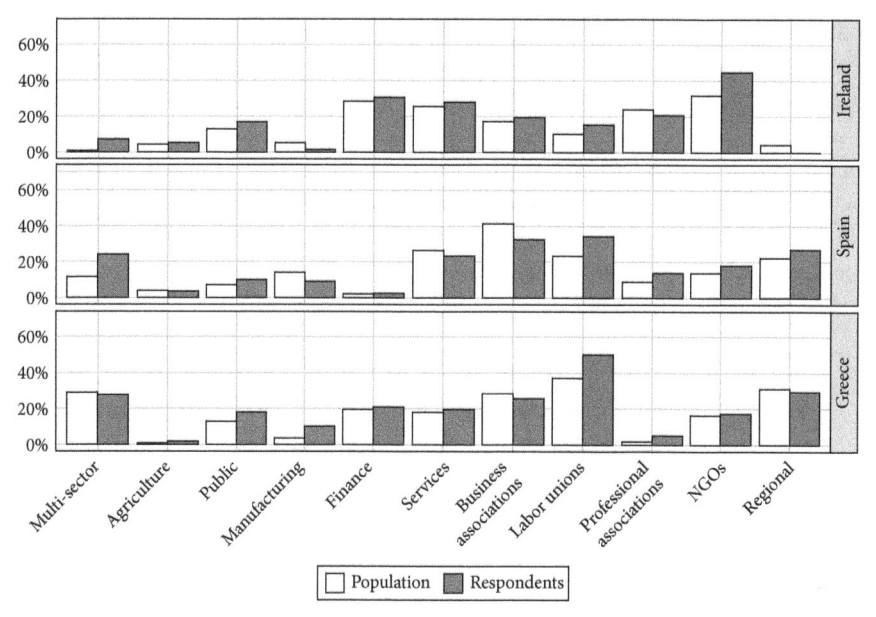

Figure 3.2 Aggregate interest group characteristics per country: population vs. respondent sample

suggest a rather similar distribution, which increases our confidence in the generalizability of our findings.

We conducted the survey in 2017; that is, at a time during which the Eurozone crisis was either largely over, such as in Ireland, or was in its final stages, such as in Spain and Greece, both of which were still suffering from sluggish growth and high unemployment at the time of our survey. In Greece, the survey took place while the country's third bailout program was underway. This relatively late point in time raises concerns about the possibility of groups displaying systematic hindsight bias, because many of our survey questions asked respondents to evaluate their preferences retrospectively. To assess to what extent interest group responses in our survey might diverge from interest group preferences at the peak of the crisis, we compared survey responses to the contents of press reports and other publications, which groups themselves issued during the prolonged crisis period (2008–12). These comparisons make us reasonably confident that the responses capture the thrust of interest group positions during the crisis, but the timing of the survey is to be borne in mind when interpreting the results.

Structure of the Analysis

Our empirical analysis proceeds in three steps. The next section begins with an analysis of groups' overall and policy-specific assessments of external adjustment, internal adjustment, and financing and shows that there is significant variation in how interest groups evaluate different policies within each of these strategies. We then aggregate these absolute preferences to explore interest groups' general support for overall crisis strategies, that is, external adjustment, internal adjustment, and financing and show that, in absolute terms, large majorities of groups across all three countries oppose both internal and external adjustment, whereas they view financing more favorably. Diving in more closely on adjustment preferences under constrained choice, the final section thus looks at crisis-related trade-offs and relative preferences in more detail.

Policy-Specific Preferences on Eurozone Crisis Management

To assess how interest groups evaluate different policies that would facilitate external adjustment, internal adjustment, and financing, we presented interest groups with a list of these policies and asked them to both rate and rank them. In this section, we explore interest groups' ratings of different crisis strategies and of specific policies, and show that there is considerable variation in opposition and support not just with regard to different strategies, but also within each strategy.

Preferences about Overall Crisis Management Strategies

We start with an aggregate analysis of how interest groups evaluated the broader crisis management strategies available for managing the Eurozone crisis. To this end, we calculated the average of groups' responses on all policy responses for external adjustment, internal adjustment, and financing, respectively, and recoded these averages on a 3-point scale: *In Favor, Neutral,* and *Opposed*.[8] This approach allows us to gauge interest groups' average assessments of the three different crisis strategies. Figure 3.3 plots the distribution of these preferences in Spain, Greece, and Ireland.

The results show that among deficit country interest groups, external adjustment was clearly the least favored policy and was overwhelmingly rejected by a vast majority of groups. In Ireland, Spain, and Greece, respectively, 80 percent, 89 percent and 76 percent of interest groups opposed external adjustment. At the same time, internal adjustment was equally contested in Spain (89 percent of groups opposed) and Greece (83 percent opposed), and to a lesser extent in Ireland (62 percent opposed). This is in line with our finding from Chapter 2, that Irish vulnerability to internal adjustment was lower than in Spain and Greece.

---

[8] Neutral responses were coded as being neither opposed nor in favor; strongly opposed/in favor and opposed/in favor evaluations were coded as being opposed and in favor, respectively.

DISTRIBUTIVE CONFLICT 81

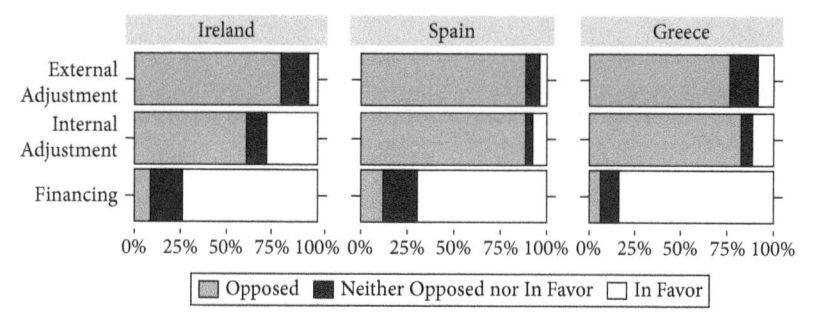

Figure 3.3 Evaluations of different crisis strategies in Ireland, Spain, and Greece

But given that all three countries nonetheless exhibited a high vulnerability to external and internal adjustment, interest groups in all countries exhibited a significant reluctance to adjust macroeconomic policies. Against this backdrop, it is hence not surprising that interest groups were much more positive toward financing measures. Of Irish groups, 74 percent favored or strongly favored financing policies, Spanish groups 69 percent, and Greek groups 84 percent.

Yet, because each strategy can usually be implemented in a variety of ways, we next delve into analyzing the more specific policy preferences of interest groups. We will see that, despite the clear aggregate picture, there is considerable variation in how interest groups evaluate concrete policy proposals, both across countries and across policies.

External Adjustment Policies

Policy options for external adjustment are relatively limited: All involve a break-up of the Eurozone, and several are beyond the control of individual deficit countries. Nonetheless, multiple scenarios of how such a break-up might occur were discussed during the euro crisis and we presented interest groups with five of these scenarios, as shown in Table 3.1. The most obvious type of external adjustment is a unilateral exit from the Eurozone, whereby a crisis country decides to leave the currency union. This is not the only scenario that is under full control of a deficit country government, but also the scenario in which the effects of external adjustment are likely to be the strongest. We then probed interest groups' evaluations of two scenarios in which another country unilaterally leaves the Eurozone, either another deficit country, or a surplus country (Germany). The final two scenarios asked how interest groups assessed a more far-reaching proposal in European monetary policy architecture, one in which the Eurozone would be split into a "Southern" and a "Northern" currency union. We asked interest groups to evaluate both a scenario in which their home country joins the "Southern"

Table 3.1 External adjustment scenarios in the Eurozone

Home country leaves the Eurozone
("[IE/ES/GR] leaves the Eurozone and reintroduces the Irish Pound/Spanish Peseta/Greek Drachma; the rest of the Eurozone remains intact")

Other deficit country leaves the Eurozone
("[GR/GR/IT] leaves the Eurozone and reintroduces the Greek Drachma/Greek Drachma/Italian Lira; the rest of the Eurozone remains intact")

Germany leaves the Eurozone
("Germany leaves the Eurozone and reintroduces the German Mark; the rest of the Eurozone remains intact")

Home country joins a Southern European Monetary Union.
("The Eurozone splits into two parts, and [IE/ES/GR] joins the 'Southern' European monetary union")

Home country joins a Northern European Monetary Union.
("The Eurozone splits into two parts, and [IE/ES/GR] joins the 'Northern' European monetary union")

Note: "Since the onset of the euro crisis in 2008, experts have argued that the Eurozone consists of member states that are too economically diverse. They predict that the Eurozone may well break up in the future. *If the Eurozone were to break apart, how would your organization evaluate the following break up scenarios?*"

monetary union, and one in which it joins the "Northern" monetary union. Groups were asked to rate their assessment of each scenario on a five-point Likert scale, ranging from "Strongly opposed" to "Strongly in favor."

Figure 3.4 displays the distribution of interest group responses in the three countries. It shows that external adjustment was, on average, viewed negatively in all three countries and by a majority of interest groups. Interest groups in all countries were strongly opposed to a unilateral exit of their home country from the common currency area. The figures for 'opposed' or 'strongly opposed' to this most straightforward form of external adjustment are 82 percent of Irish groups, 85 percent of Spanish groups, and 76 percent of Greek groups. However, there is considerable variation with regard to the remaining four scenarios. In Ireland and Spain, for example, opposition to a Greek exit from the Eurozone was much less pronounced, with one-quarter of all Irish groups (strongly) favoring this scenario. The most favorably rated scenario in Spain was that of the country joining a Northern EMU (28 percent (strongly) in favor) and almost one-third (29 percent) of Greek interest groups rated a German Eurozone exit from the Eurozone favorably.

That said, despite these differences, a picture of clear opposition to external adjustment emerges, especially with the options that were more feasible from a deficit country perspective. In line with evidence from firms and individuals from deficit countries (Fernández-Albertos and Kuo 2016; Walter et al. 2018), there was virtually no support for significant external adjustment among interest groups in all three deficit countries.

DISTRIBUTIVE CONFLICT 83

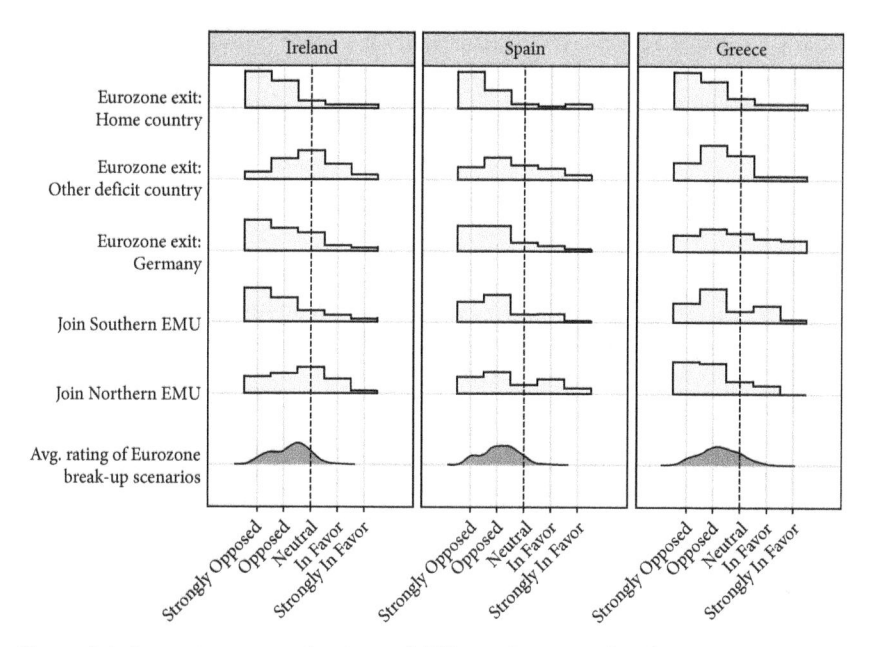

Figure 3.4 Interest group evaluations of different Eurozone break-up scenarios
Note: Dashed line highlights point at which groups are neutral to a given policy change.

Internal Adjustment Policies

Internal adjustment is the crisis strategy that offers governments most options in designing the specific contours of their crisis policy package. To explore this variety of options and interest groups' assessment of these options, we asked interest groups to rate and rank a large variety of possible options regarding austerity (public spending cuts and tax increases) and structural reforms. We asked interest groups in all three countries to rate the same set of proposed spending cuts and tax increases, but presented them with country-specific structural reform proposals to take into account that such reform measures are to a large extent shaped by each country's context and regulatory environment.[9] We thus asked groups to evaluate structural reforms that were particularly salient in each of the three countries (Table 3.2). Because proposed reforms often become salient when they face substantial domestic opposition, this may result in more negative preferences of groups toward structural reforms, but it allows us to attain a good understanding of interest group positioning themselves towards policies that were highly relevant in domestic adjustment debates.

---

[9] These structural reforms were derived from analyzing the frequency of national newspaper coverage in the three countries and validated by means of our interviews with domestic interest group actors.

84 THE POLITICS OF BAD OPTIONS

Table 3.2 Internal adjustment policies in Eurozone deficit countries

Austerity (Spending cuts)[a]	Austerity (Tax increases)[b]	Structural reforms[c]
Reduce Public Sector Employment ("Lower public sector wages and/or fewer public sector employees.") **Reduce Public Investment** ("Lower private sector subsidies and/or public contributions to infrastructure projects.") **Reduce Social Assistance and Unemployment Benefits** ("Reduce child benefit payments, disability payments, unemployment benefits, etc.") **Lower Public Pensions** ("Reduce pension pay-outs and/or increase the legal retirement age.") **Reduce the Minimum Wage** ("Reduce minimum wage rates for workers and trainees.") **Reduce Spending on Higher Education** ("Increase student tuition fees and/or cut wages of academic staff.")	Raise the VAT Rate Social Security Contributions Raise Personal Income Taxes Raise Corporate Tax Raise Capital Gains Tax	**Privatization Measures** Privatization of Water Provision *(Ireland)* Privatization of Hospital Administration Services *(Spain)* Privatization of Airports *(Spain)* Privatization of Airports and Ports *(Greece)* Privatization of Utility Services *(Greece)* Privatization of Postal Services *(Greece)* **Labor Market Deregulation** Reform of Unemployment Benefit Schemes *(Ireland)* Reform of Employment Contracts *(Spain)* Abolition of Geographic Employment Restrictions *(Greece)* **Product Market Deregulation** Deregulation of Medical and Pharmaceutical Sectors *(Ireland)* Abolition of Professional Licenses in Service Sectors *(Greece)*

[a] "Between [2008–12/2010–12], the [IE/ES/GR] government also attempted to lower government debt and improve national competitiveness. *How did your organization position itself towards less public spending* and/or efforts to reduce *labor costs* in the following areas?" Note: given that the Irish financial crisis erupted earlier than the crises in Spain and Greece, the temporal prompt given to Irish respondents was altered in the Irish survey.

[b] "During the post-2008 economic crisis in [IE/ES/GR], the [IE/ES/GR], government set out to collect additional state revenues. A number of different policy options were discussed—below you will find a list of them. *How did your organization position itself to raising the following tax rates/contributions?*"

[c] "Finally, the [IE/ES/GR] government also made attempted to deregulate labor and product markets during the crisis years. At the time, how did your organization position itself towards these structural reforms?"

How did interest groups position themselves with regard to different internal adjustment policies? In our aggregate analysis (see Figure 3.3), we discovered that interest group opposition toward internal adjustment was nearly as high as opposition towards external adjustment, particularly in Spain and Greece. In analyzing policy-specific preferences toward internal adjustment, we, however, uncover substantial variation in group attitudes toward spending cuts, tax increases, and structural reforms.

We begin our analysis by focusing on group assessments of different possible austerity policies, displayed in Figure 3.5. The average rating of all austerity policies shows that, overall, a majority of groups in all three countries were opposed to austerity. This was especially true for spending cuts, and to a lesser degree also tax increases. Cuts to public investment and higher education were very unpopular in all three countries, whereas cuts in public employment, while unpopular, was the most accepted. This measure was supported by 33 percent and 27 percent of Irish and Spanish groups, respectively, as well as 40 percent of Greek groups. But there is also variation across countries. Irish interests opposed cuts in public investment (68 percent) the most; instead, Spanish groups supported public pension cuts (88 percent) and Greek groups were most opposed to cutting social assistance and unemployment benefits (87 percent). Country-differences pertaining to spending preferences thus resonate with theoretical work on the political economy of Southern European, which emphasizes that political actors in these countries are typically strongly oriented toward sustaining domestic consumption, by means of minimal cuts in passive social transfers (Iversen and Soskice 2018; Rueda et al. 2015).

Tax increases were also generally unpopular among interest groups, although we see significantly more variation here, both across countries and across types of tax increases. Interestingly, opposition to tax increases decreases with tax progressivity in all three countries, with increases to capital and corporate taxes facing least opposition: 40 percent of Irish, 47 percent of Spanish, and 18 percent of Greek interest groups supported such tax increases. At the same time, opposition was highest to increasing the highly regressive VAT (45 percent in Ireland, 86 percent in Spain, and 87 percent in Greece). Nonetheless, we also see considerable country differences: Overall, Irish interest groups were much more accepting of tax increases than Greek interest groups, with Spain somewhere in the middle. Interest group differences pertaining to tax policy on the level of interest groups are particularly notable, given that multiple studies have found national public opinion toward tax increases tends to be relatively positive and, most importantly, similar across most European countries (see, e.g., Busemeyer and Garritzmann 2017, and Bremer and Bürgisser 2019).

Interest groups were generally much more divided, but also (with the exception of Spain) more positive about the desirability of structural reforms in all three countries, as Figure 3.6 shows. In Ireland, the deregulation of the medical and pharmaceutical sectors was strongly supported by interest groups, whereas the other two reform measures (increased private involvement in water provision services and reforms to the unemployment and benefit schemes) were less

86　THE POLITICS OF BAD OPTIONS

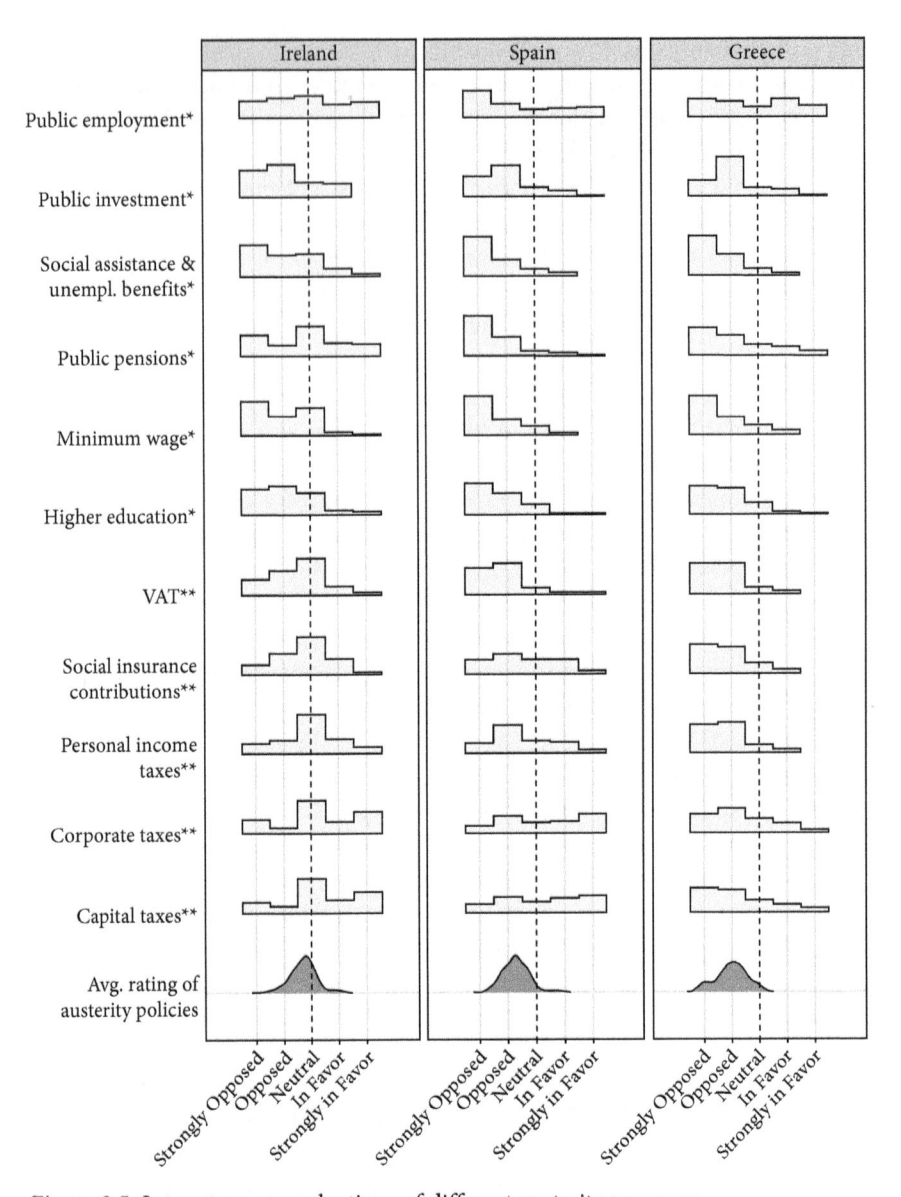

Figure 3.5 Interest group evaluations of different austerity measures

Note: *Spending cut, **Tax increase. Dashed line highlights point at which groups are neutral to a given policy change.

popular, albeit did not face major opposition. In contrast, Spanish interest groups were largely opposed to all reform proposals (between 53 percent and 67 percent (strongly) opposed policies, across the three policy areas). Finally, Greek groups were the most polarized in their preferences, and also showed the largest variation

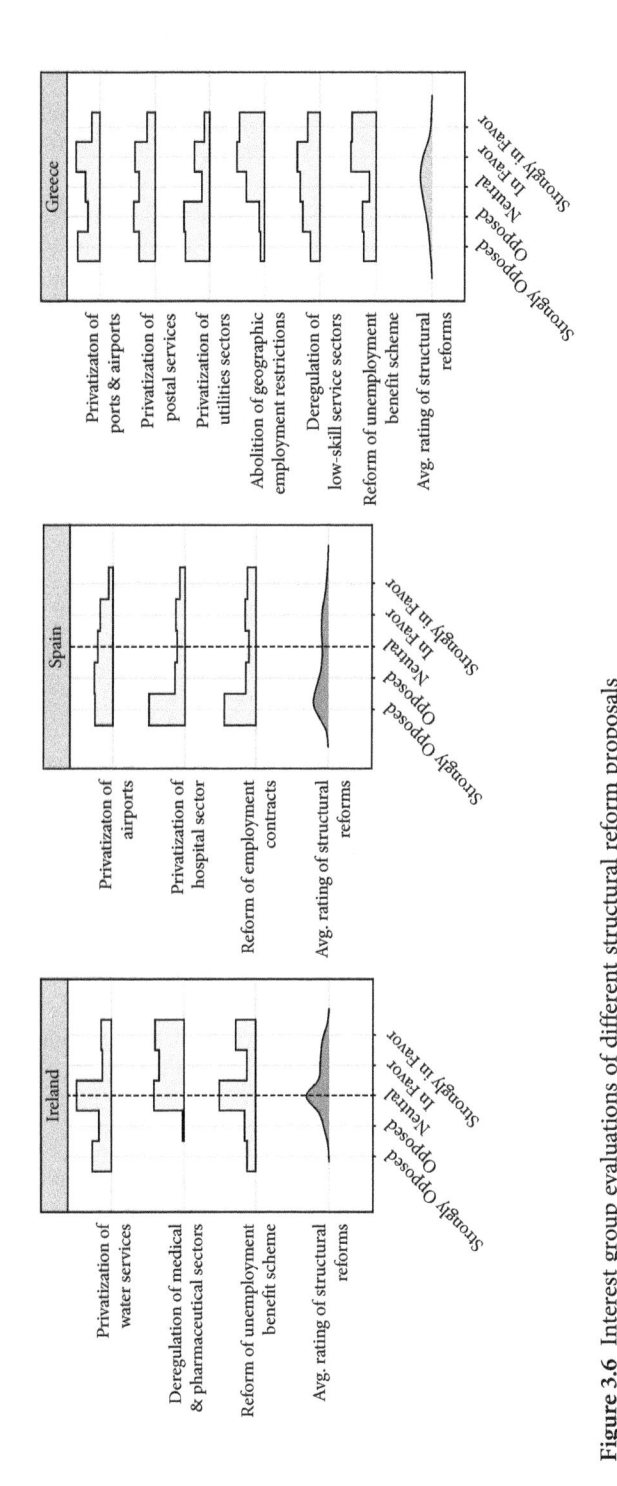

Figure 3.6 Interest group evaluations of different structural reform proposals

Note: Dashed line highlights point at which groups are neutral to a given policy change.

in the evaluation of different policy proposals. Although they displayed strong support for efforts to deregulate labor markets (supported by 66 percent of groups in total) and reform of unemployment benefit provision (61 percent), opposition toward privatization measures was considerable (opposed by 43–63 percent across sector-specific reforms).

In sum, we thus detect that while some forms of internal adjustment are almost universally rejected, interest groups have much more divided opinions about others. Broadly speaking, however, internal adjustment was not evaluated particularly positively by groups, with only very few policies receiving favorable overall ratings. To some extent, this may be because we asked interest groups of their policy preferences retroactively. At the time our survey was fielded, crisis-afflicted government had already enacted the vast majority of the internal adjustment policies included in our questionnaire, the most notable exception being the Irish corporate tax rate, which remained unchanged throughout the crisis.

Financing Policies

Finally, we asked interest groups to evaluate a number of financing measures that featured in both national and international policy debates during the crisis: Two measures that were actually implemented—government bailouts and an ECB bond-buying program (OMT)—and three that were not, or only partly, implemented—debt relief, debt default, and fiscal transfers in the form of a pan-European unemployment scheme (Table 3.3). These policies also vary in the extent to which they are likely to be subject to conditionality. Whereas government bailouts and debt relief are likely to be conditional on the enactment of adjustment policies, this is less the case for fiscal transfers, OMT, and unilateral debt default.[10]

Figure 3.7 shows that deficit country interest groups were overwhelmingly positive toward receiving financing, regardless of the policy that would achieve this. Only two policies—debt default in Spain and fiscal transfers in Greece—received an overall negative rating.

The most favored financing measure in both Ireland and Greece was the use of sovereign bailouts (favored by 71 percent of Irish groups and 86 percent of Greek groups). In Spain, however, fiscal transfers received more support from interest groups (72 percent). Conversely, most disliked in both Ireland and Greece was the establishment of fiscal transfers, which was opposed by 26 percent of Irish groups and 57 percent of Greek groups. Spanish groups were most opposed to defaulting on public debt (64 percent).

---

[10] Though we note that the exact extent of conditionality may depend to some extent on concrete policy design.

Table 3.3 Financing policies in Eurozone deficit countries

Sovereign bailouts
("Eurozone countries collectively grant sovereign bailouts subject to repayment, to member states facing crisis.")

EMU monetary policy
("The introduction of ECB bond buying programs in crisis countries [e.g., OMT].")

Debt relief
("Debt relief for countries that have accepted Eurozone Troika bailouts.")

Debt default
("The Irish/Spanish/Greek government unilaterally defaults on its sovereign debt.")[a]

Fiscal transfers
("Introduction of a pan-European unemployment benefit scheme.")

---

[a] In the Irish survey, this question was formulated as: "As a result of the Irish government's debt guarantee, a large amount of Irish private debt became nationalized in 2009 as Irish banks were facing bankruptcy. At the time, how did your organization find the decision to nationalize private debt?" Given the formulation of the question, in this instance we use inverted response values to improve interpretability.

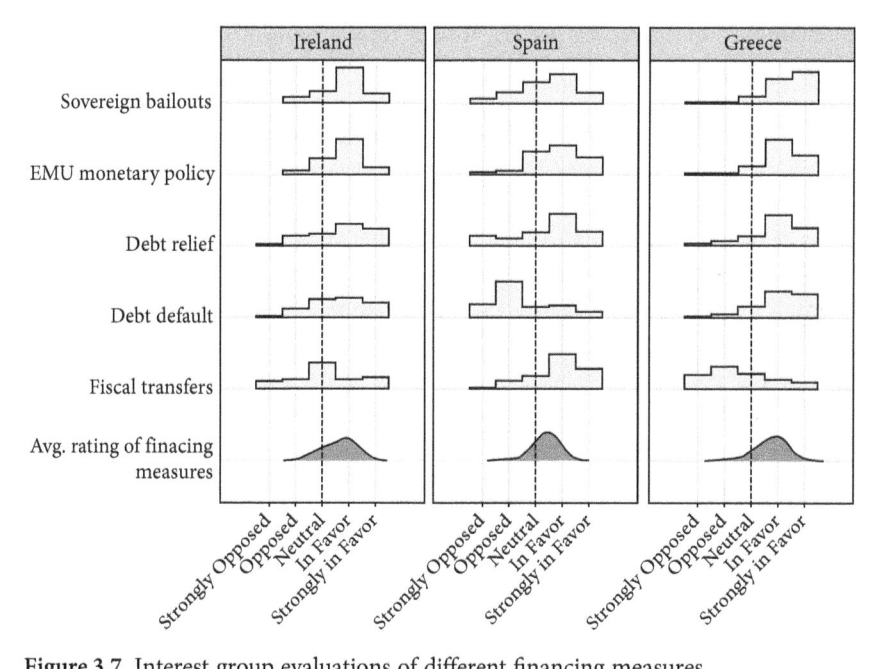

Figure 3.7 Interest group evaluations of different financing measures
Note: Dashed line highlights point at which groups are neutral to a given policy change.

The fact that interest groups across all countries were generally positive toward financing measures, squares with our expectation that countries in the "misery corner," in which all of the three crisis countries found themselves in the Eurozone crisis, prefer financing over macroeconomic adjustment.

In sum, data on the absolute preferences of interest groups have highlighted that interest groups were negative toward both external and internal strategies of adjustment, while displaying more favorable opinions toward financing. That said, we also find that, on the level of policies, groups displayed more varied preferences toward specific austerity measures and structural reforms. This suggests that internal adjustment may well have represented an easier course of action for deficit country policymakers than external adjustment, particularly in cases where they had leeway to shape the policy composition of internal adjustment packages.

While examining absolute interest group preferences already unearths certain political dynamics that underscored the politics of adjustment in Eurozone crisis countries, it also opens up new questions. In reality, political actors such as interest groups have to make relative assessments of which strategy they *most prefer* among undesirable options during crises, particularly in instances where financing measures cannot fully resolve a crisis country's current account deficit. Taking this into account, the next section explores specifically how individual interest groups positioned themselves when facing the choice between external and internal adjustment, by looking at their relative adjustment preferences.

Vulnerability Profiles and Preferred Eurozone Crisis Management Strategies

What explains the variation in support for different adjustment strategies among interest groups? Our argument suggests that these differences should be related to interest groups' vulnerability profiles. We therefore next examine groups' vulnerabilities to internal and external adjustment and examine how these relate to their overall assessment of different adjustment strategies. We do so in two steps. In a first step, we focus on groups' absolute preferences regarding each of the three possible crisis strategies. Because crisis politics is characterized by difficult choices among bad options and trade-offs, however, we then turn to an analysis of relative preferences and explore how groups evaluate different strategies *against each other*.

Vulnerability Profiles of Deficit Country Interest Groups

To identify interest groups' vulnerability profiles, we use interest groups' subjective assessment of how vulnerable they saw themselves toward internal and external adjustment, respectively, and construct, on this basis, group-specific vulnerability profiles. We measure groups' subjective, self-reported vulnerabilities to a breakup of the Eurozone (external adjustment) with two survey items (see

Table 3.2). We first asked each group how the financial market volatility that would be likely to emerge in the context of a Eurozone exit would affect their members on a five-point scale ranging from 1 ("very positively") to 5 ("very negatively"). We then asked respondents to set aside the financial market consequences of a Eurozone exit and to consider only how the effects of such an exit on international trade would affect their members. In a final step, we calculated the average of respondents' answers to these two questions and we use this average as a measure of self-reported vulnerability to external adjustment. The more negatively groups evaluated the effects of external adjustment, the higher their vulnerability to this adjustment strategy.

We used a third survey item to gauge group-specific vulnerability to internal adjustment. This item asked groups to assess how they were affected by the implementation of austerity measures during the crisis (see Question 2 in Table 3.4). Responses to this question were scaled on the same five-point scale as those used to operationalize vulnerability to external adjustment, from 1 meaning "very positive," to 5 indicating "very negative," and hence a high vulnerability to internal adjustment.

Figure 3.8 presents the distribution of group-specific vulnerability profiles in Ireland, Spain, and Greece. The upper panels identify vulnerability profiles by placing all groups that evaluate an adjustment strategy as negative and very negative into the "high vulnerability" category, and those with neutral or positive assessments in the low vulnerability category. Combining these two categories for internal and external adjustment yields a picture in which a vast majority—approximately two-thirds—of interest groups in all three countries end up in the "misery corner," where they are cross-pressured because they self-assessed

Table 3.4 Survey items used to operationalize interest group vulnerability profiles

Question 1A. *Vulnerability to external adjustment*	"Imagine that Spain had left the Eurozone. This would likely have made stock markets more volatile and increased the risk of bank closures. With this in mind: what economic effects would an exit from the Eurozone have had on those your organization represents?"
Question 1B. *Vulnerability to external adjustment*	"Now assume that it would be possible for Spain to exit the Eurozone without experiencing substantial financial turmoil. Leaving the Eurozone would also have allowed for a Spanish exchange-rate devaluation. Devaluation makes it more expensive to import foreign goods into Spain, while raising the demand for Spanish exports. With this in mind: what economic effects would a devaluation have had on those your organization represents?"
Question 2. *Vulnerability to internal adjustment*	"What economic effects has the introduction of austerity measures had on those represented by your organization?"

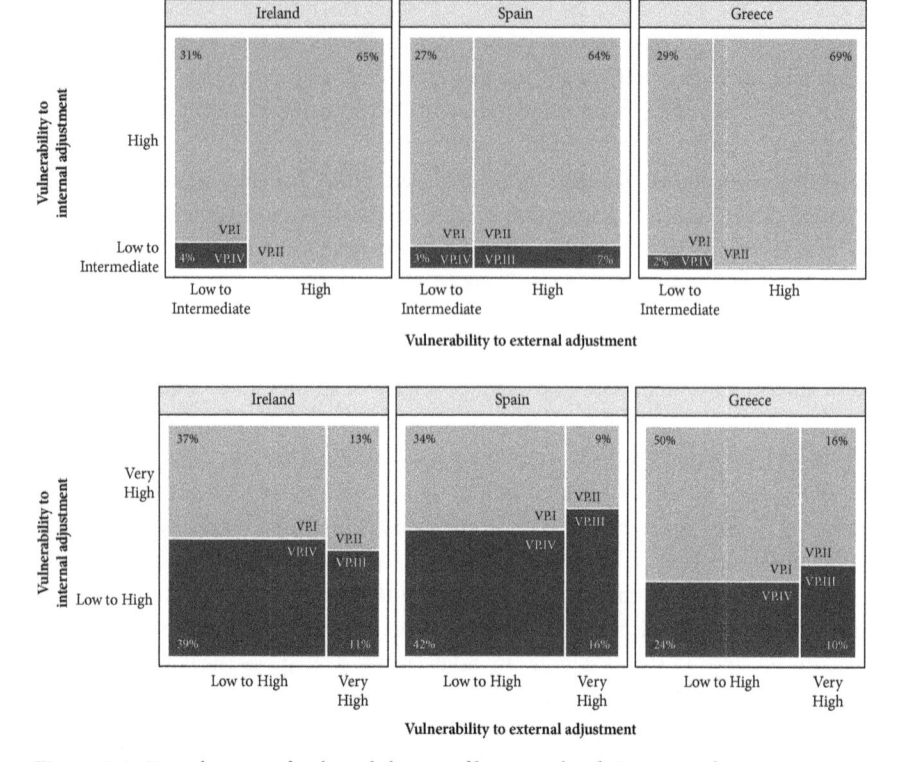

Figure 3.8 Distribution of vulnerability profiles in Ireland, Spain, and Greece

themselves to be vulnerable to both external and internal adjustment. These high rates of interest groups in the "misery corner" reflect the high level of vulnerability to both internal and external adjustment of the three countries on the aggregate level that we documented in Chapter 2. What is surprising, however, is that there is relatively little variation among countries, and the fact that so many interest groups in Ireland view themselves as vulnerable to internal adjustment, even though the macro-level analysis suggested that Ireland's vulnerability to internal adjustment was lower than that of both Spain and Greece.

Of course, adjustment in crisis countries is very rarely a process through which groups of firms and voters gain economic benefits in absolute terms. Rather, it is usually a question about relative pain, whereby some groups are less negatively affected than others. The lower panel in Figure 3.8 therefore differentiates between groups that assessed themselves as "very negatively" (5) affected by a given adjustment strategy, and all other groups. This yields a more differentiated picture, in which vulnerability to external adjustment appears considerably reduced. Between 34 percent (Spain) and 50 percent (Greece) of groups are now categorized as having a vulnerability profile I, with vulnerability to internal adjustment exceeding vulnerability to external adjustment. Only between

10 percent (Greece) and 16 percent (Spain) exhibit a vulnerability profile III, more vulnerable to external adjustment than internal adjustment. Vulnerability profile IV, in which neither adjustment strategy is highly negative, has become significantly bigger 24 percent (Greece) to 42 percent (Spain). Most surprisingly, the number of interest groups in the "misery corner" shrinks significantly in this classification, ranging between only 9 percent (Spain) and 16 percent (Greece). This coding raises some questions about measurement validity, which suggest that we should consider these categories with a grain of salt. Nonetheless, as it is the best available measure, we rely on this second category to explore how vulnerability profiles are related to crisis management strategies.

Vulnerability Profiles and Evaluations of Crisis Strategies

How are interest groups' vulnerability profiles related to their evaluations of different crisis strategies? To explore this question, we perform regression analyses of groups' overall assessments of each of the three crisis strategies (internal adjustment, external adjustment and financing), ranging from 0 (strongly opposed) to 1 (strongly in favor).

We use a categorical variable denoting interest group vulnerability profile as main independent variable; groups with vulnerability profile (VP) IV (low vulnerability to both internal and external adjustment) serve as a reference category in our regression models. In a second set of models we add a categorical interest group variable to account for different interest group types. Group-differences detected on the basis of this variable can be interpreted as a more objective measure of interest group vulnerabilities, because social policy groups and trade unions tend to be more vulnerable to internal adjustment than other groups. We use business associations as a reference category.

We pool our data from the three countries in order to overcome problems of statistical power, as the number of interest groups per country is relatively small. We therefore include country fixed effects (with Spain as a reference category) to account for country-level factors, such as historical legacies or collective bargaining frameworks, which may render the preferences of groups from one country systematically different from those of another. Because the Spanish interest group population is substantially larger than those of the other two countries, we also include country-specific inverse probability weights in our regressions in order to ensure that our findings are not overly driven by the preferences of Spanish groups.[11]

---

[11] Country weights are simple inverse probability weights, derived from the following equation: $1/(n_C/n_{ALL})$, where n_C denotes the number of country-specific observations, and n_{ALL} denotes the number of observations across all countries.

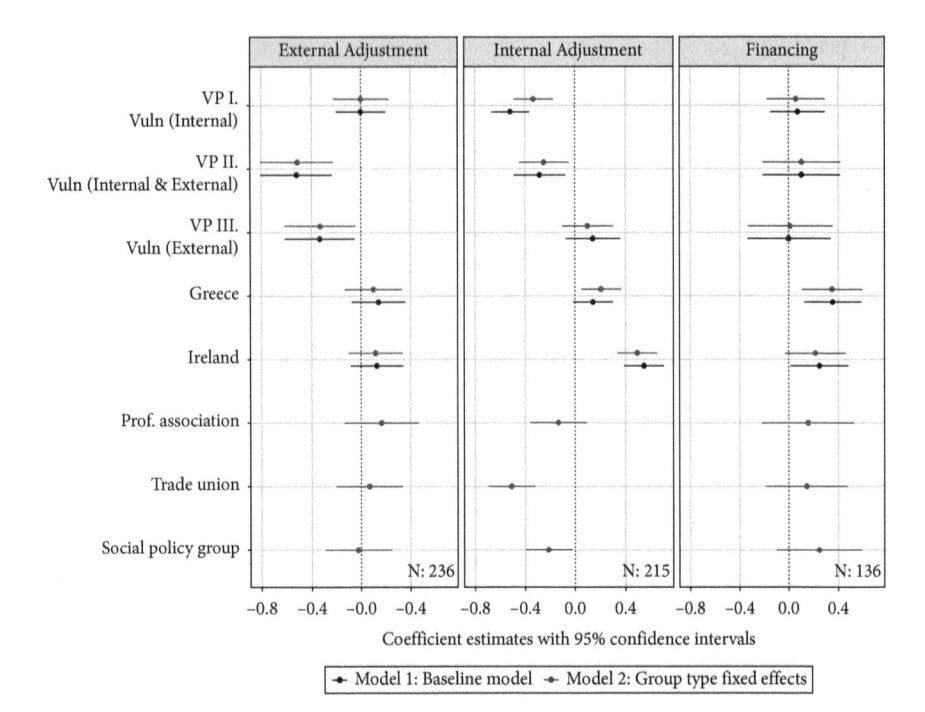

Figure 3.9 Results of OLS regression models on absolute adjustment strategy preferences

Note: Dots indicate estimated change from the reference category, VP IV (low vulnerability to external and internal adjustment), per vulnerability profile. For country controls the reference category is Spain; for group type variables the reference category is a business association.

Figure 3.9 presents the results of both sets of regression models for the three different crisis strategies. Our argument predicts that groups should oppose adjustment policies to which they are more vulnerable to, and that especially groups with a vulnerability profile II, vulnerable to any form of macroeconomic adjustment, should be opposed to such adjustment and significantly more in favor of financing instead. With the exception of financing, where we find little evidence for systematic group-specific differences in preferences, these expectations are largely borne out in our analysis. External adjustment is opposed by groups that are highly vulnerable to external adjustment, irrespective of their vulnerability to internal adjustment. Groups exhibiting a high vulnerability to external adjustment alone (vulnerability profile III), are 0.3 points more opposed to external adjustment than the baseline (business groups) on the five-point scale ranging from 0 to 4, and this difference is statistically significant ($p < 0.05$). Groups in the "misery corner" (vulnerability profile II, vulnerable to both external and internal adjustment) are most strongly opposed; on average, they rate Eurozone break-up

0.5 points more negatively, a finding that is highly statistically significant (p < 0.01). In contrast, there are no statistically significant differences between countries—in line with their rather similar aggregate levels of vulnerability to external adjustment—nor between different types of interest groups.

The picture changes when we look at group-level preferences toward austerity measures and structural reforms (internal adjustment). Here too, we find support for our argument, because groups that are highly vulnerable to internal adjustment are more likely to oppose this crisis strategy (between 0.5 and 0.3 points less support). Those highly vulnerable to internal adjustment alone (vulnerability profile I) are most opposed, followed by those who are vulnerable to any adjustment strategy (vulnerability profile II). The country differences reflect in part countries' aggregate vulnerability profiles: Chapter 2 showed that Ireland has a lower vulnerability to internal adjustment than Spain and especially Greece, and Irish groups rate internal adjustment significantly more positively than either Spanish or Greek groups. However, surprisingly, Spanish groups rate internal adjustment even more negatively than Greek groups, although Greece has by far the highest aggregate vulnerability to internal adjustment. We also find differences among interest group types, with groups representing voters, and especially workers, significantly more opposed to internal adjustment, compared with business associations.

Finally, financing preferences are not related to group-specific characteristics. There are clear country differences, with Irish and especially Greek interest groups evaluating financing significantly more positively than Spanish groups, but neither vulnerability profiles nor interest group types are associated with any significant differences in groups' general preferences toward financing. This is surprising, because our argument predicts interest groups with a vulnerability profile II (vulnerable to any type of adjustment) to be most supportive of financing. Moreover, we expected systematic differences between groups vulnerable to only one type of adjustment with regard to groups' preferences about conditional vs. unconditional forms of financing. In additional analyses (see Tables A3.1–3 and Figure A3.1 in the Appendix), we therefore explored the relationship between groups' vulnerability profile and different types of financing, but again find no statistically significant differences among groups with different vulnerability profiles nor interest group type.

Overall, our analyses show that vulnerability profiles matter especially with regard to interest groups' absolute evaluations of macroeconomic adjustment policies, but not necessarily with financing. The question that remains unanswered in this analysis, however, is how interest groups choose when confronted with a choice between crisis strategies and policies that they oppose. Which strategy do they prefer when forced to choose between such bad options, and which factors shape these relative preferences? The next section sets out to answer these questions.

Choosing Among Bad Options: Preferred Crisis Management Strategies in Trade-Off Situations

One of the key features of crisis politics is that it forces interest groups (as well as policymakers and voters) to choose between bad options. Which of these alternatives interest groups prefer does not depend only on how they evaluate each strategy of itself (their absolute preferences), but also how that strategy compares to its alternatives (their relative preferences).

To explore in more detail how interest groups choose from among bad options, we exposed respondents to two sets of customized crisis response packages, which confronted them with some of the trade-offs inherent in crisis management. In each of these sets, respondents were asked to think back to when the crisis peaked in their home country and to choose between two stylized external and internal adjustment packages (Figure 3.10). The external adjustment package suggested that the interest group's home country left the Eurozone and reintroduced a national currency at a heavily devalued rate, which would lead to a substantial increase in interest rates and a heavy decline in access to international capital. At the same time the government's need to implement austerity and structural reforms would be reduced.[12] In contrast, in the internal adjustment package, the

| [IE/ES/GR] leaves the euro zone, which means the following happens in Spain:

• [IE/ES/GR] reintroduces the [Irish Pound/Spanish Peseta/Greek Drachma] at a heavily devalued rate
• Interest rates increase substantially
• The [IE/ES/GR] government's need to implement austerity and fiscal reforms is reduced
• Access to international capital heavily declines | [IE/ES/GR] remains in the Eurozone and accepts a bailout from European Institutions/IMF.

The Troika insists that the following reforms be undertaken:

• *Most/least preferred* spending cut policy
• *Most/least preferred* tax increase policy
• *Most/least preferred* structural reform policy |

Figure 3.10 Choice between customized internal and external adjustment packages
"Please think back to [2012 (Spain)/2010 (Ireland and Greece)], when the Eurozone bailout of the [Spanish/Greek/Irish] government was being negotiated. In [2012 (Spain)/2010 (Ireland and Greece)], which of the below scenarios would your organization have preferred?"

Note: Policies in italics were customized by respondent-specific rankings of internal adjustment policies.

---

[12] In reality the effects of Eurozone exit may in fact be much more detrimental to the national economy than we postulate, but designing the exit scenario to be minimally costly allows us to see if there is in fact *any* trade-off situation in which groups would favor Eurozone exit over internal adjustment.

home country would remain in the Eurozone, but would accept a bailout from European Institutions and/or the IMF and would implement three policies designed to cut spending, increase taxes, and to implement structural reforms in an effort to achieve internal adjustment.

The internal adjustment package presented to groups varied, however, with regard to the types of policies that would have to be implemented in order to achieve internal adjustment in a customized, group-specific way. In a first set, the internal adjustment policies proposed were those that the interest group had ranked as their most preferred policies in the first part of the survey. This customized *most preferred internal adjustment scenario* contrasts with the second scenario, in which the trade-offs were much more pronounced: In this *least opposed internal adjustment scenario*, respondents faced the choice between external adjustment, or internal adjustment through the policies they had previously ranked as their least preferred adjustment policies. This second scenario thus confronted respondents with a choice between very bad options.

How did groups choose among these internal and external adjustment packages? Figure 3.11 shows the share of interest groups that opted for external adjustment and internal adjustment, respectively, or who refused to answer the question—both for the choice between bad options (most liked internal adjustment policies, upper part) and the choice among very bad options (most opposed internal adjustment policies, lower part).

Whereas our analysis of absolute policy ratings showed strong domestic opposition against internal adjustment across all our country cases, Figure 3.11 suggests that interest groups became much more accommodative of the prospect of austerity and structural reform when they were confronted with the trade-off between internal adjustment and leaving the Eurozone. In both scenarios, a majority of interest groups preferred internal adjustment to leaving the Eurozone. That said, the design of the internal adjustment package had a noticeable effect on the relative adjustment preferences of interest groups. Faced with a "soft" trade-off between Eurozone exit and an internal adjustment package that contained the policies to which an interest group was least opposed, internal adjustment was by far the most preferred crisis strategy, supported by 68 percent,

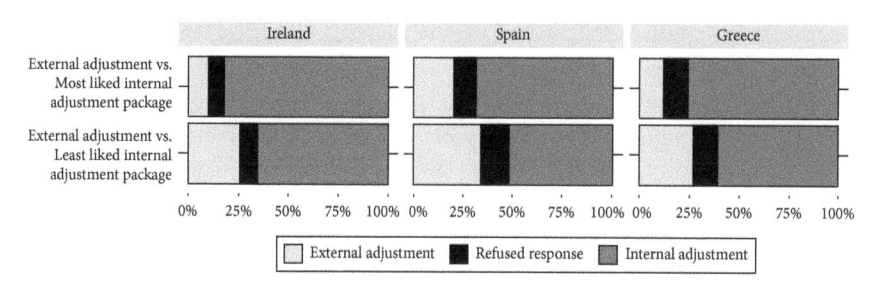

Figure 3.11 Choices between external and internal adjustment packages

76 percent, and 82 percent of groups in Spain, Greece, and Ireland, respectively. Only a few interest groups (20 percent in Spain, 12 percent in Greece, and 10 percent in Ireland) preferred Eurozone exit to internal adjustment under these conditions.

As the costs of internal adjustment rose in the second scenario, however, interest groups became substantially more amenable to the thought of Eurozone exit, even if it continued to be supported by only a minority. In the difficult trade-off scenario, the share of groups favoring Eurozone exit rose to 34 percent in Spain, 27 percent in Greece, and 25 percent in Ireland. Nonetheless, even when faced with internal adjustment policies they strongly disliked, a majority of interest groups continued to support this painful crisis strategy. The internal adjustment package containing the policies that interest groups least preferred still garnered support by 52 percent of interest groups in Spain, 60 percent in Greece, and 65 percent in Ireland.[13]

As a substantially large number of groups refused to state their relative adjustment preferences, we do not suggest that aggregate country findings are fully representative of the median policy preferences of interest groups in deficit countries during the crisis. Still, we note that interest group opposition to external adjustment in our survey echoes voter preferences during the crisis, where only a minority of voters grew so disenchanted with the euro itself that they wanted to leave it. For example, even at the peak of the crisis in spring 2011, only 33 percent, 20 percent, and 15 percent of voters opposed the common currency in Spain, Greece, and Ireland, respectively (Hobolt and Wratil 2015; Roth et al. 2015). Even in Greece, where the crisis has taken its strongest toll, only 13 percent of respondents wanted to leave the euro on the eve of the 2015 bailout referendum (Walter et al. 2018). The finding that interest groups grow more accepting of austerity when confronted with the choice between internal and external adjustment also sheds light on why, in Fall 2015, Greek voters re-elected a government that had agreed to significant new austerity measures just two months after it had called a referendum to fight against these very policies. When faced with the choice between Grexit (external adjustment) and austerity (internal adjustment), a large majority of Greeks opted for the latter (Jurado et al. 2020).

In sum, our analysis thus underscores the importance of considering the alternatives and trade-offs involved in policymaking. It suggests that an important answer to the puzzle of why deficit countries implemented painful austerity and far-reaching structural reforms is that although interest groups disliked these policies, they recognized that the alternative—external adjustment—would leave them even worse off. Even when faced with choices between bad options, interest groups evaluate which of these options is worse and choose accordingly.

---

[13] Between 8% and 14% of groups refused to respond to the trade-off-questions, highlighting the difficulties of choosing between these two highly painful crisis strategies.

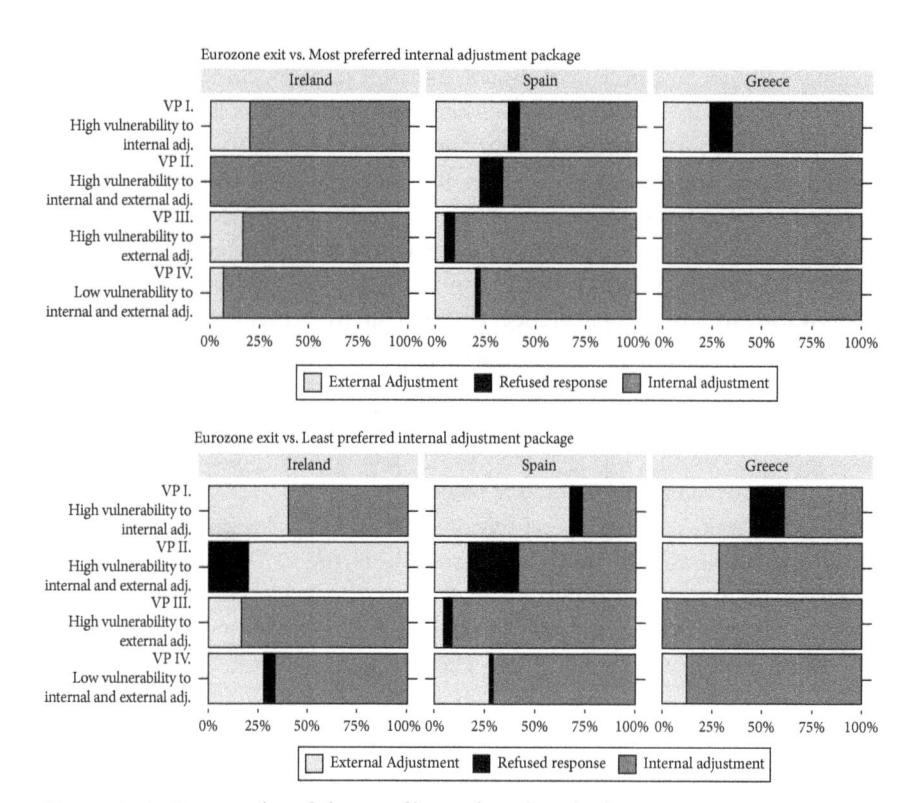

Vulnerability Profiles and Preferred Adjustment Strategies

How are interest groups' vulnerability profiles related to how interest groups decide in the difficult trade-off situations that characterize the politics of macroeconomic adjustment? Figure 3.12 displays the distribution of preferred adjustment strategies by groups' vulnerability profiles, both for the easy trade-off that includes groups' most preferred internal adjustment policies (upper panel) and the difficult trade-off that puts Eurozone exit against the groups' three internal adjustment policies they opposed the most.

The analysis shows that, overall, internal adjustment is by far the most preferred crisis strategy when interest groups weigh their most liked internal adjustment policies against Eurozone exit, but this support shrinks considerably when the choice becomes more difficult. Yet we also observe considerable differences between groups with different vulnerability profiles. For example, and in line with our expectations, interest groups with a vulnerability profile I (more vulnerable to internal adjustment than external adjustment) are most supportive of external

Figure 3.12 Group vulnerability profiles and preferred adjustment strategies

adjustment. This holds across both sets of choices, but is particularly evident when groups were confronted with the hard trade-off, where 40 percent of Irish, 67 percent of Spanish, and 44 percent of Greek interest groups with this vulnerability profile favored leaving the Eurozone to implementing very painful reforms. As expected, support for exit is much lower for those who are more vulnerable to external than internal adjustment (vulnerability profile III).[14] Unsurprisingly, their preferences also changed the least as we altered the contents of the internal adjustment package to tailor it more to their specific internal adjustment preferences.

The choice between internal and external adjustment is particularly difficult with regard to those groups with a vulnerability profile in the "misery corner." Nonetheless, among this group a vast majority consistently favored internal adjustment to leaving the Eurozone, both in the easy and in the difficult trade-off scenario. The hard trade-off scenario also demonstrates the difficulties these groups face in making their choice. Even though a majority of groups opted for internal adjustment, even in the hard trade-off scenario, the number of groups refusing to answer rose substantially in this scenario, showing how difficult it is to make a choice when the trade-off is difficult. Finally, groups with low vulnerability to both adjustment strategies (profile IV) were generally more supportive of internal adjustment, especially in the soft trade-off scenario. Once more, however, support for external adjustment rose when confronted with policy packages that contained groups' least-preferred policy options.

The differences in choices between the easy and hard trade-off scenarios demonstrate the importance of examining the details of different adjustment strategies. After all, even among groups that were predominantly vulnerable to internal adjustment, reform packages containing internal reforms that were more aligned with groups' own preferences (the most-liked scenario) resulted in a clear majority in support of internal adjustment (58 percent of Spanish groups, 65 percent of Greek groups, and 80 percent of Irish groups) over an exit from the common currency. This suggests that it is possible to design austerity policies and structural reforms in a way that reduces contestation even from groups that are predominantly vulnerable to internal adjustment.

To evaluate the relationship between interest groups' vulnerability profiles and their adjustment choices more systematically, Figure 3.13 presents the results (odds ratios) of two logit regression analyses of the choice between internal and external adjustment. The dependent variable is a dichotomous measure that takes the value of 1 if an interest group chooses Eurozone exit over an internal adjustment package (0). Figure 3.13 shows how interest groups' vulnerability profiles are related to the odds of preferring Eurozone exit over internal

---

[14] Surprisingly, a considerable number of Irish interest groups in this category nonetheless favors external adjustment.

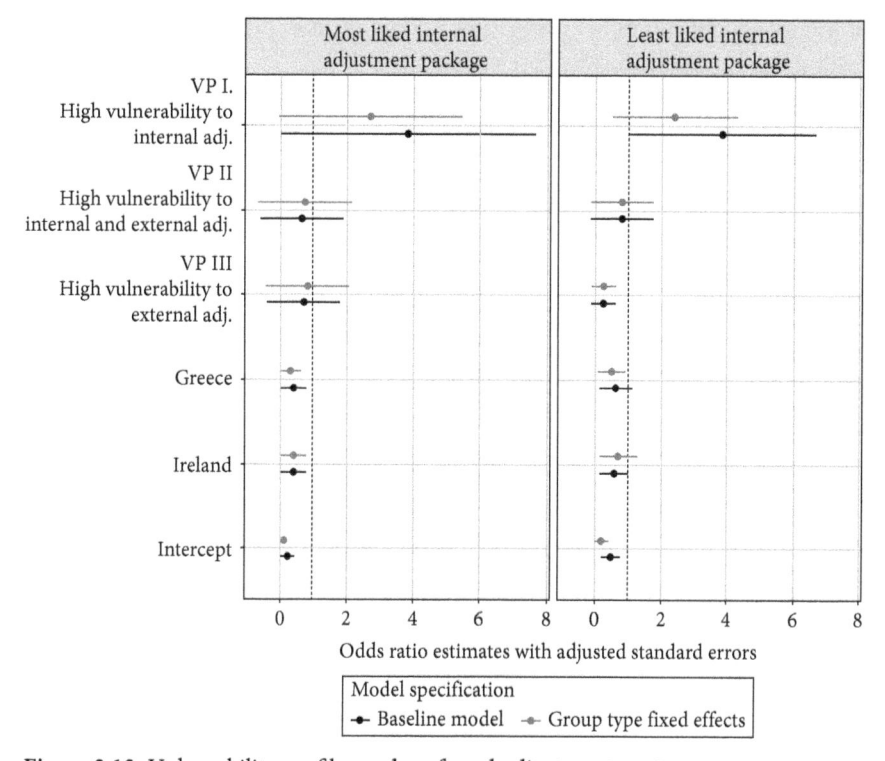

Figure 3.13 Vulnerability profiles and preferred adjustment strategy

Note: Odds ratio estimations derived from logistic regressions. Points indicate estimated change in odds of favoring Eurozone exit above internal adjustment per vulnerability profile, as compared to the reference category (groups with vulnerability profile IV). In particular country coefficients should be interpreted with caution as non-response is excluded from the estimations. Country weights are included; reference category for country fixed effects is Spain.

adjustment in each of the two trade-off scenarios. In the easy trade-off scenario, we do not find any statistically significant differences between interest groups based on their vulnerability profiles, even though those with vulnerability profile I are, as expected, more likely than any other group to choose external over internal adjustment. The differences become more pronounced in the more difficult trade-off scenario in which internal adjustment consists of the policies to which an interest group is most opposed. Here, groups vulnerable to internal adjustment alone (profile I) are between two to four times more likely to favor the prospect of leaving the Eurozone than groups that are not vulnerable to any type of adjustment (profile IV). In contrast, interest groups highly vulnerable to Eurozone exit alone (profile III) are almost twice as likely to oppose external adjustment than those not vulnerable to any adjustment strategy. For the most conflicted group, with vulnerability profile II and vulnerable to any adjustment, the choice is difficult in both scenarios, placing them in between the two groups with the more straightforward preferences.[15]

The bottom line of our analysis is threefold. First, interest groups' vulnerability profiles are indeed related to their preferences about crisis management and macroeconomic adjustment. Second, although interest groups opposed both external and internal adjustment in absolute terms, they are much more likely to opt for internal adjustment when confronted with a choice between the two. And finally, this choice is policy-specific. Interest group choices varied considerably, depending on how they assessed the specific policies proposed in a given internal adjustment package. This, in turn, implies that deficit country governments had some space to create winning pro-internal adjustment coalitions among domestic interest groups during the Eurozone crisis.

Conclusion: From Adjustment Preferences to Adjustment Policies

In Eurozone deficit countries that suffered from the financial crisis, interest groups played a key part in both the adoption as well as the implementation of crisis policies. What kind of policies did they prefer? This chapter has examined this question in detail for interest groups in three strongly crisis-afflicted countries: Ireland, Spain, and Greece, with five key findings.

First, across all three countries, large majorities of interest groups perceived themselves to be highly vulnerable toward internal and external adjustment, or both. As such, both of these adjustment strategies were largely opposed by domestic interest groups in all three countries, whereas financing policies were viewed much more favorably. Second, these absolute preferences for crisis strategy hide considerable variation in groups' evaluation of specific policies within each of these crisis strategies. Third, interest group preferences about different crisis strategies are related to their vulnerability profiles: Rather unsurprisingly, groups tend to favor the strategies to which they are less vulnerable. Fourth, even though interest groups were equally opposed to both external and internal adjustment in absolute terms, they exhibited a clear preference for internal over external adjustment in relative terms. And finally, fifth, the concrete design of adjustment strategies matters; some internal adjustment strategies are much harder to swallow for interest groups than others, suggesting that if governments use the policy discretion that they have, even in constrained situations such as the Eurozone crisis, they have a chance to build reform coalitions that allow them to implement

---

[15] We also find that Spanish interest groups are roughly 50% more in favor of Eurozone exit than their Greek and Irish counterparts ($p < 0.1$).

austerity and structural reforms even though interest groups overall dislike this strategy.

Assessing domestic adjustment preferences represents an important first step in gaining a better understanding of the domestic drivers of crisis policy in the Eurozone periphery, but is of course subject to its own limitations. Interest groups do not dictate policy in their own right. Their role is sooner one of preference mediation, whereby they attempt to influence policymakers with partisan affiliations, and subject to electoral constraints. The translation of interest group preferences into policy should therefore be seen in light of factors that shape both interest group and government behavior. All interest groups exhibit a given set of adjustment preferences, but power and influence are not symmetrically distributed across all interest groups in a given country. Some groups have preferential access to policymakers, or possess disproportionate bargaining power in adjustment negotiations simply because they have greater capacities of mobilizing political support for their cause. Related to this, the willingness of interest groups to act upon their preferences varies widely. Adjustment policies may activate interest groups that stand to gain a lot or lose substantially by their enactment, but others, who remain to a larger extent unaffected, will likely remain silent. And finally, governments are more likely to take interest group preferences into account under some circumstances than under others (Peltzman 1976).

Adjustment outcomes, such as the implementation of specific policies as well as the degrees of contention surrounding this enactment, thus need to be seen in light of both structural and institutional constraints to the political behavior of interest groups and the willingness of governments to respond to their concerns. The next chapter, therefore, examines in more detail how political parties, interest groups and voters interact in the context of crisis politics and how this shaped crisis politics and distributional conflict in Ireland, Greece, and Spain.

Appendix

Table A3.1 OLS regression results—absolute preferences toward adjustment strategies

	Dependent variable:					
	Avg. rating of: External adjustment		*Avg. rating of:* Internal adjustment		*Avg. rating of:* Financing	
	(1)	(2)	(3)	(4)	(5)	(6)
VP I (IN)	−0.002	−0.001	−0.515***	−0.332***	0.071	0.056
	(0.104)	(0.113)	(0.079)	(0.081)	(0.113)	(0.120)
VP II (IN +EX)	−0.521***	−0.515***	−0.282***	−0.248**	0.100	0.101
	(0.148)	(0.149)	(0.107)	(0.101)	(0.160)	(0.161)
VP III (EX)	−0.336**	−0.330**	0.143	0.097	−0.002	0.008
	(0.146)	(0.146)	(0.111)	(0.105)	(0.173)	(0.174)
Professional association		0.161		−0.132		0.154
		(0.154)		(0.115)		(0.192)
Trade union		0.065		−0.506***		0.141
		(0.137)		(0.096)		(0.169)
Social policy groups		−0.023		−0.211**		0.242
		(0.135)		(0.094)		(0.174)
Greece	0.142	0.099	0.144*	0.204**	0.353***	0.348***
	(0.110)	(0.116)	(0.082)	(0.081)	(0.120)	(0.125)
Ireland	0.124	0.117	0.544***	0.490***	0.244**	0.213*
	(0.109)	(0.112)	(0.082)	(0.078)	(0.120)	(0.125)
Constant	1.240***	1.211***	1.472***	1.667***	2.344***	2.208***
	(0.093)	(0.116)	(0.070)	(0.082)	(0.104)	(0.156)
Observations	236	236	215	215	136	136
R^2	0.082	0.089	0.339	0.427	0.077	0.091
F Statistic	4.090*** (df = 5; 230)	2.766*** (df = 8; 227)	21.396*** (df = 5; 209)	19.169*** (df = 8; 206)	2.171* (df = 5; 130)	1.598 (df = 8; 127)

Note: *p ** p *** p < 0.01

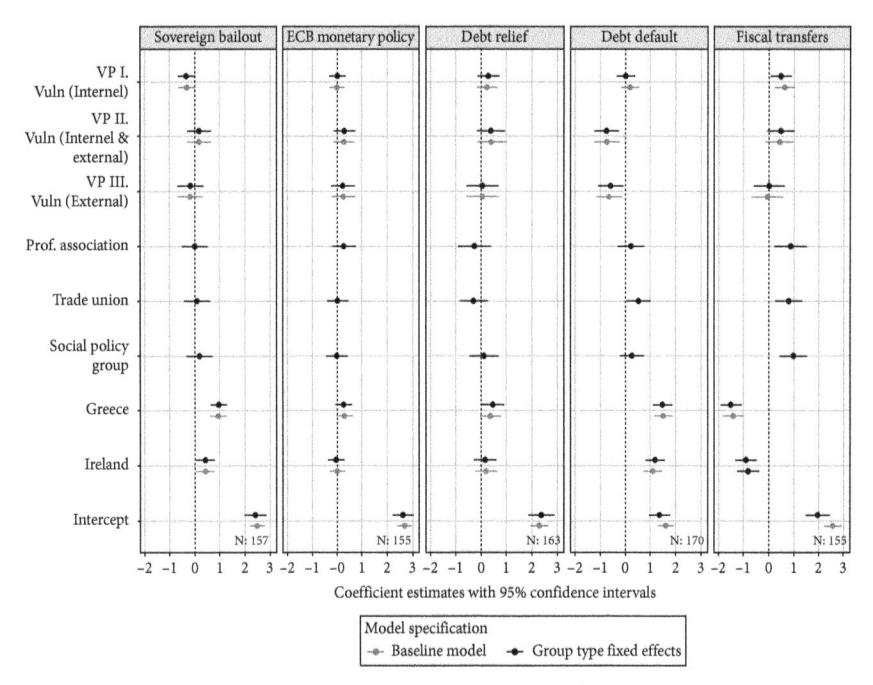

Figure A3.1 Results of OLS regression models on absolute financing policy preferences

Note: Dots indicate estimated change from the reference category, VP IV (low vulnerability to external and internal adjustment), per vulnerability profile. For country controls the reference category is Spain; for group type variables the reference category is a business association.

Table A3.2 OLS regression results—absolute preferences toward financing policies

Dependent variable:	Sovereign bailout		ECB monetary policy		Debt relief		Debt default		Fiscal transfers	
	(1)	(2)	(3)	(4)	(5)	(6)	(7)	(8)	(9)	(10)
VP I (IN)	−0.304* (0.173)	−0.320* (0.186)	−0.014 (0.160)	0.017 (0.171)	0.231 (0.212)	0.288 (0.226)	0.174 (0.183)	0.006 (0.198)	0.617*** (0.210)	0.479** (0.219)
VP II (IN +EX)	0.181	0.183	0.282	0.299	0.397	0.391	−0.748***	−0.765***	0.421	0.468*
	(0.246)	(0.248)	(0.219)	(0.222)	(0.290)	(0.291)	(0.256)	(0.255)	(0.289)	(0.282)
VP III (EX)	−0.184 (0.267)	−0.166 (0.271)	0.259 (0.246)	0.240 (0.249)	0.070 (0.323)	0.064 (0.325)	−0.650** (0.263)	−0.597** (0.263)	−0.045 (0.323)	0.017 (0.316)
Prof. association		0.015		0.277		−0.247		0.223		0.857***
		(0.289)		(0.256)		(0.334)		(0.281)		(0.327)
Trade union		0.065 (0.253)		0.029 (0.226)		−0.293 (0.291)		0.523** (0.248)		0.789*** (0.286)
Social policy group		0.185 (0.260)		−0.005 (0.231)		0.114 (0.296)		0.251 (0.244)		0.965*** (0.292)
Greece	0.937*** (0.181)	0.958*** (0.191)	0.333* (0.169)	0.268 (0.177)	0.375* (0.221)	0.472** (0.232)	1.509*** (0.192)	1.474*** (0.199)	−1.402*** (0.220)	−1.496*** (0.223)
Ireland	0.431** (0.185)	0.420** (0.194)	0.008 (0.170)	−0.035 (0.175)	0.193 (0.224)	0.166 (0.231)	1.093*** (0.193)	1.178*** (0.198)	−0.812*** (0.223)	−0.890*** (0.223)
Constant	2.494*** (0.156)	2.415*** (0.231)	2.677*** (0.147)	2.643*** (0.214)	2.309*** (0.190)	2.393*** (0.266)	1.613*** (0.169)	1.354*** (0.224)	2.598*** (0.191)	1.978*** (0.263)
Observations	157	157	155	155	163	163	170	170	155	155
R2	0.173	0.178	0.053	0.065	0.039	0.060	0.355	0.373	0.236	0.294
F Statistic	6.338*** (df = 5; 151)	3.997*** (df = 8; 148)	1.675 (df = 5; 149)	1.268 (df = 8; 146)	1.274 (df = 5; 157)	1.228 (df = 8; 154)	18.042*** (df = 5; 164)	11.991*** (df = 8; 161)	9.194*** (df = 5; 149)	7.584*** (df = 8; 146)

Note: *p **p ***p < 0.01

Table A3.3 Logit regressions on relative adjustment preferences: likelihood of preferring Eurozone exit (1) to an internal adjustment package (0)

	Dependent variable:			
	Most liked internal adjustment package		Least liked internal adjustment package	
	(1)	(2)	(3)	(4)
VP I (IN)	1.345***	0.998*	1.338***	0.869**
	(0.508)	(0.520)	(0.380)	(0.407)
VP II (IN+EX)	−0.462	−0.334	−0.229	−0.254
	(1.051)	(1.025)	(0.610)	(0.624)
VP III (EX)	−0.372	−0.221	−1.453*	−1.433*
	(0.838)	(0.823)	(0.784)	(0.788)
Prof. association		−1.039		0.305
		(1.425)		(0.704)
Trade union		1.557**		1.727***
		(0.714)		(0.565)
Social policy group		0.861		0.912
		(0.726)		(0.567)
Greece	−1.028*	−1.256**	−0.501	−0.733
	(0.533)	(0.544)	(0.422)	(0.445)
Ireland	−0.937*	−0.883*	−0.573	−0.387
	(0.517)	(0.519)	(0.410)	(0.427)
Constant	−1.634***	−2.327***	−0.775**	−1.554***
	(0.450)	(0.660)	(0.342)	(0.498)
Observations	177	177	198	198

Note: *p < 0.1 **p < 0.05 ***p < 0.01. Coefficients presented as log odds.

4
Crisis Politics in Deficit Countries

How did deficit country interest groups position themselves toward different means of crisis resolution during the Eurozone crisis? The findings of Chapter 3 highlighted the difficulties faced by these countries when attempting to converge domestically on a strategy to overcome the crisis. By examining the adjustment preferences of organized interest groups, we uncovered that both external and internal adjustment strategies were met with stark discontent from politically mobilized interest groups, majorities of which were mutually vulnerable to both these forms of crisis resolution. Instead, the main form of crisis management toward which they displayed positive attitudes was one of financing, a strategy contingent on the willingness of neighboring surplus countries to lighten their adjustment burden. Chapter 3 also highlighted the importance of opportunity costs for interest groups in deficit countries: When faced with a choice between leaving the Eurozone and enacting policies of internal adjustment, the latter adjustment strategy clearly won favor among most interest groups in crisis-afflicted deficit states. A strong factor facilitating this preference was likely the pure adaptability of internal adjustment policies, which unlike other adjustment strategies, could be enacted in a myriad of ways: Here our analysis revealed substantial variation concerning the policy-level preferences of interest groups with regard to spending cuts, taxation increases, and structural reforms.

While our results thus bring us far in understanding the preference constellations about crisis management in Eurozone deficit countries, it of course opens up the questions of how crisis politics played out in deficit countries and which adjustment policies were ultimately enacted—and why. To answer these questions, this chapter therefore traces how the preferences of interest groups shaped the design and contentiousness of crisis policies in the three Eurozone deficit states, Ireland, Spain, and Greece, over the period 2008 to 2015. These comparative case studies focus on how domestic voters, interest groups, political actors, and external creditor institutions positioned themselves and influenced the domestic adjustment debates and conflicts about policies of external adjustment, internal adjustment, and financing. The case studies incorporate policies that were discussed, including those that were adopted and others that ultimately were not enacted. For this purpose, we draw on a combination of primary data such as newspaper coverage, public opinion data, and sovereign and bank bailout documentation, as well as original qualitative evidence from seventeen in-depth interviews with national interest group representatives. The interview partners were

The Politics of Bad Options: Why the Eurozone's Problems Have Been So Hard to Resolve. Stefanie Walter, Ari Ray, and Nils Redeker, Oxford University Press (2020). © Stefanie Walter, Ari Ray, and Nils Redeker.
DOI: 10.1093/oso/9780198857013.001.0001

selected based on their size and the importance of their members to the overall economy.[1] The latter aimed at corroborating our survey results and expanding our understanding of interest groups' positions and actions during the Eurozone crisis. We complement the insights gained from this data with other sources, ranging from protocols of parliamentary debates and committee discussions to newspaper articles and other secondary sources.

We structure the case study analysis along country lines, examining domestic adjustment policies and politics in first Ireland, then Spain and finally Greece. In each case, we start by providing an overview of the country's trajectory into crisis as well of its broadly classified crisis response. We then delve deeper, looking at distributive conflict lines surrounding, in turn, policies pertaining to external adjustment, internal adjustment, and financing. As we have emphasized throughout this book, all three crisis strategies can in principle be enacted via multiple policies. In our discussion, we particularly focus on two things: First, policies that were deemed impossible given uncooperative positions taken by external actors, such as Eurozone creditors, as well as policies that were discussed domestically during the crisis period. Among the latter, we thus not only explore adjustment policies that were actually adopted by governments facing crisis, but also adjustment ideas that failed to materialize into policy outputs.

Given the depth of the crisis and the stark distributive conflicts we identified in previous chapters, it is not surprising that crisis politics in the crisis countries we study took place in the context of considerable political volatility, although to differing degrees (Figure 4.1). Our analysis focuses on the crisis responses of two consecutive liberal-conservative minority governments in Ireland—the Fianna Fáil Cowen government (supported by the Irish Green Party), which held power from 2008 to 2011, and the Fine Gael cabinet that succeeded it, led by Enda Kenny, who governed from 2011 to 2015 with the Labour Party as a minority coalition member in government. In Spain, the crisis was initially addressed by the social democratic Spanish Socialist Workers' Party (PSOE) Zapatero III government (2008 to 2011), which was supported by a number of smaller regional left-wing parties. In 2011, it was replaced by the liberal-conservative People's Party (PP) government, led by Mariano Rajoy, which was in power between 2011 and 2015. Finally, Greece is the country where crisis politics was characterized by extreme party-political volatility. Between 2008 and 2015, six governments were formed, two of which were transitory technocratic cabinets. With the exception of the second left-wing SYRIZA cabinet which began its tenure in September 2015, all parties were forced to rely on support votes from individual extra-party parliamentarians, many of which shifted party allegiances in the midst

---

[1] We also made sure to conduct interviews with groups from a variety of economic sectors as well as trade unions representing workers of different skill and income levels. A complete list of all our interview partners can be found in Table A4.1 at the end of this chapter.

Ireland

Fianna Fáil[C] | Fine Gael[C]

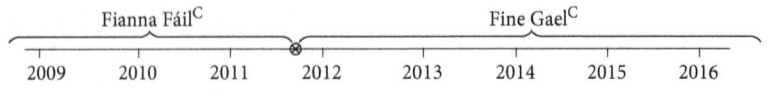

2009 — 2010 — 2011 — 2012 — 2013 — 2014 — 2015 — 2016

Spain

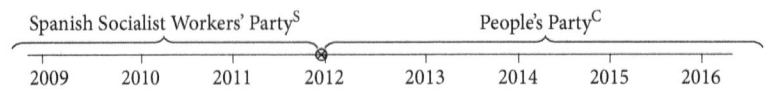

Spanish Socialist Workers' Party[S] | People's Party[C]

2009 — 2010 — 2011 — 2012 — 2013 — 2014 — 2015 — 2016

Greece

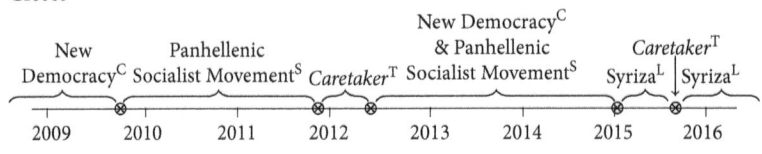

New Democracy[C] | Panhellenic Socialist Movement[S] | Caretaker[T] | New Democracy[C] & Panhellenic Socialist Movement[S] | Caretaker[T] Syriza[L] | Syriza[L]

2009 — 2010 — 2011 — 2012 — 2013 — 2014 — 2015 — 2016

⊗ = Snap election

Figure 4.1 A timeline of crisis-time governments in Ireland, Spain, and Greece

Note: Timelines are scaled to reflect real cabinet tenure lengths. Superscripts indicate party families of main cabinet party where: L = Radical Left, S = Social Democratic, C = Conservative, and T = Technocratic.

of parliamentary terms (Dinas 2010; Dinas and Rori 2013; Tsatsanis and Teperoglou 2016).

As our cases vary in a multitude of ways, our approach is exploratory in nature. We discuss the politics surrounding adjustment policy adoption, highlighting in particular distributional conflict lines that emerged in light of specific policy debates. In tandem with these accounts, we draw attention to how existing theory has conceived the causes of specific adjustment outcomes, such as the distribution of adjustment costs across socioeconomic groups and/or levels of conflict surrounding the enactment of specific policies. To conclude our discussion, we finally turn to a country-comparative perspective, examining in particular theoretical interpretations of crisis politics that can account for adjustment outcomes across the broad range of all three country cases.

Overall, we find that external adjustment in the form of Eurozone exit was entirely off the table in each of the three countries we examine. While voter minorities favored this adjustment strategy, it was never actively supported by domestic interest groups—nor was it ever picked up by any major political party. In contrast, distributive conflict pertaining to the design of internal adjustment, and to a smaller extent also financing, was noticeable in all cases. Business interests in Ireland, Spain, and Greece consistently emphasized that a low tax climate, compressed wages, and labor market deregulation would be the only means to effectively resolve the crisis at hand—all policies that lessened adjustment costs for firms. In contrast, labor unions and social policy groups were skeptical of this fiscal adjustment strategy, given that it disproportionately placed high shares of the adjustment burden on workers and socioeconomically disadvantaged voter groups. Finally, financing policies were highly delimited by Eurozone creditors, leaving deficit country policymakers unable to choose between a full range of financing policies. Rather, they were left with decisions concerning under which conditions they would accept sovereign bailouts, and more broadly, the lengths that they were willing to go in order to forcibly impose losses on foreign creditors. Similarly to internal adjustment outcomes, financing policies enacted more frequently aligned to the preferences of business interests that, unlike other interest groups, favored cautious bargaining tactics, disapproved of debt restructuring, and were more accepting of bailouts under strict loan conditionality.

The cumulative findings of this chapter thus teach us a number of things. Most importantly, interest groups representing employers were highly successful in attaining their preferred adjustment outcomes, particularly in Ireland and Spain. In these countries, business groups representing firms with highly mobile asset portfolios or whose economic activity generated substantial jobs, had significant structural bargaining power among policymakers, the latter being weary of making policy decisions that could induce investment outflows or raise unemployment. Neither the ideology of political parties nor their ties to specific interest groups seem to have affected this cost–benefit calculation of policymakers, as even social democratic parties with traditionally close ties to unions, such as PSOE in Spain, adopted adjustment reforms that aligned more strongly to the inclinations of firms' interests. External intervention by creditor institutions was much stronger in Greece during the crisis, than in Ireland and Spain, making it especially hard for ruling governments to form pro-adjustment coalitions across interest groups. It was partly for this reason that distributive conflict led to much wider scale of political outrage in Greece than in the other two contexts, with negative effects on the ability of successive governments to implement announced adjustment reforms.

Ireland in Crisis

In the early years after adoption of the euro, Ireland experienced a prolonged growth spurt, commonly referred to as the "Celtic Tiger" years (Donovan and Murphy 2013; Riain 2014). In the period 2001–7, the Irish economy grew on average 5.3 percent of GDP annually and the national unemployment rate, which had peaked at nearly 16 percent in 1993, stabilized at around 5 percent (World Bank 2016b, 2016a). The underlying causes of the boom years were manifold. Since the mid 1980s, successive Irish government had introduced reform packages aimed at boosting foreign direct investment via significant privatization schemes and the lowering of corporate taxes (Hardiman 2017), a strategy which bore significant fruit after the turn of the millennium, when an increasing number of large multi-nationals, such as Intel, Microsoft, and Google decided to place their headquarters on the island (Brazys and Regan 2017). Euro adoption facilitated Irish transition into a high-tech stronghold (Sweeney 2008). As an English-speaking Eurozone country with close links to Great Britain, Ireland could position itself as an ideal home base for big corporations looking to penetrate the European market. In brief, Ireland was perceived as a low-tax country, with access to the European common market and a strong anchor for macroeconomic policy discipline in the form of the euro (Sweeney 2008). Initially, the Celtic Tiger years as such struck observers as the natural conclusion of a prolonged structural shift away from an agriculturally oriented economy, to one that rather operated an export-led growth model (Honohan and Walsh 2002).

Under the hood, however, significant balance of payments problems were looming. Fueled by low European Central Bank (ECB) interest rates, Ireland experienced large inflows of not only foreign direct investment (FDI), but also more liquid forms of investment capital in the years preceding the crisis (Lane 2012; Obstfeld 2011; O'Rourke and Taylor 2013). Those years were characterized by increased access to cheap credit that fueled rising wages, high levels of consumption and growing asset price inflation, the result of which was the formation of a large housing bubble (Conefrey and Gerald, 2009). As a result, the Irish current account deficit peaked at −6.5 percent of GDP in 2007 (OECD 2019a). When the domestic housing market showed signs of slowing down in the fall of 2007, the Irish government reacted quickly: Already in the fall of 2007, a relatively comprehensive fiscal consolidation package was agreed upon between Irish employers, unions, and the government (Regling and Watson 2010). This, combined with very low government debt prior to the onset of the global financial crisis, meant that even though state borrowing went up by 18.5 percentage points, it only stood at 42 percent of GDP in 2008 (Eurostat 2019a).

The Irish descent into crisis thus had little to do with a prolonged legacy of public debt issues. Instead, Ireland's path into crisis began with rushed economic policy, designed to lessen negative spillovers from the US subprime crisis, inflated by problems in the design of the domestic tax base. Immediately after the bankruptcy of Lehman Brothers in September 2008, Ireland started experiencing large outflows of investment capital as a result of increased investor speculation; in other words, a sudden stop (Aizenman, Hutchison, and Jinjarak 2013). Two weeks later, in an effort to regain market sentiment, the Irish Fianna Fáil government unilaterally decided to implement a blanket guarantee for two large Irish banks, tainted by particularly worrying balance sheets: Anglo-Irish and Irish Nationwide Building Society (INBS) (Nyberg 2011). The guarantee was designed as a last-minute effort to bolster financial market sentiment among investors who were rapidly retracting their capital from the country. Paradoxically, it was installed in order to avoid a scenario whereby problems in the domestic banking sector would spill over to the real economy. However, in the end it would lead to the conversion of private into public debt and, in extension, push Ireland from a banking crisis into a full-blown sovereign debt crisis (Donovan and Murphy 2013).

By early 2010, onset by a combination of rapidly declining tax revenues which were highly sensitive to declines in construction activity, and a second spell of declining financial market confidence sparked by the unfolding crisis in Greece, markets started speculating against the solvency of the Irish state (Lane 2012:56; Figure 4.2). Fears that the Irish government would have to engage in substantial bank bailouts, as well as the possibility of the country being forced to exit from the Eurozone, raised investor alarm. Throughout 2010, the Irish government therefore grew increasingly reliant on emergency liquidity assistance (ELA) provided by the ECB—so much that once the ECB declared its intention to stop ELA financing in November of that year, the country was immediately forced into applying for a Troika bailout (Trichet 2010a, 2010b). This sovereign bailout was

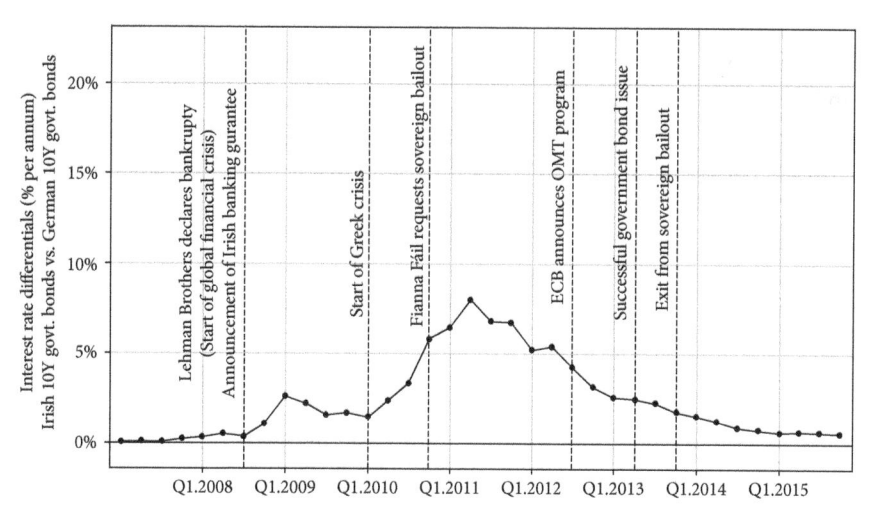

Figure 4.2 A timeline of government bond interest rate differentials and key events in the Irish crisis (2007–16)

Note: Interest rate on German 10Y government bonds are used as reference value, as the German state was conceived of as being at no risk of default throughout the entirety of the crisis.

Source: OECD (2019b).

conditional on the adoption of a number of adjustment reforms listed in a contractual Memorandum of Understanding (MOU). The creditor–debtor relationship between the Irish government and the Troika increased external influence on Irish adjustment policies. As in most instances throughout the Eurozone crisis, Troika institutions monitored the continued implementation of those reforms and disbursed loan tranches successively in order to ensure the implementation of the agreed upon loan conditions.

The Irish crisis episode stands out for two main reasons: First, the rapid pace at which governments could both adopt and enact adjustment packages, and second, the low degree of contestation displayed by Irish voters and trade unions (Genovese et al. 2016; Pappas and O'Malley 2014), both of which were opposed to many of the policies that the crisis packages contained. In part because of low levels of political conflict, Ireland became the first country to successfully exit their Troika-monitored bailout. This happened already in December 2013—less than a year after the Irish state had successfully re-entered bond markets (IMF 2013a, 2013b).

Policies and Conflict Lines Surrounding External Adjustment in Ireland

External adjustment was never seriously discussed as a crisis resolution option in Ireland. Policymakers entirely dismissed any idea of addressing the crisis by means of Eurozone exit. The common currency enjoyed immense support from both voters and interest groups alike. Amid Irish interest groups, strong support for remaining in the Eurozone was voiced by employer associations, trade unions, and social policy groups. This is in line with our survey findings which suggest that 82 percent of all Irish respondent groups opposed an Irish Eurozone exit. Most noticeably, the prospect of abandoning the common currency was a highly unattractive proposition for multinational firms in tech and pharmaceuticals sectors. Tax incentives had mainly brought them to the country, and as such a substantial part of their financial assets were stored on the island solely for tax purposes (Brazys and Regan 2017; Seabrooke and Wigan 2017). An Irish Eurozone exit would thus only serve to increase exchange-rate risk and reduce purchasing power while having relatively small positive demand-side effects, given lower levels of manufacturing situated in Ireland. Within trade unions and social policy, there was also limited willingness to engage in debates about leaving the Eurozone. From our interviews in spring 2017, we found that their preference rather was to see that firm assets remained in Ireland, so as to ensure state revenues which in the medium to long run could enable the increased progressivity of personal income taxation and added spending on social policy. An Irish Eurozone exit was conceived of merely as a risk of jeopardizing this policy trajectory.

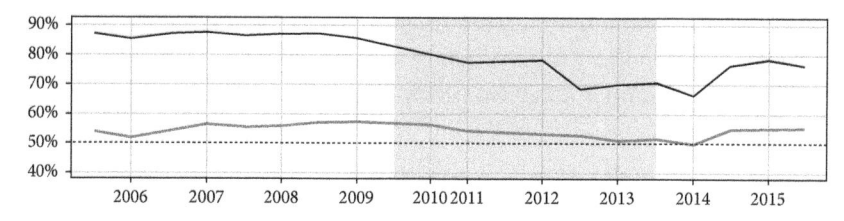

Figure 4.3 Irish vs. EMU country average public support for the euro, 2005–16

Note: Upper line shows average euro support among Irish voters over time; lower bold-marked line depicts average euro support across EZ-15 countries over time. Grey block highlights the most intense phase of the crisis in Ireland (H1 2010 to H2 2013).

Source: Data taken from Standard Eurobarometer surveys Nos 64 to 84 (European Commission 2019a).

Largely mirroring the preferences of domestic interest groups, Irish voters were strongly pro-Euro throughout the crisis. Based on data from the bi-annual Standard Eurobarometer survey of the European Commission, Figure 4.3 displays the share of Irish respondents that stated they favored the common currency, compared to the average share across countries that were full Eurozone members as of January1, 2008 (EZ-15). Although public support for the euro, which had historically been very high, dropped considerably during the crisis, this never translated into any concerted efforts among voters to advocate an Irish Eurozone exit (Simpson 2019). Even in the first half of 2014, when euro confidence was at an all-time low both in Ireland as well as in the Eurozone overall, 67 percent of Irish voters still stated they were in favor of the common currency, compared to the Eurozone average share of 50 percent (European Commission 2019a).

Given this strong domestic support for retaining the common currency, exchange rate adjustment by means of Eurozone exit was never advocated by any major political party in Ireland throughout the crisis either (Gallagher and Marsh 2011; O'Malley and Carty 2017). The common currency, rather than a cause of the crisis, was instead portrayed as an underlying driver of the Celtic Boom years. Policymakers were keen to emphasize that a return to pre-crisis growth could only come about as Ireland rectified its debt and current account imbalances, rather than via the country leaving the currency union (Cowen 2008; Kenny 2012). As a result, the politics of adjustment tin Ireland centered more strongly on the two other means by which country could resolve its crisis, namely policies of internal adjustment and financing.

Policies and Conflict Lines Surrounding Internal Adjustment in Ireland

Although internal adjustment was more contested in Ireland than the rejection of external adjustment, the crisis strategy was met with relative acceptance among both Irish voters and interest groups when contrasted to other Eurozone deficit countries. This is in line with the country's overall vulnerability profile as shown in Chapter 2. The profile exhibited a very high vulnerability to external adjustment, but only a moderate vulnerability to internal adjustment, which was also considerably lower than Spain's and particularly Greece's vulnerability to internal adjustment. Nonetheless, distributive struggles flared up on the question as to how the burden of internal adjustment should be distributed across domestic socio-economic groups. For one, these debates centered on how voter groups with varying types of employment contracts and income, were heterogeneously affected by various internal adjustment policies. Second, they revolved around the question of how the costs of austerity were to be absorbed by taxpaying citizens vs. firms. Particularly controversial issues were to what extent public sector employees would have to accept wage and pension cuts (Armingeon and Baccaro 2012b; Cawley 2012) and whether the country's competitively low rates of corporate taxation should be raised (Irish Department of Finance 2009, 2010, 2011). Far less contentious were the introduction of structural reforms. Irish labor markets were already highly flexible at crisis onset and after successive rounds of privatization in the 1990s, state-owned assets were relatively moderate in size (IEO of the IMF 2016).

Starting very early on in domestic negotiations between Irish wage social partners, in 2008, employer organizations simply pointed to "inability to pay" clauses in Irish collective wage bargains, leading to rapidly declining wages in the private sector (Armingeon and Baccaro 2012b). These clauses, which essentially enabled firms to cut wages below negotiated rates in times of exceptionally large profit losses were, however, not an option open to the Irish government, and the state was therefore unable to cut public sector wages without reopening wage rate bargaining. Given this, public sectors unions stalled negotiations in an attempt to bargain for wage freezes and extended unpaid leave for their constituents, as an alternative to direct cuts in wages (Armingeon and Baccaro 2012b).[2] Initially, this strategy seemed to work for the unions but as the topic became salient in the Irish news media (Cawley 2012), public sentiment toward the public sector's stalling efforts strongly declined (Regan 2012). In the end, the government decided to implement unilateral pay cuts without the support of unions. Fearing a backlash in the following year, however, the government instead decided to negotiate a separate peak-level agreement with the public sector unions in the run up to the announcement of the 2010 national budget (Armingeon and Baccaro 2012b). The result was the Croke Park agreement, a deal which allowed the government to implement substantial cuts in wages and benefits, but only to new hires (Hardiman and Regan 2013). Having been able to shelter its core

---

[2] In face of future deflation, this would have allowed for very smaller changes to the real income of public sector employees.

constituency of existing employees, public sector unions thus promised to uphold the industrial peace for the following five years (Armingeon and Baccaro 2012b). However, the end effect of front-loading wage cuts onto new hires effectively placed a disproportionally high burden of adjustment on younger, junior workers who were effectively entering the Irish labor market.

Organizations such as Social Justice Ireland (FKA CORI Justice), which represented the preferences of the working and non-working poor during the crisis, argued fervently against cuts in social spending throughout the crisis (CORI Justice 2008a; Social Justice Ireland 2009b, 2010, 2011). From early on the trade union movement also made clear that social spending should not be cut in ways that would disproportionally harm precarious workers or non-workers (ICTU 2009, 2011; Irish Department of Finance 2010). Both groups, unlike employer associations, also clearly opposed reductions to the national minimum wage (De Breadan 2009; *Irish Examiner* 2011; Social Justice Ireland 2009a), a policy which had been proposed by the International Monetary Fund (IMF) during bailout negotiations (Kinsella 2017: 53). Finally, public opinion data from 2011 suggests that voters were strongly opposed to investment-oriented spending cuts, particularly wanting to see increased expenditure dedicated to health care, education, and industry support, as shown in Figure 4.4 (Marsh et al. 2017, 246). These positions aligned most closely with the views of the Irish labor movement, which also favoured additional spending on these three budgetary headings (ICTU 2009, 2011; Irish Department of Finance 2009, 2011). While employers also sought to increase industry support, the majority of their proposals centered on the introduction of tax credits and exemptions rather than added spending (Irish Department of Finance 2010, 2011, 2012).

In line with the preferences of both unions and social policy groups, social transfer rates to the poor were not substantially cut during the crisis by any of the Fianna Fáil or Fine Gael governments. The Irish national minimum wage was also not significantly reduced; instead, it remained fixed at mid 2007 levels throughout

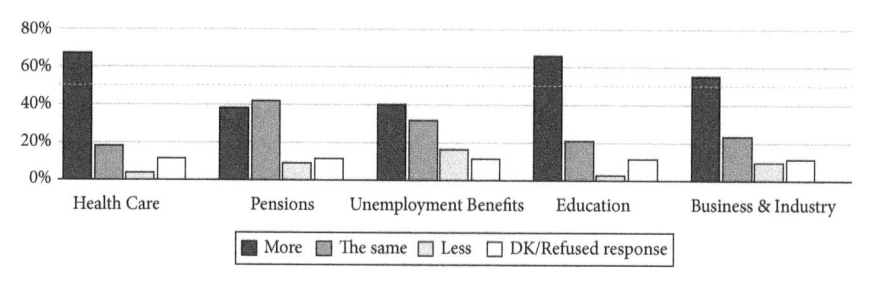

Figure 4.4 Irish voter attitudes toward level of spending across policy areas

Note: Authors' calculations based on data from the Irish National Election Study, collected in January 2011.

Source: based on Marsh et al. (2017).

the crisis, being only raised by mid 2015 (Eurostat 2019b). However, conforming to the preferences of employer associations, retrenchment measures were undertaken by significantly tightening eligibility criteria for a number of social policies, including unemployment and child benefits as well as housing allowances (Irish Department of Finance 2010). Moreover, a reported €2.7 billion were cut from Ireland's Health Service between 2009 and 2014 (Ó Cionnaith 2014). Substantial cuts to education spending were also enacted, affecting in particular primary and secondary schools set up for socioeconomically disadvantaged children, as well as students in higher education, which were charged tuition fees starting in 2011 (OECD 2013, 4, 16).

On the side of taxation, strong conflicts emerged about the issue of Irish corporate taxation, personal income taxation, and VAT rates. Our discussions with interest group representatives in Ireland suggest that it was clear from the onset of the crisis that neither of the two main political parties would favor any policy that entailed any form of direct increase to Ireland's 12.5 percent corporate tax rate—this in spite of pressure, particularly from the European Commission, to raise the competitively low rate (Winnett and Waterfield 2010). Employers in exporting sectors strongly opposed any increases in corporate tax rates, fearing that this would lead to an outflow of foreign investment capital (Irish Department of Finance 2010, 2011). Moreover, in budget discussions they highlighted that increasing the progressivity of personal income tax bands might result in problems for firms in high-tech sectors, relying strongly on being able to attract high-skilled labor from abroad into Ireland. Instead, they supported the introduction of a new expat income tax credit (Irish Department of Finance 2010). In contrast, both labor unions and social policy groups attempted to further stem public transfer losses to workers mainly by calling for the introduction of a minimum effective corporate tax rate of 12.5 percent (ICTU 2013), and by favoring a temporary 2.5 percent levy on corporate profits (ICTU 2011, 2013). Moreover, they repeatedly urged for increased progressivity in personal income and wealth taxes (CORI Justice 2008b; ICTU 2009). These policies, they argued, were much more preferable over increases to the standard VAT rate, which in end-effect was highly regressive in nature (Lynch et al. 2017).[3] Although additional taxes were also drawn from income, a larger reform to ensure progressivity of income taxes was never implemented throughout the crisis. New taxes rates did not proportionally affect individuals that belonged in the highest income bands, placing higher burdens on the middle and upper working classes (Whelan and Maitre 2014). Furthermore, a large amount of additional revenues were collected by means of special one-off tax levies, such levies on public sector pensions

---

[3] In fact, in the early stages of the Irish recession, the Irish Congress of Trade Unions (ICTU) actively proposed a decrease in the standard VAT rate from 21% to 20% (Irish Department of Finance 2007).

(Alesina et al. 2019) as well as an 8 percent Universal Social Charge leveraged directly from worker pay-checks (European Commission 2019b). Both policies ran directly counter to the preferences of labour unions (*Irish Examiner* 2009).

Likewise, employers were also more successful in shaping VAT policy than social policy groups and unions. Overall, the Irish VAT rate was successively raised by both Fianna Fáil and Fine Gael, from 21 percent in 2008 to 23 percent by 2012 (European Commission 2019b). Moreover, additional compensatory tax cuts for trade-sheltered sectors were also introduced in 2011, as the government introduced a special reduced 9 percent VAT rate for services offered in the hospitality sector (European Commission 2019b). While the reduced VAT rate likely improved bottom lines for firms in the sector, there was far less evidence to suggest that these cuts were conducive to compressing the prices of these services (Irish Department of Finance 2018). The change was thus criticized by the Irish Congress of Trade Unions (ICTU) as operating mainly as an indirect form of subsidy for firms in hotel and accommodation industries (Hospitality Ireland 2016).

Finally, the Fine Gael-led Kenny government also implemented additional tax policies to relieve firms from problems associated with the financial downturn, particularly in the construction and housing sectors. As the collapse of the Irish housing market substantially lowered demand for construction services, the sector's employers' association requested a one-year extension of mortgage relief for first-time property buyers in 2010 in order to stimulate demand (Irish Department of Finance 2010). The Irish government met this request as well as restored a stamp exemption on non-residential properties, in order to reduce costs of new construction (Alesina et al. 2019).

In sum, employer interests were highly successful in attaining their preferred forms of fiscal adjustment both in terms of spending and of taxation. Among the two likely drivers of this outcome, one is the progressive weakening of the Irish labor movement. The other is contrariwise the increasing structural power of business interests in the Irish political landscape. Crisis-time coordination problems haunted the Irish union movement, which was relatively unsuccessful in lobbying for its preferred internal adjustment policies. Organized labor suffered from problems in representative legitimacy, given that workers in particularly multinational firms were not a part of the union movement (Culpepper and Regan 2014). Moreover, the workers' movement fragmented during the crisis as collective bargaining collapsed, and public unions grew more effective in stemming income losses via sectoral agreements than their private industry counterparts. To some extent, this can explain why Irish labor unions made much fewer attempts to organize in opposition to austerity measures to the same extent as they did in other crisis-afflicted countries, such as Greece, Portugal, and Spain (Genovese et al. 2016). In tandem with a weakened domestic labor movement, business interests gained significant bargaining power throughout the crisis. Business lobbies had for a longer period of time built up relatively close links to both Fianna Fáil and Fine Gael at the onset of the crisis, thus improving their access to decision-making. Perhaps more centrally, however, multinationals headquartered in Ireland maintained large and highly mobile asset portfolios, providing them with credible exit options. In other words, these firms could thus effectively threaten policymakers by signaling their desire to move out of Ireland if they perceived the domestic policy climate to be growing too unfavorable (Culpepper and Reinke 2014; Frieden 2015b).

Policies and Conflict Lines Surrounding Financing in Ireland

With regard to policies of financing, domestic elites and citizens alike were less engaged in debates concerning the Irish decision to accept the bailout itself. Discussions rather centered on whether the Irish government should indeed make investors of failing domestic banks whole, and whether such a default on sovereign debt would be possible under the auspices of a Troika-monitored bailout. However, neither the ECB, the European Commission, nor important creditor countries, such as Germany and France, entertained any possibility of Irish sovereign debt repudiation (Breen 2012, 84)—in spite of this being actively proposed by both IMF technical staff, as well as a number of external economic policy experts (Eichengreen 2010a; Krugman 2010; Mody 2018). Moreover, there was a strong reluctance on the part of the ECB to discuss the possibility of policy measures that would have signaled its willingness to act as a Lender of Last Resort at the early stages of the Euro crisis (Schelkle 2017). Instead, the bank argued that any measures to ensure liquidity in the Irish financial system would be contingent on the Irish government undertaking substantial fiscal consolidation (Trichet 2010b). Domestic discontent with the adjustment program was thus in part rooted in this strongly un-accommodative stance of Troika institutions with regard to combining the bailout with other, low conditionality forms of financing.

It was mainly interest groups—particularly business lobbies representing multinationals, but also trade-sheltered sectors such as construction—that desired to see a bailout "at all costs," once it became clear that the ECB was no longer willing to support Irish banks by means of emergency liquidity assistance. Their key priority was to ensure a path toward the restoration of domestic financial market stability and, in extension, a return to economic growth. They viewed comprehensive fiscal consolidation and structural reform as vital steps in this direction, whereas they believed that efforts to negotiate debt relief would serve mainly to spook financial markets, thus inducing negative effects on their access to foreign credit. In contrast, labor unions and some social policy groups who were particularly active in fiscal policy debates were more vocal in communicating that debt restructuring would better distribute adjustment costs across firms and citizens than a package based solely on austerity and structural reform. Both actively

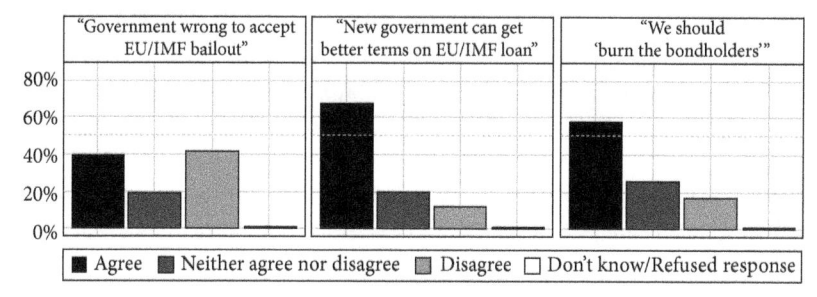

Figure 4.5 Public support of sovereign bailouts and defaults in Ireland (2011)
Note: Authors' calculations based on data from the Irish National Election Study, collected in January 2011.
Source: based on Marsh et al. (2017).

favored the government taking a harder stance on bailout negotiations in order to attain partial debt relief (Social Justice Ireland 2011; *The Irish Times* 2012).

Irish voters had mixed feelings toward the bailout package, as displayed in Figure 4.5. Pre-election polls taken in January 2011 suggest that Irish voters were split in their assessment of the Fianna Fáil government's decision to accept financial assistance, with 41 percent of voters condoning it, while 39 percent perceived it to have been a mistake. In the survey, 67 percent of voters believed that a new Irish government could negotiate better terms with the Eurozone Troika, and 57 percent thought that the new government should write down state debt (Marsh et al. 2017). Both the conservative Fine Gael and the social-democratic Labour Party actively made debt relief centerpieces of their party programs (Suiter and Farrell 2011, 36–7). And in line with voters' openness toward debt relief, both parties made strong electoral gains in the February 2011 election (Marsh and Cunningham 2011, 189).

In the end, however, no sovereign default or debt relief ever happened in the Irish case. Bailout loan conditionality focused heavily on the specifics of winding down failed Irish banks and less on policies aimed at addressing the country's fiscal position (Kinsella 2017; Pisani-Ferry et al. 2013). Moreover, demand compression policies and structural reforms that were in fact addressed by loan conditionality, drew heavily from a National Competitiveness Plan proposed unilaterally by the Irish government earlier in 2010 (Kinsella 2017; Pisani-Ferry et al. 2013), suggesting a high level of policy ownership in the Irish bailout program (IEO of the IMF 2016). That said, however, loan conditionality clearly privileged the preferences of Irish business interests over those of other domestic social partners, such as trade unions and social policy groups.

Very few efforts were seemingly taken by any of the Fianna Fáil or Fine Gael governments to push for increased burden-sharing across Ireland and other Eurozone creditor states, even though both Fine Gael and Labour, the party's minor coalition partner, had made debt write-downs a core part of their election campaigns in 2011, and a strong consensus among particularly economists and policy experts thought that it would be highly beneficial overall for the Irish economy. The low desire of Fine Gael to engage in efforts to renegotiate the terms of their bailout agreement should arguably be seen in light of two factors. As the Irish economy started rebalancing and growing relatively soon after the February 2011 election, there clearly were strong incentives for the government to refrain from upsetting the macroeconomic status quo by giving reasons for investors to grow spooked. Equally important, however, was the strong bargaining power of particularly foreign multinationals rooted in Ireland—these firms vehemently opposed the idea of renegotiating bailout terms or engaging in discussions about debt restructuring.

Crisis Politics in Ireland: Conclusion

In sum, external adjustment by means of Eurozone exit was never actively considered in Ireland. Instead, the country rapidly initiated efforts to engage particularly policies of internal adjustment by means of primarily fiscal consolidation. Conflicts pertaining to the policy-level enactment of this were substantial, as interest groups attempted to shelter their own constituencies. Business groups preferred spending-based consolidation efforts and were wary of changes to Irish corporate tax burdens. Unions and social policy groups conversely favored more strongly revenue-oriented policy in order to sustain higher levels of public spending, while starkly opposing increases to the regressive VAT. Eurozone creditors only ever entertained the idea of providing Ireland financing by means of bailouts, subject to loan conditionality, and rapidly shut down discussions surrounding the potential of debt repudiation. This, however, conformed to the preferences of business interests, which feared that debt write-downs would reduce investor confidence. Employers were far more successful than other groups in getting their fiscal positions translated into policy output in Ireland. But in spite of this, the Irish workers' movement, or indeed the domestic population more broadly, undertook relatively few political actions in opposition of enacted fiscal policy.

Spain in Crisis

During the immediate years preceding the crisis, the Spanish economy, like Ireland's, grew at a rapid pace. After it had adopted the euro in 1999, the unemployment rate sank by 48 percent to reach 8.2 percent in 2007 (World Bank 2016b). In the four years preceding the onset of the great recession in 2008, Spain recorded an average annual growth rate of 4.2 percent of GDP (World Bank 2016a). In parallel with these developments, however, the economy was characterized by rapidly mounting current account deficits, caused by strong inward capital inflows, wage inflation in particularly trade-sheltered sectors and high levels of domestic consumption (Neal and García-Iglesias 2013). As a result, following 2003, the Spanish current account deficit grew, reaching −9.4 percent of GDP by 2007 (OECD 2019a).

The Spanish crisis itself was triggered by the onset of the US subprime crisis in September 2007. Spain, like Ireland, then faced the collapse of a domestic housing bubble, onset by freezes in international interbank lending markets (Quaglia and Royo 2015). The collapse uncovered a number of structural problems in the country's financial sector that made the Spanish economy particularly sensitive to sudden stops of foreign investment capital. First, a substantial portion of the domestic banking sector—in particular smaller savings banks, also known as "cajas"—maintained insufficiently diversified asset portfolios, strongly concentrated in Spanish property (Fernandez-Villaverde et al. 2013; Royo 2013).[4] Moreover, almost the entire Spanish mortgage market, which had grown particularly rapidly since the introduction of the euro, was priced on variable interest rates. Rapid increases in interbank interest rates, thus quickly translated into the deterioration of domestic firm and household balance sheets, an immense share of which had invested in property during the housing boom (Fernandez-Villaverde et al. 2013). As the crisis progressed, the combination of contracted housing demand and rising interest rates fueled firm insolvencies and unemployment, thus effectively raising the number of non-performing loans on bank balance sheets (Fernandez-Villaverde et al. 2013). By September 2012, three relatively small cajas, Bankia, CatalunyaCaixa, and Novagalicia, had run up capital deficits of €54 billion—a sum constituting over 5 percent of Spanish GDP at the time (Garicano 2012).

The Spanish government's immediate reaction to the unfolding crisis was similar to that of most other industrialized economies, addressing the bursting of the bubble through fiscal expansion in an effort to restore market confidence (Hardiman and Dellepiane 2012; Royo and Steinberg 2019). Only in spring 2010, as the balance sheets of semi-public Spanish banks started deteriorating rapidly, did internal adjustment by means of austerity and structural reform become part of the Spanish crisis-resolution agenda (Royo 2013). By then interrelated factors such as the fledgling domestic construction sector, the general slow-down of the global economy and increased speculative pressure in the aftermath of the commencement of the Greek crisis early 2010, weighed down heavily on smaller, over-leveraged Spanish savings and loans banks (Garicano 2012). Moreover, unemployment had soared as a result of mass bankruptcies in the construction

---

[4] The cajas maintained no shareholders but were rather governed by managerial boards, specifically selected by regional and local governments. Political pressure to finance electorally popular construction and property projects, which promised to generate both local employment and infrastructure, may thus arguably have influenced financial mismanagement on the part of these banks (Fernandez-Villaverde et al. 2013; Markgraf and Rosas 2019).

and housing sectors, reaching more than 40 percent of the domestic working-age population (World Bank 2016b).

The Spanish turn to internal adjustment was politically arduous and came about under immense domestic opposition from both loosely coordinated voters and trade unions. Both took action against unpopular spending cuts, tax increases, and structural reform (Anduiza et al. 2014; del Rio Loira and Fenger 2019). During the tenure of the PP, Spain embarked upon significant fiscal consolidation based on cuts in public wages and regional state budgets, as well as hikes to VAT rates, significant regulation of labor markets and targeted privatization efforts (MacInnes and Pinedo 2011; Royo and Steinberg 2019). Yet, in the end, austerity and structural reform alone could not address the Spanish crisis. In May 2012, after prolonged efforts from both PSOE and PP cabinets to avoid a sovereign bailout, the Spanish government accepted a partial banking bailout from the Eurozone Troika designed specifically to restore the solvency of its fledgling financial sector (Royo and Steinberg 2019). By August of the same year, the ECB announced a comprehensive scheme to purchase government bonds in secondary markets, in order to further aid the Spanish government in the issuance of new debt: Outright Monetary Transactions, more commonly referred to as OMT (ECB 2012). The resulting combination of dramatic fiscal consolidation, structural reform and low conditionality financing managed to lift Spain out of crisis by 2013. In January 2014, the Spanish government exited its bailout agreement with the Eurozone creditor institutions (Pérez 2014) (Figure 4.6).

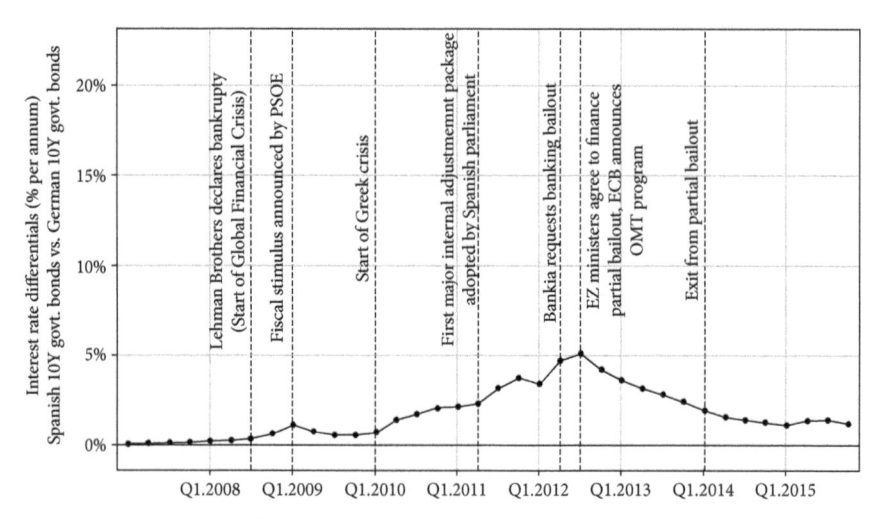

Figure 4.6 A timeline of government bond interest rate differentials and key events in the Spanish crisis

Note: Interest rate on German 10Y government bonds are used as reference value, as the German state was conceived of as being at no risk of default throughout the entirety of the crisis.

Source: OECD (2019b).

Policies and Conflict Lines Surrounding External Adjustment in Spain

Much like in Ireland, there was a strong consensus among Spanish political actors that Spain should remain in the monetary union (Fernández-Albertos and Kuo 2018). As highlighted in Chapter 3, 85 percent of interest groups that participated in our Spanish survey were opposed to a Spanish exit from the Eurozone. Throughout our discussions with representatives of business groups, trade unions, and social policy groups in the spring of 2017, not a single person stated they had ever favored a Spanish Eurozone exit. The overwhelming support by businesses toward the euro is also shown in other work: In a 2014 survey, 88 percent of business managers favored retaining the euro (Fernández -Albertos and Kuo 2016, 2018).

While the preferences of the Spanish electorate were subject to more variation than those of interest groups, public opinion data from the crisis period suggests that a clear majority of voters was always in favor of retaining the euro. This is highlighted by Figure 4.7, which depicts how nationally representative samples of voters positioned themselves with regard to the choice of keeping the euro or returning to previous Spanish currency, the peseta, throughout the crisis. In spring 2012, support for the common currency declined notably, after the crisis peaked in Spain throughout 2011—at this point 36 percent of respondents preferred to return to a national currency. But, similar to other Spanish public opinion data from the period, it underlines the fact that comfortable majorities of Spanish voters persisted in wanting to remain in the Eurozone (Fernández-Albertos and Kuo 2016; Hobolt and Wratil 2015; Roth et al. 2016).

These societal preferences regarding external adjustment were well-represented by parties on both sides of the left–right divide. The Spanish government's

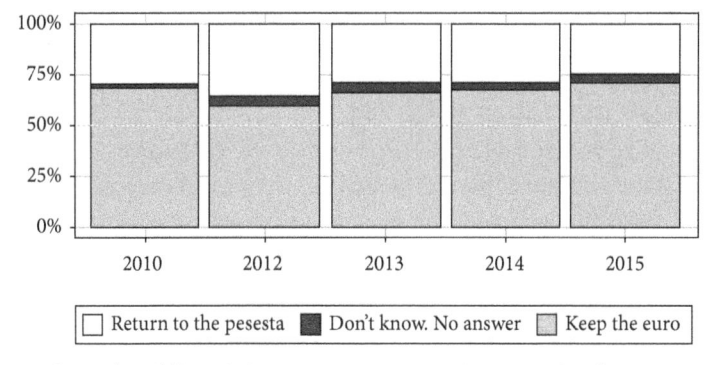

Figure 4.7 Spanish public opinion on euro vs. returning to national currency

Note: Authors' calculations based on 2012, 2013, 2014 and 2015 annual spring surveys on "Global Attitudes and Trends" from the Pew Research Center

Source: based on Pew Research Center (2019).

commitment to the euro was strong from the onset of the crisis, and never faltered throughout the entire crisis. In early 2010, then social democratic prime minster José Luis Zapatero made clear that "nobody is going to be leaving the Euro" (Willis 2010). His successor, the conservative Mariano Rajoy was even less inclined to entertain the possibility of a Spanish Eurozone exit, stating rather that "Europe has to transmit to the world that the Euro is an irreversible project" (Dowsett and Stonestreet 2012). This strong consensus about the importance of avoiding a euro exit thus left Spanish policymakers with but two options—internal adjustment and/or financing.

Policies and Conflict Lines Surrounding Internal Adjustment in Spain

Unlike in Ireland, the Spanish crisis response to the downturn was inconsistent, shifting dramatically particularly between 2008 and 2010. The initial strategy of the PSOE government in power at the start of the great financial crisis was one of fiscal expansion and demand stimulus rather than internal adjustment. The government initially launched a comprehensive public investment plan aimed at generating jobs especially for individuals formerly employed in the construction and services sectors, who were hard-hit by the collapse of the domestic housing bubble (Royo 2013; Wölfl and Mora-sanguinetti 2011).[5] While the stimulus package was opposed by centrist and conservative opposition parties in parliament, who argued that it failed to sufficiently address the country's underlying financial problems, the bill passed without significant opposition from interest groups on either side of the employer–labor divide. Low conflict about the stimulus package was predictable, as it was expansionary—and therefore also did nothing to address the country's current account deficit by means of internal adjustment. Instead, the combination of increased fiscal cost outlays from the stimulus package combined with additional spending triggered by automatic fiscal stabilizers, such as increasing unemployment benefit outlays, hit Spanish public finances hard (Fernández-Albertos and Kuo 2018; Royo 2013): By 2009, the Spanish public deficit had risen to 9 percent of GDP (World Bank 2016a). Between 2010 and 2011, the PSOE Zapatero government was thus forced to effectively reverse the initial policy agenda and to introduce fiscal consolidation and reform-based bills to replace the party's initial stimulus program.

PSOEs sharp fiscal U-turn came at immensely high political costs. Both of Spain's main trade unions, the General Union of Workers (UGT) and the Workers' Commissions (CCOO), initially signed agreements aimed at cutting

---

[5] For an overview of most important policy components of this package, see Royo (2013, 61).

back particularly state expenditures on pensions and public wages in the early stages of crisis, in efforts to avoid political confrontation (de Guzmán et al. 2016). But by late summer 2010, social dialogue between employers, unions, and the government broke down, after which Zapatero's PSOE decided to legislate austerity measures unilaterally, without the involvement of unions. As a result, all Spanish unions launched general strikes in September of that year, in order to oppose Zapatero's proposed cutbacks (Molina and Miguélez 2014). These cutbacks included a 5 percent reduction in civil servants' wages; pension freezes; a €6 billion cut in public sector investment; a €1.2 billion cut to the budgets of regional and local governments; increases in VAT; and significant savings on pharmaceutical subsidies (Fernández-Albertos and Kuo 2018; Mallet 2010). Participation rates in strikes were incredibly high, garnering roughly 10 million participants (Govan 2010).

Throughout the first half of 2011, the PSOE government attempted in successive negotiations to introduce further fiscal consolidation and structural reform packages. Union involvement in these efforts was mixed. Together with employers, both major unions signed a tripartite social pact in January 2011, centering on pension reform, and which allowed for a staggered increase in the Spanish retirement age from 65 to 67, as well as a noticeable increase in the minimum contribution period (Rainsford 2011). But already in spring 2011, negotiations between unions and the government had broken down again, this time over a comprehensive bill to deregulate labor markets which, among other things, would allow for a temporary suspension of collective agreements in case of economic downturn as well as enable firm-level bargaining of wages (Sanz de Miguel 2011).[6] The main proponents of the bill were the main Spanish business associations, the Confederation of Small and Medium-Sized Enterprises (CEPYME) and the Confederation of Employers' Organizations (CEOE), who saw it as a necessity that would help to bolster domestic wage compression (Sanz de Miguel 2011). Ultimately, the government managed to pass the reforms through parliament—but public outrage grew intensely.

By July 2011, the party's parliamentary support coalition, which consisted largely of smaller regional parties, broke down (Dellepiane-Avellaneda and Hardiman 2015). In effect, the strongly social-democratic PSOE had implemented an economic policy which ran counter not only to the preferences of a substantial part of its core electorate—but also simply the Spanish median voter. Figure 4.8 displays preferred levels of public spending among Spanish voters in the summer of 2011. The Spanish median voter at this point essentially wanted additional spending across all main budgetary headings, with the one exception of public works (CIS 2011). Moreover, voter discontent had started to manifest itself in

---

[6] For an overview of the main bill components, see Bentolila, Dolado, and Jimeno (2011, 19–21).

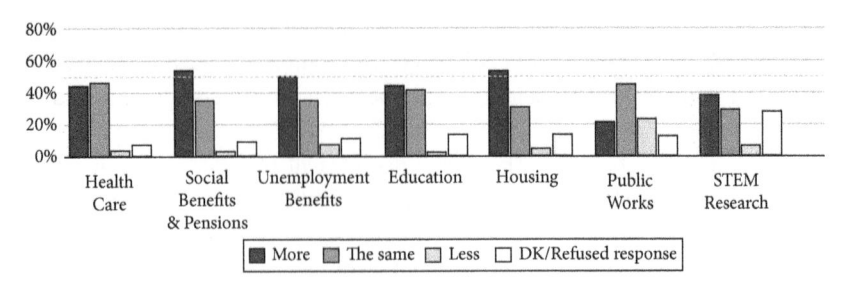

Figure 4.8 Spanish voter attitudes toward level of spending across policy areas
Note: Authors' calculations based on fiscal barometer data collected in July 2011 by the Centro de Investigaciones Sociológicas.
Source: based on CIS (2011).

collective action in the form of both coordinated strikes announced by unions, but also less organized, yet vast street protests.

The total number of popular protests in Spain had already more than doubled between 2009 and 2010, from roughly 10,000 to 25,000, the vast majority of which were organized to oppose austerity measures and labor market reform (Medina 2015). But a second protest wave started on May 15, 2011 in Madrid—a week before the local and regional elections—in opposition to the PSOE's newly adopted fiscal consolidation agenda (Orriols and Cordero 2016). This movement, conventionally dubbed the 15-M movement, received substantial popular support from voters. Public opinion polls taken in spring suggest that roughly 60 percent of Spanish voters were sympathetic to the movement, which, in addition to protesting against the proposed measures, also championed significant legislative changes to improve the direct influence of voters in Spanish political institutions (Sampedro and Lobera 2014, 66). Moreover, support for new social movements remained strong for a prolonged period of time: 50 percent of voters remained supportive of similar protest actions undertaken over one year later, in September 2012 (Sampedro and Lobera 2014).

In light of these developments, the party was forced to announce a premature election in July 2011 (Martín and Urquizu-Sancho 2012). In the November 2011 election that followed, outrage among former PSOE voters was immense. Overall, 3.9 million of them transferred their vote to other parties and half a million abstained from voting at all (Kennedy 2012: 679). In total, the party lost 34 percent of its vote share (Martín and Urquizu-Sancho 2012: 348). By December 2011, the liberal-conservative Spanish People's Party (PP) managed to form a minority government with the help of smaller regional parties, having campaigned on being more fiscally competent than their social-democratic rivals. PP's proposed policy agenda of privatization, VAT expansion, and labor market deregulation were favored by domestic business associations (Cioffi and Dubin 2016), but engendered immense opposition, most importantly from the organized trade union movement (de Guzmán et al. 2016), and newly formed social movements (Orriols and Cordero 2016).

Starting in 2012, Spanish consolidation efforts were thus intensified, as the new government adopted successive austerity packages. The government implemented further spending cuts by cutting public employment, eliminating Christmas bonuses granted to civil servants, and cutting a significant amount of municipal jobs in the public sector. Decreases in social spending were mainly achieved by cutting unemployment benefits both in size and in distribution by tightening eligibility criteria. Moreover, the government also enacted significant cuts to higher education spending by raising tuition fees, increasing classroom sizes, and slashing professorial wages (Royo 2013). On the revenue side, the government both raised standard VAT rates and reduced VAT rates by 2–3 percentage points, but sustained the super-reduced rate applied to essential consumer goods (European Commission 2019b).

Perhaps most noteworthy about PP's internal adjustment agenda was, however, the depth of labor market reforms that the party undertook in terms of deregulating the domestic economy's heavily dualized labor market (Picot and Tassinari 2017). In line with employer preferences, the party pushed through drastic reductions in worker dismissal costs (Bulfone and Afonso 2019) as well as a significant reform of collective bargaining frameworks, effectively enabling employers to negotiate firm-level agreements on working hours, wages, and task structures (Cioffi and Dubin 2016). Within business associations, this generated a split in the preferences of smaller vs. larger firm members. The former preferred sector-level agreements in order to maintain industrial peace, while the latter had a clear preference for firm-level bargaining (Bulfone and Afonso 2019: 16–17).

To conclude, in much the same way as in Ireland, distributive conflict lines on internal adjustment also pitted employers against organized labor in Spain. Struggles centered most strongly on labor market reforms designed to rapidly compress domestic wages, where unions were starkly opposed while employers saw reforms as necessary for the resumption of growth. Unlike in the Irish context, union positions were also advanced by other, more loosely coordinated voter groups that mobilized in great numbers to oppose cutbacks to the Spanish welfare system and increases in regressive forms of taxation, particularly after the PSOE's Zapatero government intensified fiscal consolidation efforts in 2011. It was arguably the birth of these large-scale social movements—not directly linked to unions and often critical of union organizational structures—that indirectly toppled the first social-democratic PSOE party from its traditionally strong position in Spanish party politics. Internal adjustment did not, however, end with the demise of the PSOE government, but was rather accelerated upon the arrival of the liberal-conservative PP government that superseded it. While both governments made clear that fiscal consolidation efforts and structural reforms were informally imposed by Eurozone Troika institutions, some argue that the crisis rather generated a window of opportunity for particularly PP to introduce neoliberal reforms that had been on their economic policy agenda for a long time (Cioffi and Dubin 2016; Royo and Steinberg 2019).

Policies and Conflict Lines Surrounding Financing in Spain

In addition to internal adjustment, the Spanish crisis response also relied on foreign financing. Financing policies discussed, proposed, and enacted in Spain during the crisis years were mainly designed to prevent a situation akin to Ireland's, where the domestic banking sector distress would morph into a full-blown Spanish sovereign debt crisis. Having observed the Eurozone bailouts in Greece, Ireland, and Portugal in 2010 and 2011, opposition to this form of financing grew in Spain, especially among Spanish employer associations. They argued that Troika-monitored government bailouts, possibly including some sovereign debt restructuring, would only exacerbate the crisis and prolong the Spanish recession (Schirm 2018). Financial sector interests feared that state bailouts had the potential of inducing downward spirals of investor confidence, rather than signaling that crisis-afflicted countries were on the path to recovery—particularly in the Eurozone context, which in early 2012 was characterized mainly by a stark absence of a formalized EMU banking union or a Lender of Last Resort (Schelkle 2017). Although these sentiments were somewhat shared by the trade unions and social policy group representatives we interviewed, they predominantly feared that adjustment costs would be disproportionally placed on middle-to-low-wage workers under the auspices of a Troika-monitored bailout, as financing would be tied to loan conditionality that would mandate far-reaching and rapid internal adjustment.

In the end, the Spanish government did end up accepting a sovereign bailout—but one that departed substantially in its shape and contents from those of its Greek, Irish, and Portuguese predecessors. Fears about the need for a Spanish banking bailout culminated in early 2012, when investors started speculating not only against smaller savings banks, but also against the stocks of larger Spanish retail banks such as Santander and BBVA, as well as Spanish government bonds (Royo 2013). By the end of May 2012, the most troubled bank, Bankia, requested a formal bailout from the Spanish government. Shortly thereafter, in July 2012, Spain became the first country in the Eurozone to receive a partial European Stability Mechanism (ESM) bailout, subject to no formalized loan conditionality, solely for the purpose of recapitalizing the domestic banking sector (Copelovitch and Enderlein 2016). At the time, the partial bailout was a form of compromise in order to appease both the Spanish government and the German government, the latter strongly opposed to monetary financing of troubled sovereigns. The limited funds of the ESM, however, worried the European Commission, which thought the bailout would lack credibility among private investors (Jones et al. 2016). Sure enough, unable to moderate financial market speculation, the bailout was soon combined with significant monetary assistance. In September 2012, the ECB ultimately stepped up in order to act as a Lender of Last Resort, by introducing a bond-repurchasing scheme specifically designed to stabilize sovereign interest rates (ECB 2012).

The cost of the banking bailout was far from fully covered by borrowed ESM funds. Ultimately, half of drawn recapitalization funds, or €53.6 billion, were provided by the Spanish state itself (De Barón 2016; Pérez 2014). The distributive effects of this state contribution were largely clouded by the PP government, which in 2012 repeatedly emphasized that the bank rescue was organized so that it would not "cost taxpayers one single Euro" (De Barón 2016). In retrospect, this was an optimistic assessment at best. By 2016, it was clear that bailed-out banks would be unable to pay back 95 percent of the funds they had received during the banking recapitalization of 2012 (*Financial Times* 2016). Still, in part because of the obfuscation of the distributive effects of the banking bailout, discussions about debt relief and default were largely muted in the Spanish political context, never having been taken up by unions or even social policy groups.

It is clear now that successive Spanish government cabinets—led by both PSOE and PP—explicitly wanted to avoid a scenario where the Spanish state would have to appeal to the Eurozone Troika for a sovereign bailout such as those requested by Greece, Portugal, and Ireland (Royo and Steinberg 2019; Zapatero 2013). Prime Minister Rajoy insisted until the very last minute that Spain would not require any financing in the form of a sovereign bailout, rather emphasizing the importance of alternative financing measures aimed at breaking risk exposures between Eurozone banks and sovereigns—policies such as generating a Eurozone-level deposit guarantee scheme and introducing mutual debt in the form of Eurobonds (Dowsett and Stonestreet 2012). Yet these policies were for a long time met with fierce opposition from Eurozone surplus countries such as Germany and the Netherlands, who worried that they would signal a step toward a European transfer union to which they would have to contribute regularly, a prospect which was deeply unpopular among electorates of these member states at the time (Mody 2018; Sandbu 2015), as we discuss in detail in Chapter 7.

On the one hand, the low conditionality financing package was arguably attributable to the systemic importance of the Spanish economy. Fears of negative financial sector spillovers between smaller Spanish banks, which displayed worrying balance sheet positions, as well as financial sectors in other Eurozone member states, may well have driven the Eurozone Troika to agree to providing a partial banking bailout subject, as well as ultimately to procure ECB monetary support measures. Equally, timing likely mattered. After a succession of four sovereign bailouts in the

Eurozone characterized by strong loan conditionality, all of which failed to convince financial markets of the solvency of deficit country member states, creditors were likely more willing to take an accommodative stance in bailout discussions.

Crisis Politics in Spain: Conclusion

In sum, as in Ireland, no organized political actor came out in favor of leaving the Eurozone in Spain throughout the entire crisis—voters, political parties, or any major interest group. Instead, the wish to avoid external adjustment made internal adjustment attractive in relative terms to policymakers, employers, and unions alike—a clear majority of Spanish voters wanted to remain even when the crisis was at its worst. As a result, the country resorted to comprehensive internal adjustment, with a particularly noteworthy emphasis on labor market deregulation (del Rio Loira and Fenger 2019). Conflicts pertaining to this were substantial, generating clear preference divides between reform-friendly employers and oppositional unions. Throughout the crisis, union positions were largely shared by new, anti-austerity movements that managed to generate immense public support for their cause.

Interestingly, parties from both sides of the left–right divide undertook large internal adjustment efforts. Particularly the behavior of the social-democratic PSOE, in adopting substantial and rapid internal adjustment programs, raises questions for multiple reasons. First, austerity and structural reform ran contrary to the preferences of both voters as well as the two main unions, to which the party was traditionally close. Second, massively unpopular internal adjustment measures were not undertaken under the auspices of conditionality-bound bailouts. In fact, Spain held out longer in adjustment negotiations with creditors, refusing to accept a government bailout, and successfully attained a partial bank bailout subject to no formalized loan conditionality—as well as, eventually, even guarantees of monetary support from the ECB.

Greece in Crisis

Unlike Ireland and Spain, the causes of crisis in Greece were rooted more strongly in problems of public rather than private borrowing. The Greek government had already run up considerable public debt prior to the onset of the global financial crisis of 2007/8, having issued substantial amounts of bonds in the early euro years to finance its rising outlays on public transfers, particularly pensions (Featherstone and Papadimitriou 2008; Panageas and Tinios 2017, 466–9). This went hand in hand with a substantial current account deficit, which peaked at −14.5 percent of GDP in 2008: This is an indication of the extent to which the government was relying on foreign investment capital when designing its fiscal policy (IMF 2016a). By the end of 2009, Greek public borrowing had reached roughly 127 percent of GDP, more than double the 60 percent threshold stipulated by the Fiscal Stability and Growth Pact (Eurostat 2019a).

While financial markets had already been somewhat weary of the Greek public debt hangover throughout 2009, the real blow to financial market confidence came in December 2009. At that time, the newly elected Panhellenic Socialist Movement (PASOK) government considerably revised upwards the debt estimates set by the former ruling party, New Democracy (Aizenman, Binici, et al. 2013), from an original estimate of 7 percent of GDP to 12 percent (it would ultimately end up at 15.6 percent) (Zettelmeyer et al. 2013, 518). The cumulative effects of the rising Greek public debt burden as well as this direct announcement were immense, leading to a string of Greek government bond downgrades by international rating agencies. Within twelve months, by February 2010, Greek ten-year bonds had moved from A+ to BBB+ status on Standard & Poor's credit score index (Gibson et al. 2012, 505). At this point, Greek reserves were depleted, rendering it impossible for the government to ensure solvency without external financial assistance. In February 2010, the Greek government thus formally applied for a joint financial assistance program from the IMF and the European Union (Lynn 2011). Faced with considerable reluctance from surplus countries such as Germany, however, it took until May 2010 for the first Greek bailout to materialize (Schneider and Slantchev 2018).

In the five-year period that followed, Greece experienced an economic depression as deep as the US Great Depression (Pagoulatos 2019). Financial markets, policymakers, and pundits repeatedly speculated about the possibility of a so-called "Grexit", a scenario whereby Greece would end up having to leave the Eurozone. Yet, domestic support for remaining in the Eurozone was strong from both interest groups and voters. As such, successive internal adjustment packages were adopted. They included fiscal consolidation policies centering specifically on cuts in pensions, public employment, and health care spending (Matsaganis 2011; Pagoulatos 2019), combined with increases to, most centrally, VAT rates and property taxes (Flevotomou et al. 2017). Moreover, these packages contained comprehensive structural reform agendas targeting labor and product markets—both by means of regulatory change and via the sales of state assets, for example via full or partial privatizations (Katsoulacos et al. 2017; Lyberaki et al. 2017; Skreta 2017).

The Greek internal adjustment agenda was far from solely a domestic affair. Many policies were stipulated as loan conditions to EU/IMF bailouts that the Greek government agreed upon three times within a six-year window—a first in May 2010, a second in March 2012, and a third in August 2015 (Pagoulatos 2019). However, not all loan conditions specifically pertained to internal adjustment. The criteria for loan disbursal under the second bailout program stipulated concrete private sector involvement (PSI) (Lütz et al. 2019b), whereby private investors in

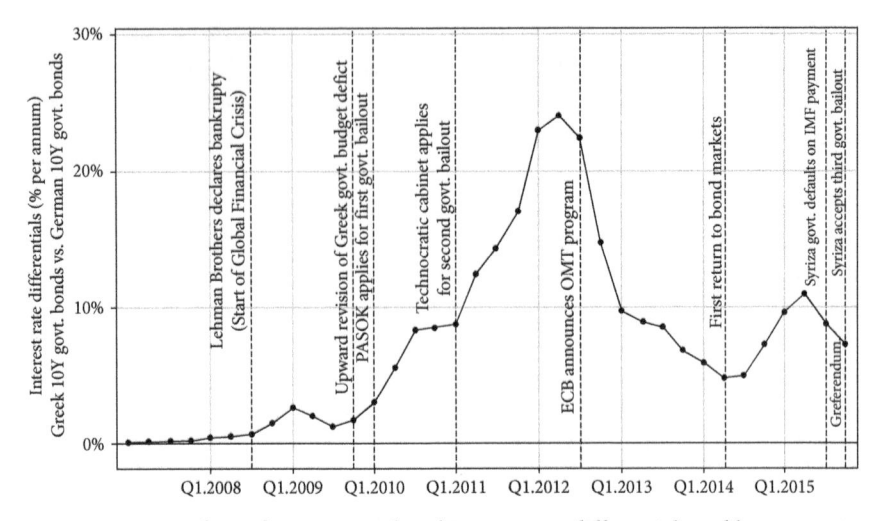

Figure 4.9 A timeline of government bond interest rate differentials and key events in the Greek crisis (2007–16)

Note: Interest rate on German 10Y government bonds are used as reference value, as the German state was conceived of as being at no risk of default throughout the entirety of the crisis.
Source: OECD (2019b).

ownership of Greek government bonds would have to accept a 53.5 percent write-off of the face value of their assets (Eurogroup 2012, 2).[7] In other words, financing policies adopted by Greece were not only linked to applications for sovereign bailouts, but went so far as to include a partial sovereign default.

The possibility of additional sovereign debt write-downs after 2012, whether unilaterally undertaken in the form of a state-led default or an orderly managed plan for debt forgiveness with creditors, loomed throughout the rest of the crisis. Only in the early fall of 2015, after both an August referendum on whether Greece should accept a revised EU/IMF bailout package extension and an early election, did it become clear that the ruling party SYRIZA would refrain from unilaterally imposing additional losses on Greek debt holders (Tsebelis 2016). By then, capital controls had already been introduced in the summer of 2015, and the outlook for the Greek economy looked bleak (IMF 2016b) (Figure 4.9).

The distributive effects of adjustment policies undertaken in Greece were substantial. Fiscal retrenchment and structural reforms stripped a broad range of interest groups of fiscal privileges during the crisis, causing outrage and motivating groups to engage in a long series of economic strikes (Hamann et al. 2013; Lorenzini and Hunger 2019). Among groups that were particularly active

---

[7] According to Zettelmeyer, Trebesch, Gulati, et al. (2013), this write-off was roughly equivalent to an overall loss of between 59% and 65% of asset values.

were unions, traditionally representing older prime-age workers, pensioners, and civil servants (Kretsos 2011). All these groups lost substantial income in absolute numbers during the crisis, but were relatively sheltered from adjustment when compared to the Greek youth (Matsaganis and Leventi 2013). Younger voters, while less represented on the level of organized interest groups, also coordinated to display their discontent in a multiplicity of forms. The prevalence of mass protests grew strongly during the crisis period, particularly as a response to the perceived Troika-mandated policy change (Altiparmakis and Lorenzini 2019). Already by 2010, estimates suggested that every third voter had participated in a political protest of some sort (Rüdig and Karyotis 2014). In essence, political dissatisfaction was widespread and manifested itself in a number of ways, ranging from electoral backlashes against mainstream parties in voting booths (Bremer et al. 2019), to outright violence and civil disobedience (Andronikidou and Kovras 2012). In what follows, we shed light on the distributive conflict lines that underscored these developments.

Policies and Conflict Lines Surrounding External Adjustment in Greece

Throughout the entire crisis, the possibility of Grexit was often discussed in scholarly settings, among policymakers as well as by the general public. In the summer of 2015, when the salience of a potential Grexit was immense in light of the August bailout referendum, Nobel Prize-winning economists Paul Krugman and Joseph Stiglitz both made statements to suggest that leaving the Eurozone might well be preferable to the enactment of further internal adjustment measures (Krugman 2015; Stiglitz 2015). The German Chancellor of Finance at the time, Wolfgang Schäuble, famously brought up the idea of a "temporary Grexit" (Ehlers et al. 2015).

In reality, however, there was very little willingness among domestic political actors to return to a national currency. In Chapter 3 we showed that 76 percent of Greek interest groups that responded to our survey opposed a Eurozone exit. These responses square well with statements made by representatives of both Greek employers as well as organized labor, both at the time and after the crisis was largely over. The SEV was strongly opposed to Grexit throughout the crisis, arguing that speculation about the potential of a Grexit was itself exacerbating the depth of the Greek crisis (Mitsopoulos and Pelagidis 2015). While both public and private sector unions were less clear in their support of the common currency, favoring renegotiations of adjustment packages with the Eurozone Troika (Maltezou 2011; Papachristou 2011), they too never came out clearly in favor of a Grexit. During our June 2017 interviews with Greek interest groups—spanning business associations, trade unions, pensioners associations, and social policy

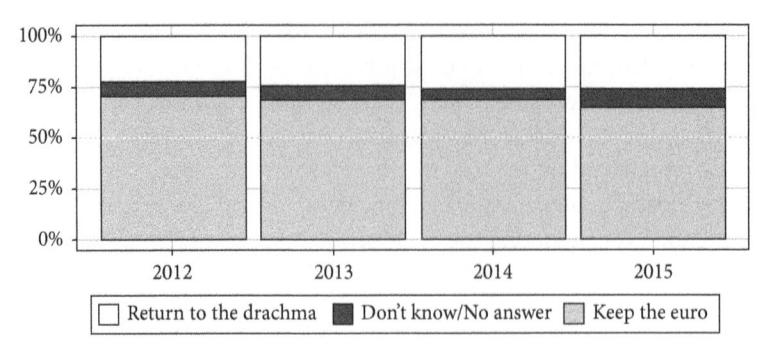

Figure 4.10 Greek public opinion on euro vs. returning to national currency

Note: Authors' calculations based on 2012, 2013, and 2014 annual spring surveys on "Global Attitudes and Trends" from the Pew Research Center.

Sources: based on Pew Research Center (2019); 2015 data from Walter et al. (2018).

groups—not one single interest group representative stated that they had ever favored a Greek exit from the Eurozone.

Negative sentiment toward Grexit was also echoed among the national electorate more broadly (Jurado et al. 2020). Figure 4.10 displays variation over time in public support of the Euro among Greek voters, gathered by the Pew Research Center (2015) and Walter et al. (2018). It highlights the same pattern uncovered in Irish and Spanish electoral contexts. Euro support among voters declined somewhat over time, but a comfortable majority of the Greek electorate persistently favored remaining in the common currency area throughout the entire crisis period. Although the share of voters toying with the idea of a Euro exit increased throughout the crisis, these voters always remained a minority. Through the period 2012–15, only between 23 percent and 27 percent of Greek voters stated that they preferred a return to the drachma over retaining the euro.

Between 2009 and 2015, no political party actively and consistently proposed that Greece should abandon the euro. Some parties, notably SYRIZA—the party governing Greece from January 2015 onward—sometimes seemed to signal an increased willingness to consider a Grexit (Vasilopoulou and Halikiopoulou 2013). The exact position of the party on the issue was relatively hard to determine—even during the summer of 2015, when the topic of Grexit was most salient (Tsatsanis and Teperoglou 2016). Sections of the party's leadership, notably the country's finance minister Yiannis Varoufakis, actually engaged in Grexit preparations such as planning for the introduction of a new parallel Greek currency (Smith 2015). In reality, however, only a minority of the SYRIZA electoral base favored this adjustment strategy above others (Walter et al. 2018). After the August 2015 bailout referendum, the party's Grexit hardliners either left or were pushed out of the party's leadership, rendering it a de facto "pro-Euro" party (Tsebelis 2016; Vasilopoulou 2018). In sum, in line with Greece's high vulnerability to external adjustment, Grexit was never considered a viable option throughout the crisis.

Policies and Conflict Lines Surrounding Internal Adjustment in Greece

With external adjustment off the table, internal adjustment and financing became the dominant crisis responses in Greece. During the crisis, cuts were made to all broad categories of Greek public spending. And both firms and citizens, at some point or another, suffered from raised tax burdens, as the Greek government attempted to improve the state's fiscal fundamentals. Given Greece's unusually high vulnerability to internal adjustment (see Chapter 2), this approach seems surprising at first, especially as it was met with fierce resistance, political turmoil, and significant costs to large parts of Greek society. Yet, internal adjustment was the price to pay for both avoiding Grexit and for receiving financial assistance. In short, considering the alternatives provides a compelling explanation for why a "bad" policy option was chosen.

Not surprisingly, internal adjustment was a difficult choice for Greece. In a survey conducted in December 2015, four in five respondents reported that they had lost at least 20 percent of their income over the course of the crisis, with almost a quarter reporting income losses of over 50 percent (Jurado et al. 2020). These numbers show just how significant the effects of the crisis were perceived subjectively by ordinary Greeks. Likewise, however, firms were also highly negatively affected by the recession, as the vast majority of them targeted domestic demand prior to the onset of crisis. Interviewed interest group representatives from both labor and employer sides, across a wide span of sectors, all agreed that price and wage compression had gone too far, too rapidly in Greece as a result of multiple, successive internal adjustment packages.

After the onset of the Greek crisis, initial adoption of fiscal consolidation efforts was relatively swift. Upon accepting the first Greek financial assistance program in 2010, the social-democratic PASOK government undertook large cuts in public spending, particularly with regard to public employment (Matsaganis and Leventi 2013) and public sector pensions (Panageas and Tinios 2017; Tinios 2015). At the same time, and unlike particularly in Ireland, Greek labor unions were extremely quick in mobilizing and displaying their discontent toward these measures. Already in February 2010, the main public sector union, the Civil Servants' Confederation (ADEDY) had announced its first comprehensive twenty-four-hour strike to oppose cuts in public sector salaries and pensions. Most of their 500,000 employees participated (CNN 2010). By July 2010, five major union-led strikes had been held in Greece, organized by both ADEDY and its private sector counterpart, the General Confederation of Greek Workers (GSEE), in many instances leading to rioting and police teargas counteraction (Reuters 2010). In contrast, Greek employers were significantly more strongly in favor of improving rationalizing wage inefficiencies in the Greek bureaucracy, as well as cutting public transfers that took the form of pensions.

Significant strike activity continued until 2014 (Altiparmakis and Lorenzini 2019), but concerted efforts by organized labor did relatively little to influence policy during the first five years of the crisis. By summer 2010, public sector salaries were frozen at 2009 levels and capped. Special allowances to civil servants were slashed, affecting public sector workers and retirees, who had until then benefited from receiving 13th and 14th month salaries, but then lost access to these additional salaries, which were instead replaced by a flat-rate vacation allowance.[8] Ad hoc cuts, particularly in pension expenditures such as these, garnered substantial media attention not only in Greece but also abroad in, for example, Eurozone surplus countries. In Eurozone countries they were frequently portrayed as shallow retrenchment efforts undertaken in a country infamous for fiscal profligacy (Kutter 2014; Ojala and Harjuniemi 2016). In reality, however, legal changes to the Greek pension system had been highly comprehensive already from an early stage of the crisis.[9] Overall, pension spending was cut through changing pensionable incomes, reducing replacement rates, and raising statutory retirement ages (Matsaganis 2011; Petmesidou 2013).[10]

The PASOK government's attention to cutting spending on pensions was understandable: At crisis onset, pension expenditure constituted over 13 percent of GDP—twice as much as spending on health care services, which amounted to 6.5 percent of GDP (OECD 2012, 5). Cuts in public pension provision thus effectively reduced the Greek government's projected fiscal deficits. Moreover, they were relatively progressive as they were income-level adjusted, targeting mainly individuals with high incomes and substantial asset holdings (Matsaganis 2011; Matsaganis and Leventi 2013). Still, cuts in both pensions and

---

[8] Salaries were capped at €5,981 per month—special allowances to civil servants were slashed by 20% (Matsaganis and Leventi 2013). The flat-rate vacation allowance was set to €1,000, granted only to workers with salaries of lower than €3,000 per month (ibid.). This two-month "bonus" had also been accessible to public sector pensioners prior to 2010, but was also cut for retirees and replaced by a similar flat-rate allowance of €800 per year—payable only to retirees aged 60 and above and earning below €2,500 per month (Matsaganis 2011).

[9] PASOK-led changes to pension legislation in the summer of 2010 were arguably one of the largest singular fiscal consolidation efforts undertaken during the crisis in Greece—and they were not the last to address pension spending. After this, laws were further altered to contract pension spending and improve pension fund efficiency in at least four instances by the end of 2014 (Panageas and Tinios 2017).

[10] Pensionable incomes, which were calculated based on a worker's last five years of earnings, were changed and instead defined on the basis of full career-span earnings (Petmesidou 2013). Replacement rates were more closely linked to individual contributions and, in extension, the number of contribution years. The statutory retirement age, which had previously enabled specific subsets of workers to receive full pensions in some instances already at age 45 (Matsaganis 2011), was raised first to 65 years in 2010, and later to 67 years in 2012 (Panageas and Tinios 2017).

public employment came at a high societal cost. Predictably, cuts in public employment asymmetrically affected atypical workers with fixed-term contracts, who instead of receiving pay-cuts lost their jobs (Matsaganis 2011). Political stagnation and impediments to pension reform in decades prior to the crisis had led to a welfare state constructed around pension transfers (Featherstone and Papadimitriou 2008; Tinios 2015), distributed to a narrow subset of retired workers (Matsaganis 2007). Little funds were allocated to social programs targeting economically vulnerable low-income groups (Matsaganis 2011; Petmesidou 2013). At crisis onset, social provision such a housing support, child benefits, and minimum income schemes were highly under-developed. Instead, social redistribution was commonly practiced by means of intra-family transfers, whereby singular breadwinners—often civil servants—provided informal financial support to both seniors and juniors in their households to cover basic needs (Reher 1998). Trade unions, which in Greece also maintain large sub-factions representing pensioners, thus argued throughout the crisis that cuts to relatively well-off prime age workers and retirees would have substantial negative spillovers to other, more financially precarious parts of the Greek electorate. Conversely, Greek employer associations were more keen to see a transition of the social welfare system. They typically favored the replacement of pension transfers with other forms of social transfers, such as targeted support for particularly women and younger workers, in order to bolster domestic labor market participation.

Finally, already two years into the crisis, austerity fatigue was immense among Greek voters. Figure 4.11 shows that the median voter wanted more rather than less public spending—and that to essentially all forms of social and investment policy. But in the end public desire for increased spending failed to manifest into any real policy outcomes. Cuts to particularly pensions and public employment conformed more closely to the preferences of larger Greek firms than to those of unions which vehemently opposed contractions to these budgetary headings. But even Greek business interests were discontented with the extent to which

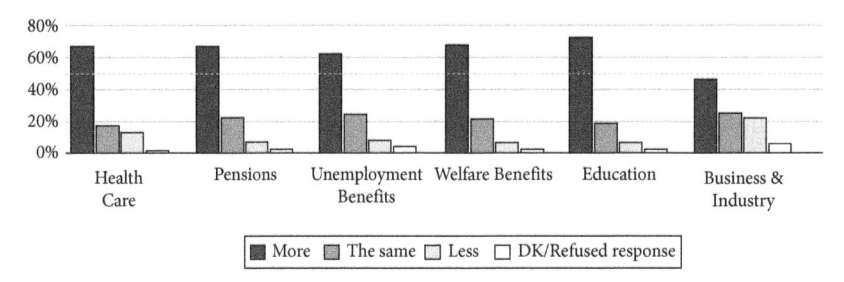

Figure 4.11 Greek voter attitudes toward level of spending across policy areas

Note: Authors' calculations based on data from the Hellenic Election Study 2012.

Source: based on Andreadis et al. (2016).

spending was cut, arguing that spending cuts should rather be phased in at a slower pace to allow for additional spending in social investment policies.

The social costs of declining wages and public transfers were arguably further exacerbated by tax-side policies adopted during the crisis. Relative to other EU member states, Greece suffered from substantial problems of tax fraud and legal tax evasion already prior to the Eurozone crisis (Alt et al. 2014; Matsaganis et al. 2012). The Greek strategy to collect additional tax revenues thus centered mainly on two things: (a) attempts to close loopholes in the domestic tax code, as well a (b) raising tax rates particularly on "easy to collect" tax policies, such as consumption taxes (Flevotomou et al. 2017). Rectifying the Greek tax code, plus improving the enforcement of tax collection were measures supported by all major political parties. They were met with broad support from both employer associations and trade unions. Institutional impediments to improving tax collections were, however, substantial. Legal complexities made it hard for public authorities to penalize tax evasion. Cuts to local administrative budgets made it difficult for agencies to improve tax monitoring and compliance in a country characterized by high levels of self-employment and small firms (Featherstone 2015; Kaplanoglou and Rapanos 2013). While ambitious targets pertaining to improving the tax collection process were thus set forth in tandem with Greece's first bailout agreement, these would later be subject to substantial downward revisions (Featherstone 2015).

The main chunk of additional state revenues thus instead came from a combination of VAT unification, increased property taxes, and progressive increases to personal income taxes (Flevotomou et al. 2017). In order to meet fiscal criteria set forth by the first Greek MOU, the Greek government enacted ad hoc tax policies starting 2012, such as one-off solidarity contributions to pensions (Matsaganis and Leventi 2013). In contrast, corporate taxation in Greece was effectively lowered throughout the crisis, as were both employer and employee social security fees under both PASOK- and New Democracy (ND)-led cabinets (European Commission 2019b). The rationale for this was simple: Encouraging private investment and employment in a context of contractionary growth. However, the result was in effect also reduced public revenue streams from firms, which translated into a lower capacity to finance public spending and a larger emphasis on regressive changes to VAT. Upon the urging of the Eurozone Troika, the Greek government decided to enact a staggered unification of domestic VAT rates (Papaconstantinou 2016), which in 2009 consisted of a 19 percent standard rate, a 9 percent reduced rate applicable mainly to food and medicine, and a 4.5 percent rate for hotel accommodation, books, and newspapers (European Commission 2019b). In addition to these rates, a number of tourism-based islands in the Aegean Sea were subject to further discounted VAT rates. In order to bolster tax revenue, Greek VAT rates were thus progressively raised throughout the crisis, reaching at the end a standard rate of 24 percent, and reduced rates at 13.5 percent and 6.5 percent, respectively, in 2013 (European Commission 2019b). Tax rates were set to increase even further in 2015, but the left-wing SYRIZA government refused to adopt this policy.

Neither unions nor employers were content with stop-gap measures in taxation enacted by successive Greek governments in order to bolster state revenues. Raised and unified VAT rates raised immense alarm among unions, which in likeness to their Irish and Spanish counterparts, disliked that they placed disproportional tax burdens on low-income workers and other socioeconomically disadvantaged voter groups. Business groups even in tradable industries found increased VAT rates problematic. While raised VAT rates in, for example, the hospitality sector should in theory have compressed domestic tourism while increasing state revenues collected by foreign tourists, the process by which smaller Greek hospitality actors were forced to adjust to rapidly changing consumer tastes was immensely costly. Large and relatively isolated hotel resorts, often foreign-run, started being constructed in order to attract foreign demand, effectively crowding out large numbers of smaller firm actors who could not offer price-competitive full-service experiences. As such, while changes to tax policy did not directly affect firms via rate increases, they distorted demand patterns in ways that generated large losses particularly for many small Greek small and medium enterprises (SMEs) and family businesses.

Finally, spending cuts and tax increases were not the only internal adjustment policies which successive Greek governments attempted to adjust internally. During the crisis period, a substantial number of structural reforms were also made to the Greek labor and product market laws. Addressing wage compression most directly, policies were designed to compress minimum wages. The PASOK government formally cut minimum wages by 22 percent in 2012, in tandem with Greece's second EU bailout. After this, the monthly minimum wage remained stagnant at roughly €684 for seven years (Eurostat 2019b).[11] In addition, the government reduced both employee and employer social security contributions as well as introduced special sub-minimal wages for young workers aged 18–25 in an effort to encourage employment (Kakoulidou et al. 2018). Moreover, PASOK also introduced substantial reforms to Greek wage-rate bargaining procedures, in order to move away from sectoral-level collective wage-rate agreements to a system where wages would be increasingly negotiated at the firm level: This included, most importantly, new procedures for the setting of future minimum wages (Lyberaki et al. 2017). GSEE, the umbrella private sector union, strongly opposed both the introduction of sub-minimal wages as well as changes in collective bargaining arrangements (ILO 2011). In contrast, larger Greek

---

[11] The minimum wage was then formally raised to €758 in the second half of 2019 (Eurostat 2019b).

employers largely welcomed reforms which were aimed directly at reducing red tape and cutting labor costs.

All of this occurred in a setting of decreasing employment protection legislation, which aimed not only at reducing hiring and firing costs (Lyberaki et al. 2017), but additionally reducing oligopolist structures particularly in service sectors with high levels of self-employment. Prior to the crisis, service sector professions in Greece were strongly regulated. Occupational groups ranging from lawyers to stevedores were subject to geographic employment restrictions, capped numbers of professional licenses and compulsory fees (Katsoulacos et al. 2017). In 2013, a New Democracy-led government, supported by PASOK, effectively managed to deregulate a broad range of professions—though critics argued that insufficient monitoring by authorities lagged behind the actual enactment of new market rules (Katsoulacos et al. 2017). Occupational deregulation, while generally popular among the Greek public, generated concentrated losses for a number of professional groups such as lawyers, engineers, and doctors, all of which were resilient in obstructing the implementation of new market-liberalizing legislation (Pagoulatos 2019).

Perhaps the most electorally salient part of the Greek structural reform agenda were state-led efforts to privatize public assets, which included the founding of an entirely new agency dedicated to this task in 2011—the Hellenic Republic Asset Development Fund (HRADF) (HRADF 2019). Since the early 1990s, successive Greek governments had begun to initiate large-scale privatization schemes. In the period January 1991 to June 2011, when the HRADF was founded, the Greek state privatized roughly €31 billion of assets by selling off percentage shares and issuing partial public offerings in economic sectors including banking, manufacturing, telecommunications, utilities, and shipping (Skreta 2017). By the time Greece applied for a second sovereign bailout in spring 2012, these efforts were rapidly accelerated. In the three-year period that followed, a string of high-profile privatizations took place, engendering outrage from both interest groups and voters alike. Privatization efforts were problematic for a number of reasons. First, the Greek government had substantial problems in selling off assets at their planned price targets, in part because of administrative issues. More substantially, however, foreign investors could attain state assets at relatively low cost given the Greek state's terrible bargaining position—a position which was worsened after the government accepted the terms of its second bailout, when privatization efforts became the main locus of loan conditionality (Manasse 2014). This in particular engendered outrage among Greek business groups which, moreover, in light of the immense scale of the domestic recession, were unable to make competitive bids during crisis-time privatization auctions. Second, cost-cutting measures under new private owners were often designed in ways that directly harmed the employees of newly privatized enterprises whose contracts were converted from public to private sector ones. For example, logistical workers in the privatized Piraeus Port, suffered from cuts in both salaries and working hours (Meunier 2015). Moreover, labor unions argued that its new owners were rapidly loading up with non-unionized workers in efforts to stave of the risk of collective action (Reguly 2019).

In sum, as our discussion has shown, several key internal adjustment policies generated significant political uproar in the Greek political landscape. On the side of fiscal policy, particularly unions fought hard against cuts to public employment and pension provisions, clashing with the views of creditor institutions and, partially, employer groups representing larger firms. Policies of increased taxation, which targeted mainly consumption, pension incomes, and asset ownership, generated less clear-cut cleavages than those associated with spending cuts. Institutional flaws made it hard for the Greek state to widen the domestic tax base. As such, policymakers seemingly considered the ease of de facto tax collection when deciding on policy, in order to meet tough fiscal consolidation targets set by the Troika during bailout negotiations. Greek cabinets also engaged in wide-ranging structural reform; perhaps most unique in the Greek case, immense efforts to privatize state-owned enterprises engendered outrage from all corners of Greek society. Unionized workers in newly privatized sectors feared a significant downgrading of their employment conditions—which manifested as soon as state assets were sold off to private sector interests. Employer associations were, however, also critical at the speed, timing, and enactment of these measures: First, state asset sales were poorly managed and second, they were conducted in the midst of a prolonged recession, allowing foreign firms to attain significant assets at below market value.

In brief, internal adjustment measures undertaken in Greece were on the one hand so large and undertaken at such a rapid pace that they failed to conform very clearly to the preferences of any domestic socioeconomic groups. Unsurprisingly, they were as such met with immense opposition—particularly from labor groups that were more effective in mobilizing collective action than their employer counterparts. This strong opposition of interest groups toward internal adjustment in addition to domestic low willingness to leave the Eurozone, makes sense when seen in light of the country's vulnerability profile. As we showed in Chapter 2, Greece was highly cross-pressured in that the country displayed very high vulnerabilities to both external and internal adjustment. Countries with this vulnerability profile, we have argued, are significantly more likely to seek external financing in order to resolve their crises; as we show in the discussion that follows, this held true also in Greece.

Policies and Conflict Lines Surrounding Financing in Greece

The Greek crisis response was characterized not only by wide-ranging internal adjustment measures, but also by historically large sovereign bailouts: More specifically, three consecutive ones accepted in May 2010, February 2012, and

August 2015. Only in August 2018 did the country finally graduate from its adjustment programs, after having spent over eight years being monitored by the Eurozone Troika and enacting substantial fiscal and structural reforms as part of conditions attached to the adjustment loans (Pagoulatos 2019). In what follows we discuss the path to and particularly surrounding the three bailouts, one of which concretely stipulated that financial investors indeed accept a "haircut" of their government bond holdings—and none of which entailed any form of reciprocal debt forgiveness, which would have allowed for stronger burden sharing between Greece and Eurozone surplus states.

The first Greek financial assistance program was heavily ad hoc in nature. It was signed through in May 2010, by the first PASOK-led Papandreou cabinet that had come to power in fall 2009. At signing, rapidly increasing bond spreads for Greek government bonds and dwindling foreign reserves had essentially forced the government to request external financial assistance (Papaconstantinou 2016). The MOU signed by the Greek government at this point centered squarely on the enactment of comprehensive and expedient fiscal consolidation efforts in the realms of public employment, public pensions, and health care spending—it also envisaged substantial increases in state revenues as a result of raised VAT rates and the abolition of tax credits.

The package was mainly generated via bilateral contributions from individual creditor countries (€144.7 billion), but also included substantial funds from the IMF (€19.8 billion) (Pagoulatos 2019). Moreover, adjustment support was also indirectly provided by the ECB, which in January 2010 launched the Securities Markets Programme (SMP), as a stop-gap measure to bolster Greek interest rates (Schelkle 2013). Rich Eurozone surplus countries, such as Germany and France, were thus represented in a multiplicity of arenas during adjustment negotiations, both as direct creditors as well as on the executive committees of both the IMF and the ECB (Copelovitch and Enderlein 2016; Papaconstantinou 2016). From the outset, these states made it very clear that there would be no discussion of a default on Greek state arrears during discussions about the first Greek assistance package (Kincaid 2019; Mody 2018). To say that an early default was avoided *solely* due to the desires of external actors would, however, be a stretch. Leaked IMF meeting notes from the fund's early meetings with Greek interest group representatives suggest that domestic willingness to entertain a potential default was very low at the time (*Wall Street Journal* 2013). Greek employers later contested these meeting notes, stating rather that they had severe concerns pertaining to the exact design of a potential debt restructuring.

Unlike the first bailout, the second financial assistance package of 2012 made a partial default of Greek sovereign debt a key component of the Greek crisis response. Private sector involvement (PSI), by which private investors incurred losses on their Greek government bond holdings, was announced and debt restructuring negotiations took place between investors and the Greek state from March to April 2012 (IEO of the IMF 2016). Infamous in this process was the ratification of so-called collective action clauses in February 2012 on Greek bonds. These *ex post* provisions, which were not in place at the time investors purchased their bonds, ensured that a qualified majority of bondholders could make decisions that contractually obliged all bondholders. Importantly, the clauses were not only fitted into novel debt issues, but also retroactively inserted into existing bonds (Zettelmeyer, Trebesch, Gulati, et al. 2013).

It would be hard to argue that the complex distributional effects of the PSI agreement were fully transparent to interest groups or the public in advance of its passing—but after its enactment some aspects of it became highly controversial. First, the delay in Greek debt restructuring, which should arguably have taken place at crisis onset, had effectively allowed foreign banks to sell off Greek debt well in advance of the PSI deal (Merler 2015).[12] In effect, a belated debt restructuring thus contributed to lower burden-sharing between the Greek state and its foreign creditors (Schelkle 2017). Domestic Greek investors, in particular pension funds that were regulated to hold large shares of "low risk" financial assets such as government bonds, instead incurred disproportionate losses (Georgiopoulos and Papadimas 2012). Conversely, Greek banks were compensated to a larger extent via a mechanism of bank recapitalization, which was paradoxically financed via the second Greek financial assistance package (Zettelmeyer, Trebesch, Gulati, et al. 2013). This aspect of the PSI deal became the center of a general discussion about social justifiability of the Greek crisis response, where Greek taxpayers were effectively forced to foot the bill for banking sector losses via the Greek government's acceptance of adjustment aid. By late fall 2012/early winter 2013, public opinion data (displayed in Figure 4.12) suggests that 67 percent of the Greek

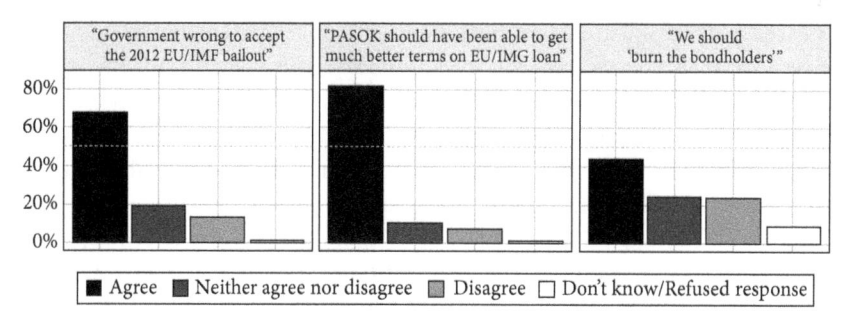

Figure 4.12 Public support of sovereign bailouts and defaults in Greece (Nov. 2012–Feb. 2013)
Note: Authors' calculations based on data from the Hellenic Election Study 2012.
Source: based on Andreadis et al. (2016).

---

[12] Indeed, Merkel and Sarkozy pre-announced that future ESM bailouts would require PSI clauses during their famous "Deauville walk" in October 2010, thus effectively increasing outflows of foreign investment capital from Greece (Mody 2014).

electorate found it was wrong of the Greek government to accept the second EU/IMF bailout package. Moreover, 81 percent thought that a better deal could have been negotiated by the Greek state. Unlike in the Irish case, however, there was no clear majority favoring a sovereign debt default (44 percent)—possibly given levels of contention surrounding the Greek PSI deal.

The strings attached to the first two loans in particular were many, engendering immense anger and distributional conflict among both organized interest groups as well as voters in Greece, so much so that the SYRIZA government, which came into office specifically to cut them in the winter of 2015, refused to enact planned fiscal cuts that were stipulated in Greece's second bailout agreement (Pagoulatos 2019). This populist government was determined to negotiate financing with less austerity and internal adjustment conditionality than the previous governments. What followed were intense months of negotiations with the Troika, which did not, however, result in major concessions on the part of the latter. To increase his bargaining leverage, SYRIZA prime minister Alexis Tsipras, in a surprise move, stopped the negotiations about terms for an extension of the second bailout package, and instead called a referendum on exactly these terms. Understanding exactly just how fed up Greek voters were with austerity, he recommended to vote against the bailout package, arguing that this would provide him with bargaining leverage and ultimately financing with less austerity for Greece. Eurozone policymakers, however, quickly pointed out that the choice was not between financing with or without internal adjustment, but rather one between financing with internal adjustment (conditionality) or external adjustment: Grexit. A majority of Greek voters did not believe this treat, however, and voted against the bailout agreement, even though a majority had a clear preference for remaining in the Eurozone (Walter et al. 2018).

Faced with a situation in which Eurozone policymakers forced the Greek government to choose between conditionality-bound financing and Grexit, Tsipras decided for the former. As a result, the left-wing government ended up accepting a third bailout less than two weeks later, with only moderately altered loan conditions.[13] Once more, this choice can only be understood against the backdrop of Greeks' strong opposition to leaving the Euro. By having brought the country to the brink, however, Tsipras had not only signaled to Greek voters that austerity was non-negotiable after all, but also that he had done everything in his power to reduce it. This secured him a comfortable re-election in an early election in the fall of 2015 (Dinas et al. 2015).

---

[13] To some extent, the third bailout departed from its two Greek predecessors in that it allowed for a smoother pacing of deficit and debt criteria—and importantly allowed for the rehiring of public sector workers (Pagoulatos 2019), which represented a core section of the SYRIZA electorate.

Crisis Politics in Greece: Conclusion

In spite of immense speculation about the possibility of Grexit, there was never any strong desire by interest groups or voters to abandon the euro in Greece. That said, there was also low domestic willingness to engage in rapid and comprehensive internal adjustment. As a result, Greece became the first country in the Eurozone to request a formal sovereign bailout from the Troika and did so an additional two times throughout the crisis. Loan conditionality attached to in particular the first two bailouts were, however, immensely stringent—rendering it difficult for policymakers to structure internal adjustment measures in ways that aligned closely with the overall policy preferences of any interest group. Political discontent was therefore immensely widespread in Greece throughout the crisis, often preventing ruling governments from implementing adjustment reforms that were in fact adopted.

Conclusion

How did the adjustment preferences of deficit country interest groups influence how deficit countries responded to the Eurozone crisis? To what extent did external actors curtail and affect domestic policy decisions? And which policies did the governments in countries facing crisis ultimately implement? Drawing on a combination of primary and secondary sources, this chapter has examined these questions across three diverse deficit countries within the Eurozone: Ireland, Spain, and Greece.

A number of findings deserve to be highlighted. First, throughout the crisis, external adjustment was never seriously considered as a policy option by deficit country governments. This reflected the preferences of wide sets of domestic interest groups and voters who opposed the idea of external adjustment by means of Eurozone exit by a great margin and corresponds to the countries' high vulnerability to external adjustment that we documented in Chapter 2.

Second, in line with our prediction for countries that find themselves in the misery corner at the outset of a balance of payments crisis, all three countries opted for financing. The type of financing—sovereign bailouts subject to considerable conditionality—did, however, force these countries to simultaneously engage in considerable internal adjustment. Particularly in Ireland, and repeatedly in Greece, Eurozone policymakers forced ruling governments to choose between remaining in the Eurozone and accepting a bailout under conditions offered—or risk being forced out of the common currency area, as a result of aggravated financial market pressure. Given the strong support the euro enjoyed in all the countries we analyzed, policymakers always opted for the latter. Eurozone creditors thus were able to leverage their bargaining power to narrow down adjustment choices available to crisis countries. While left-wing governments tended to hold out longer in adjustment negotiations, they too ultimately opted for this strategy in efforts to avoid an overall exacerbation of crisis dynamics. In essence, tipping points were seemingly higher for left-wing policy makers than for their right-wing counterparts—but when the opportunity costs of bargaining for less austerity and structural reform with creditors were made sufficiently high they ultimately paved in adjustment negotiations.

Finally, with the exception of Ireland, whose vulnerability to internal adjustment was somewhat lower than that of Spain's and Greece's, internal adjustment was associated with considerable distributive conflicts that manifested in protests, strikes, and electoral upheavals. These conflicts squared centrally on how the costs of adjustment would be distributed across socioeconomic groups within crisis countries. Proposals for wage and spending cuts induced strong conflicts between, in particular, younger vs. older workers, the former of which were far more exposed to transfer and wage cuts. Discussions surrounding tax policy pitted firm interests against domestic labor movements and social policy groups, as business associations tendentially preferred increases in regressive forms of taxation, such as VAT rates, above more socially equitable ones on capital and income. Both structural reforms, by means of labor market deregulation and privatization schemes, were met with stark opposition especially from organized labor groups. Overall, the positions of business associations were more likely to translate into policy output throughout the crisis. Across all cases, adjustment measures were largely spending- instead of revenue-based; additional tax revenue was collected from heavy VAT increases, and both Spain and Greece saw the undertaking of comprehensive labor market deregulation as well as privatization measures. The relative mobility of firm assets, as well as links to ruling parties—particularly in Ireland and partially in Spain—likely facilitated these outcomes.

In sum, our analysis shows just how difficult crisis politics are in countries which find themselves in the "misery corner" that makes both internal and external adjustment costly and thus forces the government into many difficult and painful decisions. Of course, these decisions could have been less painful if the burden of adjustment had been shared more equally among countries. Why creditor-surplus countries were reluctant to pursue such a course of action therefore is the focus of the next three chapters of this book.

Appendix

Table A4.1 List of interview partners

Ireland	
Interview IE1	Mr. David Begg, Ph.D. Head of Irish Trade Union Confederation, 1990–2014
Interview IE2	Mr. Kevin Callinan General Secretary of Fórsa, formerly at IMPACT Trade Union
Interview IE3	Mr. Hubert Fitzpatrick Director of the Construction Industry Federation
Interview IE4	Mr. Brian Murphy Head of Trade Services at Irish Exporters' Association
Interview IE5	Ms. Michelle Murphy Research and Policy Analyst at Social Justice Ireland
Spain	
Interview ES1	Ms. Graciela Malgesini, Ph.D. Head of Policy Advocacy at the European Anti-Poverty Network in Spain
Interview ES2	Mr. Juan Carlos Delrieu Managing Director of the Spanish Banking Federation (AEB)
Interview ES3	Mr. Antonio Deusa, Vice Secretary of External Affairs at UGT-FICA (Industry, Construction, and Agriculture)
Interview ES4	Mr. Daniel Barragán Burgui Secretary of Union Action at CCOO—Construction and Services
Interview ES5	Mr. Manuel Vicente Gómez Journalist at *El País* newspaper
Greece	
Interview GR1	Mr. Giorgos Kourasis Secretary General of The Hellenic Confederation of Professionals, Craftsmen & Merchants (GSEVEE)
Interview GR2	Mr. Spyridon Kapitsinas General Manager at the General Panhellenic Federation of Tourism Enterprises (GEPOET)
Interview GR3	Mr. Samaras Panagiotis Union Representative of the Aviation Transport Personnel at Athens Airport
Interview GR4	Mr. Nikolaos Moulinos President of the Higher General Pension Confederation of Greece (AGSSE)
Interview GR5	Mr. Mihalis Mitsopoulos Senior Advisor of Macroeconomics and EU Politics at the Hellenic Federation of Enterprises (SEV)
Interview GR6	Mr. Theodoros Mallios President of the Greek Federation of Kiosk Renters
Interview GR7	Mr. Ioannis Athanasiadis Manager of Fiscal Affairs at Papastatos (PMI Greece)

5
Surplus Country Vulnerability to Rebalancing
A Comparative Analysis

Raphael Reinke, Nils Redeker, Stefanie Walter, and Ari Ray

Introduction

Sometimes, the relevance of political conflicts becomes most apparent when they spill into other arenas.[1] When in the summer of 2012 football fans from all over Europe gathered in Poland and the Ukraine for the European soccer championship, the international political repercussions of the crisis were difficult to ignore. Few commentators forwent the chance to employ flowery metaphors of Holland's "austere" and "unforgiving" style of playing football or the fact that one needed to "give Italy credit" for the team's "recklessness." From all over Europe, Irish fans were applauded for holding up banners saying "Angela Merkel thinks we are at work!" And when, during a symbolic face-off in the quarterfinals, German fans welcomed Greek supporters by singing "Without Angie, you wouldn't be here," the other side quickly responded, chanting "We will never pay you back."

Besides stressing the political character of big sport events, the episodes illustrate an important aspect of the Eurozone crisis: Though the most severe consequences of the Eurozone crisis—sharp recessions, skyrocketing unemployment and sovereign debt problems—were centered on the deficit countries, much of the international politics of the crisis was characterized by the position of surplus states. This is surprising as the consequences of the crisis were much milder in countries with sustained and substantial current account surpluses. In these surplus countries, economic growth slowed down in 2012, but—except for the Netherlands—remained positive. Between 2011 and 2014, unemployment increased only slightly in such countries. In Germany, unemployment even fell throughout this period. In 2014, it fell below 5 percent and even lower thereafter.[2]

---

[1] Raphael Reinke is currently employed by the Swiss National Bank. However, the views expressed in this text are those of the authors and do not necessarily represent those of the Swiss National Bank.
[2] World Development Indicators, World Bank, available at https://datacatalog.worldbank.org/dataset/world-development-indicators [accessed 10.23.2018].

The Politics of Bad Options: Why the Eurozone's Problems Have Been So Hard to Resolve. Raphael Reinke, Stefanie Walter, Ari Ray, and Nils Redeker, Oxford University Press (2020). © Raphael Reinke, Nils Redeker, Stefanie Walter, and Ari Ray.
DOI: 10.1093/oso/9780198857013.001.0001

The funding costs for deficit and surplus states moved squarely in the opposite directions. Debt costs rose for deficit countries, while surplus countries could raise new funds at little or no costs (Bundesfinanzministerium 2013, 13). Judging from the economic data about surplus countries one could have asked, "what crisis"?

This absence of direct economic problems is common for the position of surplus countries in balance-of-payment (BOP) crises. During such episodes, deficit countries are confronted with the direct economic repercussions of a major debt crisis. Problems for surplus countries are much more indirect, however, and center around lack of external demand, financial market turbulence, and value losses in foreign assets (Frieden and Walter 2017; Hünnekes et al. 2019). Yet, as we have seen in Chapter 1, surplus countries contribute to the problems underlying BOP crises. These countries export more than they import. In consequence, they are often accused of pricing competitors out of the market while contributing little to global demand. At the same time, they consume or invest less than they earn. Therefore, they provide deficit states with cheap money, fueling excessive credit taking and speculative bubbles abroad. From a global macroeconomic perspective, this position is as similarly destabilizing as running large deficits (IMF 2017a). Nonetheless, as Figure 5.1 shows, running large and persistent current account surpluses is a common feature of many countries and by no means confined to the Eurozone.

As much as surplus countries are part of the problem underlying BOP crises, they could also be part of the solution by bearing at least some of the adjustment costs. Against this background, international conflicts about the adjustment of current account imbalances have shaped much of international economic history

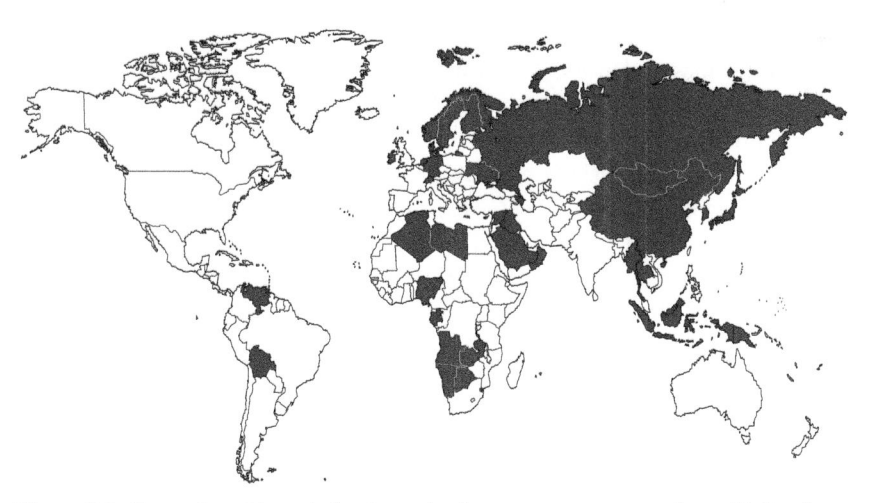

Figure 5.1 Countries with periods of sustained current account surpluses (defined as a surplus of more than 3 percent of GDP which is sustained for at least 3 years) since 1980

in the last century. Already in the interwar years of the early twentieth century, such conflicts weighed heavily on world politics (Simmons 1997). In the 1970s and 1980s, they produced heated disputes between the United States, Japan, and Germany (Kinderman 2008a; Kreile 1977; Putnam 1988). Consequently, they were a main liability for the European Monetary System (EMS) (Eichengreen and Frieden 2001; Frieden 2015b). Most recently, they have turned into a main justification for Donald Trump's return to trade wars (Fetzer and Schwarz 2019).

Thus, rather than being a one-of-a-kind, *sui generis* event, the Eurozone crisis stands in a long line of debt and balance-of-payment crises. Much can be learned from putting this most recent crisis into a comparative perspective. In order to understand the approach that countries like Germany, the Netherlands, or Austria took in the management of the Eurozone crisis, this chapter starts our analysis of surplus countries in Europe by examining their positions in the broader context of surplus countries in other BOP crises.

This is especially important, as the pressure to contribute was unusually high for surplus countries in the Eurozone. On the one hand, the common currency bound deficit states and surplus countries together. Any policy response undertaken by Eurozone deficit countries was going to affect the surplus countries in the common currency area—and vice versa. One possible crisis resolution strategy for deficit countries was to exit the Eurozone and return to national, depreciated currencies. External adjustment is common for deficit countries in balance-of-payment crises but only in the Eurozone it also implied external adjustment for surplus countries. Their currency, regardless of whether they would have kept the remaining euro or reintroduced their national currencies, would surely have appreciated. On the other hand, surplus countries in the Eurozone faced the risk of substantial losses in their foreign assets. This is a common problem for surplus countries in most balance-of-payment crises. However, the deep financial integration within the Eurozone concentrated the claims of deficit countries in the block's surplus countries in an extraordinary way. Surplus countries' banks held a large amount of Greek debt (see Figure 1.2 in Chapter 1), and their balances in the European payment system (TARGET2) had multiplied. For instance, Germany's balance in TARGET2 had increased from €115 billion in 2008 to €655 billion in 2012.[3] A debt default by Greece, which probably would have accompanied the euro exit would thus have inflicted high costs on surplus countries' banks and taxpayers.[4] Such a break-up of the Eurozone would have caused further damage to all member states by endangering the European Union and its hard-wrought achievements of the past decades. By mapping the specific position of surplus

[3] TARGET balance of participating National Central Banks, ECB, available at https://www.ecb.europa.eu/stats/policy_and_exchange_rates/target_balances/html/index.en.html [accessed 10.23.2018].

[4] The exposure to Greek debt changed during the crisis, mostly from private banks to the public sector (see Chapter 1).

countries in the Eurozone against the backdrop of their predecessors in other balance-of-payment-crises we can thus uncover what makes this specific crisis so hard to resolve.

As in other balance-of-payment crises, the principle resolution strategies for Eurozone countries were external adjustment, internal adjustment, or financing (see Chapter 1). External adjustment for surplus countries means letting the currency appreciate. For members of the Eurozone, this option would have required leaving the Eurozone or forcing the deficit countries out of it. Internal adjustment, as suggested by the International Monetary Fund (IMF) at the time (IMF 2014, 20, 28), includes surplus countries spending more domestically, increasing wages, and ultimately letting prices rise. In brief, allowing higher inflation. Finally, financing refers to supporting deficit and debtor countries with financial support programs.

Even though internal adjustment yields several benefits, the surplus countries agreed to a restrictive type of financing. These benefits include higher wages, which are generally popular among workers. Another component is increased public investment, which can stimulate growth, renovate infrastructure, and improve education. Still, surplus countries granted the crisis-ridden deficit countries financial rescue programs. These programs included billions of euros, with Greece receiving the largest financial assistance package in history.[5] Conditions for financial support were reform requirements for deficit countries which included reductions in public expenditure, privatizations, and labor market reforms (see Chapter 3). In surplus countries, this financial support was unpopular (see Chapter 6).

Why was this approach so contentious and why would the Eurozone surplus countries rather pay deficit countries than adjust internally? Why has it until today proven to be so difficult to arrive at a more balanced approach to resolving the current account imbalances underlying the crisis in the Eurozone? In this section of the book, we address these questions by developing vulnerability profiles for 61 surplus countries over 272 periods of sustained current account surpluses and by comparing them to the positions of surplus countries during the Eurozone crisis. Especially, we compare the vulnerability profiles of Eurozone crisis countries to the experience of countries with large surpluses outside the Eurozone and during the EMS crisis in 1992/3. This juxtaposition reveals that surplus countries in the Eurozone were exceptionally vulnerable to both internal and external adjustment. It also shows why they were willing to engage in grand-scale bailouts but at the same time pushed the burden of adjustment largely onto deficit states. Before turning to the vulnerability profiles of surplus countries, we turn to existing answers to this question in the literature.

---

[5] European Stability Mechanism, "Greece emerges from crisis," available at: https://www.esm.europa.eu/assistance/greece [accessed 11.05.2018].

Surplus Country Preferences and National Interests in the Eurozone Crisis

A core premise of this book is that we can learn a lot about the Eurozone crisis by putting it into a comparative perspective. Research on the politics of current account adjustment in surplus countries in times of crisis remains relatively scarce. This is mainly because—contrary to deficit states—countries with large savings and exports are under no inherent pressure to adjust (Frieden 2015b). However, a growing literature has started to analyze this question. A special focus lies on why surplus countries tend to be so reluctant in addressing their large export overhangs even under huge political pressure. Two approaches are especially prominent: The role of ideas and the importance of structural growth models.

First, idea-based explanations emphasize how strongly held beliefs about the axiomatic merits of prudent fiscal policies and limited state involvement in the economy (Bulmer 2014; Dullien and Guérot 2012; Matthijs 2016c; Wendler 2014; Young 2014) as well as the causes of past crises (Aizenman 2007; Chin 2010; Haffert et al. 2019; Howarth and Rommerskirchen 2013; Mendoza 2004) influence policymaking by providing coherent narratives for why adjustment is not the surplus country's responsibility or in their interest. As we will discuss in more detail in the next two chapters, during the Eurozone crisis, surplus countries often evoke orthodox economic ideas. These are commonly summarized under the header of ordoliberalism. In order to address the Eurozone's problems, deficit states need to reform their economies to regain competitiveness. Stimulating growth and inflation in surplus countries would only risk surplus countries' hard-earned standing on international markets and endanger price stability. This particular reading of the sources and cures for the crisis are often seen as a major reason for the lack of current account adjustment in countries like Germany or the Netherlands (Dullien and Guérot 2012; Ferrara et al. 2018; Matthijs and Blyth 2015; Schäfer 2016). Similarly focusing on the role of ideas, research studying the reluctance of East Asian countries to re-balance their large trade surpluses in the 2000s has emphasized the belief that a repeat of the 1997 Asian financial crisis and the subsequent dependence on foreign institutional lenders must be avoided at all costs. This drove these countries to keep accumulating large savings and trade surpluses (Aizenman 2007; Chin 2010; Dooley et al. 2004; Mendoza 2004).

A second explanation emphasizes the importance of growth models and focuses on the structural importance of the export sector for surplus economies. Going back to studies on the persistence of current account surpluses in Germany and Japan under Bretton Woods, scholars have pointed to the structural importance of the export industry in many surplus countries as a major impediment for the adjustment of current account surpluses (Kinderman 2008b; Kreile 1977). Regarding emerging economies with current account surpluses, studies in this vein emphasize that persistent current account surpluses reflect export-oriented growth strategies (Chinn et al. 2014; Dooley et al. 2009; Prasad 2011). Recent research on the lack of adjustment among surplus countries in the developed world, however, mainly builds on the literature on comparative capitalisms (Baccaro and Pontusson 2016; Hall and Thelen 2009). What unites these approaches is the idea that the structural need to preserve export competitiveness in surplus countries creates a broad coalition of policymakers, employers, and workers, all of whom are opposed to measures that would lead to internal adjustment (Hall 2012; Höpner and Lutter 2018; Iversen and Soskice 2018; Leupold 2016).

Existing work provides valuable insights into surplus country resistance to adjustment, but some questions remain. For one, the two dominant explanations paint a picture of surplus countries being united in their resistance toward macroeconomic adjustment. This is either due to the dominance of ideas and economic narratives that frame adjustment as irresponsible and harmful or because safeguarding the export-led growth model constitutes the national interest. Yet, adjustment policies in surplus countries also generate significant domestic distributive conflicts (Frieden and Walter 2017) analogous to the distributive struggles that characterize balance of payments adjustment in deficit countries (Eichengreen 1992; Simmons 1997; Walter 2013a). Decisions whether to engage in re-balancing by boosting domestic demand (e.g. through cutting taxes or stipulating wage growth) or to do nothing at all, will hurt some domestic actors and benefit others. The questions whether, on aggregate, internal adjustment is desirable, who wins and who loses from (non-)adjustment and how these distributional effects influence politics are, thus, crucial for understanding the political economy of (non-)adjustment in surplus countries.

Second, existing approaches concentrate predominantly on fiscal and monetary policy as well as wage-setting issues. In contrast, we emphasize that macroeconomic adjustment decisions are multidimensional. Surplus country resistance to adjustment has significant consequences abroad, which puts global and regional financial stability in question and increases the financing needs of those countries running large current account deficits. This is especially relevant when private capital inflows into these countries dry up. Understanding why surplus countries opt against adjusting internally thus requires a more multidimensional understanding of how surplus country decision-makers evaluate these alternatives relative to the option of adjusting domestic policies in a way that reduces the current account surplus.

Vulnerability Profiles—Concept and Argument

To complement existing research, our argument centers on distributional considerations as well as the multidimensional trade-offs inherent to episodes of crisis. In previous chapters, we have focused on deficit countries and argued that their policymakers—when faced with balance-of-payment problems—weigh the potential costs associated with internal and external adjustment. We argue that similar considerations also occur during crises in surplus countries. For the purposes of this comparative chapter, we define surplus country episodes as those with a current account surplus of more than 3 percent GDP in the current year and, on average, in the last three years. In effect, we speak of surplus countries only when the surplus is substantial and sustained, not merely accidental and transitory.

The surplus countries in the Eurozone did not suffer from a debt crisis, but they shared the common currency. Any resolution strategy of deficit countries creates mirrored effects for surplus countries. Thus, surplus countries' basic options of responding to the crisis were to (i) adjust externally, by breaking up the Eurozone and revaluing their currencies; (ii) adjust internally, by spending and letting wages and prices rise relative to those in deficit countries; or (iii) try to gain time by financing the other countries' deficits. In our view, the policymakers in surplus countries consider the positive and negative consequences of each of these strategies for important socioeconomic and political groups as well as the national economy as a whole, and compare their overall vulnerabilities associated with each of the adjustment strategies. They then choose the option to which they are least vulnerable.

We argue—as in the case of deficit countries and based on Walter (2008, 2013a, 2016)—that this choice is ultimately between the potential costs of internal adjustment *relative* to the potential costs associated with external adjustment. The combination of these costs is reflected in a country's "vulnerability profile" (Figure 5.2). The horizontal axis in Figure 5.2 represents the vulnerability to external adjustment; that is, the costs that would result from exiting or breaking up the Eurozone with an implicit appreciation of the surplus countries' currencies—be it a "Northern" Euro or reintroduced national currencies. The vertical axis denotes the vulnerability associated with internal adjustment. For surplus countries, internal adjustment means increasing public spending, stimulating wage increases, and/or letting domestic prices rise. A country's vulnerability profile results from its location in this cost matrix.

Surplus countries have a different strategy to respond to the crisis: Provide deficit countries with financing. However, this strategy has the crucial drawback of leaving the structural problems underlying the surpluses and deficits unresolved or even worsen them, only for them to reoccur later. Accordingly, policymakers following this strategy run the risk of (i) losing the provided funds as repayment is uncertain and (ii) eventually having to resolve an even larger imbalance (Frankel and Wei 2004; Walter and Willett 2012). For this reason, financing is often viewed as a temporary measure to alleviate the actual adjustment—internal or external. In the specific case of the Eurozone crisis, some policymakers and experts advocated

	low	high
high	**I** Only vulnerable to internal adjustment • External adjustment	**II** Vulnerable to internal and external adjustment ("misery corner") • Delay • Mixed adjustment • Extensive financing
low	**IV** Not very vulnerable to adjustment • No clear predictions on policy response	**III** Only vulnerable to external adjustment • Internal adjustment

Vulnerability to internal adjustment (increasing domestic demand, e.g. higher public spending)

Vulnerability to external Adjustment (exchange rate appreciation, Eurozone: euro exit)

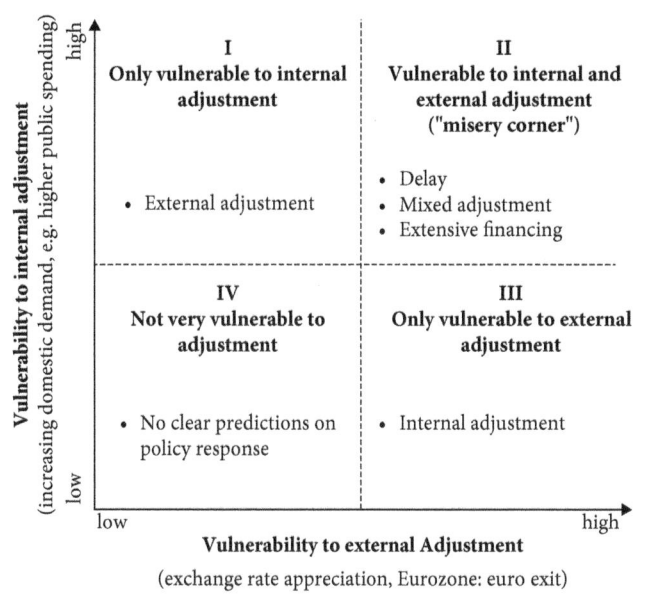

Figure 5.2 Vulnerability profiles and crisis response for surplus countries

permanent financing mechanisms, such as European unemployment insurance (e.g., Dullien 2014). We expect financing as the preferred solution when vulnerabilities to the other adjustment strategies are high.

There are four ideal-type vulnerability profiles. We argue that a country's vulnerability profile shapes its crisis response. The profiles result from the combination of high and low vulnerabilities to internal adjustment (top or bottom half in Figure 5.2) and high or low vulnerabilities to external adjustment (left or right half in). On the downward diagonal (profiles I and III) are the cases of countries being vulnerable to only one type of adjustment. In these cases, the cost–benefit analysis is straightforward and we expect countries to choose the resolution strategy to which they are not vulnerable, for example, external adjustment with profile I. On the upward diagonal (profiles II and IV), we find the countries whose vulnerabilities to both types of adjustment are similar. Profile IV is in the lucky position to either form of adjustment. We expect a relatively quick resolution that is not very contentious. Countries with profile II are much less fortunate. They find themselves in the "misery corner" of having high vulnerabilities to either strategy. Given the high vulnerability to any of the resolution strategies, we expect a highly contentious process and a strong push toward delaying adjustment—even if it means providing funding for other countries. In short, we argue that the position of a country in the matrix of vulnerabilities will determine its crisis response and how controversial the response will be.

Weighing Bad Options: Vulnerabilities to External and Internal Adjustment

In general, contributing to crisis resolution for surplus countries requires adjustment in the opposite direction as compared to deficit countries. In deficit countries, external adjustment means lowering the value of the currency. In surplus countries, external adjustment means letting the currency appreciate.

As in the case of deficit countries, *external adjustment* has positive and negative consequences. A positive consequence of appreciation is that the purchasing power of domestic households increases. Real incomes rise because the appreciation of domestic goods makes foreign goods and services cheaper. The flipside of this effect is the lower competitiveness of the exporting sector. The appreciation of the currency renders domestically produced goods and services more expensive abroad. This downside is especially important for countries with large exporting sectors. Similar to the exchange-rate effect for deficit countries, it is likely to be shaped by additional factors, such as the level of the exchange-rate pass-through on product prices (Frieden 2002; Kinderman 2008) and producers' reliance on imported goods (Helleiner 2005). Another drawback of external adjustment concerns the country's balance sheet, particularly regarding assets and debt in foreign currencies. The appreciation of the currency lowers the domestic value of foreign-denominated assets. External adjustment thus implies losses for investments and savings in other currencies. At the same time, the domestic value of foreign-denominated debt decreases. This effect on debt, however, is likely to be less important for surplus countries. Continuous current account surpluses—by way of the corresponding capital flow abroad—amass foreign assets and lead the country to become a net creditor. Accordingly, the negative balance sheet effect from foreign assets should be larger than from foreign debt. Indeed, an actual rebalancing—or adjustment—between deficit/debtor and surplus/creditor countries implies losses for the latter.

Surplus countries share an impediment of external adjustment with deficit countries. The cost of adjusting the currency tends to be higher if countries adhere to a fixed exchange-rate regime as compared to a floating exchange-rate regime. Giving up a fixed exchange-rate regime creates volatility and uncertainty that are costly both economically and politically (Barro and Gordon, 1983; McKinnon and Pill, 1999; Willett, 2007). Particularly, these costs occur for members of a common currency union. For countries in a currency union, adjusting the exchange rate requires them to give up the common currency. Such a radical step involves significant costs. The necessary infrastructure, like minting coins, printing bills, and creating a national electronic payment system, needs to be established. It would also require rewriting financial contracts to refer to the new currency. The uncertainty caused by these fundamental changes would itself be costly. Accordingly, the costs of exiting a currency union, like the Eurozone, go beyond those from merely adjusting the value of the currency. Nevertheless, there are multiple instances in history that witnessed the breakup of currency unions (Cohen, 1993; Rose, 2007). In sum, costs from external adjustment are likely to be higher for countries with (i) a larger export sector, (ii) more net foreign assets, especially foreign-currency denominated assets, and (iii) a fixed exchange-rate regime, particularly when the country is part of a monetary union.

Another crisis resolution strategy is to adjust internally. *Internal adjustment* aims at lowering the current account surplus by adjusting relative prices and boosting domestic demand. It can be achieved by raising prices and wages, loosening monetary policy, increasing public spending or cutting taxes. Particularly in a recession, such expansionary policies can be beneficial to households and the overall economy. Policymakers following Keynesian thought have implemented them in their own right, irrespective of trying to adjust current account imbalances of a surplus country (Armingeon and Cranmer 2017; Raess and Pontusson 2015). There are, however, factors that impede internal adjustment and influence benefits and costs.

The effectiveness of domestic fiscal stimulus varies with trade openness. As the stimulating effect of increased public spending, or reduced taxes, "leaks" through imports to the trading partners, fiscal stimuli are more effective for the economy in larger countries and in those with lower levels of imports (Batini et al. 2014). Accordingly, policymakers should be more reluctant to use public funds to stimulate domestic demand when the propensity to import is high. Internal adjustment by increasing public spending, or by collecting less tax revenue, requires the government to run higher budget deficits and incur more public debt. This expansionary fiscal policy is easily possible at a low debt burden and with low budget deficits, but it is problematic when they are high. An already high budget deficit means less leeway for additional spending. Additionally, funding costs for the government tend to increase with increasing levels public debt. The costs of internal adjustment for surplus countries thus increase with larger public deficits and higher levels of public debt. Taken together, it is less beneficial, or costlier, for surplus countries to adjust internally when the effectiveness of fiscal stimuli is low and when the fiscal space of governments in terms of debt and deficit is constrained.

Research Design

This chapter focuses on analyzing Eurozone surplus countries comparatively. To this end, we develop a quantitative measure of countries' vulnerability profiles. With these profiles, we can compare surplus countries in the Eurozone crisis to those in other crises. These profiles consist of countries' vulnerabilities to internal and external adjustment, for which we construct indices. We then analyze and compare the vulnerability profiles of Eurozone countries to those outside the Eurozone as well as to countries in the 1992 European Monetary System (EMS) crisis.

Sample Selection: Identifying Surplus Countries during Balance-of-Payments Crises

To establish a comparative perspective for Eurozone deficit countries, we chose other countries in balance-of-payment crises. Finding appropriate comparisons for Eurozone surplus countries is more complicated. The reason for this difficulty is that the BOP crises rarely have clear surplus counterparts. While there are always corresponding international surpluses to a country's deficit in the current accounts, these surpluses are usually broadly distributed. Furthermore, countries with surplus are usually not tied to the deficit countries by a common currency union. For instance, in the run up to the Asian financial crisis, there were countries with surpluses as well. However, these countries were not directly affected by the imbalance or obligated to remedy it. As the current account surplus is often shared among many countries and because none of them may have a particularly strong economic or institutional connection to the deficit country, there is little connection to the deficit country. Only in some cases is a connection evident. Examples include the United States and Mexico in its 1982 debt crisis. As a result, there is no broad sample of episodes that we can use as comparisons to the Eurozone surplus countries.

For our analysis, we select countries with sustained and substantial current account surpluses from a broad universe of cases. This broad universe consists of 122 developed and emerging economies since 1995. As mentioned above, we chose a current account threshold of 3 percent GDP, in the current year and on average in the latest three years. We exclude the oil-exporting countries whose surpluses lie outside the adjustment logic and may unduly affect the results.[6] Due to data availability, we also exclude microstates from our sample, as well as least-developed countries (LDCs) and Cuba, Libya, Iraq, and North Korea. The better data availability for OECD countries allows us to include them since 1990—rather than 1995. These selection criteria identify—by definition—current account surplus countries. More broadly, they capture the countries that are generally exposed to capital inflows and experience upward pressure on their exchange rate. This identification is agnostic about the adjustment strategy. The countries are selected irrespective of whether they choose to adjust internally, externally, or

---

[6] In fact, conducting the principal component analysis (PCA) on the sample including oil-exporting countries gives no material changes to the presented results.

delay adjustment. Following this methodology, we identify 61 countries which together experienced 272 episodes of sustained surpluses. While for some countries like, for example, Belgium or Argentina, we only observe one episode of sustained surpluses since 1990, other countries like, for example, Switzerland or Norway, have run large surpluses for almost the entire episode that we study.

A potential alternative to identify relevant cases would be to use the inverse of the exchange-rate market pressure, that is, picking country episodes with large inflows of capital. In practice, the inverse exchange market pressure (EMP) does not identify surplus countries, but countries with sharp surges in reserves or exchange rates. Such movements can also occur in deficit countries immediately after a crisis incident. Typically, inflows to the largest surplus countries, like Germany or China, occur slowly over time. This process does not create spikes in the EMP index. Accordingly, the EMP index would not allow identifying surplus episodes in a consistent manner.

Operationalization: Vulnerability Profiles

In a setting like the Eurozone crisis, the resolution strategy of a surplus country depends—as we argue it does for deficit countries—on the trade-off associated with adjusting internally or externally. We conceptualize this trade-off as vulnerability profiles. The profiles consist of two dimensions, expressing the potential costs of internal and external adjustment. For these two dimensions, we chose indicators that we find applicable to a broad set of countries and are most relevant for the aggregate vulnerabilities. Of course, such aggregate profiles cannot capture the whole gamut of vulnerabilities, especially not the entire domestic constellation of interests. In the following chapters, we delve more deeply into these issues. We use these two dimensions to illustrate the profiles on a simple Cartesian plane (as presented in Figure 5.2).

The potential costs of external adjustment are larger for a surplus country, the more it relies on exports, and the lower its rate of inflation. The costs also increase with a higher level of net foreign assets, especially foreign-currency-denominated assets, and an increased rigidity of the exchange-rate regime. We measure these dimensions of external adjustment costs as follows (the exact data sources and definitions are shown in Table 5.1):

- *Competitiveness.* Because currency appreciation lowers the competitiveness of domestically produced exports and import-competing products, the cost of external adjustment is likely to be higher in countries with a large tradables sector and lower in countries with a large nontradables sector (cf. Frieden 1991b, 2014 for deficit countries). To capture this dimension, we use the size of exports, measured as share of GDP.

Table 5.1 Indicator operationalization for surplus countries

Cost	Variable	Operationalization and Sources
External adjustment		
Competitiveness	Exports	The value of a country's goods and services provided to the rest of the world in percent of GDP. Source: World Development Indicators, World Bank.
Inflation	Consumer price changes	The annual percentage change of the consumer price index, logarithmically transformed according to the formula $x' = \log(x + (\sqrt{x})^2 + 1)$, which attenuates outlines and allows negative values.
Balance sheet effects	Net foreign assets	The sum of foreign assets held by monetary authorities and deposit money banks, less their foreign liabilities, in percent of GDP. Source: World Development Indicators, World Bank.
Leaving a fixed exchange-rate regime	Exchange-rate regime	Coarse classification of exchange rate regimes (1–4; coded 1 for currency unions (no separate legal tender), currency boards, pre-announced pegs or bands that are at most +/− 2 percent). Source: Ilzetzki, Reinhart, and Rogoff (2017).
Internal adjustment		
Fiscal conditions	Government deficit	Cash deficit (or surplus) is revenue (including grants) minus expense, minus net acquisition of nonfinancial assets, in percent of GDP. Source: World Bank: World Development Indicators.
	Government debt	Government debt in percent of GDP. Source: World Bank and IMF Historical Debt Database.
	Domestic savings	Gross domestic savings as GDP less final consumption expenditure (total consumption), in percent of GDP. Source: World Development Indicators, World Bank.
Effectiveness of fiscal spending	Imports	Imports of goods and services, in percent of GDP. Source: World Development Indicators, World Bank.
	Size of the economy	GDP in constant 2010 US dollars. Source: World Development Indicators, World Bank.
Organized interests	Union density	Union density rate, net union membership as a proportion of wage and salary earners in employment. Sources: ILO, OECD, ICTWSS Database.

- *Balance sheet effects.* The cost of external adjustment increases with a country's net value of foreign assets. More assets abroad imply higher losses when the domestic currency appreciates, and foreign currencies—relative to the domestic currency—lose in value. To measure net foreign assets, we use the sum of foreign assets held by monetary authorities and deposit money banks, less their foreign liabilities (relative to GDP).

- *Inflation.* Letting the currency appreciate creates deflationary pressures due to cheaper imports. This downward shift of prices may be particularly costly when inflation is already low. We measure inflation as the annual change of the consumer price index.
- *Leaving a fixed exchange-rate regime.* The costs of external adjustment are particularly high in countries with a fixed exchange-rate regime. Market actors do not expect a devaluation of the currency and a devaluation badly damages a government's credibility (Blomberg et al. 2005; Sattler and Walter 2010; Stein and Streb 2004; Willett 2007). We use Ilzetzki, Reinhart, and Rogoff's (2017) coarse classification of de facto exchange-rate regimes. The category of fixed exchange-rate regimes covers countries with no separate legal tender, currency boards, pre-announced pegs, or bands that allow fluctuations of at most +/− 2 percent.[7] Note that this operationalization represents a conservative approach to coding currency unions. Currency unions, such as the Eurozone crisis, are coded in the same way as pegged exchange-rate systems (for all countries except the one with the anchor currency), such as the EMS. We choose this conservative coding to avoid assigning Eurozone members a high vulnerability to external adjustment by construction. Our index is thus likely to underestimate the external vulnerability of the Eurozone countries, because we would like to examine to what extent other factors than simply the cost of exiting the Euro may have influenced a Eurozone member's decision calculus.

The costs for surplus countries to adjust internally are especially large when poor public finances—both debt and deficit—allow little leeway to reflate the economy, when the effect of fiscal spending leaks due to a small economy and a high level of imports, or when unions as organized interest in favor of reflation are weak. As indicators for these sources of costs, we use (i) the level of government debt, (ii) the government deficit, (iii) domestic savings, (iv) the size of the economy, (v) imports, and (vi) union density.

- *Fiscal conditions.* Reflating the economy with more public demand requires the government to increase its deficit and debt. This expansionary fiscal policy is easily possible at low levels of public debt and deficit, but it is problematic at high levels. Thus, the costs of internal adjustment for surplus countries are higher when the public deficit and public debt are larger. We include these two measures as the level of overall government debt relative to the size of the economy (i.e., in percent of GDP) and the annual government deficit in percent of GDP. Similarly, high domestic savings facilitate policies

---

[7] For "freely falling" exchange rates (category 14 in the fine classification), we use the coding of the last preceding categorization in order to assess the effect of the country's original exchange-rate regime.

that aim at increasing spending household level, through policy incentives like the cash-for-clunkers program, for example. We measure this household financial cushion as the level of domestic savings in percent of GDP.

- *Effectiveness of fiscal spending.* Increasing fiscal spending contributes to adjustment by increasing aggregate demand and thereby not only directly lowering net exports but also by raising relative prices. It is less costly politically if the fiscal multiplier is high and the stimulus results in faster growth and greater income. A fiscal stimulus tends to be more effective for larger economies and for countries with lower levels of imports (Batini et al. 2014). We account for these effects by including the size of the economy (as the log of GDP) and imports (as share of GDP).
- *Organized interests.* The key beneficiaries of fiscal stimuli are workers and employees as they benefit from the positive effect on employment and wages. Thus, increasing fiscal spending should be politically easier where unions are strong to provide their support despite its downsides, like its higher levels of debt or taxation, and against opposition from other interest groups. We measure this positive effect on internal adjustment with union density.

Creating the Cost Indexes Using PCA

As in Chapter 2, we calculate an index for external and internal vulnerability by conducting a principal component analysis (PCA) on a set of variables measuring the different sources of adjustment costs (Walter 2016). For instance, we use the net value of foreign assets to reflect the extent to which an appreciation of the currency would result in balance-sheet losses. More assets abroad result in higher losses when the domestic currency appreciates, and foreign currencies—relative to the domestic currency—lose in value. In the next sections, we go into more detail about how we arrive at the vulnerability profiles.

Table 5.2 presents the PCA results for potential costs of both external and internal adjustment. The estimated PCA weights (or loadings) for these variables

Table 5.2 PCA results for surplus countries

External Adjustment	Loadings	Internal Adjustment	Loadings
Exchange rate regime	−0.39	Government debt	0.34
Net foreign assets	0.59	Government deficit	0.67
Exports	0.62	Domestic savings	−0.63
Inflation	−0.33	Size of the economy	−0.03
		Imports	0.17
		Union density	−0.10
Proportion explained	0.46		0.63
N	272		272

are consistent with their theorized contributions to adjustment costs. A more flexible exchange-rate regime reduces external adjustment costs for surplus countries, while more net foreign assets and a higher reliance on exports increases them. Higher inflation reduces the costs of external adjustment. Internal adjustment costs increase with higher government debt and deficit as well as with lower levels of domestic savings. Costs are also higher for smaller countries and for countries with more imports. A higher union density—as a measure for organized interests in favor of internal adjustment—decreases the political costs of internal adjustment. The first components explain about half of the sample variation (46 percent and 63 percent). The loadings are substantially important for most variables.

We use these indexes to locate the surplus country episodes in the two-dimensional space of adjustment vulnerabilities shown in Figures 5.3, 5.4, and 5.5. In Figure 5.3 we first present the vulnerability profiles of Eurozone surplus countries as well as of the entire sample of surplus episodes. Next, we use the vulnerability profiles to compare the European surplus countries inside with those outside the Eurozone. Finally, we move back in time to contrast the crisis in the Eurozone with the one in the European Monetary System in 1992/3.

In these figures, the quadrants represent the different types of vulnerability profiles: Countries in the upper left-hand corner (quadrant I) are more vulnerable to internal than external adjustment. In the lower right-hand corner (quadrant III), countries face the reverse profile. They are more vulnerable to external than to

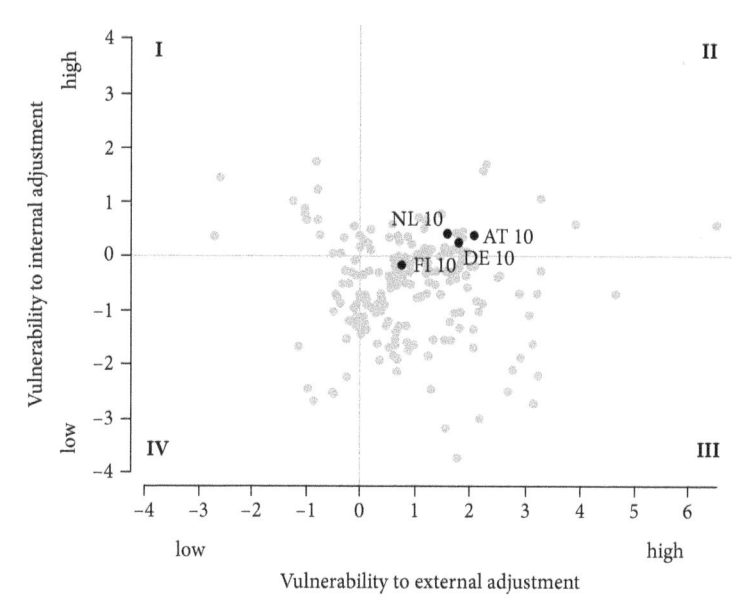

Figure 5.3 Vulnerability profiles of the Eurozone surplus countries compared to other episodes with sustained current account surpluses

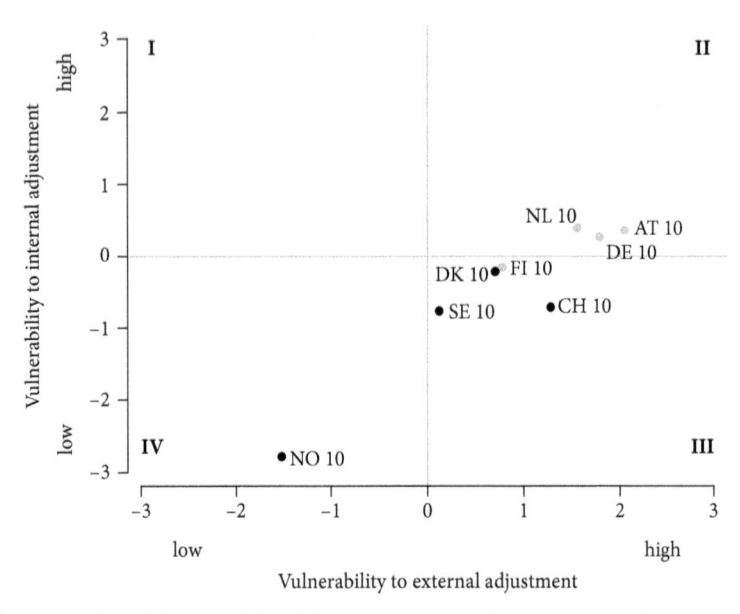

Figure 5.4 Vulnerability profiles of the European surplus countries at the outset of the Eurozone crisis

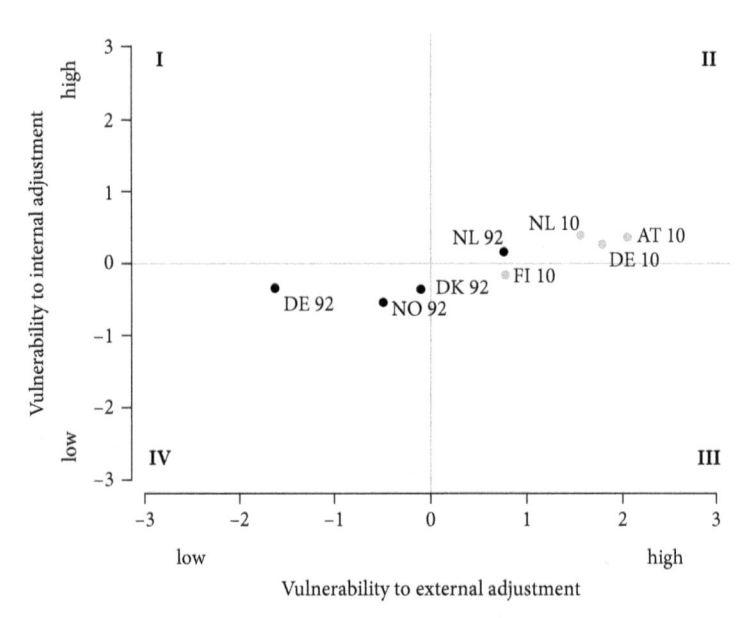

Figure 5.5 Vulnerability profiles in the 1992 EMS and the Eurozone crises

internal adjustment. Countries in the lower left-hand corner are less vulnerable than average to both internal and external adjustment. The final, upper right-hand corner represents the profiles with higher-than-average levels of vulnerabilities to both internal and external adjustment—hence the "misery corner."

Vulnerability Profiles of Surplus Countries in the Eurozone Crisis

The Eurozone surplus countries found themselves in a difficult position when the Eurozone crisis erupted in deficit countries. In fact, comparing them to other surplus countries in crises situation illustrates the particular difficulty. Figure 5.3 shows that the Eurozone surplus countries found themselves in a similar situation as the deficit countries. For them, both internal and external adjustment was difficult. This result helps explain the resistance of surplus countries to resolve the crisis and to accommodate the adjustment burden of deficit countries. First, we provide a short overview of their responses to the crisis. In a second step, we show how their vulnerability profiles help in explaining those responses.

How did the surplus countries respond to the crisis? None of the surplus countries actively pursued an external adjustment strategy, for instance by trying to leave the Eurozone and thereby obtaining a stronger, appreciated currency. The closest these countries came to this strategy was the German finance minister suggesting that Greece should exit the euro (Wagstyl 2015; see also Chapter 7). However, this suggestion never came to fruition. An external adjustment with a more direct impact on the surplus countries, such as them exiting, was never seriously on the table. The expansionary monetary policy of the ECB during the crisis further supported exports by depreciating the euro against other currencies, rather than help eliminate the imbalances.

Overall, the surplus countries pursued tight fiscal policies. Germany stuck to its goal of achieving a "schwarze Null" ("black zero," meaning a balanced government budget). Even as Germany gained additional fiscal space from increasingly lower interest rates, it preferred to pay back debt rather than to spend and invest. Finland and the Netherlands also tightened their purses. Only Austria slightly loosened fiscal policy. However, Austria lowered taxes to counter a weak economy rather than to reverse the current account balance (OECD 2015b, 16). The picture for wages is similar. In surplus countries, relative wages changed only slightly. Particularly, German relative labor unit costs, which had been decreasing over the past decade and had contributed to the country's large current account surplus, remained at low levels (OECD 2016a).

Instead of pursuing either adjustment strategy, the Eurozone surplus countries resisted a fast crisis resolution. Their crisis strategy was to delay their adjustment and complement it with emergency financing of deficit countries. These countries, together with the European Commission and the IMF (the so-called Troika), set strict conditions for reforms that put high costs onto deficit countries. The Troika stipulations required from these countries for instance, to increase taxes and cut spending, which, in the short term, contributed to a harsh recession and higher unemployment (Sapir et al. 2014).

What do the vulnerability profiles reveal about the Eurozone surplus countries and their reluctance to engage in crisis resolution? Compared to other countries with sustained surpluses, Eurozone surplus countries (shown in black) were—except for Finland—in the "misery corner." At the beginning of the crisis in 2010, Austria, Germany, and the Netherlands had high levels of vulnerabilities to internal and external adjustment. The situation in these countries was that any adjustment entailed economic costs and was therefore politically unappealing. On the one hand, exiting the Eurozone and letting the currency appreciate would have created uncertainty, hurt the important export sectors and created losses for assets abroad. On the other hand, adjusting internally through increased demand was difficult right after banking crisis of 2008/9. Their fiscal space was curtailed by a first round of fiscal stimuli to counter the recession and bailout banks. In addition, their large reliance on trade meant that the effect of further increased spending would be considerably weakened. Politically, the diminished clout of unions contributed to prohibit a consensus on measures of boosting internal demand. Overall, this analysis highlights the particularly difficult situation for surplus countries. They faced high vulnerabilities to any type of adjustment.

As we have seen in Chapter 2, the deficit countries were in the misery corner as well. They too were highly vulnerable to either adjustment strategy. Therefore, there was no quick crisis resolution through decisive responses in deficit countries. Internal and external adjustment posed high costs to both deficit and surplus countries.

This "miserable" vulnerability profile—especially in combination with the same profile in deficit countries—matches the protracted process of resolving the crisis and the surplus countries' preference to resort to bailouts. Instead of opting for either internal or external adjustment, they preferred to delay crisis resolution and grant emergency funding to deficit countries. By attaching strict conditions to these funds, they placed the adjustment burden on the deficit countries (see Chapters 4 and 7). In effect, the surplus countries shifted the costs of the crisis resolution to the deficit countries. This distribution of costs indicates that, even with such high interdependence, the bargaining power still rests with surplus countries. They would suffer from a break-up, but they did not face the same hard limits that markets had created for deficit countries.

Figure 5.3 depicts somewhat lower internal adjustment costs for Finland, where we consequently expect internal adjustment. This depiction is in line with two aspects of the Finnish crisis experience. First, Finland saw an internal adjustment in its current account balance due to a loss in competitiveness—even though it mostly stemmed from a loss in productivity and from structural changes in the Finnish economy (OECD 2016b). Second and more importantly, Finland was one of most vociferous critics of the bailouts. This criticism may be explained by its preference for internal adjustment. While the other surplus countries found emergency funding a relatively attractive way out of the misery corner, Finland preferred internal adjustment as a collective crisis resolution. Still, the relatively small difference in the vulnerability profiles should not be over-interpreted. In Chapters 6 and 7, we delve deeper into the different country positions.

Vulnerability Profiles of Non-Eurozone Surplus Countries during the Eurozone Crisis

What would the European surplus countries have done without membership in the common currency? For Germany and the Eurozone countries, this question remains hypothetical. However, it is interesting to compare them to the EU surplus countries outside the Eurozone. To this end, in Figure 5.4, we show the vulnerability profiles of Denmark, Norway, Sweden and Switzerland in addition to those of the Eurozone surplus countries. They, too, are surplus countries. Since the late 1990s, these three countries have run consistent current account surpluses. Again, we first turn to the crisis response and then to the vulnerability profiles.

Norway and Sweden, two surplus countries with flexible exchange rates, responded to the crisis by adjusting externally. They let their currencies appreciate. Norway, with its fortunate vulnerability profile, accompanied the external adjustment with some reflationary measures. Yet, adjusting externally was not the only option. Denmark went along with the Eurozone countries and kept its krone pegged to the euro. Switzerland, which had adopted a flexible exchange rate regime and saw its currency increasingly appreciate, introduced an exchange-rate floor and effectively fixed its currency at 1.20 CHF/EUR in 2011. The Swiss central bank abandoned the floor only in January 2015, when the European Central Bank was expected to launch a further round of loosening its monetary policy and when the rising value of the dollar cushioned the franc's appreciation against the euro.

In the vulnerability profiles graph of Figure 5.4, Denmark, Sweden, and Switzerland are in the lower right corner, with relatively low vulnerabilities to internal adjustment, but a relatively high vulnerability to external adjustment. Among these three, Switzerland has the highest vulnerability to internal adjustment and Sweden the lowest (close to the lower left corner). Norway had low vulnerabilities to both types of adjustment. These profiles match well with their crisis strategies.

Evidently, being outside the Eurozone gave these countries the flexibility to pursue their individual strategies that corresponded best to their trade-offs. Of course, they had lower costs to external adjustment: Exiting the Eurozone and re-introducing their national currency was not a pre-requisite to letting the value of their currency adjust. But more generally, the interdependencies they faced were smaller and allowed differing strategies. While some countries kept the value of their currencies pegged to the euro as well, others let them appreciate.

Vulnerability Profiles of Surplus Countries in the 1992/3 EMS Crisis

As in the case of deficit countries, the crisis in the European Monetary System (EMS) in 1992 and 1993 provide another insightful comparison. At the time, the members of the European Communities (EC) did not form a monetary union, but they the maintained a system of fixed exchange rates as part of the EMS, the so-called Exchange Rate Mechanism (ERM). Generally, they had to keep their currency within a band of +/− 2.5 percent around a weighted basket of the participating currencies. Several additional countries chose to peg their currencies to the system's anchor currency, the Deutschmark.

The crisis started after Danish voters rejected the Maastricht Treaty in June of 1992. This happened against the background of Germany tightening its monetary policy in response to increasing wages and prices in the aftermath of its reunification. Several countries that maintained fixed exchange rates came under pressure. In the fall of 1992, Italy and the United Kingdom withdrew from the ERM and devalued their currencies. Further speculative attacks followed until the participating countries extended the ERM fluctuation band to +/− 15 percent.

How did the countries respond to the EMS crisis? Germany focused on its domestic price stability and tightened monetary policy in the wake of its reunification—which worsened the pressure on the other countries. Thereby it effectively gave up the integrity of the EMS and let the Deutschmark appreciate. Denmark and the Netherlands both stuck to the fixed exchange rate vis-à-vis the Deutschmark, which meant an appreciation of their effective exchange rates of about 5 percent (OECD 1993b, 38). The two countries followed German monetary policy by trying to maintain moderate wage growth and exercise fiscal restraint (OECD 1993a, 90ff., 1993b). Essentially, the two countries fended off any internal adjustment and accepted external adjustment by letting their currencies appreciate relative to the ones of their trading partners.

Figure 5.5 plots countries with current account surpluses in the EMS crisis (in black) alongside the surplus countries in the Eurozone. The vulnerability profiles lie in those two quadrants where we cannot make strong predictions about the choice of adjustment strategies. Nevertheless, they are insightful when considering the difference to the Eurozone crisis.

The countries in the early 1990s generally faced lower vulnerabilities to both internal, but especially to external, adjustment. The difference in vulnerability profiles between the EMS and the euro crisis was largest in Germany. In 1992/3, its vulnerability to external adjustment was much lower than later on during the euro crisis. In 2010, Germany was more integrated in the European and global economy, with more net foreign assets and a much higher export volume. Of course, membership of the monetary union—in comparison to a system of fixed exchange rates—had also increased the costs of external adjustments. The lower vulnerability to external adjustment is consistent with the German strategy to implement external adjustment. They used the adjustment that came from realigning the exchange rate between deficit and surplus countries.

Another difference between the EMS and the Eurozone crisis is the vulnerability of deficit countries. The vulnerabilities to external adjustment for deficit countries were lower during the EMS than during the Eurozone crisis. Accordingly, there was less impetus to resort to financing. It was easier for both surplus and deficit countries to achieve a resolution through rebalancing exchange rates.

Conclusion

In comparison to deficit countries, surplus countries suffered much less economic upheaval during the crisis: Growth, unemployment, and governments' cost of capital developed positively. But even for surplus countries, the crisis implied costs. Most directly, they had to fund the bailouts for the deficit countries. Achieving this response was a drawn-out political struggle. The vulnerability profiles on the macro-level help explain this outcome. Internal and external adjustment were politically costly. The Eurozone surplus countries had no easy way out. At the same time, they shifted much of the adjustment burden onto deficit countries.

Putting surplus countries in the Eurozone crisis in a comparative perspective thus gives some first indication as to why the crisis was so hard to resolve. The broader comparison among surplus countries of balance-of-payment crises shows that the Eurozone posed a particularly complicated challenge for both deficit and surplus countries. Outside—and before—the Eurozone crisis resolution was less difficult.

However, the macro-level vulnerability profiles are necessarily broad and cannot capture the various constellations of domestic interests. Moreover, by conceptualizing aggregated vulnerabilities at the country-level, we cannot account for the fact that different societal groups would be affected very differently by the various options for internal and external adjustment. In the following two chapters, we closely examine these constellations in surplus countries. We show that internal adjustment—even if macroeconomic benefits may be clear—also depends on a consensus about how to translate it into a concrete set of policies.

6
Distributive Conflict and Interest Group Preferences in Surplus Countries

One of the most puzzling aspects of the Eurozone crisis has been the limited amount of burden sharing amongst the members of the monetary union (Blanchard et al. 2017; Frieden and Walter 2017). Rather than write-off substantial parts of the accumulated debt, boost domestic demand to revive economic growth in the Eurozone, and rebalance their export overhangs, surplus countries were content to see the crisis-ridden deficit countries shoulder the brunt of the pain of crisis resolution. Most strikingly, surplus countries have been reluctant to rebalance their current accounts. In theory, such rebalancing could be achieved in two ways. In practice, surplus countries never seriously entertained the first option, external adjustment, which would have involved a breakup of the Eurozone and, subsequently, an appreciation of their nominal exchange rates. However, surplus countries were also reluctant to engage in internal adjustment as a second option—that is, a boost in domestic demand, for example through more public investment or wage increases—which leads to more domestic consumption, more imports, and, as a result, a reduction of the export overhang. Instead, they opted for a restrictive type of financing: They provided deficit countries with bailouts.[1] What explains this resistance to rebalancing in surplus states?

Research on the sources of this reluctance has only recently begun to emerge. Some authors have argued that surplus countries have been led by ordoliberal ideas: The belief that the Eurozone's problems could be resolved if deficit states reformed their economies to regain competitiveness, whereas a stimulation of growth and inflation in surplus countries would only risk surplus countries' hard-earned standing in international markets and endanger price stability (Brunnermeier et al. 2016; Dullien and Guérot 2012; Matthijs and McNamara 2015; Schäfer 2016; Young 2014). Some even argue that these ideas were so strong that they trumped surplus states' material interests in a more cooperative approach to euro-crisis management (Matthijs 2016a). A second strand of research contests this notion and argues that surplus countries refused to share

---

[1] These bailouts mostly took the form of loans, which have to be repaid fully to the creditor countries. There are some debates as to whether the favorable conditions on these loans, including long maturities and low interest rates, amount to indirect transfers to deficit countries (for a discussion see Gourchinas et al. 2018), but in any case, these potential transfers remained rather limited.

the adjustment burden precisely because it benefitted the economic interests of core economic sectors in these countries, such as the financial and the export industries (Hall 2012; Leupold 2016; Steinberg and Vermeiren 2015). This structural perspective is rooted in the literature on the varieties of capitalism, especially research on different growth models (Baccaro and Pontusson 2016; Hall and Soskice 2001). It argues that the need to preserve export competitiveness in surplus countries creates a large coalition of policymakers, employers, and workers, all of whom are opposed to measures that would lead to internal adjustment, expanded domestic demand, higher inflation, and increased domestic wages (Hall 2012, 2014; Höpner and Lutter 2014; Leupold 2016; Mahnkopf 2012; Thompson 2015). This research suggests that in the international negotiations about the terms of the bailouts, adjustment programs, and economic policy reforms, surplus country governments acted in line with the dominant concerns of their domestic economies (Schimmelfennig 2015; Streeck and Elsässer 2016; Thompson 2015).

Both approaches have greatly advanced our understanding of the politics of the Eurozone crisis. Yet they also have some blind spots. For one, existing explanations suggest that domestic actors in surplus countries tend to be rather homogenous in their pursuit of certain crisis policies, either because of the dominance of economic ideas or because safeguarding the export-led growth model constitutes the national interest. Yet, analogous to the distributive struggles in deficit countries (Eichengreen 1992; Simmons 1997; Walter 2013a), adjustment politics in surplus countries generate diverging interests. By focusing on a homogenous national interest or economic ideology, existing approaches cannot account for divergent societal preferences and their influence on policymaking. Second, both structural and ideational approaches have not investigated the empirical framework conditions of their theory. While scholars stressing the role of ordoliberal ideas have provided compelling arguments for the relevance of economic orthodoxy for surplus-country policymaking, there is little work on the questions under what circumstances these ideas were particularly influential. Similarly, structural approaches rest on a number of micro-level assumptions about interest group preferences, which authors in this research tradition have themselves identified as being treated as a "black box" (Baccaro and Pontusson 2016, 200–1). Third, existing approaches concentrate on singular aspects of crisis management such as bailout conditions or wage-setting issues. Macroeconomic adjustment decisions are, however, multidimensional. Resistance to internal adjustment, for example, has significant consequences abroad. It risks global and regional financial stability and increases the financing needs of deficits states, especially when private capital inflows into these countries dry up. Understanding why surplus countries opt against adjusting internally thus also requires understanding how surplus country decision-makers evaluate these alternatives relative to the option of adjusting domestic policies in a way that reduces the current account surplus. Finally, and perhaps most importantly, we still know relatively little about how ideational and structural forces interact in shaping crisis politics and policies.

Our analysis in this chapter and Chapter 7 seeks to address these issues by conducting a systematic empirical analysis of the preferences of interest groups and voters and the way in which they interacted with the ideas of policymakers in shaping crisis outcomes. It thus complements existing approaches and sheds more light on the mechanisms and interactions between the different actors who shaped policymaking in surplus countries during the Eurozone crisis.

We start our investigation of domestic crisis politics in surplus countries by studying the preferences of important economic interest groups in this chapter. The structural approach suggests that economic interest groups played a key role in the domestic politics of the Eurozone crisis. In most surplus countries in the Eurozone, economic interest groups are traditionally deeply involved in economic policymaking. Countries such as Germany, Austria, Finland, and the Netherlands are often characterized as neo-corporatist or coordinated market economies (Hall and Soskice 2001; Nölke 2015; Schmitter and Streeck 1991; Streeck and Thelen 2005). In these countries, close and often institutionalized networks exist between state actors, unions, and business groups. To overcome collective-action problems, these networks provide market actors with privileged access to policymakers. Organized interest groups are actively integrated into national policymaking processes and, in turn, help with the implementation of reforms and other economic policy outcomes (Martin and Thelen 2007). Many of the economic questions underlying the management of the Eurocrisis in surplus countries directly affected the core interests of trade unions, employer associations, or industry groups, and they often had an important voice in important economic political decisions in the crisis years. When discussing whether to expand domestic public investment, the German government in 2014, for example, established a commission that included major trade unions, industry groups, and insurance associations to discuss existing needs and priorities.[2] Given the institutional context in coordinated market economies, economic interest groups were, thus, in prime positions to have an active say in how their governments approached key policy questions of the crisis.

Interest groups also matter in the context of ideas-based approaches because voters often use heuristics, such as cues by economic interest groups, to form opinions on complex matters, such as financial crises (Kim and Margalit 2016; Mcdermott 2006). Metal industry workers will likely not invest their evenings reading into the macroeconomics of balance-of-payments crises. However, they may consider the position of their trade union when thinking about whether their government should support international bailouts or not. There are numerous examples of such clue rendering in the crisis. During the run-up to the Dutch parliamentary elections of 2012, for example, a large coalition of Dutch employer

---

[2] See https://www.bmwi.de/Redaktion/DE/Pressemitteilungen/2016/20160914-expertenkommission-zur-steigerung-der-investitionen-in-deutschland-zieht-bilanz.html.

associations ran a huge public campaign emphasizing the importance of Europe for the Dutch economy and to counter widespread skepticism about the bailouts and integration more generally.[3] Economic interest groups thus often provide important information to broader electoral groups; they transport their ideas and interests into the wider electoral politics.

Despite broad agreement that organized interests played an important role in surplus countries' management of the Eurozone crisis, virtually no systematic and comparative empirical research on the specific preferences of these groups exists. A deep understanding of these preferences and the constraints they impose on policymakers is important, however, for a substantive analysis of the role of interest groups in Eurozone politics. This chapter addresses this lacuna. It analyzes interest groups' policy preferences on Eurozone policies using unique data we collected with an online survey of more than 350 employer associations, trade unions, and social policy groups in Germany, Austria, and the Netherlands. In addition, it leverages information from more than thirty in-depth interviews with interest group representatives and policymakers in these three countries.

Employing the vulnerability profile framework developed in this book, we show that analyzing the distributional conflicts amongst different societal groups in surplus countries helps to understand some important features of the management of the crisis. We find that a large majority of economic interest groups in all surplus countries opposed a breakup of the Eurozone (i.e., external adjustment) and supported internal adjustment through strengthened domestic demand. However, while interest groups uniformly rejected all Eurozone breakup scenarios, they disagreed heavily about the policies through which internal adjustment should be achieved. The resistance against macroeconomic adjustment in surplus states was largely rooted in distributive struggles about the design of possible adjustment policies. Importantly, in contrast to the highly politicized issues of external and internal adjustment, financing was a low-salience issue. Taken together, the polarized views on the specificities of internal adjustment, the broad consensus to avoid breaking up the Eurozone, and the low-salience of financing policies amongst economic interest groups, thus turned financing into an attractive strategy for surplus country governments.

Domestic Trade-Offs, Vulnerability Profiles, and Adjustment in Surplus Countries

To study the domestic politics of adjustment in surplus countries, we once more use the general vulnerability profile concept developed in this book to analyze the

---

[3] See https://www.vno-ncw.nl/campagnes/europa.

preferences and trade-offs faced by economic interest groups. Mirroring our analyses of deficit country interest group politics discussed in Chapter 3, we expect domestic economic interest groups to form their crisis preferences based on the relative costs and benefits they associate with each of the two possible adjustment strategies that surplus countries have in a balance-of-payments crises: Internal adjustment and external adjustment—in the case of the Eurozone crisis, a breakup of the monetary union—and the net costs of engaging in financing. Their policy preference will be for the adjustment strategy that benefits them the most or, if all options are costly, the one that costs them the least.[4]

Grouping interest groups by their net vulnerability to the two possible adjustment strategies, we can distinguish between four main ideal types. The first type (quadrant I) is vulnerable to internal adjustment but not to external adjustment (see Figure 1.5). As an example, one could think of an interest group representing the poor—a highly inflation-averse group whose purchasing power is enhanced by an appreciated currency. This first type is likely to prefer external adjustment over any other form of crisis management. The second type (quadrant III) would be hurt by a Eurozone breakup but is likely to benefit from a boom in domestic demand. Because internal adjustment creates net benefits for the group but its financing is costly, interest groups of this type will favor internal adjustment over external adjustment or financing. The third type (quadrant II) is vulnerable to both internal and external adjustment. An example for an interest group in this "misery corner" is a group that represents export-oriented firms, who would lose out from both a reorientation toward the non-tradable sector and an appreciated exchange rate. This type of interest group should be the most willing to provide deficit countries with some form of financing rather than supporting macroeconomic adjustment in their own country. Finally, groups that are neither vulnerable to internal nor external adjustment constitute the fourth ideal type (quadrant IV). For these groups, macroeconomic adjustment should be a low-salience issue, and they are likely to prefer adjustment over financing.

These straightforward predictions face one major complication. Each of the three main crisis strategies—internal adjustment, external adjustment, and financing—can be achieved in a variety of ways. Take, for example, internal adjustment, in which the range of possible policies is largest, because it can be achieved in very different ways in surplus countries (Bernanke 2015; Eichengreen 1992). For example, policymakers intent on boosting domestic demand might increase public investment in infrastructure and schools; these policymakers could also reduce corporate taxes or cut red tape for businesses to incentivize private

---

[4] We use a stylized example in which governments must choose between the three types of strategies. Of course, combinations of these options are also possible (e.g., some policies increasing domestic demand, some exchange-rate appreciation, and some financing). The underlying distributional considerations are likely to be the same in these situations, however.

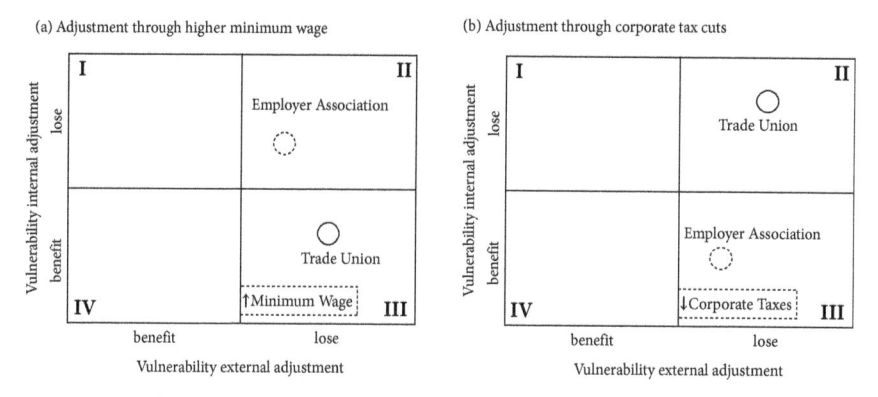

Figure 6.1 Policy-specific vulnerability profiles to internal adjustment

investment. Or they could raise the minimum wage, increase pensions, or expand unemployment benefits. Even though all these measures help to rebalance the economy, their distributional implications differ widely. As a result, interest group vulnerabilities to internal adjustment are likely to be policy-specific (Redeker and Walter 2020). While one group may benefit from one type of internal adjustment policy, the same group could, at the same time, be hurt by another policy aimed at boosting domestic demand. Depending on the specific policy under consideration, groups will, therefore, end up in different quadrants of our vulnerability profile. Figure 6.1 illustrates this point with a stylized example. It shows the vulnerability profiles of two hypothetical groups—one group representing employers and one group representing low-wage workers, for example a service sector trade union. We assume that both of our fictional groups are vulnerable to the breakup of the monetary union, putting them on the right-hand side of the vulnerability profile. Whether or not they support internal adjustment will then depend on the specific policy under consideration. In Panel A, internal adjustment is achieved through an increase in the minimum wage. Because members of our hypothetical trade union would benefit from higher minimum wages, the group falls in quadrant III and is likely to support internal adjustment. The employer association, on the other hand, is vulnerable to this form of internal adjustment, perhaps because it represents firms that rely on low-paid workers. This puts it in quadrant II. Since it is vulnerable to both a breakup and to the specific form of internal adjustment on the table, we expect it to oppose both external and this type of internal adjustment, and to be more supportive of financing instead. The situation is reversed when the internal adjustment policy under consideration is a reduction in corporate taxes meant to stimulate private investment. Panel B shows that the trade union now finds itself in quadrant II because it is likely to oppose the loss in tax revenue associated with tax cuts for businesses, whereas the employer association is now located in quadrant III and turns into a proponent of internal adjustment.

In the same vein, interest group vulnerabilities towards financing, and to a lesser extent external adjustment, are also policy-specific. The costs that financing puts on different societal groups in surplus countries depend on how exactly funds are provided to deficit states. Bailout packages, for example, are largely borne by the taxpayer, whereas debt relief and haircuts on private surplus country loans to deficit country governments and market actors impose costs on surplus country investors. (Copelovitch and Enderlein 2016; Frieden and Walter 2017). However, for many forms of financing, it is much more difficult to predict who exactly is going to have to pay the costs of these policies and how high these costs will actually be. The distributive consequences of Eurobonds, the provision of emergency liquidity assistance by the European Central Bank, or its bond-buying program for surplus country interest groups are likely to be much more opaque. Even for bailout packages, many question marks remain as to which taxpayers will have to pick up the bill and at what point in time. In sum, none of the financing measures are free, but a majority of them do not produce well-defined groups that will be clearly hurt by these measures. Politically, this means that many of these policies are likely to be less contested than adjustment policies with clearer distributive consequences.

Policy options for external adjustment, in contrast, are much less diverse. Of course, it will make a difference whether a crisis-ridden deficit country, such as Greece, leaves the monetary union, whether the Eurozone as a whole breaks down, or whether a surplus country leaves the club. But despite these different breakup scenarios, any change in the composition of Eurozone membership would result in some form of market upheaval and an appreciation of surplus countries' exchange rate (Åslund 2012; Eichengreen 2010b). Few groups are, therefore, going to benefit from one form of external adjustment but be hurt by another.

Overall, this discussion suggests that we should expect some variation in how interest groups evaluate different policy options for internal adjustment and financing, and less variation regarding to external adjustment. Especially concerning internal adjustment, policy proposals will garner support from some groups but will also provoke fierce opposition from others based on their policy-specific vulnerability profile. Moreover, we expect the two possible strategies leading to macroeconomic adjustment and rebalancing—internal and external adjustment— to be much more salient for interest groups than financing policies.

The expectation that interest group preferences about surplus country crisis management, and especially internal adjustment, are policy-specific and polarized adds some important alternative predictions to the perspectives suggested by the growth model and the ideas-based approaches. Both of these approaches suggest that rebalancing in surplus states is blocked by a broad societal coalition that shares either the common goal of safeguarding the country's export competitiveness (Hall 2012; Iversen and Soskice 2018) or a general skepticism toward political demand management (Brunnermeier et al. 2016; Dullien and Guérot 2012;

Matthijs 2016a). Although our argument shares this prediction for external adjustment, it makes a different prediction for internal adjustment. Here, our argument suggests that for most types of internal adjustment, some economic interest groups will be supportive, whereas others will be opposed. Rather than representing a general opposition to internal adjustment, interest group preferences diverge on how to adjust internally.

Research Design: Studying Interest Group Preferences in Surplus Countries

To examine how the distributional concerns of interest groups shaped their preferences on crisis resolution strategies for the Eurozone crisis, we pursue a two-pronged, mixed-method empirical approach that uses data from an original online survey of interest groups and in-depth interviews with interest group representatives and policymakers in Germany, Austria, and the Netherlands. In the next section, we justify our case selection, describe the sample of interest groups we contacted, and provide detailed information on the design of our survey.

Our empirical analysis concentrates on Germany, Austria, and the Netherlands. We selected these cases from all Eurozone countries running a current account surplus in the years leading up to the crisis, based on two considerations. As the attractiveness of internal adjustment depends on how well the economy is running in the first place, the first consideration is how well surplus countries' own economies did during the Eurozone crisis. Some of the surplus countries experienced robust GDP growth throughout the crisis years, whereas others faced economic problems of their own. It is plausible to assume that the situation of the national economy shapes groups' evaluation of the different crisis strategies. Measures aimed at boosting domestic demand, for example, are likely to seem much more attractive if business at home is doing poorly than if domestic markets are humming. Second, interest group support for or opposition to providing deficit countries with financial support is likely to be influenced by whether a surplus country ends up on the receiving end of international financing in the future. While some surplus countries in the Eurozone have run persistent trade surpluses for decades, others have a history of running both surpluses and deficits (Manger and Sattler 2017). Countries that are more likely to run deficits again in the future are also more likely themselves to need some financing support in a future crisis. Interest groups in such countries thus might be more generous than interest groups in countries with persistent current account surpluses.

To compare interest group preferences and politics across these different contexts, we select countries that differ with regard to these two issues. Figure 6.2 plots the countries' position regarding their average growth rates

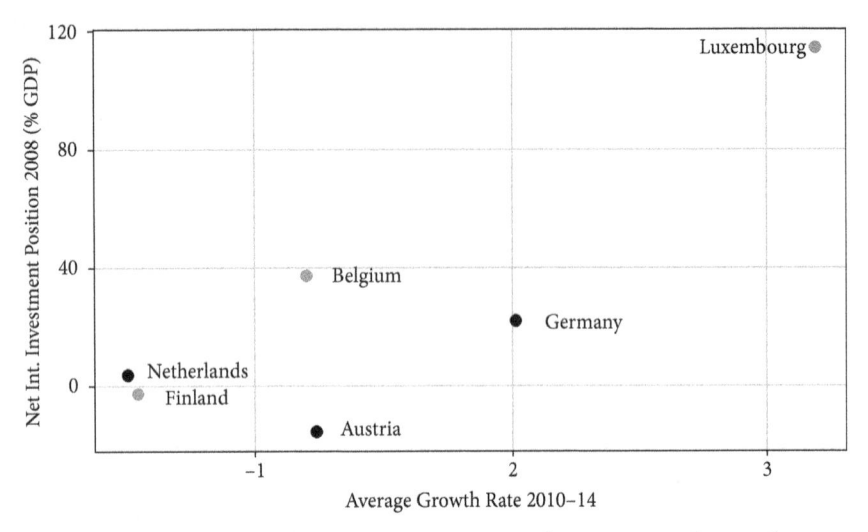

Figure 6.2 Net international investment positions and average growth rates for Eurozone surplus countries

between 2010 and 2014 and their net international investment positions in 2008 (i.e., prior to the crisis). Because countries with a current account surplus are by definition always capital exporters, they will over time accumulate financial assets in the rest of the world. The net international investment position—the stock of foreign assets an economy has with the rest of the world—will, therefore, be higher the longer a country has been running a current account surplus. Thus, it proxies for how long countries have been running a current account surplus.

Figure 6.2 shows that Austria, Germany, and the Netherlands vary on both of these dimensions. Austria's economy was doing moderately well between 2010 and 2014. However, its current account had only turned positive at the beginning of the 2000s, so its international investment position remained negative until 2012. Germany showed robust growth throughout the Eurozone crisis and has had a persistent current account surplus for decades.[5] Germany is also a substantively important case, as it was one of the most prominent and powerful actors involved in managing the Eurozone crisis and was widely criticized for running massive current account surpluses. Finally, the Netherlands also had a stable current account surplus, but the country struggled with stagnating growth rates and rising unemployment during the Eurozone crisis.[6]

---

[5] A short exception to this was Germany's period as a deficit country in the 1990s as result of German reunification. See Manger and Sattler (2017) for a discussion.

[6] Although Luxembourg would maximize variation on these two indicators, the country's unusual and small economy limits the inferences we can draw from this case.

Much research on the role of societal interests in economic policymaking makes strong assumptions about the preferences of different interest groups, but either they do not empirically examine these assumptions (Hall 2018b; Iversen and Soskice 2018; Nölke 2015) or they use only broad proxies to operationalize these preferences (e.g., Frieden 2002). We follow a different approach. Rather than inferring policy preferences on theoretical grounds, we conducted large-scale online surveys of Austrian, German, and Dutch interest groups in which we asked them about their specific policy preferences and reactions to the trade-offs inherent in crisis management. The surveys were conducted between September 2016 and October 2017—that is, after the crisis had calmed down but at a time when discussions over different financing approaches, Eurozone reforms, and macroeconomic imbalances were still ongoing in all three countries. Nonetheless, several of our questions asked respondents to answer retrospectively about their policy preferences at the peak of the crisis. To ensure that this did not systematically skew the responses, we validated survey answers with press releases, reports, and other interest group publications on similar topics between 2010 and 2015 whenever possible. We did not find any evidence that interest group responses differed due to the timing of our survey.

We contacted "sectional interest groups," that is, groups that represent the interest of a well-defined subset of societal interests (Giger and Klüver 2016). We concentrated on interest groups that engage with economic or social policy issues and disregarded all other groups, such as environmental groups, civil rights, and religious groups. We also contacted only groups organized at the national level where most policy decisions regarding the crisis were made.[7] Respondents were contacted via email, through three rounds of reminder emails, and finally by an individual phone call. Among the contacted interest groups, 357 completed our questionnaire (136 from Germany, 116 from the Netherlands, and 105 from Austria), resulting in response rates of 28 percent in Germany, 26 percent in Austria, and 29 percent in the Netherlands, which corresponds to typical response rates for interest group survey research (Marchetti 2015). Among the interest groups who responded to our survey, 54 percent are employer associations, 30 percent are professional associations, 8 percent are trade unions, and 8 percent are social policy groups. This distribution comes close to the overall distribution of these types of interest groups within the three countries.

We also conducted 30 in-depths interviews with interest group representatives and policymakers in Germany (13 interviews), Austria (9 interviews), and the Netherlands (8 interviews).[8] The main goal of our conversations was to

---

[7] The details of the sample construction in our three cases can be found in the online appendix at https://forsbase.unil.ch/project/my-study-overview/16230/.
[8] The interviews in Germany took place between November 27 and December 8, 2017. Interviews in Austria and the Netherlands took place between June 18–22 and July 2–6, 2018.

understand what motivated their preferences regarding possible policy responses to the Eurozone crisis and how they pursued these interests politically. We selected groups based on their size and the importance of their members to the overall economy; we made sure to cover groups representing a wide range of sectors, including manufacturing and services, domestic- and export-oriented associations, and trade unions representing workers at different income levels. A complete list of interview partners can be found in the appendix to Chapter 7: see Table A7.1.

Our analysis examines the preferences of economic interest groups about the management of the Eurozone crisis in surplus countries. It proceeds in three steps. The next section explores how interest groups evaluate different policy options within internal adjustment, external adjustment, and financing. We analyze not just how these preferences vary but also to what extent they are related to material considerations. Our results show that, overall, a large majority of groups opposes a Eurozone breakup and are positive toward internal adjustment, although groups strongly diverge in policy-specific preferences for internal adjustment. Moreover, most economic actors are relatively indifferent about various measures of international financing. We then turn to the inherent trade-offs of crisis management and apply the vulnerability profile framework empirically to investigate the preferences of economic interest groups when confronted with policy-specific trade-offs. We show that internal adjustment is the strategy of choice for a large majority of interest groups, especially when a reduction of the current account surplus is achieved through policies suiting their interests. It is only in scenarios in which all adjustment strategies are costly that financing becomes an attractive alternative. In the third step of our analysis, we finally explore the salience of the different crisis strategies and find that financing carries much less salience for interest groups than strategies aimed at macroeconomic adjustment.

Policy-Specific Preferences on Eurozone Crisis Management

How did surplus country interest groups evaluate the different policy options within the three general strategies—external adjustment, internal adjustment, and financing—available to resolving the Eurozone crisis? To examine this question empirically, we presented interest groups in our survey with a set of policies that were actually discussed in policy circles during the Eurozone crisis as options to achieve a rebalancing or to finance deficit states. Among these policies, we chose those policies that were actively discussed in all three of our country cases and that are general enough to remain comparable across the three countries.

Table 6.1 provides an overview of the different policies included in our survey. The possible scenarios for external adjustment all involve the breakup of the Eurozone, and we presented respondents with three variants of how such a

Table 6.1 Policy options by crisis strategy

Internal Adjustment Policies	Financing Policies	External Adjustment Policies
Public infrastructure spending("Expand public investment, for example in education or infrastructure.")	**Provision of bailouts** ("Provide financial assistance and loans through the European rescue funds.")	**Deficit countries leave the EMU**("Deficit countries like Spain or Greece leave the Eurozone.")
Higher minimum wage ("Increase low wages, for example by raising the minimum wage.")	**European unemployment insurance**("Introduce European unemployment insurance.")	**North/South division** ("The EMU divides into a North and a South bloc with different currencies.")
Public spending on welfare ("Expand public spending on social welfare programs.")	**ECB bond purchases** ("Purchases of government bonds and other assets by the European Central Bank.")	**Germany leaves the EMU** ("[DE, AT, NL] leaves the Eurozone.")
Decreasing VAT("Reduce the rate of the value added tax.")	**Haircuts on public sector debts**("Grant reliefs on debt that crisis countries' owe the [DE, AT, NL] state as a result of the European bailout packages.")	
Decreasing corporate taxes ("Reduce taxes for companies.")	**Haircuts on private sector debts**("Grant reliefs on debt that crisis countries' owed the [DE, AT, NL] private banks at the beginning of the crisis.")	

breakup could come to pass: Eurozone exit by a deficit country such as Greece; dividing the monetary union into a "Southern" and a "Northern" Eurozone, or their own country's exit from the Eurozone—a policy that was touted, for example, by the German populist-right party Alternative for Germany (AfD).

Regarding internal adjustment, for example, socialist and social democratic parties in Austria, Germany, and the Netherlands all pushed for policies that aimed at raising the incomes of low-wage workers. We, therefore, included "higher minimum wage" as a possible adjustment policy that captures group preferences toward low-wage policies more generally. Likewise, the International Monetary Fund (IMF) and the European Commission repeatedly called for overhauls of the corporate tax systems in surplus countries to boost private investment. While the specific tax recommendations differed slightly across countries, we included "decreasing corporate taxes" to measure preferences toward corporate tax incentives more generally.

Policy options for financing also covered very different approaches. They included government-based financing in the form of sovereign bailouts and loans; more indirect forms of financing, such as European Central Bank (ECB) bond purchases; long-term EU-wide schemes, such as the introduction of a European unemployment insurance, to a bail-in of private investors. As discussed above, the policy options for internal adjustment and financing range much more widely than policy options for external adjustment, and we presented interest groups with a selection of five different policies for both of these crisis strategies. Respondents were asked to evaluate each policy on a scale from 1 (strongly oppose) to 5 (strongly support). Interest groups' evaluations of each of these policies allow us to explore in considerable detail how they evaluated not only the overall crisis strategies available to policymakers but also the concrete policies associated with each of these policies.

We begin by analyzing interest groups' average assessment of the different policies that were discussed during the crisis as possible ways to rebalance the economy or finance deficit countries. Figure 6.3 shows the average policy support or opposition to these policies for each of the three crisis strategies in Austria, Germany, and the Netherlands. This analysis suggests that, overall, most interest groups opposed any breakup of the Eurozone, took a rather benevolent view of internal adjustment, and were quite indifferent with regard to financing. In contrast to both the ideas-based (Brunnermeier et al. 2016; Matthijs and McNamara 2015) and the growth-model-based research strands (Iversen and Soskice 2018; Steinberg and Vermeiren 2015), which both assume a broadly shared opposition to internal adjustment among surplus country interest groups, we find a generally positive attitude toward internal adjustment.

This finding is corroborated by our interviews. In Germany especially, a large number of interest groups felt that the country's large current account surplus was problematic. These groups are not only major trade unions but also a wide range of employer associations, including those representing export-oriented industries, such as the association of the metal industry (Interviews DE2; DE7; DE8). Even groups that rejected the notion that Germany's export overhang had played a role in the Eurozone crisis stated that the German economy had underperformed in terms of private and public investment in recent years and voiced their support for specific policies that would serve to counter this trend (Interviews DE3; DE6). Debates about the general effects of current account surpluses were more muted in Austria and the Netherlands. In both countries, most major economic interest groups did not perceive their national trade balances to be problematic. Discussions about the macroeconomic imbalances within the Eurozone were largely seen as a German problem; the surpluses of the Netherlands or Austria played only a minor role (Interviews AT1; AT4; NL1; NL4). However, most interest groups similarly pointed at the lack domestic demand as well as the shortage of private and public investments as major policy

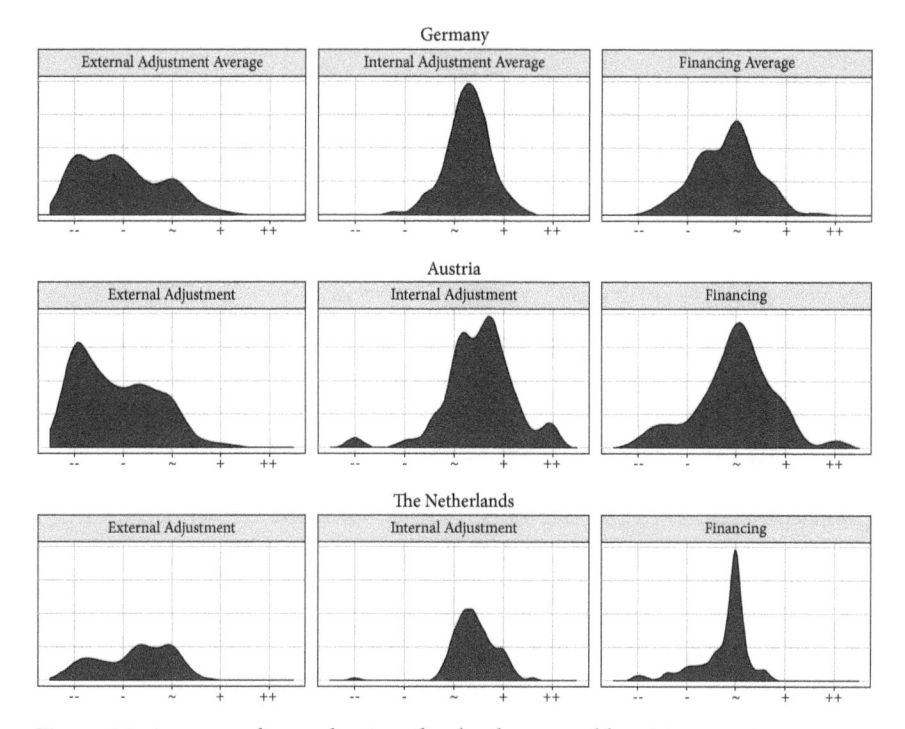

Figure 6.3 Average policy evaluations for the three possible crisis strategies

concerns that needed to be addressed (Interviews AT1; AT4; AT5; NL1; NL4; NL3). Instead of building a unified front in favor of preserving export surpluses, most of the actors we interviewed were in favor of some measures that would increase domestic demand and reduce current account surpluses.

While these average assessments are insightful, our argument suggests that interest groups' preferences about macroeconomic adjustment should be policy-specific. We therefore next turn to a more disaggregated analysis.

External Adjustment Preferences

How did interest groups evaluate different breakup scenarios for the Eurozone? Figure 6.4 displays density plots of groups' assessment of each of the three options of external adjustment. In all our analyses, we distinguish between the four main types of interest groups—employer associations, professional associations, social policy groups, and trade unions—because the material interests of these groups are likely to differ.

Our analysis shows that on average all interest groups in all three countries opposed a breakup of the Eurozone in any form, even though Dutch interest

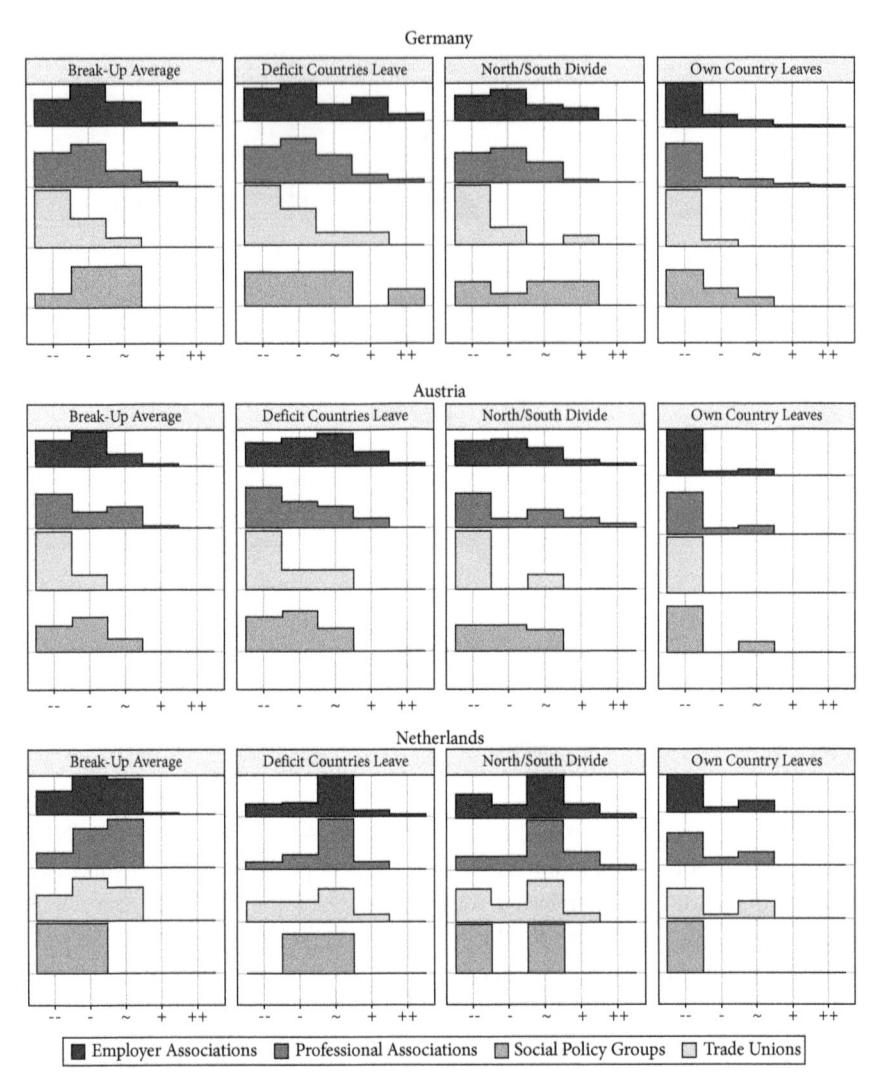

Figure 6.4 Interest group evaluations of different Eurozone breakup scenarios
Note: Density plots. Ratings range from − − (strongly oppose) to ++ (strongly support).

groups were slightly less opposed than Austrian and German groups. There is some variation regarding the various breakup scenarios. While groups unequivocally rejected a Eurozone exit of their own country and mostly opposed dividing the Eurozone into a Northern and a Southern bloc, the assessments of a deficit country exit were slightly more mixed. Nonetheless, only about 21 percent of all the groups in our sample stated that they would support some form of a Eurozone breakup.

These findings are consistent with qualitative evidence on interest group preferences on external adjustment. In our interviews, major employer associations and trade unions in all three countries univocally stated that their members depended crucially on the stability of the monetary union in its current form. Groups in tradable sectors mainly feared that a breakup would lead to unforeseeable exchange-rate and market volatilities, disruptions on financial markets, as well as threats to European economic integration more generally. They also often mentioned the return of trade barriers as a possible long-term consequence of a Eurozone breakup (Interviews DE1; DE2; AT1; AT4; NL1).[9] However, even nontradable sector interest groups, such as those focused on retail or construction, emphasized that a breakup would have extensive negative effects on their members. Main concerns were a general depression of the economic climate as well as higher credit and refinancing costs for their members due to insecurity and friction in the financial markets (Interviews DE5; NL3). One important exemption to this general opposition to a Eurozone breakup was a potential exit by Greece. While almost all trade unions and employer associations we interviewed said that they had supported keeping Greece in the Eurozone at the beginning of the crisis—mainly due to potential contagion effects on other member states under stress—most of them also pointed out that the potential economic costs of a Grexit for their members had become negligible by 2017.

Nonetheless, the overall picture confirms research that assumes a general opposition among surplus country interest groups to external adjustment (Hall 2018b; Iversen and Soskice 2018; Nölke 2015). During the Eurozone crisis, an important objective of these groups was to safeguard the Economic and Monetary Union (EMU).

Internal Adjustment Preferences

The picture is decidedly more mixed when it comes to internal adjustment. Despite the rather favorable overall assessment of internal adjustment, Figure 6.5 shows that there are clear differences in interest groups' evaluations when it comes to the specific policy alternatives. While, for example, a large majority of trade unions, social policy groups, and professional associations in Austria, Germany, and the Netherlands stated that they would support a higher minimum wage or more spending on social welfare, most employer associations were clearly opposed to such policies. The picture looks exactly the opposite way when it comes to lower taxes for businesses. Our analysis shows that every policy

---

[9] For press statements confirming this position see (Habit 2011; Inacker 2012; Meyer 2011; VNO-NCW 2014).

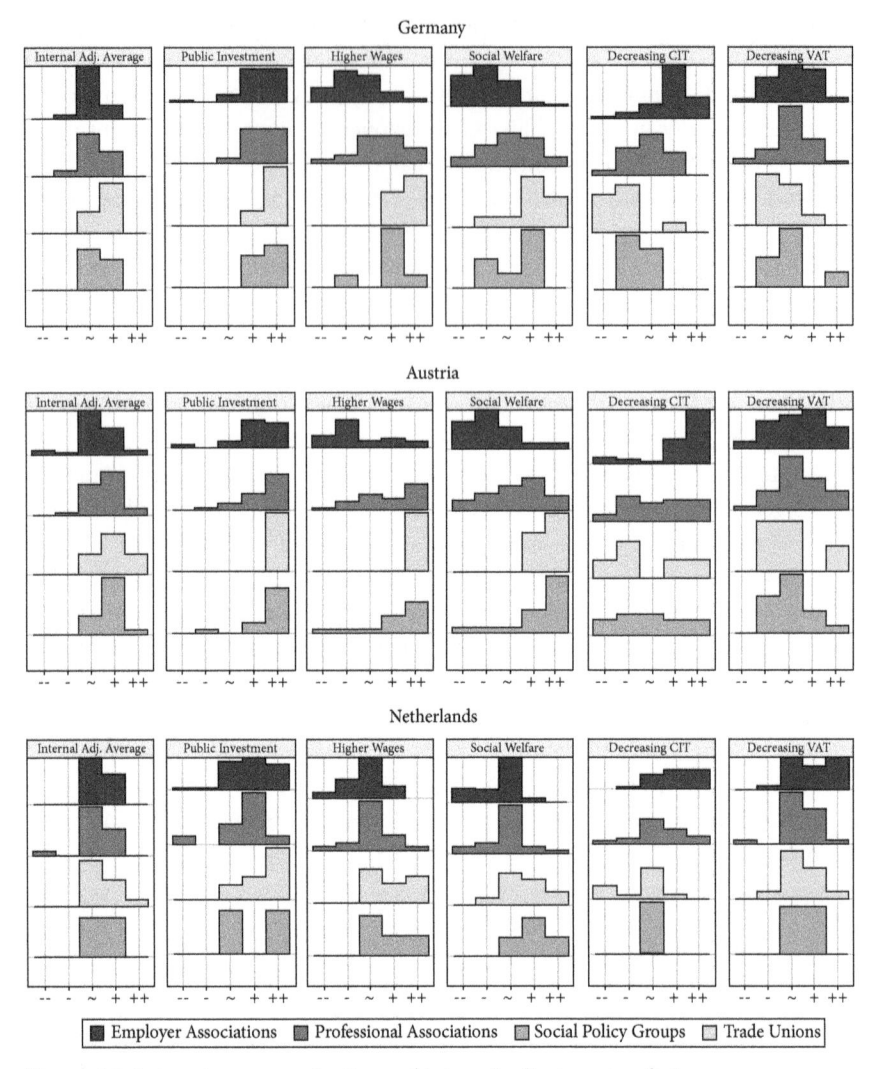

Figure 6.5 Interest group evaluations of internal adjustment policies
Note: Density plots. Ratings range from − − (strongly oppose) to ++ (strongly support).

is supported by some groups, but also opposed by others. The only exception is a policy of increasing public investment, which almost no interest group rejected and for which support was particularly high in Germany. These findings corroborate our argument that interest group evaluations of different internal adjustment strategies are likely to be policy-specific because the costs and benefits of internal adjustment for a socioeconomic group depend on the specific policy under consideration.

While we find a generally positive attitude toward internal adjustment, we also find a considerable degree of variation in policy-specific assessments, which results in rather polarized policy preferences regarding internal adjustment. This finding is corroborated by our interviews. All the trade unions we talked to stressed the need to increase wages—for example through higher minimum wages, expanded coverage of the negotiated tariff commitments, and a re-regulation of opt-out clauses and temporary employment contracts (Interviews DE7; DE8; AT4; AT5; NL4).[10] At the same time, they fiercely rejected any form of tax break for companies or any efforts to deregulate the service sector in order to stimulate private investments—the last one being a concern that they shared with representatives of the craft association. Many employer associations, on the other hand, emphasized the expansive effects of corporate tax cuts, reductions of red tape in service industries, and less-regulated credit provisions (Interviews DE1; AT1; NL1).[11] At the same time, most German industry groups had fought the introduction of the minimum wage in 2013, and employer associations in three countries said that they would lobby against further attempts to strengthen the bargaining positions of employees in wage negotiations. As a representative of a large umbrella organization put it, "of course the main employer associations, for microeconomic reasons, have to come out against such measures [such as higher minimum wage or re-regulating contracts]. But then in tripartite exchanges, trade unions say 'But that's exactly what we want.' [. . .] Nobody is thinking about these things in an overall macro-economic context. So that's what makes it difficult" (Interview DE1).

One of the most surprising findings from our survey is the strong support for public investment by almost all interest groups. This support was also evident in our interviews, where all interest groups agreed that more public investment was needed. However, opinions again diverged on what kind of public investments should be prioritized and on how these investments should be financed. While some groups stressed the need for more public services, such as investment in education and daycare, others prioritized investments in road, energy, and digital infrastructure. Regarding the financing of more investments, similar distributional conflicts arose. Whereas trade unions and craft associations demanded financing through tax money and possibly new public debt, many employer associations insisted they be financed by private–public partnerships, which would also provide new investment opportunities to large institutional investors (Interviews DE13; DE8).

In sum, our analysis shows that surplus country interest groups are not opposed to internal adjustment per se. In fact, among all three potential crisis strategies, internal adjustment was the strategy that interest groups viewed most favorably on

---

[10] See also (DGB 2013; ORF 2012).
[11] See also (BDI 2014; Christoph Schneider 2013; VNO-NCW 2014, 2016).

average. However, our analysis also shows that interest groups were heavily divided on how such adjustment should be achieved.

Financing Preferences

Given that interest groups were opposed to any form of a Eurozone breakup and were deeply polarized on how to achieve internal adjustment, we now turn to their assessments of the third possible crisis response—financing. Figure 6.6 shows how Austrian, German, and Dutch interest groups evaluated different forms of international transfers. As in the case of internal adjustment, we see that interest groups' assessments were once more policy-specific. The dominant financing policy pursued by surplus country governments in the Eurozone crisis—the provision emergency credits to deficit states in the form of bailouts—was viewed rather favorably and supported or at least not opposed by a majority of interest groups. In contrast, evaluations of haircuts on loans extended to deficit countries by private investors, the ECB bond-buying scheme, and the introduction of EU-wide unemployment schemes were much more contested.

However, Figure 6.6 also shows that groups were much more indifferent about most forms of financing than they were about the various Eurozone breakup scenarios or internal adjustment policies. A majority of interest groups stated that they neither opposed nor supported any financing option. As discussed above, this indifference may reflect the fact that financing policies can often be designed in ways that make it difficult to predict who exactly is going to bear their cost. Of course, some options produce clear-cut winners and losers, and those are the policies where we see more polarization. For example, the choice to bailout crisis countries with emergency credits instead of haircuts on private sector investments clearly benefitted exposed banks in surplus countries at the expense of taxpayers. In many cases, however, it is hard to say in advance which domestic actors are going to pay the bill for interstate redistribution and when that bill will come due. Hence, interest groups have few incentives to form opinions, let alone fight, for or against, such financing policies.

Material Interests and Policy Preferences

The huge divergence in interest groups' policy preferences adds to ideas-based and growth-model perspectives on Eurozone crisis politics. Both of these approaches focus mainly on factors that should unite broad coalitions of interest groups in their opposition towards macroeconomic rebalancing. In contrast, the heterogeneity of interest group's policy preferences underscores that interest groups also

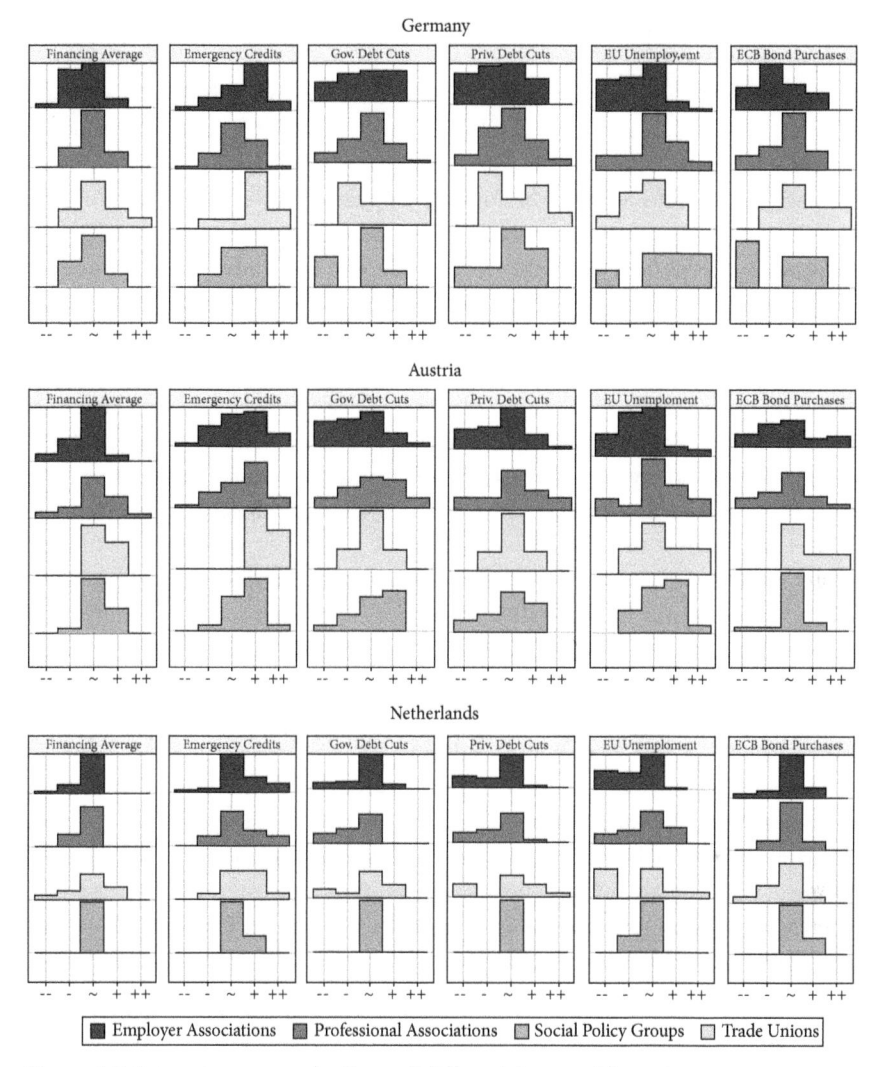

Figure 6.6 Interest group evaluations of different forms of financing

Note: Density plots. Ratings range from − − (strongly oppose) to ++ (strongly support).

form policy preferences based on their material interests (Frieden 1991b; Lake 2009; Rogowski 1989; Walter 2013a), which thus compete with ideational and structural forces in shaping surplus-country politics in the Eurozone crisis.

To corroborate this assumption, which also underpins the theoretical approach in this book, we next examine empirically how well objective measures of interest groups' material interests explain their stated policy preferences in our online survey. Do interest groups' subjective evaluations of policies broadly correspond to some rough estimates of their objective exposure to different adjustment strategies?

For this analysis we use both broad measures of how much interest groups are likely to be helped or hurt by a macroeconomic rebalancing and information on the type of people or firms they represent to gauge their material exposure to different crisis strategies. For the former, we classify groups according to their main sector of economic activity and use this classification to collect data on two measures of exposure: Interest groups' trade dependence and demand elasticity.[12] A group's trade dependence is measured as the share of the output that it exports to other countries in the Eurozone.[13] It proxies the degree to which a group would be hurt by a breakup of the monetary union. The more a group exports to other European countries, the more negatively it should be affected by the exchange-rate volatility and market insecurity that is likely to follow a breakup (Frieden 2002). For demand elasticity, we assess how much a group would benefit from the general expansion of domestic demand that internal adjustment implies. We focus on the income elasticity of demand for the goods the members of an interest group produce, because it reflects how sensitive the demand for a specific good or service is to increases in aggregate income. We construct an ordinal variable that ranges from 1 for very inelastic goods (e.g., food and tobacco) to 6 for very elastic goods (e.g., financial services and personal care activities).[14] The higher the income elasticity of demand for the main good an economic group provides, the more it should benefit from internal adjustment.

The interest groups in our sample also represent very different sets of members, and we expect this variation in material interests to be reflected in how they evaluate different policies. Trade unions and social policy groups, for example, represent individuals who benefit from progressive, redistributive policies, whereas employer organizations are more likely to benefit from policies aimed at incentivizing private firms to invest. Likewise, social policy groups are likely to be the group least exposed to a breakup of the Eurozone. Of course, it is difficult to pinpoint how exactly interest groups are affected by specific policies. For example, in general, trade unions are likely to support higher minimum wages. However, the extent to which they do so will also depend on whether they represent workers

---

[12] We use the statistical classification of economic activities in the European community (NACE) for this purpose. At the two-digit level, this categorization scheme allows us to differentiate between 99 distinct fields of economic activity. For groups that represent actors from more than one sector, we take the unweighted averages of all the sectors present among their members.

[13] NACE-level data on both measures stems from the input–output tables provided by national statistical offices (CBS 2018; Destatis 2018; Statistik Austria 2018). All variables are measured by the average values between 2010 and 2013.

[14] When people have more money to spend, the income elasticity of demand tells us how much of this money they spend to buy more of a specific good or service. We make use of several empirical studies (European Commission 2007; Copenhagen Economics 2008) as well as the COICOP categorization of the UN Statistics Division to arrive at our categorization. The details of our coding scheme can be found in the online appendix at https://forsbase.unil.ch/project/my-study-overview/16230/.

from lower or higher ends of income distribution, whether they fear that higher minimum wages could lead to layoffs in the specific sectors they represent, and whether their members are already covered by tariff wages and, thus, would not benefit from universal minimum wage increase. But on average, we should see differences in how these groups evaluate the different policy options discussed in the context of the Eurozone crisis.

To examine to what extent interest groups' policy preferences are related to these proxies of their material interests, we run regression analyses in which we examine how an interest group's policy evaluation is related to its exposure to these policies. Figure 6.7 summarizes the main findings from thirteen OLS regression analyses (one for each policy option listed in Table 6.1). All models include all 343 interest groups that answered our survey as well as robust standard errors and country fixed effects. For the group types, we compare the effects of interest group type relative to the policy evaluations of employer associations.

Our findings in Figure 6.7 confirm that groups' policy evaluations were related to their material exposure. First, it shows that groups that provided goods and services with higher levels of demand elasticity evaluated internal adjustment policies more positively. Hence, the more groups benefitted from an increase in domestic incomes, the more they supported internal rebalancing. Similarly, the groups' evaluation of different forms of internal adjustment also reflected the material interests of the type of members they represented. Compared to employer associations, trade unions and social policy groups were more supportive of measures to increase lower wages and social spending, whereas they oppose tax cuts, especially for private companies.

Second, material interests also underpin support for financing policies. The more groups relied on exports to other members of the Eurozone, the more positively they evaluated different options for providing deficit countries with financial resources. Interestingly, these effects were most pronounced for the option to grant debt relief for deficit countries' governments. Somewhat surprisingly, trade unions, social policy groups, and professional associations tended to evaluate some forms of financing more positively than industry groups. While some of this could reflect material considerations—for example, trade unions' support for the monetary expansion of the ECB could be interpreted as prioritizing employment over price stability—norms of international solidarity were also likely to play a role.

Finally, counter to our intuition, we do not find that trade-exposed groups feel more vulnerable to different breakup scenarios than groups that focus mostly on the domestic economy. As we have seen above, this is likely to stem from the fact that all groups, independent of their market orientation, were deeply concerned about the material repercussions of external adjustment.

Taken together, these findings suggest that the interest groups' evaluations of crisis policies reflect real material considerations.

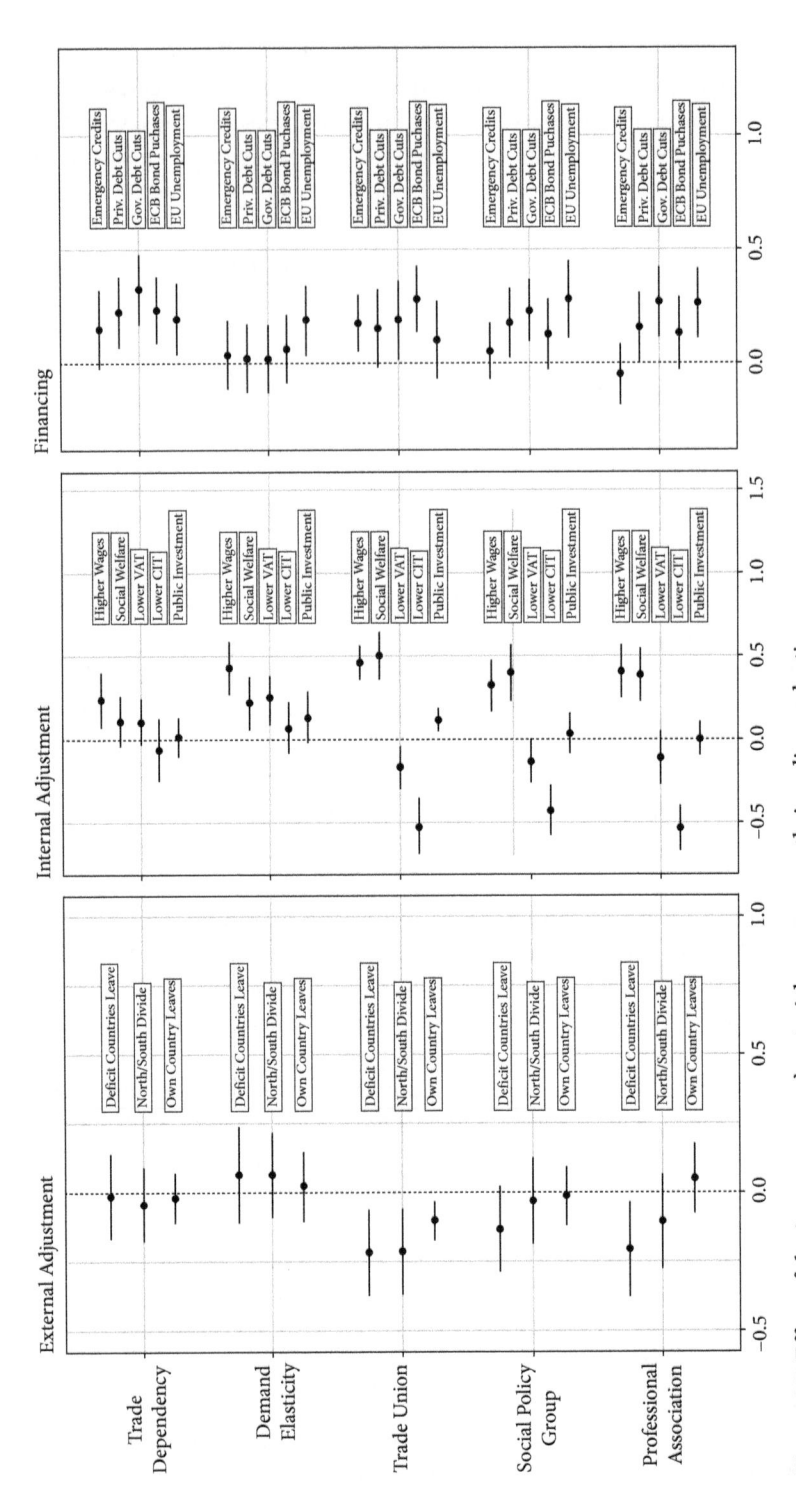

Figure 6.7 Effect of the interest groups' material exposure on their policy evaluations

Note: OLS regression coefficients. All variables are standardized; all models include robust standard errors as well as country fixed effects. The baseline category for interest group dummies is employer associations.

Policy Salience

So far, our analysis has shown that in line with our theoretical expectations, policy preferences about possible adjustment policies varied widely—especially regarding internal adjustment and, to a lesser extent, financing—and were related to interest groups' material interests. What about policy salience? We have argued above that policies that lead to rebalancing through internal or external macroeconomic adjustment are likely to be much more salient for interest groups than financing policies because the distributional effects of most forms of financing are more opaque and too long-term for interest groups to strongly care about them.

Our initial assessment of policy preferences regarding financing indeed suggested that distributional conflicts about financing were much more limited than those regarding internal adjustment. Figure 6.8a confirms this finding with a more systematic analysis. It shows boxplots of the average share of policies that interest groups stated to being indifferent about for each crisis strategy. While, on average, groups supported or rejected about 71 percent of the internal adjustment and 75 percent of the external adjustment policies included in the survey, the same was true for only about 56 percent of financing measures.

To explore this finding in more detail, Figure 6.8b presents further evidence in line with this characterization. To assess policy salience directly, we asked respondents how important each policy was for their organization's political work. Figure 6.8b shows a stark contrast in salience between internal adjustment and financing. Almost 80 percent of the groups stated that policies related to internal adjustment were

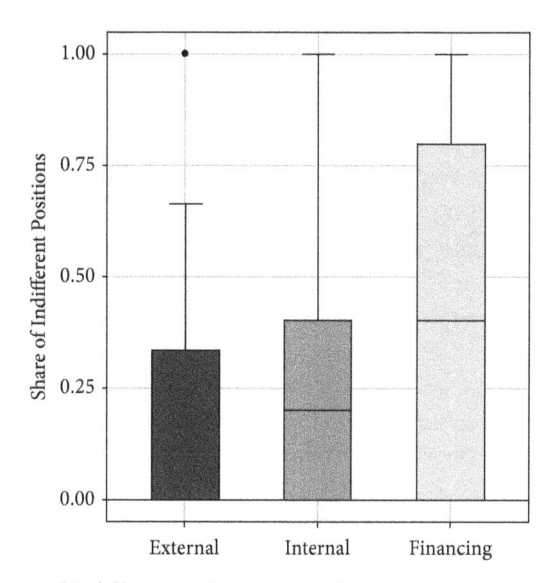

Figure 6.8a Share of indifferent policy positions by crisis strategy

[Figure: density plot with x-axis from "Not important" to "Important", showing Salience Financing and Salience Internal]

Not important   Rather Not important   Indifferent   Rather Important   Important

☐ Salience Financing   ■ Salience Internal

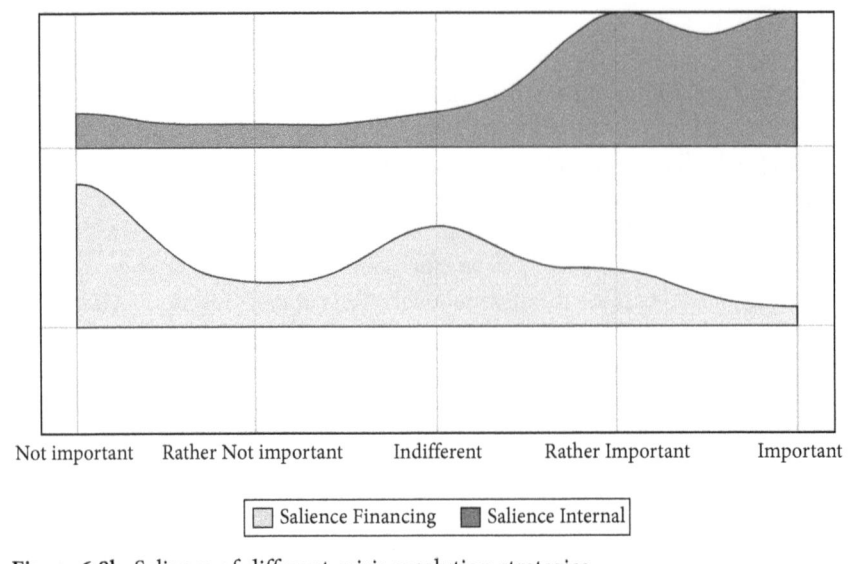

Figure 6.8b Salience of different crisis resolution strategies

Note: Based on the question "How important were the following policies for the political work of your organization?"

important or rather important for their political work. Only 19 percent of them said the same for financing policies, whereas the large majority characterized these policies as unimportant or rather unimportant for their political work.

Qualitative evidence confirms this picture. While most groups we interviewed supported financial rescue measures, the specificities of the bailout regime or the further steps to institutionalize transfers ranked very low on their political agenda (Interviews DE1; DE2; AT1; NL1). Even within large and encompassing employer associations—such as the Federation of German Industries (BDI), the Austrian Economic Chambers (WKÖ), or the Confederation of Netherlands Industry and Employers (VNO-NCW)—there was no formal consultation about the specificities of financing policies. As a representative of a large umbrella association for business groups put it: "The potential costs of these measures were never really thought of or discussed. [. . .] There are simply 50 other topics that are of much greater importance to our members (Interview DE1)."[15] In line with this characterization, none of the policymakers we talked to could remember any consultations with interest groups about the nature of different financing measures (Interviews DE11; AT9; NL7).

---

[15] The financing questions were more important to trade unions. However, here they were mainly discussed with reference to the effects of the attached conditionality to workers in deficit countries and not so much regarding the potential distributional effects in Germany.

Trade-Offs and Difficult Choices between External Adjustment, Internal Adjustment, and Financing

Until now, we have studied interest groups' evaluations and the salience of different forms of internal adjustment, external adjustment, and financing separately. Our analysis has shown that almost all interest groups opposed any form of a Eurozone breakup. At the same time, they were quite open toward an internal rebalancing of their economies but deeply divided on how such internal adjustment should be achieved, and, overall, surplus countries did show a great reluctance to adjust internally. Regarding financing, most groups were rather indifferent about different options for financing, and, in general, interstate transfers ranked low on their political agenda.

A key argument in this book, however, is that crisis politics needs to be understood as choices among bad options, which are characterized by trade-offs. In a setting in which groups strongly disagree about the desirability of different policy options, it is hardly possible to implement forms of domestic expansion suiting everybody's interests. Understanding what drives decisions between costly alternatives is especially important in such contexts. Therefore, we now turn to a closer analysis of how interest groups responded to the trade-offs inherent in Eurozone crisis management. To examine how interest groups weighed the different policies and adjustment strategies relative to one another, we asked them to choose between different customized crisis responses that embodied these trade-offs. Respondents were asked to choose between three policy packages that correspond to the three adjustment strategies: Internal adjustment (internal adjustment policies, limited financing, and no external adjustment), external adjustment (no internal adjustment, no financing, and external adjustment, i.e., a breakup of the Eurozone), and financing (no internal adjustment, extensive financing, and no external adjustment).

Because both our theoretical argument and our empirical analysis so far suggest that interest groups' choices between these options should vary by policy, especially within the internal adjustment and the financing options, we constructed two different choice sets and asked respondents to indicate their preferred policy package for each of the two scenarios. A first set included those policies that interest groups had evaluated most favorably and, thus, presented them with a setting in which trade-offs were relatively small. A second set, however, confronted respondents with a much more difficult choice; it included only bad options—that is, those policies that interest groups had opposed most strongly.

To customize the choice sets, we asked interest groups not only to rate the different policies listed in Table 6.1 but also to rank these policy options within each crisis strategy from their most- to their least-preferred option. We then used these rankings to build customized policy packages that reflected internal adjustment, external adjustment, and financing. Figure 6.9 shows how the different

198 THE POLITICS OF BAD OPTIONS

Q: "Assume that your organization would have had the choice between the following hypothetical policy packages during the Euro crisis. Which one do you think would suit the interests of your member best?"

A	B	C
• Provision of emergency credits to crisis countries	• No changes with regard to German economic policies	• No changes with regard to German economic policies
• Highest-ranked internal adjustment policy	• No financial support for crisis countries	• Highest-ranked financing policy
• 2nd highest-ranked internal adjustment policy	• Highest-ranked Eurozone breakup scenario	• 2nd Highest-ranked financing policy
• All members of the Eurozone remain in the EMU		• All members of the Eurozone remain in the EMU

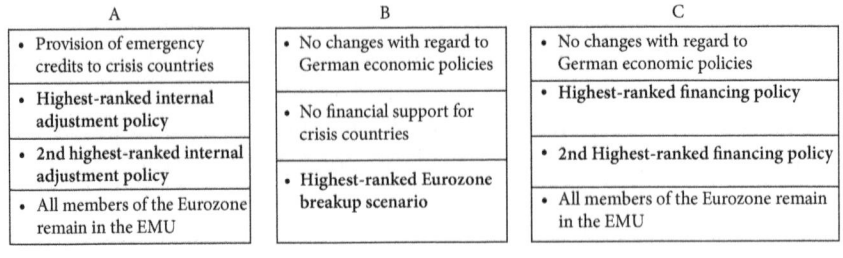

Figure 6.9 Customized construction of choice set for the three different crisis strategies

packages were presented to respondents. For each of the two choice sets, respondents were shown three hypothetical policy packages and were asked to choose one package. We use this exercise to generate two categorical variables: One that records interest groups' choice of crisis strategy in a less constrained context and one that records their choice in a highly constrained context, where interest groups are forced to choose between bad (i.e., their least preferred) policy packages.

How did interest groups choose when confronted with these different choice sets? Figure 6.9 shows their choices in each of the two scenarios. On the left-hand side, we see interest groups' preferred crisis strategies in all three countries when the policy packages include those policies that the interest group had previously ranked as its most preferred among the different options for internal adjustment, financing, and a breakup of the Eurozone. In contrast to much existing work that assumes economic interest groups in surplus countries uniformly oppose any policies that might undermine export competitiveness (Baccaro and Pontusson 2016; Hall 2012; Iversen et al. 2016; Steinberg and Vermeiren 2015), we find that an overwhelming majority of groups actually favored such internal adjustment, as long as it comes in forms meeting their interests. Support for internal adjustment ranges from about 67 percent in Germany and the Netherlands to more than 80 percent in Austria. Support for financing, on the other hand, remains below 20 percent in both Germany and Austria and below 30 percent in the Netherlands. Echoing our findings above, less than 10 percent of the interest groups in the three countries would support a breakup of the monetary union—even if it comes in the form they rated as the least objectionable among the different options for external adjustment.

This picture changes dramatically in the highly constrained scenario, in which we asked groups to select their preferred crisis strategy among policy packages containing only bad options. The panels on the right-hand side of Figure 6.10 show that the popularity of internal adjustment drops substantially when the

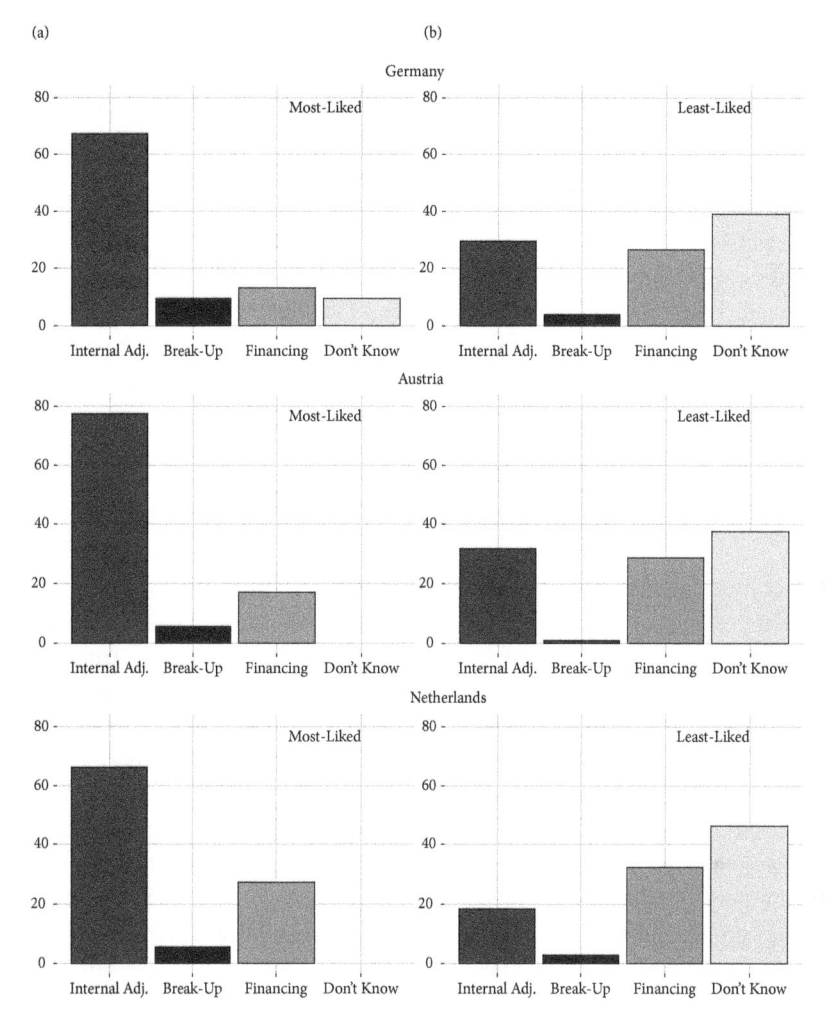

Figure 6.10 Choice between most-preferred (left) and least-preferred (right) crisis strategies

Note: Choice between customized policy packages containing most-preferred (left) and least-preferred (right) policies.

policy packages contain only the options least preferred by the interest groups. In Germany and Austria, only 30 percent of the respondents remain supportive of internal adjustment in this scenario, whereas in the Netherlands support drops below 20 percent. At the same time, external adjustment becomes even less popular. Less than 5 percent of interest groups in all three countries would support their least-preferred form of a Eurozone breakup in this scenario. While support for internal and external adjustment is reduced, financing becomes significantly more attractive. In Germany and Austria, it is almost as high as support for domestic expansion, and in the Netherlands, it turns into the most popular crisis response. When the trade-offs are difficult and all choices are bad, interest groups also find it significantly harder to voice clear preferences. In all three countries, the modal response is "don't know"—many interest groups simply declined to choose in such a highly constrained context.

Our analysis underscores once more that support for different adjustment strategies is policy-specific. Whether or not an interest group supports internal or external rebalancing, or financing hinges on how these crisis strategies are designed. When internal adjustment comes in the form of policies they support, most groups support such a rebalancing. But when they are confronted with difficult choices among bad options, support for internal adjustment drops and financing becomes more attractive.

Vulnerability Profiles and Preferred Crisis Responses

Rather than exhibit a fundamental opposition to internal rebalancing of the economy, surplus country interest groups seem finely attuned to the distributive consequences of different possible crisis policies and strategies. To explore how interest groups deal with the trade-offs inherent in crisis management, we next explore how interest groups' vulnerability profiles shape how interest groups make difficult choices among bad options. As discussed above, we expect domestic economic interest groups to form their crisis preferences based on the relative net costs or benefits of internal and external adjustment and the net costs of engaging in financing. This suggests that when pressed to choose, they should opt for the policy package that benefits them the most and costs them the least. As long as groups benefit from the internal adjustment policy under consideration, we expect them to support domestic rebalancing. Financing, on the other hand, should become attractive when interest groups are confronted with trade-offs between bad options that push them into the "misery corner" of the vulnerability profile in which they are vulnerable to both the specific policies proposed for internal adjustment and a Eurozone breakup.

To explore how the interest groups' vulnerability profiles are related to how they make difficult choices, we thus need to construct these profiles in a policy-specific way. To proxy the interest groups' policy-specific vulnerabilities, we construct their vulnerabilities to their most-preferred and least-preferred policy options, drawing more on their ratings and rankings of the policy options shown in Table 6.1. Because our analysis has shown that interest groups' policy evaluations are related to their material interests, we use their policy evaluations of their most-preferred and least-preferred policy options, respectively, as proxies for these policy-specific vulnerabilities. We assume that groups would benefit from policies they support and are vulnerable to policies they oppose, which allows us

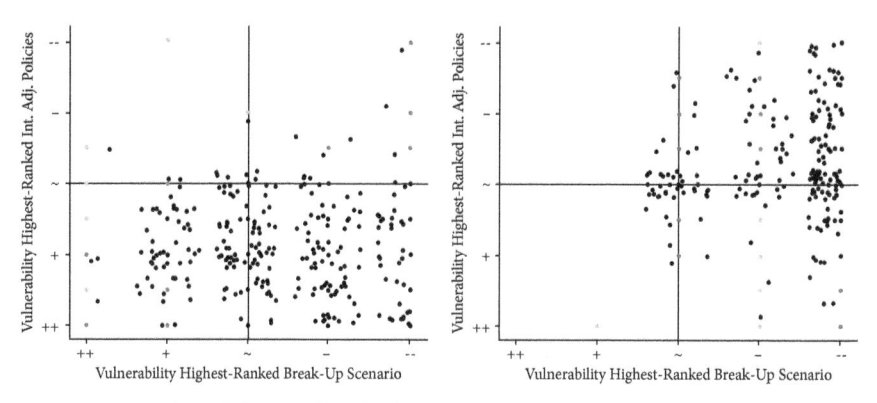

Figure 6.11 Vulnerability profiles for highest-ranked (left) and lowest-ranked (right) policies

to plot each group's vulnerability profiles for its most-preferred and its least-preferred policy options.

Figure 6.11 shows the results of this exercise. It plots interest groups' policy-specific vulnerability to external adjustment on the horizontal axis and plots vulnerability to internal adjustment on the vertical axis. The left-hand panel shows interest groups' vulnerability profiles vis-à-vis their most-preferred types of internal and external adjustment. This panel illustrates that almost 52 percent are located in quadrant IV and would thus benefit from internal adjustment but be hurt by the proposed form of a breakup. Another 28 percent combine benefitting from internal adjustment with being indifferent about the suggested form of external adjustment. Taking these groups together, it is not surprising that almost seven out of ten interest groups support a macroeconomic rebalancing through domestic expansion in this scenario.

The picture changes drastically, however, when we examine vulnerabilities toward the interest groups' least-preferred policies for internal and external adjustment. We see not only a strong increase in those that are very vulnerable to external adjustment but also a significant increase in interest groups who are vulnerable to internal adjustment. As a result, a large number of interest groups (42 percent) cluster in quadrant II, the misery corner, and would be hurt by both internal and external adjustment. Not surprisingly, as we have seen in Figure 6.10, this scenario corresponds to a massive drop in support for boosting domestic demand and an increase in support for financing.

Our data also allow us to analyze the relationship between interest groups' vulnerabilities and their choices between different crisis strategies more systematically. For this analysis, we focus on choices in the constrained trade-offs scenario in which groups have to choose between crisis strategies that contain their least-preferred policies. Because not even 3 percent of our respondents chose a Eurozone breakup in the least-preferred scenario, we focus on analyzing interest groups' choices for internal adjustment and financing. We recode our dependent variables into two dummy variables that take the value of 1 if a group chose internal adjustment or financing, respectively, and 0 if it did not. Because our argument suggests that adjustment decisions are driven by policy-specific vulnerabilities, our main independent variables are each group's policy-specific vulnerabilities (proxied by the respective rating) toward the least-preferred policies in the trade-off scenario. To make sure that our findings are not driven by a group's general position toward internal and external adjustment, we control for their average evaluations of all remaining policy options within each crisis strategy (i.e., all policies that are not included in the hard trade-off scenario). Because ideas-based approaches emphasize the importance of ideology, we also control for the general opinion about European integration[16] of the groups and their overall attitude toward the role of the state in the economy.[17] We also include country fixed effects.

Table 6.2 presents the results of probit regression analyses in which interest groups are more likely to choose internal adjustment (models 1 and 2) and in which they are more likely to choose financing (models 3 and 4) when confronted with difficult choices. The results show that in line with our argument, interest groups' vulnerabilities are, indeed, related to the choice of crisis strategies. The more vulnerable groups are towards the internal adjustment policies in question, the less likely they are to support domestic expansion, whereas a higher vulnerability toward external adjustment increases the propensity to support internal adjustment.[18] In contrast, interest groups' evaluations of the other internal and external adjustment policies do not have an effect. This is not surprising to the extent that these policies are not on offer, but it also suggests that the choice for internal adjustment is not driven by a general support for macroeconomic rebalancing. Interestingly, ideology has no statistically significant effect on this choice, neither regarding the interest groups' evaluation of European integration nor of state interventions more generally.

For groups that find themselves with a vulnerability profile in the "misery corner," which has a high vulnerability to external and internal adjustment, financing should be an attractive alternative. And, indeed, the more an interest group is vulnerable to internal adjustment, and to a lesser extent external adjustment, the more likely it is to choose financing as its preferred crisis strategy

---

[16] "Now thinking about the European Union, some say European integration should go further. Others say it has already gone too far. Where does your organization stand on this question?" (1 = "Has gone too far"; 5 = "Should go further").

[17] "It's a fundamental question of economic policy, whether the government should actively intervene in the economy and regulate the economy or whether economic processes should be left to the market only. Where does your organization stand on this question?" (1 = "Comprehensive interventions"; 5 = "No interventions at all").

[18] The latter effect is not always statistically significant. Recall that most groups opposed external adjustment, so this variable varies much less than the internal adjustment variables.

Table 6.2 Probit regression—vulnerabilities and likelihood of choosing adjustment strategies

	Adjustment Choice—Least-Liked Packages			
	Internal Adjustment		Financing	
	(1)	(2)	(3)	(4)
Vulnerability to lowest-ranked internal adjustment policies	−0.357***	−0.380***	0.227**	0.246**
	(0.100)	(0.108)	(0.095)	(0.101)
Vulnerability to other internal adjustment policies	0.057	0.069	−0.210*	−0.201
	(0.114)	(0.131)	(0.120)	(0.140)
Vulnerability to lowest-ranked external adjustment option	0.262**	0.194	0.237**	0.149
	(0.123)	(0.136)	(0.111)	(0.128)
Vulnerability to other external adjustment options	0.138	0.141	0.110	0.100
	(0.088)	(0.098)	(0.086)	(0.091)
Market liberalism		0.039		−0.005
		(0.080)		(0.085)
European integration		0.116		0.009
		(0.086)		(0.090)
Austria dummy	−0.035	0.045	0.066	0.149
	(0.185)	(0.204)	(0.189)	(0.202)
Netherlands dummy	−0.417**	−0.293	0.201	0.219
	(0.195)	(0.217)	(0.186)	(0.203)
McFadden R-Square	0.13	0.25	0.12	0.23
Observations	333	282	333	282

Note: * $p<0.1$, ** $p<0.05$, *** $p<0.01$

(models 3 and 4). As before, we do not find a significant effect of interest groups' vulnerability to those internal and external adjustment policies not included in the policy packages or ideological factors.

To illustrate these results, Figure 6.12 plots the predicted probabilities of choosing internal adjustment and financing across different levels of policy-specific vulnerability toward internal adjustment. Given that virtually all interest groups opposed external adjustment, these plots assume that groups' vulnerability to external adjustment is high. Figure 6.12 shows that the probability a group prefers financing increases the more vulnerable it is to the proposed form of internal adjustment. When an interest group strongly supports all internal adjustment policies, including its least-preferred one, it will choose domestic rebalancing with a predicted probability of almost 60 percent, which is in line with its vulnerability profile in quadrant III. In contrast, the likelihood that the group will opt for financing stands at less than 20 percent. Results are reversed for interest groups in the "misery corner," who are very vulnerable to both the internal and external

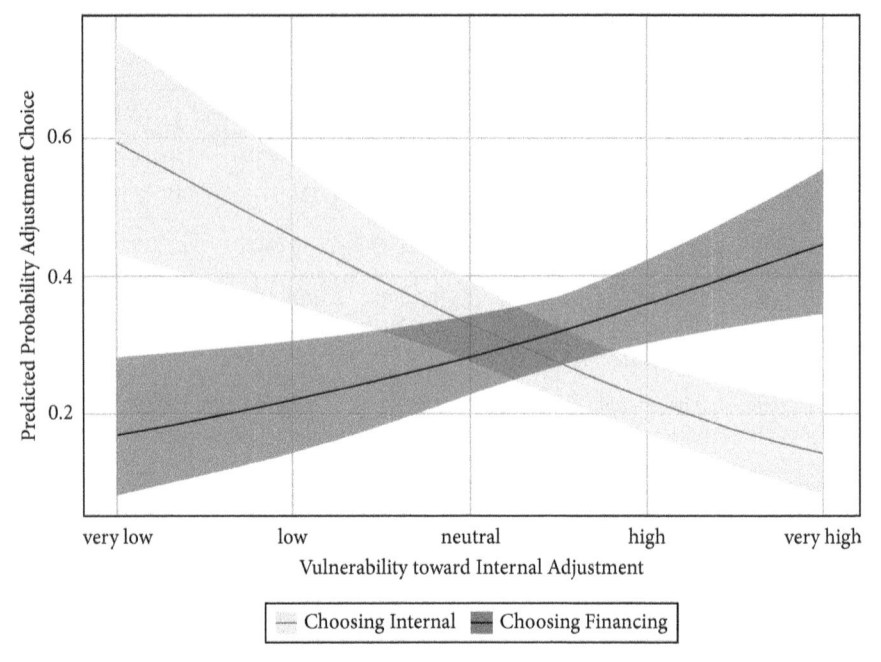

Figure 6.12 Predicted probabilities of choosing internal adjustment and financing at different levels of vulnerability toward internal adjustment

adjustment policies in the proposed policy packages. As expected, these interest groups are predicted to select internal adjustment with a probability of only about 10 percent, whereas the likelihood that they will opt for financing rises to over 40 percent.

Our analysis so far has shown that a majority of groups prefer internal adjustment over other possible crisis responses as long as domestic expansion is achieved through policies that serve their interests. The costs and benefits of different internal adjustment policies, however, differ across groups. Distributional conflicts about how to rebalance the economy thus make it a politically difficult strategy to pursue. However, opposition to specific internal adjustment policies is also associated with more support for financing, even in its unpopular variants, which is especially true, since a large majority of groups feel vulnerable to external adjustment. Together with the low salience of financing policies, this makes international transfers attractive.

Conclusion

Domestic economic interests have played a key role in the way surplus countries in the Eurozone approached the Eurozone crisis. Knowing how different economic interest groups positioned themselves during the crisis, what kind of adjustment strategies they supported, and which options they opposed is crucial to gain a thorough understanding of the politics of the crisis. In this chapter, we have used a wide range of newly collected quantitative and qualitative data to study the preferences of interest groups in Germany, Austria, and the Netherlands.

Our results show that different types of interest groups, such as employer associations, trade unions, or social policy groups, varied significantly in their support for and opposition to specific possible crisis policies, especially regarding internal adjustment and a to a lesser extent financing. Whereas a large majority of interest groups supported internal adjustment via policies that were to their advantage, support dropped significantly when internal adjustment involved policies to which they were opposed. At the same time, interest groups' vulnerability profiles informed their choice among crisis strategies, especially when confronted with difficult choices involving only bad options. For those interest groups who were vulnerable to both internal and external adjustment, financing turned into an especially attractive option.

Several findings stand out. First, we find that a large majority of economic interest groups reject any kind of Eurozone breakup. While there is some variation in the perception of different scenarios of external adjustment, most groups operate under the impression that any change in the composition of the monetary union would have enormous costs for their members. Just like in deficit states, the support for EMU also remained strong among surplus country interest groups throughout the crisis. Second, the lack of internal adjustment in such countries as Germany, Austria, and the Netherlands is not only rooted in ordoliberal ideas, but also in distributional conflicts about the design of possible adjustment policies. Although we find strong general support for strengthening domestic demand, different groups disagree heavily about how to achieve this goal, which turns internal adjustment into a politically difficult crisis strategy. At the same time, many interest groups are willing to support financing as a way to resolve the Eurozone's problems, especially as the salience of this crisis response is surprisingly low. These findings highlight new aspects of the politics of non-adjustment surplus countries and suggest that distributional conflicts about the specific forms of internal adjustment, together with a large consensus to avoid a breakup of the union, made financing the politically most attractive alternative.

However, our results also pose a number of new questions. If interest groups were so impassionate about the costs of engaging in bailouts, debt forgiveness, or more institutionalized forms of international redistribution, why did surplus country governments, nonetheless, take such hawkish positions in international negotiations? And why did some countries, such as Austria, implement expansionary policies despite the fact that distributional conflicts about the design of such measures were similar as in the Netherlands and Germany? To answer these questions, the next chapter digs deeper into how interest group preferences interacted with public opinion, ordoliberal ideas, and the general economic climate in shaping domestic politics in surplus countries.

7
Crisis Politics in Surplus Countries
Caught between Voter Pressure and Interest Group Stalemate

Why have surplus countries been so unwilling to carry a larger share of the adjustment burden in the Eurozone crisis? In the previous chapter, we showed that domestic distributional conflicts among interest groups were a key factor impeding internal rebalancing in core countries. Based on the first systematic empirical study of interest group preferences in Austria, Germany, and the Netherlands, we showed that although most interest groups supported internal adjustment in the abstract, they were deeply divided on how to achieve it. At the same time, they also agreed that a breakup of the monetary union should be avoided, but were much less opposed to financing. Moreover, this structure of interest group preferences was very similar in all three surplus countries under investigation. We therefore concluded that this constellation of interest group preferences turned financing coupled with very limited domestic adjustment into the politically most expedient strategy for surplus country policymakers.

However, this conclusion seems at odds with two characteristics of surplus country policy responses to the Eurozone crisis. First, international transfers were not at all seen as "politically expedient" by policymakers. Rather, surplus countries, and especially Germany, were initially quite hesitant to provide bailouts and emergency loans (Sandbu 2015; Christina Schneider and Slantchev 2017). Throughout the crisis, they rejected most calls for more extensive transfers or the establishment of more permanent risk-sharing mechanisms at the European level and insisted that any financial support was granted only in exchange for harsh fiscal cuts and deep structural reforms in recipient countries (Armingeon and Cranmer 2017a; Schimmelfennig 2015; Wasserfallen and Lehner 2018). If important domestic interest groups were so accepting of financing measures directed toward rescuing the monetary union, why were surplus country governments so reluctant? A second puzzle emerges from the fact that despite a similar structure of interest group preferences, Germany, Austria, and the Netherlands differed substantially in the extent to which they engaged in internal adjustment during the crisis. Despite enormous international pressure, successive German governments did little to expand domestic demand. Austria, on the other hand, implemented a surprisingly large range of policies to strengthen domestic consumption and investment. Finally, instead of boosting domestic demand, the Dutch government initially implemented contractionary (rather than expansionary) policies and did very little to reduce the country's rapidly growing current account surplus. If interest group preferences were similar in all three countries, what explains these differences?

To address these questions, this chapter takes a closer look at the politics of crisis management in these three surplus countries. We argue that to understand surplus country crisis policies, we also need to take into account the role of voters and how their preferences about all three available crisis strategies—internal adjustment, external adjustment, and financing—interacted with interest group pressures to shape the policy decisions made by governments. A wide range of authors have emphasized that public opinion played an important role in shaping Eurozone crisis politics (Bechtel et al. 2017; Beramendi and Stegmueller 2016; Bernhard and Leblang 2016; Howarth and Rommerskirchen 2013; Schneider and Slantchev 2017). This chapter builds on this work and provides a systematic analysis of how domestic voters in general evaluated the different forms of internal adjustment, external adjustment, and financing, how their preferences interacted with those of organized interests, and how contextual factors determined whether voters or interest groups had more influence on the way surplus country governments approached the management of the crisis.

We argue that both interest groups and voters shaped crisis outcomes but that their vulnerability profiles and preferences differed substantially. Given these differences, issue salience was a key factor determining whether interest group politics or public opinion had a greater influence on governments' choices between different forms of external adjustment, internal adjustment, and financing. Although both voters and interest groups opposed a breakup of the monetary union, voters were much more skeptical about most forms of international transfers than were interest groups. Given the high salience of financing issues in national debates and electoral campaigns, this skepticism trumped the more open stance of interest groups and led surplus country governments to adopt very restrictive positions in international negotiations. At the same time, most voters were very open to measures that would stimulate the domestic economy, whereas interest groups were gridlocked and could not agree on how internal adjustment should be pursued. As long as good economic conditions reduced the salience of domestic economic reforms, this gridlock among interest groups meant that neither voters nor organized economic interests strongly pushed for internal adjustment. In this context, governments had ample room to follow their own ideological economic convictions or simply focus on other policy areas which largely resulted in non-adjustment. However, in contexts in which the state of the domestic economy became a salient issue, the public's support for internal adjustment led policymakers to disregard both interest group conflict and their own ideological reservations against state expansion and to engage in certain forms of internal rebalancing.

We conduct comparative case studies of crisis politics in Germany, Austria, and the Netherlands and consider a wide range of quantitative and qualitative evidence to examine this argument in detail. Our analysis proceeds in two steps. First, we draw upon a rich set of available public opinion data that allows us to trace how voters in surplus countries evaluated different policies that fell into the categories of internal adjustment, external adjustment, and financing. Based on this analysis, we show that voter preferences were remarkably similar across the three countries but that their preferences differed substantially from those of surplus country interest groups. Second, we conduct in-depth case studies of Eurozone crisis politics in our three surplus countries. Building on existing studies of the interplay between voters and interest groups, we use evidence from over thirty in-depth interviews with policymakers and interest group representatives and numerous primary sources to trace the dynamics and contextual factors that determined whether voters or interest groups were more influential in guiding how policymakers approached different crisis strategies.

Overall, our analysis shows that given the broad opposition of both voters and interest groups, external adjustment never became a politically viable option for surplus countries. Vocal and clear opposition from voters in all three countries blocked the route toward more encompassing financing approaches. Finally, more accommodating economic policies were pursued only in Austria, where the salience of the state of the domestic economy made expansionary policies electorally expedient and led the government to force economic interest groups to accept domestic reforms.

Voter Preferences about How to Resolve the Eurozone Crisis

Our book's central premise is that a full understanding of the politics of the Eurozone crisis requires an understanding of how key societal actors and policymakers evaluated all potential crisis responses, including those not chosen. For surplus countries, these options were threefold: First, external adjustment in the form of a breakup of the monetary union, second, internal adjustment via a boost to domestic demand that would increase imports and domestic inflation, and third, financing the current account deficits of countries in the Eurozone's deficit countries through financial transfers. In Chapter 6, we showed that interest group preferences about the desirability of each of these strategies differed considerably.

We now turn to voters and examine how surplus country voters evaluated these different policy options for managing the crisis, focusing on the same three surplus countries (Austria, Germany, and the Netherlands). To generate a comprehensive picture of voters' policy preferences, we combine data from multi-country surveys, such as the Eurobarometer, with a large number of national surveys that allow us to gauge voter preferences with respect to more specific issues in the domestic arena and as well as to trace the trajectory of public opinion over time. We first discuss voter preferences regarding each crisis strategy, starting with their positions on external adjustment and moving on to their positions on domestic rebalancing and finally financing. We then draw together this evidence and discuss what it means in the context of the book's vulnerability profile framework. We find that voters largely opposed a breakup of the monetary union, were quite supportive of a wide array of measures that could have contributed to internal adjustment, and remained deeply skeptical of virtually any form of international financing.

External Adjustment: Surplus Country Voters and a Breakup of the Eurozone

How did surplus country voters evaluate external adjustment? How did they view different scenarios of how the Eurozone might break up? To answer these questions, we explore three aspects of public opinion about the euro in our three surplus countries: The public's overall support for the euro, voters' support for their own country's exit from the common currency, and the public's views about an exit of individual deficit and debtor countries from the Eurozone.

In line with existing research (Hobolt and Leblond 2013; Roth, Jonung, and Nowak-Lehmann 2016), Figure 7.1 shows that an overwhelming majority of voters in surplus countries viewed the euro positively and retained this positive view of the common currency throughout the crisis. On average, about 68 percent of voters in Germany, 65 percent in Austria, and 60 percent in the Netherlands stated that overall the euro was a good thing for their country. That said, there was a sizeable increase in the share of surplus country voters who believed that the euro was a bad thing for their country between 2010 and 2013, when the

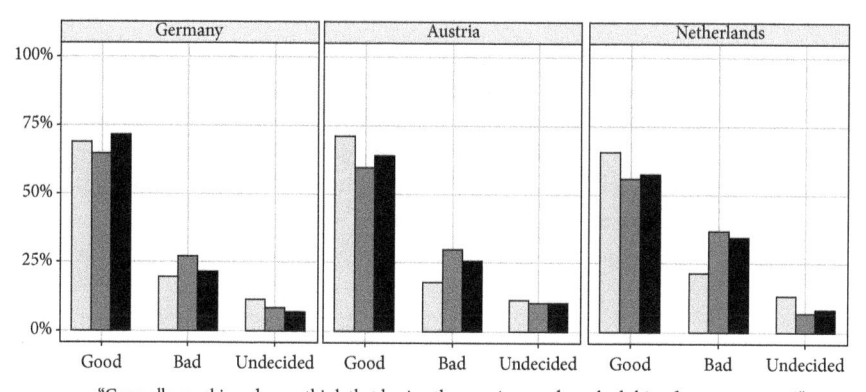

Figure 7.1 Overall evaluation of the Euro between 2013 and 2015

Eurozone crisis peaked. Nonetheless, throughout the crisis those with a generally positive view of the euro remained the clear majority in Germany, Austria, and the Netherlands.

This positive of evaluation of the euro was also mirrored by the fact that a clear majority of surplus country voters wanted their respective countries to keep the common currency. A wide range of studies has emphasized that Euroskepticism in Northern Europe increased throughout the crisis (Braun and Tausendpfund 2014; Hobolt and de Vries 2016a; De Vries 2018). Nonetheless, this did not translate into broad support for an exit from the monetary union. Various national surveys show that those who actually wanted their country to leave the Eurozone remained the clear minority. Yet that minority was not negligible, and it was much more pronounced than among interest groups. For example, every third respondent in both a 2011 survey in the Netherlands (De Hond 2011b) and a 2012 survey in Austria (OGM 2012) stated that their country should abandon the euro and return to a national currency.[1] And in Germany, every fourth respondent favored a German exit from the Eurozone in 2013 (Jung et al. 2015). Importantly, however, this support for a national withdrawal from the common currency was more concentrated among supporters of far-right parties such as the Alternative for Germany (AfD), the Freedom Party of Austria (FPÖ), and the Dutch Party for Freedom (PVV). In contrast, 79 percent of those voting for the government parties Christian Democratic Union (CDU) and Free Democratic Party (FDP) in Germany in 2013, and 65 percent of those voting for the People's Party for Freedom and Democracy (VVD) and the Labour Party (PvdA), which governed the Netherlands in 2011, wanted to remain in the Eurozone. To the extent that policymakers pay particular attention to the preferences of their own party's voters (Walter 2016), this means that surplus country governments confronted voters that overwhelmingly supported a continuation of their country's membership in the Eurozone.

Overall, voters in surplus countries also opposed an exit of other countries from the Eurozone. Rather than supporting an "external adjustment through the backdoor" by allowing or asking deficit countries to leave the Economic and Monetary Union (EMU), surplus country voters exhibited a strong aversion to such proposals. The best data available on this issue stems from a July 2011 poll in Germany. Figure 7.2 shows that a large majority of German respondents supported the continued membership of almost all crisis countries in the common currency.[2] Greece is the only case in which opinions on a potential exit from the

---

[1] In the Netherlands, 32%; in Austria, 35%.
[2] Although we lack surveys that asked similar questions about deficit countries to respondents in Austria and the Netherlands, given the consistency voters from the three countries showed on other items, we have little reason to believe that public opinion in these countries was dramatically different.

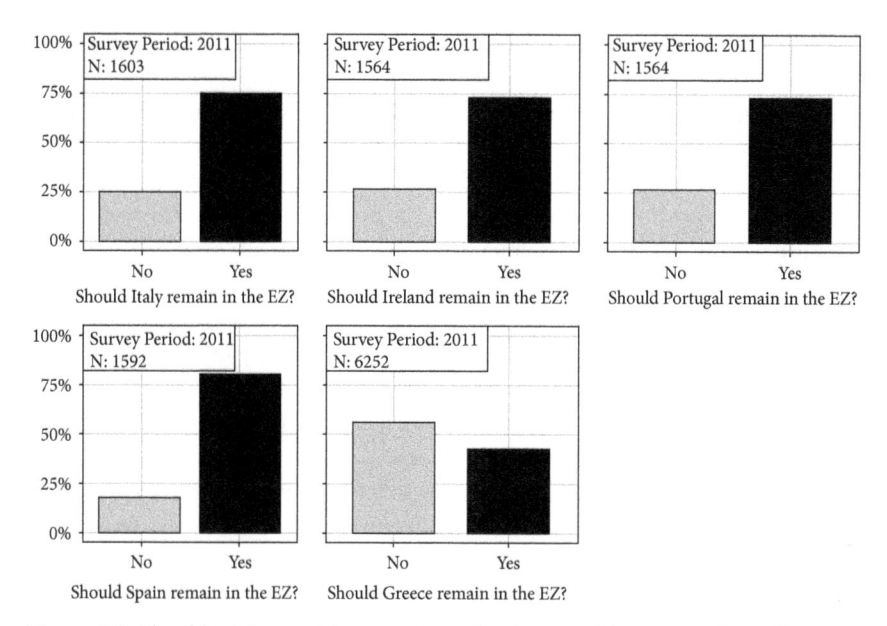

Figure 7.2 Should crisis countries remain in the Eurozone? Responses from Germany
Source: Jung, Schroth, and Wolf (2013)

Eurozone were more divided. But even in the case of Greece, there was not a clear popular push for Grexit. In 2012, a slight majority (53 percent) of German respondents stated that Greece should abandon the common currency. This sentiment remained quite stable over time, and the number of Grexit supporters did not even change during the spectacular negotiations about the third bailout in the summer of 2015 (Forschungsgruppe-Wahlen 2016). Surveys from Austria and the Netherlands point in a similar direction. In the Netherlands, supporters of a Grexit varied around 45 percent throughout the crisis period (De Hond 2011a, 2012, 2015). In Austria, the share of citizens that supported a Grexit actually decreased throughout the crisis. In 2012, more than 60 percent of Austrian respondents—a clear majority—were in favor of Greece leaving. However, by 2015 the share had decreased significantly to 45 percent (OGM 2015).

Our analysis thus leads us to conclude that in the Eurozone's three major surplus countries, public support for external adjustment was quite limited. Even though sizeable minorities supported a breakup of the monetary union in one form or another, this support was concentrated among those who voted for populist-right opposition parties. The parties in government, in contrast, were confronted with voters who—in line with surplus country interest groups— overwhelmingly rejected external adjustment.

Internal Adjustment: Public Opinion on Domestic Rebalancing

What did public opinion on internal rebalancing look like? Research emphasizing the role of ideas has often argued that the road toward an expansion of domestic demand in surplus countries is blocked by fiscally austere voters, who subscribe to the argument that domestic wage restraint is necessary to safeguard their country's export competitiveness (Bulmer 2014; Sattler and Haas 2018) and who love low government debts (Blyth 2013; Haffert 2016; Howarth and Rommerskirchen 2013; Matthijs 2016a). This suggests that during the Eurozone crisis, voters in surplus countries should on average have opposed expansionary measures designed to rebalance the economy, such as increases in government spending, efforts to increase wage growth, tax cuts, or new incentives for generating more private investment in the domestic economy.

However, national polls show that at the policy level, voters in surplus countries actually seemed to be very open to different forms of domestic expansion. Figures 7.3–7.5 depict public opinion on potentially expansionary policies, which were discussed in Germany, Austria, and the Netherlands, respectively, over the course of the Eurozone crisis. It shows that voters were quite supportive of a wide range of possible measures for domestic expansion.

In Germany, for example, public opinion was not overly orthodox in terms of public spending. In a 2010 survey, more than half (55 percent) of respondents stated that additional tax revenues should be used for tax cuts or more government spending, whereas only 43 percent were in favor of using such revenues to repay debts (Infratest-dimap 2016). The public also supported various policy measures designed to raise domestic wages. Panel (a) in Figure 7.3 shows that between 2011 and 2013, a strong and growing majority of ultimately over 70 percent of respondents supported the introduction of a nationwide stationary minimum wage, which became a major policy issue during that time and was eventually implemented in 2013. Voters were also supportive of wage growth in

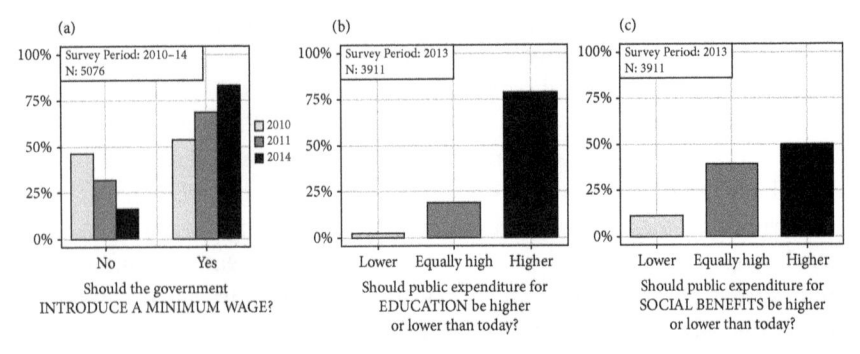

Figure 7.3 Public opinion on various forms of internal adjustment in Germany

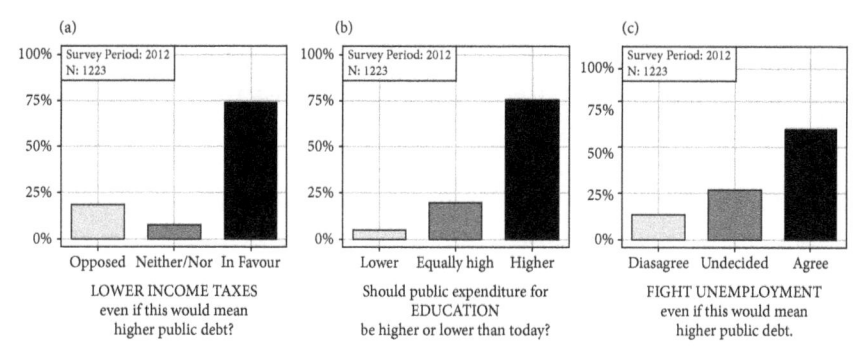

Figure 7.4 Public opinion on various forms of internal adjustment in Austria

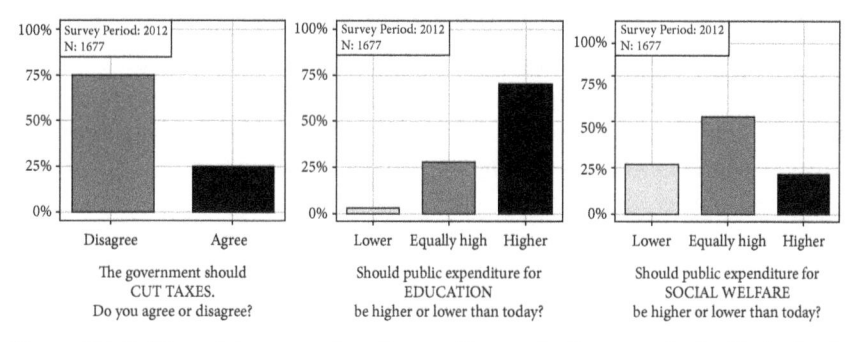

Figure 7.5 Public opinion on various forms of internal adjustment in the Netherlands

other segments of the income distribution. In a survey from 2010, about two-thirds of all respondents supported the statement that the economic recovery should first and foremost be used to increase the wages of workers in Germany (Infratest-dimap 2011). At the same time, German voters were also surprisingly favorable to increasing public spending. In 2013, more than 75 percent wanted the government to increase public investment in education, and there was even majority support for substantial increases of public spending on social welfare (see panels (b) and (c) in Figure 7.3). This support was also very broad. With the exception of supporters of the liberal FDP, support for the minimum wage, more spending on education, and increased expenditure for social welfare reached across party lines (Forschungsgruppe-Wahlen 2016; Jung et al. 2013, 2015; Rattinger et al. 2018).

The public was quite positive about internal adjustment in other surplus countries as well. In Austria, three-quarters of respondents in a 2013 survey agreed that the government should lower income taxes, even if such measures would lead to higher public debt, and that the state should invest more in education (panels (a) and (b) in Figure 7.4). And more than 60 percent of respondents felt that the government should fight unemployment even if this would lead to higher budget deficits (panel (c) in Figure 7.4).

Only in the Netherlands did public opinion exhibit less enthusiasm about policies designed to foster internal adjustment. In 2012, a clear majority opposed tax cuts (panel (a) in Figure 7.5), and only 25 percent supported increasing government spending on social welfare (panel (c) in Figure 7.5). As we will see later in the chapter, a possible explanation for this more restrictive stance is the fact that in 2012, the Netherlands itself struggled with rising levels of public debt and financial market pressures. However, even in these fiscally difficult times, a clear majority of voters favored more public spending in some areas, such as education (panel (b) in Figure 7.5).

Altogether, this evidence suggests that the lack of internal adjustment in surplus countries can hardly be explained by public skepticism and fiscal orthodoxy. Just like surplus country interest groups, the public seems to have been surprisingly open to implementing some forms of internal adjustment. Especially in Germany and Austria, there was plenty of room to garner public support for expansionary domestic policies, and even in the Netherlands, voters would have welcomed some expansionary measures.

Financing: Public Opinion on Financial Transfers to Deficit States

Voters were much more skeptical with regard to financing as a third possible crisis response. Most research on surplus country voter preferences on this issue finds that voters generally opposed the idea of redistributing money from surplus countries to deficit states (Beramendi and Stegmueller 2016; Hobolt and de Vries 2016a). There was considerable opposition not only to bailing out individual crisis countries (Bechtel et al. 2014, 2017) but also to the creation of European rescue funds (Stoeckel and Kuhn 2018), the provision of debt reliefs for struggling countries (Rathbun, Powers, and Anders 2018), and the establishment of more institutionalized transfer mechanisms such as European unemployment schemes or Eurobonds (Daniele and Geys 2015; Dolls and Wehrhöfer 2018; Kanthak and Spies 2018; Koller 2018).

One of the reasons for the widespread opposition among voters was that, contrary to our findings for interest groups, financing preferences at the individual level seemed to have been shaped largely by noneconomic factors. Extensive research has shown that opposition to different forms of international transfers was closely linked to voters' nationalist attachment and in-group loyalty (Bechtel et al. 2014; Daniele and Geys 2015; Kuhn et al. 2017), limited altruism (Kleider and Stoeckel 2018), conservative and Euroskeptical political attitudes (Bauhr and Charron 2018; Stoeckel and Kuhn 2018), and moral questions about fairness and retribution (Rathbun, Powers, and Anders 2018). Importantly, these cultural factors seemed to matter more for voters' preferences than did the individual material costs and benefits they attached to financing policies. In general, however, extensive research has shown that public opinion in surplus countries was characterized by widespread opposition to financing and that although some voters reacted to partisan cues on the issue (Stoeckel and Kuhn 2018), rejection did not seem to be correlated with political sophistication, general political interest, or media consumption. Against this background, public opposition to transfers was relatively stable over time and, once established, hard to move into a more generous direction (Rathbun, Powers, and Anders 2018.).

Yet it is also important to note that respondents were quite attentive to the type of financing provided. For example, German respondents were much more likely to support smaller bailout packages for Greece and packages in which Germany's relative share of the financial burden was smaller. Also, voters' grew more supportive of financial transfers, if bailouts were linked to strict economic conditionality (Bechtel et al. 2017).

A brief review of national polls confirms that surplus country voters were deeply skeptical about financing. Figure 7.6 shows that throughout the crisis, a clear majority of voters opposed even the general idea that their countries should financially support other member states in times of crisis. In Germany, more than 60 percent stated that their country should not support other member states in need. Other surveys show that the German electorate was not more forthcoming when asked about more specific forms of financing. More than 80 percent opposed the expansion of the European Financial Stability Facility in 2011, and more than 70 percent were against providing additional resources to the European Stability Mechanism in 2012 (Jung et al. 2013, 2014). Furthermore, 84 percent of all Germans opposed the introduction of Eurobonds, and 56 percent thought the German government should not have agreed to the haircut on Greek debt owed to

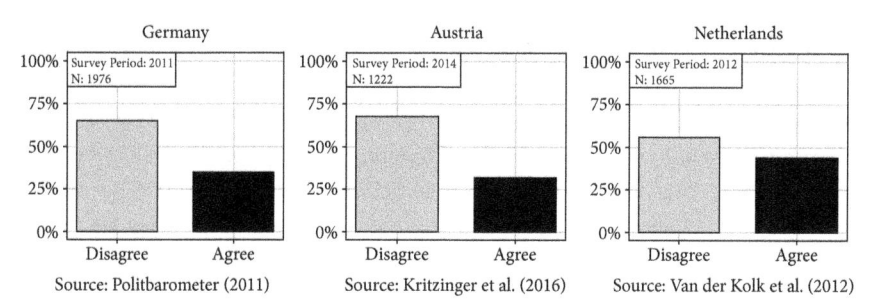

"In times of crisis [your country] should financially support EU member states that suffer from economic and financial distress."

Figure 7.6 Public opinion on financing

private banks in 2011 (Jung et al. 2013, 2014). Importantly, this distribution did not differ substantially across party lines. With the exception of Green parties, a majority of supporters of all major parties opposed the general premise of international financial support in times of crisis.

Moreover, Figure 7.6 illustrates that even though much of the existing literature on financing preferences has focused on Germany, skepticism regarding international transfers also characterized public opinion in Austria and the Netherlands. Almost 70 percent of all Austrians and a majority of Dutch respondents opposed the provision of financial support to crisis countries.[3] Other surveys confirm this picture. In 2011, 64 percent of all Austrians opposed the creation of new rescue funds at the European level,[4] and in the same year about 60 percent of Dutch voters stated that their government should stop lending money to countries in crisis (Austria Presse Agentur 2011; De Hond 2011).

Overall, voters in all surplus countries throughout the crisis remained deeply skeptical of financing as a response to the euro crisis. Although public opinion on external and internal adjustment was similar to interest groups' views regarding potential crisis policies, they differed significantly with regard to the financing strategy: Whereas financing was mostly a low-salience issue for interest groups, more far-reaching reforms for international transfers and risk sharing elicited the support or at least a lack of opposition from a majority of interest groups. In contrast, financing was a salient issue for voters, and public support for redistributive measures that benefitted deficit countries was quite limited.

Diverging Preferences: Public Opinion and Interest Group Preferences in the Euro Crisis

Table 7.1 summarizes how voters evaluated the three possible strategies followed by surplus countries in the management of the Eurozone crisis. First, the crisis did spark a significant proliferation of anti-European sentiments in all surplus countries. However, the group of voters who actually would have welcomed a breakup of the monetary union remained a clear minority, and on aggregate, surplus countries' electorate opposed external adjustment. Second, at the policy level, voters would have welcomed a wide array of measures designed to stimulate domestic demand and wage growth. Although we lack detailed information on interest group preferences for comparable polices across all countries for voters, national surveys show that public opinion did not constitute a major hurdle for

---

[3] In the Netherlands, respondents were asked whether their country should "lend money to" instead of "financially support" member states suffering from economic and financial distress (Kolk et al. 2012). This wording might explain the slightly higher share of supporters.

[4] https://diepresse.com/home/wirtschaft/economist/704181/Oesterreicher-lehnen-EURettungsschirm-ab

Table 7.1 Voter and interest group preferences on crisis strategies

	External Adjustment	Internal Adjustment	Financing
VOTERS	↓	↑	↓
INTEREST GROUPS	↓	↑↓	↑

internal adjustment. Finally, extensive academic research and public opinion polls show that a large majority of voters in surplus countries remained very skeptical about international transfers. Given that most voters wanted to avoid a breakup of the monetary union, public opposition to financing might seem surprising. However, existing studies have also shown that in contrast to the attitudes of economic interest groups, voters' attitudes toward international redistribution and risk sharing were driven much more by nonmaterial factors such as national attachment and redemption than by cold cost–benefit analyses.

The overview in Table 7.1 also allows for a comparison of the preferences of voters with the positions of interest groups, which we analyzed in Chapter 6. Although both voters and interest groups opposed a breakup of the monetary union, their preferences diverged with respect to the other two possible crisis responses. Contrary to voters' welcoming stance, distributional conflicts about the microeconomic effects of various expansionary policies made internal adjustment a costly strategy to pursue for economic interest groups. Moreover, interest groups did not share voters' skepticism with respect to financing and would have been open to a wide array of potentially stabilizing measures.

Given the differences in preferences between voters and interest groups, it becomes important to identify the preferences responsible for setting the more vigorous constraints for policymakers and to determine how the influence of voters and interest groups differed across various policies and adjustment strategies. Before we discuss our case studies of crisis politics, the next section therefore builds on existing studies of interactions between voters and interest groups to guide our theoretical expectations.

Voters, Interest Groups, and Eurozone Crisis Politics in Surplus Countries

Our analyses have shown that although both voters and interest groups in surplus countries rejected external adjustment as a path to Eurozone crisis resolution, they differed significantly in their assessments of the merits of internal adjustment and financing. A key question for the study of crisis politics in surplus countries is therefore whose preferences were more influential in guiding policymakers' decisions regarding the management of the euro crisis.

Existing research on the politics of the euro crisis has been divided on this question. One set of studies has emphasized that public opinion and voter preferences were key determinants of the way surplus countries responded to the Eurozone's problems. These studies have built on the general idea that, in democracies, politicians are responsive to the interests of potential voters, because citizens use the ballot box to hold governments and legislators accountable for their political decisions (Dahl 1971; Downs 1957; Esaiasson and Wlezien 2017). As a result, democratically elected policymakers, even in the context of European policymaking, have strong incentives to turn voters' preferences into policy (Hagemann et al. 2017; Schneider 2018).[5] From this perspective, the decisions made by surplus country governments during the Eurozone crisis were therefore shaped primarily by domestic electoral considerations (Armingeon and Cranmer 2017a; Bernhard and Leblang 2016). Concerns about public opinion and rising levels of Euroskepticism made surplus countries hesitant to support international bailouts (Schneider and Slantchev 2017) and further fiscal integration (Börzel and Risse 2018), both of which were largely rejected by a majority of voters. Likewise, especially in Germany—the most extensively studied surplus country—the lack of internal adjustment reflected voters' fiscal conservatism, inflation aversion, and preference for balanced budgets (Bonatti and Fracasso 2013; Bulmer 2014; Haffert 2016; Howarth and Rommerskirchen 2013) but also voters' beliefs that current account surpluses were a desirable sign of economic strength (Iversen and Soskice 2018; Sattler and Haas 2018). In sum, this first line of research has argued that surplus country policies reflected voter preferences in these countries.

A second line of research has emphasized the influence of special interests on surplus countries' policy responses to the Eurozone crisis. Starting from the observation that the congruence between public opinion and policy outcomes is often limited (Matsusaka 2010; Wlezien and Soroka 2012), these studies have built on a large body of research on the influence of organized interest groups on political outcomes (Dür and Bièvre 2007; Gilens and Page 2014; Grossman and Helpman 2001; Hacker and Pierson 2010; Klüver 2013). Such groups have at their disposal a wide array of means to shape policies. They can directly sway policymakers through campaign contributions (Baumgartner et al. 2009; Kalla and Broockman 2016) and by mobilizing the electoral support of their members (Klüver 2018). They can influence policy outcomes by providing expertise and special knowledge on complex issues (Culpepper 2011), by shaping the (expected)

---

[5] We leave aside here the debate about the extent to which voters' policy preferences can be shaped by elite cues (see, for example, Steenbergen, Edwards, and Vries 2007).

economic consequences of certain policy decisions (Culpepper and Reinke 2014; Lindblom 1977), or even, especially in corporatist settings, through direct involvement in bodies of formal consultation and institutions for governmental decision-making (Martin and Swank 2012; Schmitter and Streeck 1991). Economic interest groups thus also shaped surplus country policymaking in the Eurozone crisis. A number of studies have argued that governments' willingness to engage in limited international bailouts was largely a tool for protecting the interests of exposed domestic banks (Blyth 2013; Frieden and Walter 2017; Hall 2012; Tarlea et al. 2019). This research has maintained that the initial opposition of Germany, Austria, and the Netherlands to any form of debt forgiveness for deficit states reflected the need to buy their own banks the time to eliminate risky assets from the periphery (Steinberg and Vermeiren 2015; Thompson 2015). At the same time, the road toward more encompassing fiscal transfers was blocked by producer groups in export industries, which perceived more far-reaching transfers as detrimental to their interests in austere fiscal policies and wage restraint at home (Hall 2018b; Höpner and Lutter 2014; Steinberg and Vermeiren 2015). Similarly, these studies argue that surplus countries' unwillingness to rebalance their current accounts was rooted in a broad coalition of domestic employer groups and trade unions that depended either directly or indirectly on the performance of the export sector (Hall 2012; Iversen et al. 2016). According to this literature, the need to preserve competitiveness on international markets thus led a powerful coalition of both employer associations and trade unions in affected industries to lobby against any internal adjustment measures that could produce higher inflation, and a rise of the domestic wage level (Bonatti and Fracasso 2013; Hall 2014; Moravcsik 2012; Stockhammer 2016).

Existing research has thus demonstrated that both electoral concerns and interest group pressure influenced the way surplus country governments chose to manage the Eurozone crisis. At the same time, our own analysis of interest group and voter preferences shows that neither of these groups were fully successful in shaping policy outcomes in line with their preferences. Had surplus country governments cared most about implementing policies in line with voter preferences, they would have been more restrictive in terms of financing and would have instead engaged more in implementing popular expansionary policies at home. In contrast, had crisis politics been dominated exclusively by special interests, surplus countries would have been much more forthcoming about international transfers, and distributional conflicts among interest groups would have effectively ruled out any form of internal adjustment.

The fact that neither of these scenarios played out suggests that policies were the outcome of the interplay between domestic voter preferences, special interest influence, government agency, and the more general domestic and international context in which the Eurozone crisis played out. An extensive literature on the interplay between voters and interest groups in the policymaking process (Becker

1983; Dixit and Londregan 1996; Grossman and Helpman 2001; Stigler 1971) shows that both voter and interest group preferences usually matters to policymakers. Second, governments' own ideas and preferences shape the policies they implement, including crisis responses. And finally, in a setting such as an international economic crisis, policymaking is also constrained by a number of contextual factors, such as economic developments or the actions and policy positions of other countries involved in crisis management. Taken together, this suggests that governments were neither the long arm of organized interests nor did they simply bow to electoral and external pressures. Instead, national political elites in surplus countries often had and made use of the considerable room to maneuver to manage the crisis within the realm of external constraints.

This raises the question under which circumstances which considerations matter most. Existing work suggests that voter preferences constrain policymakers' room to maneuver most on issues that are highly salient to voters (Armingeon and Giger 2008; Burstein 2003; Stimson et al. 1995) and on which they have consistent views (Busemeyer, Garritzmann, and Neimanns 2020). On such salient issues, voters are likely to monitor how candidates and parties position themselves and will hold them accountable for their standpoints in future elections (Bélanger and Meguid 2008; Reher 2014). For Eurozone politics, this suggests that governments' incentives to pursue policies in line with public sentiment—even if these policies were at odds with the preferences of important economic groups or their own ideological convictions—should have been particularly strong for those crisis strategies and policies to which voters played particular attention and on which they had relatively consistent views.

However, the political clout of public opinion wanes, the more disinterested voters become. The realm of the "quiet politics" (Culpepper 2011) that characterizes nonsalient issues provides an ideal terrain for organized groups with concentrated interests (Keller 2018). In this context, the preferences and power resources of interest groups are likely to outweigh policymakers' concerns for the preferences of largely disinterested voters. For Eurozone crisis politics, this suggests that the less salient certain policies become in the eyes of the electorate, the more the preferences of interest groups should dominate the trade-offs governments face. The salience of policies can also vary within each of the three possible crisis strategies: Voters may pay attention to some aspects or forms of external or internal adjustment or financing, but not to others. This gives policymakers some room to maneuver within each of these strategies.

Finally, governments' room to maneuver is largest when neither voters nor interest groups push strongly in favor of or against specific policies. In contexts in which voters are disinterested and in which, at the same time, interest groups are unwilling or unable to shape policymaking according to their interest, policymakers experience limited concerted pressure to follow specific polices. This opens up considerable room for governments to move in line with their own preferences and ideas. In such contexts, ideational factors such as ordoliberal convictions amongst key decision makers are likely to become an important driver of crisis politics (Blyth 2002; Dullien and Guérot 2012; Matthijs 2016a; Ryner 2015). For Eurozone crisis politics, this suggests that the ideas of national political elites should have been important drivers of policymaking on issues for which issue salience was low and interest groups were disunited. Because voters and interest groups differed in their vulnerabilities to and preferences regarding various crisis strategies during the Eurozone crisis, and because these preferences had different political weights in different contexts, this suggests that we should observe considerable variation in the degree to which different interests succeeded in influencing Eurozone crisis politics in line with their preferences.

In a nutshell, we expect public opinion to shape government behavior in contexts in which adjustment strategies were saliently discussed in national politics. But in contexts in which potential adjustment strategies gained little public attention, we expect the dynamics between interest groups to be more influential. If neither voters nor interest groups push for a specific crisis resolution, we expect governments to be much more able and likely to follow their own ideas and preferences. Finally, governments are constrained not only by voters and special interests, but also by the wider policymaking context, such as the macroeconomic setting (Bernhard et al. 2002; Clark and Hallerberg 2000), international processes and financial markets (Mosley 2000, 2003; Oatley 2011), and the negotiating positions of other countries (Lundgren et al. 2018). This suggests that surplus country policy responses to the Eurozone crisis should diverge most strongly from both voter and interest group preferences where the governments' room to maneuver was most constrained by the policymaking context.

Eurozone Crisis Politics in Germany, Austria, and the Netherlands

We trace this argument through comparative case studies of the crisis politics in the three biggest surplus countries: Germany, Austria, and the Netherlands. These cases are instructive because they have many similarities but also differ in important respects. All three countries positioned themselves in similar terms with regard to many European-level proposals for crisis resolution, as our analysis in Chapter 5 has shown. More generally, their crisis responses both shared important features and exhibited significant differences, especially with regard to internal adjustment. Whereas Germany did little to address its huge current account surplus and the Netherlands even fueled its export overhang by engaging in contractionary instead of expansionary domestic policies, Austria implemented a remarkably large array of measures to strengthen domestic demand and investment. These differences are somewhat surprising, because interest groups and, to a lesser extent, voters in these countries had rather similar preferences about external and internal adjustment as well as financing.

The three countries also share a number of features that could affect the relative influence of different voter segments and interest groups. They have similar electoral institutions (Iversen and Soskice 2006) and had comparable partisan dynamics during the crisis.[6] Interest group systems in all our cases are highly centralized, and strong peak organizations wield considerable political power. Finally, all three countries are coordinated market economies with long traditions of corporatist policymaking (Dür and Mateo 2013b; Hall and Soskice 2001; Paster 2013). Differences in crisis outcomes are therefore unlikely to stem from some important political or institutional dissimilarities across the three countries. However, the three countries varied considerably in their economic experiences during the crisis: Whereas Germany experienced an economic boom, Austria struggled with stagnation and rising unemployment, and the Netherlands only narrowly escaped a full-fledged economic crisis of its own. Comparing crisis politics in the three countries thus allows us to explore how the preferences of voters and interest groups shaped crisis politics in different contexts.

We focus our analysis on adjustment politics between 2010 and 2016, during which time the Eurozone crisis was a prominent issue in domestic (and European) politics. To trace crisis politics in this period, we conducted thirty in-depth qualitative interviews with policymakers and interest group representatives in the three countries. We selected interest groups based on their size and the importance of their members to the overall economy. We also made sure to conduct interviews with groups from all economic sectors as well as trade unions representing workers at different skill and income levels. Overall, the interviews aimed at corroborating our survey results and expanding our understanding of interest groups' positions and actions during the Eurozone crisis. We also conducted interviews with twelve policymakers, who were either legislators who had been actively involved in decisions about the crisis or high-ranking officials in the responsible departments in the ministries for finance and economic affairs.[7] The main aim of our interviews with policymakers was to understand their perceptions of the different societal preferences and to trace how these preferences played into decision-making. A complete list of all our interview partners can be found in Table A7.1 in the Appendix to this chapter. We complement the insights gained through these interviews with other sources, ranging from protocols of parliamentary debates and committee discussions to newspaper articles and other secondary sources.

---

[6] During the crisis, Germany and the Netherlands were first ruled by center-right-liberal coalitions and subsequently by grand coalitions between center-right and social demoS8cratic. Austria was ruled by a grand coalition between social democrats and the center-right Austrian People's Party.

[7] Interviews in Germany took place between November 27 and December 8, 2017. Interviews in Austria and the Netherlands took place between June 18 and June 22, 2018, and July 2 and July 6, 2018, respectively.

The goal of our analysis is to explore how interest group and voter preferences jointly influenced surplus country policymaking during the Eurozone crisis. We examine surplus country politics with regard to each of the three different adjustment strategies in turn. We start with the strategy of external adjustment, the avoidance of which attracted a large societal consensus. We then turn to financing, where interest group and voter preferences diverged considerably but where all three countries opted for a similar policy approach. The final section discusses internal adjustment, the strategy on which interest groups were most divided and on which the three surplus countries differed considerably in terms of implementation. By examining how public opinion, interest group pressure, and contextual factors jointly influenced surplus country policymaking during the crisis, we also address the two puzzles about surplus country crisis strategies discussed at the beginning of this chapter: The fact that surplus countries kept a tight rein on all attempts to establish a permanent European-level system of financial transfers even though such measures would have been supported by economic interests and could have provided significant efficiency and insurance gains (Beramendi and Stegmueller 2016; Schelkle 2017) and the fact that surplus countries differed in their approaches to internal adjustment, even though similar deep distributional conflicts between interest groups about how to adjust internally existed in all surplus states.

Not an Option: External Adjustment

As we have shown throughout this book, the question of how to resolve the Eurozone crisis was hotly contested. Nonetheless, there is one issue on which a remarkable consensus emerged quickly among voters, interest groups, and policymakers: The Eurozone was to be protected. As our interest group surveys show, four out of five interest groups opposed any form of a Eurozone breakup. Although this share was somewhat lower for voters, a clear majority of voters were equally opposed to external adjustment. The euro was also a highly salient issue for voters. A representative study from 2012 shows that almost 30 percent of all respondents in Germany singled out the European Union (EU) and the euro as the most important issue the country was facing. No other issue area was mentioned with the same frequency, and in 2013, more than 85 percent of German voters stated that the management of the euro crisis would matter or matter a lot for their voting decision (Jung et al. 2012, 2013). The euro crisis was also a dominant issue in the public debates in Austria and the Netherlands. In the run-up to the Austrian election in 2014, party positions on the euro and the EU were almost as important to Austrian voters as their stance on social and tax policies. The euro crisis thus outranked usual evergreens of domestic political debates, such as crime or the environment (Kolk et al. 2012; Kritzinger et al. 2016).

Dutch election studies from 2012 show a very similar pattern (Kolk et al. 2012; Kritzinger et al. 2016).

Given this consensus among major domestic stakeholders, it is unsurprising that the possibility of external adjustment was scooped off the political agenda early on and without much resistance. Policymakers in Germany, Austria, and the Netherlands never seriously considered external adjustment in the form of either leaving the monetary union or pushing deficit countries to leave. Importantly, this happened even though external adjustment would have been in line with the ordoliberal convictions of large parts of the German, Austrian, and Dutch bureaucracies and even some political decision-makers, who were deeply convinced that keeping countries which had violated fundamental rules of sound economic policymaking in the common currency would set a dangerous precedent and weaken the monetary union in the long run (Interviews DE4; DE11; AT9; see also Feld et al. 2015). Nonetheless, none of the mainstream parties in surplus countries regarded calling for a breakup of the union as a viable political position, and although ministries in all countries planned for a breakup, these steps were always regarded as preparing for a worst-case scenario (Interviews DE9; DE10; DE12; AT7; AT9; NL5; NL6). Several policymakers argued that politically, there was simply "no alternative" to keeping the Eurozone together, not only because the expected market upheavals and potential threat to the stability of the common currency would have hurt crucial economic sectors but also because there was little popular backing for any measure that could risk the stability of the union (Interviews DE12; AT9; NL6).

The only exception to this uniform rejection of a Eurozone breakup occurred after the election of the Greek anti-austerity party SYRIZA in early 2015—and especially when the Greek people voted in a referendum against the terms of a proposed bailout agreement in July of that year. To the extent that markets had priced in a potential exit of Greece and because Eurozone policymakers feared that giving Greece softer conditionality terms as a result of the referendum might create a dangerous precedent (Walter et al. 2018), a number of high-ranking policymakers in the ministries of finance in Austria, the Netherlands, and especially Germany, concluded that Greece should abandon the common currency if it failed to comply with program conditionality (Interviews DE11; AT9; see also Mody 2018). Pressure rose to the degree that the German finance ministry Wolfgang Schäuble circulated a proposal for a temporary Greek "time-out" from the common currency among members of the Eurogroup, and some media outlets even reported on meetings among conservative European finance ministers who planned to force the Tsipras government to leave the Eurozone.[8]

---

[8] See http://www.spiegel.de/international/germany/schaeuble-pushed-for-a-grexit-and-backed-merkel-into-a-corner-a-1044259.html.

This tough stance is not completely surprising if we remember that among all possible options for external adjustment, a Greek exit from the Eurozone was the least opposed option across all societal groups and that, as we discuss below, harsh conditionality was how surplus country policymakers had sold financing to their skeptical voters. Moreover, at the time, most important economic interest groups considered the direct adverse economic effects or possible contagion risks from a Grexit to be quite limited (Interviews DE1; DE2; AT1; NL1). As such, the episode underlines the core argument that policymakers acted in line with voter and interest group preferences with regard to external adjustment.

The broad public opposition to a breakup of the monetary union also meant that anti-Euro parties gained comparably little political momentum during the crisis years. In Germany, the AfD, which was founded in early 2013 and which in its early years campaigned almost exclusively on the call for dissolving the monetary union, failed to reach the 5 percent hurdle to enter parliament in 2013 (Korte 2013). Most observers agree that in the Netherlands, the electoral chances of the radical-right PVV in 2012 were significantly hurt by the party's call for a Dutch exit from the euro (Niedermayer 2013; Pirro and van Kessel 2017). Finally, the 2013 election success of the Euro-skeptical FPÖ has been attributed to the fact that the party toned down its criticism of the euro and instead focused its campaign on classical anti-immigration issues (Dolezal and Zeglovits 2014).

All in all, the broad opposition from most voters and important economic interest groups thus meant that external adjustment was never a real political option during the crisis years.

The Vocal Politics of Financing in Surplus Countries

Whereas there was strong support for avoiding a breakup of the Eurozone among both voters and interest groups, they diverged in their preferences when it came to financing. Voters in all three countries were strongly opposed to virtually any form of financial transfers from surplus to deficit countries, and this issue was highly salient, especially in the early years of the crisis. In contrast, most interest groups were quite open or at least indifferent to various forms of international transfers. Whereas financing was a low-salience issue for some interest groups, some special interests got heavily involved in this issue. Financial sector groups in particular invested heavily in lobbying for bailouts and against debt cuts in all three surplus countries in the early years of the crisis (Interviews DE6; AT3; NL2; see also Steinberg and Vermeiren 2015; Thompson 2015).

The strong popular opposition to financing put surplus country governments in a difficult position. On the one hand, the context of the accelerating crisis meant that without financial support, the countries hit hardest by the crisis were likely to default and crash out of the Eurozone, an outcome that no one—neither voters, interest groups, nor policymakers themselves—wanted. On the other hand, the issue of financing was so heavily contested among the public that it severely limited policymakers' room to maneuver to consent to intra-European transfers.

Vocal popular opposition influenced surplus countries' willingness to provide financing in two main ways. First, it led to serious delay in and political conflicts about the creation and approval of financing measures. One striking example is the hesitation of the German government to back the first bailout package for Greece in the spring of 2010. As several analyses as well as our own interviews show, electoral concerns were one of the key reasons for Germany's foot-dragging in agreeing to a bailout (Schneider 2018; Schneider and Slantchev 2017). Motivated by the upcoming elections in North Rhine-Westphalia and the unpopularity of the bailouts among large voter segments, Angela Merkel decided to postpone any decision on Greece until after the election in order to secure success for her party in the elections. By the time the German government finally came around, the original costs of the bailout had more than doubled (Schneider and Slantchev 2017). This episode turned out to be representative of the constraints surplus countries faced in financing decisions more generally (Bernhard and Leblang 2016; Bulmer 2014; Schimmelfennig 2015; Zimmermann 2014). For example, strong public opposition to international transfers also led Dutch prime minister Mark Rutte to pledge "not a cent more for Greece" as a central campaign promise in the run-up to the Dutch 2012 national elections. This statement, at least according to a number of domestic observers, substantially contributed to his election victory and made it all the more costly to walk back from it for the third Greek bailout in 2015 (Interview NL6).[9]

Second, the intense politicization of financing and domestic popular opposition also affected the form of financing that surplus country governments were willing to provide. Both bureaucrats and party members involved in the crisis mentioned that the decisions they made always partly hinged on what was politically possible without evoking resistance from a watchful public (Interviews DE9; DE10; AT9; NL6). At the same time, most policymakers we interviewed stated that the stability of the domestic financial sector had been a key concern that motivated their actions during the crisis years (Interviews DE12; AT9; NL6). Policymakers thus confronted a difficult situation. Voters wanted the euro to survive, and they did not want to finance the European periphery, yet they were also in no way willing to support another bailout of domestic banks, which they had disapproved of heavily during the 2009 global financial crisis (Goerres and Walter 2016). At the same time, a default of the European crisis countries was likely to trigger just that (or a major domestic banking crisis), because surplus country governments had heavily invested in these countries (Ardagna and Caselli 2014), and the financial

---

[9] See https://www.ecfr.eu/article/dutch_drama_over_greek_crisis_4004.

industry therefore lobbied heavily for providing deficit countries with the funds to repay their debts.

Policymakers resolved this problem by devising financing in a way that not only pushed the potential costs for taxpayers far into the future, but also allowed them to channel the necessary funds to their domestic banks via a bailout of the peripheral countries and more indirect measures, such as allowing the Target2 balances in creditor states' central banks to grow (Blyth 2013; Frieden and Walter 2017). This feat was achieved by subjecting the bailouts to significant conditionality and by the introduction of a strong rhetoric about "profligate" debtor states who had caused the entire crisis and the need to pursue this path out of "solidarity" and in order to safeguard "European integration" (Degner and Leuffen 2016; Matthijs 2016a; Wendler 2014).

A large body of literature has shown that the emphasis on strong conditionality to avoid moral hazard, the design of strict rules in making financing available, and the moralizing framing of the bailouts, was in line with and inspired by an ordoliberal interpretation of the sources and potential cures for the Eurozone crisis (Dullien and Guérot 2012; Feld et al. 2015; Matthijs and Blyth 2015; Young 2014). However, it is important to note that this narrative remained dominant because few political actors challenged it. Although most interest groups viewed several financing variants rather favorably, the low salience of the issue for their members meant that they hardly got involved in this debate.[10] Even major opposition parties did not prominently discuss financing alternatives to bailouts. For example, although the German Greens and the Social Democratic Party (SPD) at times discussed alternative financing regimes and less austerity-oriented rescue programs, they strategically avoided campaigning on these issues given the overwhelming popularity of the hard stance that Angela Merkel's CDU took (Bauer and Steiner 2015; Korte 2013; Interview DE9). In German parliamentary debates, the far-left Die Linke was the only party to call attention to the fact that the bailouts were large redistributive programs from German and peripheral taxpayers to German and other creditor states' banks (Wonka 2016). In a similar vein, except for the right-wing populist FPÖ, most Austrian opposition parties invested little political capital in challenging the government's position on limiting international transfers and tying bailouts to strict conditionality (Dolezal 2014; Dolezal and Zeglovits 2014). Even changes in government coalitions did little to move surplus countries' restrictive position on financing. After the 2012 election, the traditionally more Keynesian Social Democrats took over the Dutch Ministry of Finance. However, although according to staff members this occasionally led to a change in tone on European issues, it did not have any effect on the substantive

---

[10] With the exception of the financial sector.

position of the ministry (Interview NL6).[11] Similarly, the German position on financing remained unchanged when the Social Democrats entered the grand coalition led by Angela Merkel in 2013 (Zohlnhöfer and Saalfeld 2017).

Other forms of financing quickly faded as options once the dominant bailout narrative had taken hold. At the beginning of the crisis, bureaucrats in the Dutch Ministry of Economic Affairs, for example, had discussed a wide range of European reforms, including institutionalized forms of financing and permanent risk-sharing measures. However, they quickly scrapped these ideas when it became apparent that they would be politically impossible to implement (Interview NL6). Public opposition to financing also caused the Austrian government to backpedal on its initial support for the idea of Eurobonds. Although Chancellor Werner Faymann occasionally expressed some support for the issuance of common bonds, public skepticism and the skepticism of his conservative coalition partner eventually led him to postpone the idea to "some point in the future."[12] And policymakers from all surplus countries emphasized that it became increasingly difficult to get popular support for the use of taxpayer money to help countries that according to much of the public discourse were themselves responsible for the troubles they faced (Interviews DE9; AT7; AT9; NL5; NL6).

Our focus on the diverging interests of different societal actors thus complements existing accounts of the politics of financing in surplus countries. In line with the structuralist interpretation that surplus countries restricted financing and tied it to strict conditionality in order to push the burden of adjustment on to deficit states and safeguard the competitiveness of their export sectors (Hall 2018b; Iversen and Soskice 2018), our interviews showed that most employer associations and industry groups in surplus countries supported imposing austerity and structural reforms on to deficit states (Interviews DE2; DE4; AT2; NL1).[13] However, the same groups would have been open to a wide range of additional financing measures and generally invested little political capital in shaping financing outcomes. Export interests were thus not at the heart of hesitant financing. Similarly, in line with the constructivist emphasis on the importance of ordoliberal ideas in guiding surplus countries' approach to financing (Blyth 2013; Matthijs 2016a), our case studies have shown that many policymakers were convinced of the merits of forcing crisis countries into fiscal prudence and structural reforms (Interviews DE11; AT9). However, even for those that did not hold these ideas, the political room to maneuver was very limited by vocal popular opposition.

---

[11] A couple of years later, the social democratic finance minister, Jeroen Dijsselbloem, famously emphasized his position on international transfers by describing Southern European budgeting as the fiscal equivalent of spending money on "liquor and women".

[12] See https://www.politico.eu/newsletter/brussels-playbook/politico-brussels-playbook-terror-in-london-dijsselbloem-strategy-mogherinis-putin-problem/; https://derstandard.at/1319183544762/Oes terreich-strikt-dagegen-Europa-hofft-auf-Heilung-durch-Eurobonds; https://orf.at/v2/stories/2122109 /2122049/.

[13] Importantly, however, trade unions—even in the export sectors—fiercely rejected such measures.

Overall, the broad support for keeping the Eurozone together, vocal and widespread public skepticism regarding international transfers, targeted lobbying by the financial sector, and little opposition from other interest groups thus came together to shape surplus countries' hesitant, piecemeal, and highly restrictive approach to financing.

Context Matters: The Politics of Internal Adjustment

Voters and interest groups diverged not only in their assessment of financing, but also in their evaluation of the desirability of internal adjustment policies. Although interest groups were open to internal adjustment in principle, they were deeply divided about how to adjust internally. In contrast, voters in all surplus countries viewed expansionary economic policies at home positively. Nevertheless, the three big surplus countries pursued very different responses to their domestic economic crises. Whereas Germany did little to boost the domestic economy, Austria implemented a range of expansionary policies. Finally, the Netherlands initially did not just resist internal adjustment, but even implemented contractionary measures that fueled rather than decreased the Dutch current account surplus— and then ignored all international calls to reduce its export overhang.

We examine the politics of adjustment for each country separately, focusing on how domestic economic developments influenced the salience of economic reforms during the crisis and on how public opinion and interest groups jointly influenced the politics surrounding internal adjustment. Our analysis suggests that the differences in surplus countries' willingness to pursue internal adjustment stem from the fact that domestic economic reforms were not equally important to voters in all surplus countries. Distributional conflicts among interest groups resulted in nonadjustment in contexts in which voters paid little attention to economic policies. The more salient such reforms became in the eyes of the electorate, however, the more likely policymakers became to override the gridlock among interest groups. This dynamic suggests that the politics of adjustment is characterized by a paradox: The better a country's economy is doing, and hence the easier it is economically to pursue internal adjustment, the less likely a government is to push for internal adjustment, because there is no political pressure to do so.

Germany

Domestic economic reforms were not a major political issue in Germany throughout most of the crisis period. Contrary to most other European countries, Germany weathered the Eurozone crisis well. Although the country had been hit hard by the global financial crisis in 2008, its export sector quickly recovered thanks to the low exchange rate of the euro and rising demand for its products, especially from Chinese and US markets (Dustmann et al. 2014). As a result, Germany experienced robust economic growth and declining unemployment rates throughout the crisis. Financial investors intent on reducing their exposure to crisis-ridden deficit countries rushed into the safety of German assets, reducing the government's debt service costs and contributing to a conversion of Germany's budget deficit into a surplus in 2012 (Figure 7.7a). Given this fiscal space, Germany was thus in a prime position to engage in meaningful internal adjustment (Elekdag and Muir 2014).

Ironically, however, the thriving economy also decreased domestic pressure to engage in domestic expansion. Figure 7.7b plots the salience voters attached to the domestic economy, measured as the share of German citizens that singled out the economy or taxation as the most important issue their country was facing. It shows that the salience of domestic economic issues decreased constantly over the span of the euro crisis. By 2015, less than a quarter of the German public thought that economic issues should be at the forefront of political priorities. This suggests that even though voters liked a wide range of expansionary policies, these preferences did not gain much political traction. In the run-up to the national election in

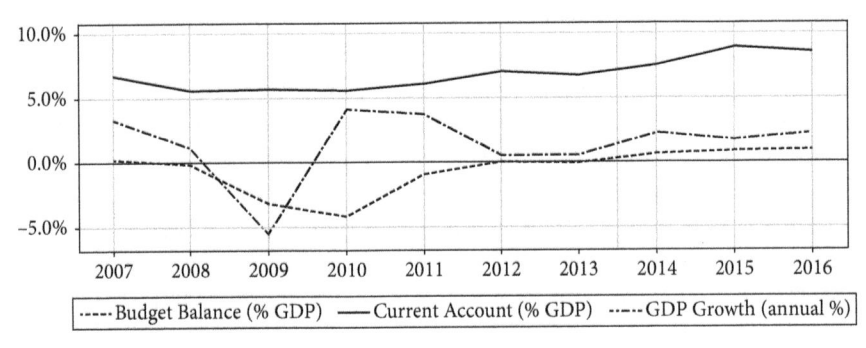

Figure 7.7a Macroeconomic developments in Germany

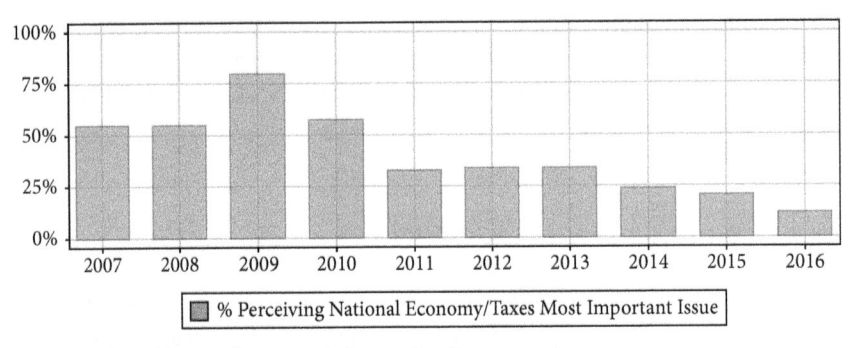

Figure 7.7b Salience of economic issues for German voters

2013, for example, a large majority of Germans evaluated the state of the domestic economy very positively. Unsurprisingly, economic issues played only a minor role during the campaign. None of the main opposition parties campaigned on a broad-based spending or investment program (Korte 2013; Steinbrecher 2014). Only Die Linke and the Green Party made Germany's large current account surplus the main subject of several parliamentary motions and often linked the existence of trade imbalances to low wages and a lack of public investment and spending in Germany. However, although they agreed in principle with much of the international criticism directed at Germany, both parties did little to publicly campaign on the matter. At the same time, interest groups and economic experts who were sympathetic to the international criticism of Germany's large current account surplus found it difficult to effectively communicate their concerns (Interviews DE1; DE7; DE8; DE13). Arguments about the effect of German reforms on disparities in the Eurozone had little effect on public opinion (Frech et al. 2015), which is perhaps unsurprising given the overwhelming public satisfaction with the contemporary state of affairs.

In this context, debates about the current account surplus and possible adjustment policies took place mainly among a small circle of political experts and economic interest groups and never entered the wider public discourse (Interview DE1). In this context, distributional conflicts between interest groups about the microeconomic effects of various adjustment measures often inhibited meaningful reforms. For example, throughout the crisis both the International Monetary Fund (IMF) and the European Commission called for Germany to fundamentally reform its corporate tax regime in order to increase private investment and reduce capital outflows (European Commission 2014; IMF 2011, 2013a, 2013b). This call was largely in line with the partisan program of the economically liberal FDP, who until 2013 was part of the ruling coalition and had made the abolition of local business taxes a core objective of their legislative period (Rixen 2015). A wide range of large employer organizations and trade associations supported the reform. However, all attempts to pass it into law failed due to intense opposition from the Association of German Cities, who feared the loss of an important source of revenues, from a wide range of trade unions, and from the fiscally conservative wing of the CDU.[14] In the end, the two coalition governments that ruled Germany during the crisis implemented fewer tax reforms than had any other German government since 1965 (Rixen 2019). Opposition from trade unions as well as craft associations also kept deregulatory reforms of the domestic service economy off the political agenda (Bandau and Dümig 2015), even though they were often proposed as another means to spur domestic demand and investment (Interviews DE5; DE8; DE11; see also IMF 2015).

---

[14] See https://www.bundestag.de/blob/409640/0f335317888ca03d9b08c4c93ac83d03/wd-4-247-10-pdf-data.pdf; http://www.dgb.de/presse/++co++e9732abe-e1ce-11df-6211-00188b4dc422.

Distributional conflicts among economic interest groups also contributed to the limited expansion of public investment. One of the striking factors discussed in Chapter 6 was that most economic interest groups favored more government spending on investment. Their opinions diverged, however, on what kind of investment should be prioritized and how such investment should be financed. When in 2014 the SPD-led ministry summoned an expert committee on infrastructure investment (composed of economic experts, industry and employer associations, and trade unions) to devise policy suggestions, these differences led trade unions to distance themselves from the committee's final report and limited the political momentum of the document in the social democratic ministry (Interviews DE8; DE13).[15] Against this background, expanding public investment never became a political priority, and the rate of public investment in Germany remained one of the lowest in the entire EU (Rixen 2019).[16]

Distributional conflicts about the specifics of internal adjustment thus rendered domestic expansion politically difficult. Nonetheless, given that a majority of interest groups supported the overall goal of boosting domestic demand, the question remains why policymakers did not invest more political capital into building compromises that would have made internal adjustment attractive for a diverse set of groups. Considering our findings from the previous chapter, a joint package of policies aimed at simultaneously strengthening wage growth, lowering corporate taxes, and financing public investment through diverse funds, for example, might have been able to garner support from a larger number of organized interests.

The absence of such a compromise becomes less puzzling when we also consider the agency of the government itself, however. Distributional conflicts amongst interest groups combined with the low salience of economic reforms for voters provided German political elites with considerable of room to maneuver in terms of domestic economic policymaking. In this context, the economic convictions and crisis interpretation of policymakers became especially relevant. In line with the dominant ordoliberal reading of the sources of the crisis in German economic academia as well as major economic institutions such as the Bundesbank and the finance ministry (Dullien and Guérot 2012; Matthijs and McNamara 2015; Young 2014), German political elites were largely convinced

---

[15] See https://www.wallstreet-online.de/nachricht/9013536-bericht-einigung-fratzscher-kommission-investitions-masterplan.

[16] Besides these distributional conflicts, policymakers also stressed the importance of institutional bottlenecks as an important hurdle for more public spending. Especially in Germany, fiscal federalism means that most public investment—for instance in education or road infrastructure—has to be undertaken at the state or even the municipal level. Although the German finance ministry—especially since the onset of the refugee crisis in 2015—had incrementally increased some of the federal resources provided to the subnational level, a lack of planning and execution capacities in German municipalities has made it difficult to effectively realize potential investments (Interviews DE11; DE12; DE13). For a similar interpretation, see Hassel (2017).

that internal adjustment in Germany would be futile (Interviews DE10; DE11; DE12). Especially amongst members of the ruling CDU, the current account surplus was mainly perceived as the outcome of market forces and a manifestation of the competitiveness of the German economy (Interviews DE4; DE10; DE11). International calls for reducing the export overhang were interpreted as attempts to deflect from necessary adjustment in deficit states (Interviews DE10; DE11; DE12; see also Zimmermann 2014) as reducing the surplus was seen as ignoring the related debt and competitiveness problems in the South. Given robust growth rates in Germany, some policymakers also feared that an additional stimulus would simply overheat the economy and endanger the country's standing on international markets (Interviews DE1; DE4; DE10; DE11; DE12).[17] As one member of parliament put it, "I simply cannot understand how making us as uncompetitive as the South would really help the Eurozone" (Interview DE10). Finally, whereas some ministerial bureaucrats generally acknowledged the German current account position to be problematic, they did not believe that any reasonable form of macroeconomic demand management would have enough impact on domestic consumption and investment to change it (Interviews DE11; DE12).[18]

Given the lack of salience of economic reforms for the German public and the gridlock between organized interest groups, this interpretation remained largely unchallenged (Interviews DE1; DE7; DE9; DE13). As a result, the government implemented domestic economic policies in line with these ideological convictions. Internal adjustment remained limited and the German current account surplus continued to grow throughout the crisis period, as Figure 7.7a shows.

Nonetheless, the German case also demonstrates that internal adjustment measures become more feasible when voters start to care about them. The only meaningful economic policy reforms that occurred during the crisis period were labor market reforms, more specifically the introduction of a minimum wage. Ever since its broad-based labor market liberalization in 2005, Germany had experienced a rapid expansion of the low-wage sector. The rising number of the working poor made the introduction of a statutory minimum wage an increasingly salient topic in the German domestic debate (Mabbett 2016). By 2013, it had become a major issue in the political arena and enjoyed overwhelming public support, especially among SPD voters (95 percent in support) and the CDU (79 percent in support) (Jung et al. 2015). Moreover, the major trade unions engaged in a broad and coordinated campaign in favor of the minimum wage, and the SPD

---

[17] This interpretation was also supported by a number of academic studies in Germany, amongst them, for example, a special report by the German Council of Economic Experts, an institutionalized group of economists which regularly consults the German government on economic policies. See https://www.sachverstaendigenrat-wirtschaft.de/fileadmin/dateiablage/gutachten/jg201415/JG14_06.pdf.

[18] Again, this interpretation finds the support of a range of prominent German economists. See, for example, https://www.bmwi.de/Redaktion/DE/Publikationen/Ministerium/Veroeffentlichung-Wissenschaftlicher-Beirat/gutachten-wissenschaftlicher-beirat-wirtschaftspolitische-probleme-der-deutschen-leistungsbilanz.pdf?__blob=publicationFile.

turned its introduction into a central campaign promise (Zohlnhöfer and Saalfeld 2017). This high salience of and support for the issue among voters eventually trumped the fierce opposition from industry groups and employer associations, and led to the implementation of a central internal adjustment policy, a statutory minimum wage, in 2013.

Austria

Boosting the domestic economy became much more important for Austrian policymakers. Although Austria sailed through the crisis better than many other Eurozone countries, the downturn in the rest of the Eurozone still weighed heavily on the country's economy. In contrast to German manufacturers, the Austrian export sector depended heavily on markets in Italy and Eastern Europe, and the slump in demand from these countries therefore took a heavy toll on many export-oriented industries (Pudschedl 2013). At the same time, economic insecurity and comparatively low wage growth also stalled domestic demand and investment throughout much of the crisis (OECD 2015a). As a result, the Austrian economy only narrowly escaped a recession in 2012 and 2013, and growth remained below 1 percent until 2015 (OECD 2015a; Figure 7.8a). Sluggish growth also resulted in rising unemployment. Although it started from comparatively low levels, the jobless rate increased throughout the crisis and had reached levels not seen since the 1950s by the end of 2015.[19]

At the same time, public finances had suffered from the costs of bank bailouts and anticyclical policies implemented in response to the global financial crisis in 2008 and 2009 and therefore missed the EU budget deficit target of 3 percent of GDP in 2010 (Figure 7.8a). The Austrian government therefore implemented a range of budget cuts and tax increases, especially in the beginning of the crisis (Lehndorff 2012).

These bleak economic developments turned the domestic economy into a salient issue for Austrian voters. Figure 7.8b shows that throughout the peak years of the Eurozone crisis (2010–13), approximately every second Austrian respondent rated the national economy and fiscal policy as the most important issue facing the country. In the run-up to the election of 2013, more than 90 percent of the respondents to the representative survey stated that spurring the economy was an important issue (Kritzinger et al. 2016). Unsurprisingly, the question of how to reform the economy dominated much of the political debate during the crisis (Dolezal 2014). The issue of economic growth and

---

[19] See https://derstandard.at/2000030145081/Oesterreich-Arbeitslosigkeit-naehert-sich-500-000er-Marke.

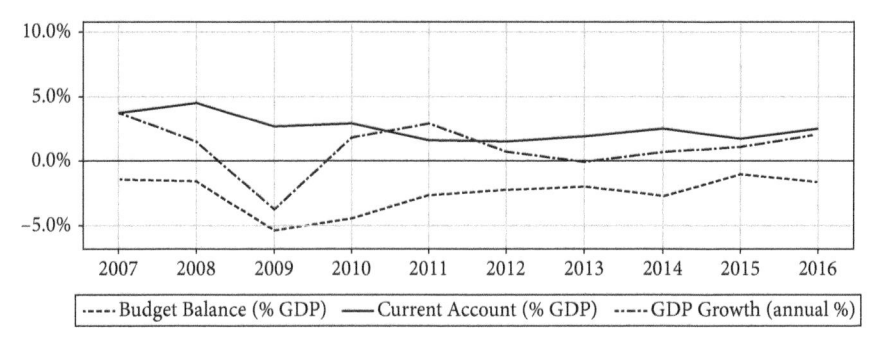

Figure 7.8a Macroeconomic developments in Austria

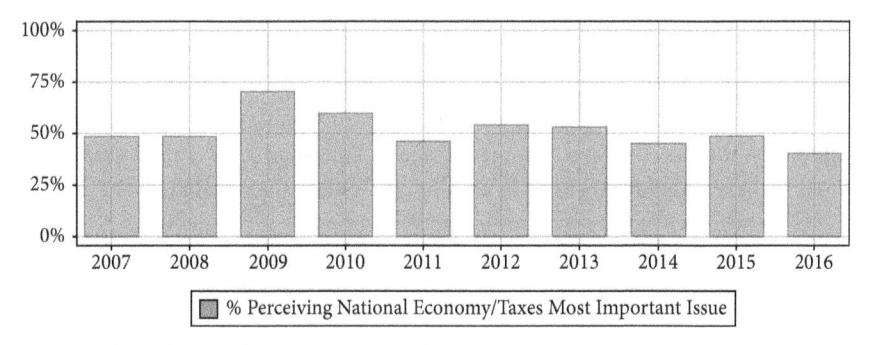

Figure 7.8b Salience of economic issues for Austrian voters

unemployment was one of the most covered topics in national media, and both the conservative Austrian People's Party (ÖVP) and the Social Democratic Party of Austria (SPÖ) focused their national campaigns almost exclusively on their respective visions of regaining growth and jobs (Dolezal and Zeglovits 2014).

The high salience of economic reforms in the domestic debate thus put Austrian policymakers under immense pressure to spur domestic job growth, demand, and investment (Interviews AT1; AT7; AT8). As in Germany, economic interest groups shared this goal but disagreed profoundly about how it should be achieved. However, because public pressure did not allow Austrian officials to sit on their hands, they not only disregarded considerable ideological reservations amongst large parts of the conservative ÖVP, whose economic program for a long time had centered on fiscal consolidation and reducing the size of the state in the economy (Dolezal and Zeglovits 2014). The government also forced interest groups to compromise. In 2013, for example, the Austrian grand coalition agreed on a large stimulus package for the domestic economy. Among other measures, the package aimed at supporting the struggling construction sector and increased resources available for public child care and health care services. Whereas employer associations in the construction sector praised the package, which also gained broad support among all major trade unions, the measures were heavily criticized by the powerful Federation of Austrian Industries, who publicly maintained that the measures would lead to market distortions and would put excessive strain on public finances.[20] However, given the high popularity of the program (less than 35 percent of voters opposed it) and the imminence of the national elections, this opposition of the major industry group gained little political momentum (Interview AT8).[21] Public demands for expansionary measures also led the Austrian government to increase spending in other areas. Among other initiatives, the grand coalition employed additional resources to promote broadband connections in rural areas and substantially raised the fiscal space available to municipalities across the country (Interview AT7). As a consequence, public investment in Austria remained above 3 percent of GDP and was substantially higher than investment rates in all other European surplus countries (Eckerstorfer and Prammer 2017).

In addition to increasing expenditures, the Austrian government sought to stimulate domestic demand through tax cuts. The biggest reform was a broad-based modification of income taxes in 2015. It amounted to cutting taxes by about €5 billion per year and was one of the single biggest tax reductions in recent Austrian history (Baumgartner and Kaniovski 2015). The long negotiation process that preceded the reform was marked by intense conflicts between the Austrian Economic Chambers and a number of large trade unions, which fought extensively about the specifics of the reform and were especially polarized on various forms of countervailing measures (Interviews AT1; AT4). In the end, the government forced the social partners into a compromise that offset some of the costs by a substantial increase of the marginal income tax rates but refrained from the parallel implementation of wealth and inheritance taxes that employee representatives had called for (Interviews AT1; AT4).[22] Although the final tax reform was evaluated negatively by a large set of companies, public pressure to implement tax relief and stimulate domestic demand was so high that it outweighed initial concerns, especially on the part of the ÖVP.[23] All these reforms occurred despite the fact that Austrian policymakers for a large part held very similar ideas about the sources and possible solution of the Eurozone crisis as their German counterparts. As in Germany, the Austrian crisis discourse largely focused on the culprits of state debts lacking competitiveness in deficit countries (Leupold

---

[20] See https://www.wko.at/branchen/gewerbe-handwerk/bau/Bauinnung-spezial—Dez-2014.pdf; https://orf.at/v2/stories/2188508/2188507/.

[21] See https://www.profil.at/home/alpine-bau-umfrage-50-konjunkturpaket-alpine-pleite-361177.

[22] See https://www.ots.at/presseaussendung/OTS_20150707_OTS0189/leitl-zu-steuerreform-einige-entschaerfungen-fuer-betriebe-erreicht-jetzt-sind-neue-konjunkturimpulse-noetig.

[23] See https://derstandard.at/2000018304405/Neos-Umfrage-Unternehmer-mit-Steuerreform-unzufrieden.

2016). Similarly, most Austrian government and party officials explicitly disagreed with the idea that adjustment in countries like Germany or Austria would contribute to stabilizing the monetary union and stressed that, at the international level, they had always defended Germany against its international critics (Interviews AT7; AT8; AT9). However, given the large public demand for a fiscal stimulus, this general agreement with the ordoliberal tenets of German crisis interpretation did not keep the Austrian government from engaging in substantial internal adjustment.

The dire prospects of the Austrian economy, coupled with high salience of domestic reforms and popular pressure to counter low growth and increasing unemployment, thus led the Austrian government to override distributional conflicts among interest groups and ideological reservations of the conservative coalition partner. As a result, Austria implemented a range of expansionary measures during the crisis years.

The Netherlands

Finally, the Dutch crisis experience can be divided into two distinct phases. Starting from 2011, the Netherlands experienced the most severe economic problems of all surplus countries in the monetary union. The reasons for this downturn were manifold, ranging from a loss of European export markets to gloomy domestic consumption due to the bursting of a big housing bubble that put heavily indebted private households in the Netherlands on a prolonged deleveraging path. As a result, the Dutch economy slid into a recession in 2012 and 2013, and unemployment rose from less than 3 percent in 2008 to almost 8 percent in 2014. Public deficits, which had dropped from a small surplus to a deficit of about 5 percent of GDP by 2009, improved only slowly, and only in 2013 did the drop fall below the 3 percent target of the EU again (Figure 7.9a). During these years, the Dutch experience was often seen as evidence that the Eurozone crisis would eventually creep to the north, and commentators as well as government officials were deeply concerned that financial markets could start turning against the Netherlands as well (Interviews NL7; NL6).[24] However, from 2014 onwards, house prices started to recover alongside foreign demand for Dutch exports (especially from the neighboring Germany). As a result, the second half of the Eurozone crisis was characterized by a steady economic recovery in the Netherlands. Only three years after the recession, unemployment in the

---

[24] See https://www.nytimes.com/2012/05/02/business/global/euro-stress-crosses-border-into-netherlands.html; https://www.reuters.com/article/us-dutch-economy/the-dutch-europes-apostles-of-austerity-feel-the-economic-pain-idUSBRE97F07F20130816; https://ftalphaville.ft.com/2016/06/16/2166258/why-is-the-netherlands-doing-so-badly/.

Netherlands was again lower than the levels with which Austria struggled, and the Dutch economy started to grow faster than Germany's (CPB 2016).

The salience of domestic economic issues in the political arena closely followed this trajectory of recession and recovery. Figure 7.9b shows that between 2012 and 2014, more than 70 percent of Dutch citizens thought that the economy was the Netherlands' most important problem. Economic issues dominated politics in those years. In 2012, the coalition government, consisting of the liberal People's Party for Freedom and Democracy (VVD) and the conservative Christian Democratic Appeal, had to call for snap elections, because the far-right PVV, who so far had supported the minority government, refused to back a new budget plan that contained €16 billion of fresh austerity measures (Evans 2013). In the following election, the economy was the central concern for most voters (CPB 2015), and parties campaigned mainly on their respective visions for the breadth and depth of measures that should bring down the deficit (Van Kessel 2015; Pirro and van Kessel 2017). Over time, however, as growth and employment recovered, the salience of economic issues waned. As Figure 7.9b shows, by 2016 less than 25 percent of Dutch respondents thought of economic problems as

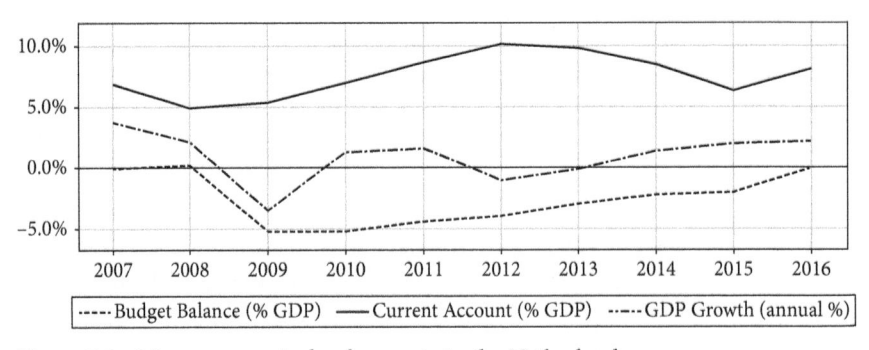

Figure 7.9a Macroeconomic developments in the Netherlands

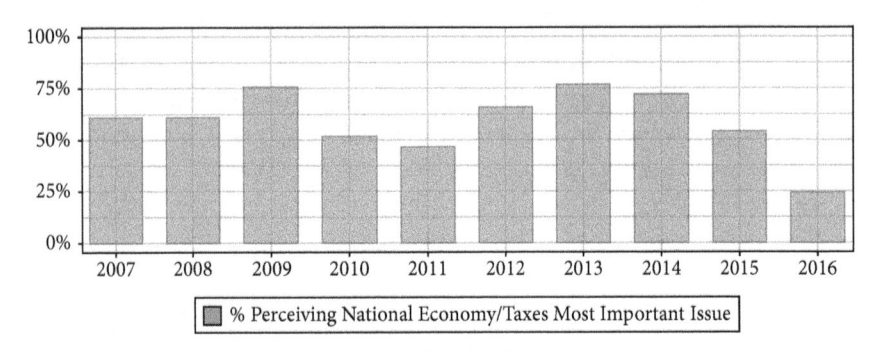

Figure 7.9b Salience of economic issues for Dutch voters

a priority, and in the 2017 elections, economic issues played a very limited role (Van der Meer et al. 2017).

What did the bifurcated crisis experience mean for the politics of internal adjustment? In the early phase of the crisis, characterized by a large budget deficit, cuts to public spending, and weak domestic demand, debates about internal adjustment were largely absent from the political arena, even though the Dutch current account surplus increased substantially in the early 2010s. On the one hand, there were domestic reasons for this absence. Prioritizing fiscal consolidation was not only in line with the ruling VVD's fiscally conservative ideology and the feeling that the government needed to practice what it had been preaching to deficit countries since the outbreak of the crisis (Interviews NL6; NL7; NL8), but it was also supported by a majority of voters (De Hond 2012) as well as almost all employer associations and even the biggest trade unions. In addition, international pressure focused on the budget deficit. At several points between 2012 and 2014, the European Commission demanded that the Netherlands extend its austerity program so as not to fall subject to an excessive deficit procedure. At the same time, none of the country reports and recommendations by either the Commission or the IMF mentioned the current account as an area of priority. Without international pressure to rebalance, and because voters and a majority of interest groups largely agreed on the need for austerity, reducing the current account surplus was not on the table at all in the early years of the crisis (Interviews NL1; NL3).[25]

Debates about internal adjustment became more prevalent from 2015 onward as the economy recovered. With the budget deficit under control, both the IMF and the European Commission started to call on the Dutch government to take steps to reduce the country's big export overhang (IMF 2016a; IMF 2017b; IMF 2018; European Commision 2015; European Commission 2016a), because most economic groups agreed that infrastructure in the Netherlands was already in a relatively good state and that the need for further public investment was therefore limited. The domestic discussion about the current account surplus, thus focused mainly on decreasing wages and high savings in the corporate sector as the main drivers of the large current account surplus (Boumans and Keune 2018; Interviews NL1; NL4). The political debate about how to rebalance was once again characterized by distributional conflicts between different interest groups. Trade unions emphasized that the labor share of income had been declining in the Netherlands for years. They therefore called for a re-regulation of labor markets in an effort to strengthen the bargaining power of workers, achieve higher wage growth and, as a result increase domestic demand (Interview NL4; see also FNV 2016). These

---

[25] Parliamentary documents between 2010 and 2016 also show that during the early period of the crisis, only the far-left Socialist Party (SP) regularly called attention to the large export overhang as a problem and linked it with calls for more domestic expansion and higher wages.

measures were, however, fiercely opposed by most employer associations, which instead advocated a wide range of tax cuts that they deemed necessary to incentivize private investment in the Netherlands by unlocking the huge amounts of savings that had accumulated in the corporate sector (Interview NL1; see also VNO-NCW 2016). These debates about the current account surplus did not take place in the wider public, which is unsurprising given that by 2015, the salience of domestic economic reforms was rapidly decreasing (Figure 7.9b). Several parliamentary meetings with social partners on the subject gained little media attention (Interview NL5; see also Boumans and Keune 2018). Without public backing for one side of the debate over the other, these conflicts among the most important interest groups meant that interest groups got bogged down in distributive struggles. Without much external pressure from either voters or interest groups, the Dutch government had ample room to navigate the discussion about internal adjustment in accordance with its own preferences, given that most economic policymakers in the Netherlands disagreed with the idea that the Dutch current account surplus was of any particular relevance to the stability of the monetary union.[26]

With the priorities of the government elsewhere, internal adjustment measures thus never gained much political momentum. The current account surplus continued to balloon.

Internal Adjustment in Eurozone Surplus Countries

Overall, our analysis of the domestic politics of (non-)adjustment in surplus countries yields two main insights. First, our study of crisis politics indicates that the lack of internal adjustment in surplus countries was rooted in distributional conflicts about how to adjust rather than a broad societal consensus to avoid expansionary measures. The resulting lack of strong interest group and voter pressure for expansionary policies opened up room for policymakers to implement domestic economic policies in line with the ordoliberal ideas prevalent amongst political elites in surplus countries. However, when the national economic context made domestic economic policies a salient issue and support for an expansionary policy became more vocal and concerted, ordoliberal ideas became much less influential for surplus country policymaking, as our analysis of the Austrian case suggests.

---

[26] This interpretation was also shared by the Dutch Bureau for Economic Policy Advice, which is part of the Ministry for Economic Affairs and Climate Policy and regularly publishes influential policy papers. See https://www.cpb.nl/sites/default/files/publicaties/download/cpb-policy-brief-2015-05-causes-and-policy-implications-dutch-current-account-surplus.pdf.

Second, our analysis also implies that the lack of adjustment in core countries is much less structurally engrained than is often assumed. Especially when voters start to care about increasing domestic growth and employment, public opinion is likely to pressure policymakers into expansionary measures even against the opposition of powerful interest groups. However, this also suggests that politics of adjustment in surplus countries are characterized by a paradox: The better a country's economy is doing, and hence the easier it is economically to pursue broad adjustment measures, the less likely such voter pressure is to occur and the more likely it becomes that the distributional conflicts among interest groups result in non-adjustment.

Conclusion

Why did surplus countries in the euro crisis not shoulder a larger share of the burden of adjustment? Why did they invest huge sums in short-term bailouts but refuse to build up a more extensive and permanent system of transfers and mutual risk sharing? And why did they allow their current account surpluses to keep rising while at the same time demanding that crisis countries take painful measures to reduce their deficits? Our book's central premise is that a full understanding of the politics of the Eurozone crisis requires an understanding of how key societal actors and policymakers evaluated all potential crisis responses, including those not chosen. In this chapter, we have therefore analyzed how voters positioned themselves with regard to external adjustment, internal adjustment, and financing, and how their preferences and policymakers' ideas interacted with the preferences of economic interests groups in shaping crisis outcomes.

A number of key finding stand out. First, neither interest groups, voters, nor policymakers wanted to risk a crashing of the Eurozone. Given this broad societal consensus to keep the Eurozone together, external adjustment was never seriously considered as a politically viable crisis strategy in any of the surplus countries we studied. Second, the politics surrounding financing illustrate how difficult it is to do politics on the back of bad options. On the one hand, financial industries lobbied heavily for bailouts and against debt reliefs, and other economic interest groups were supportive of a range of financing measures but did not make them a political priority. On the other hand, voters remained deeply skeptical about international transfers and, given the huge salience of the euro crisis in domestic debates, were difficult to ignore. Trying to satisfy both sides, policymakers only engaged in the forms of financing that were absolutely necessary to keep the Eurozone from crumbling, which further fueled market tensions and crisis tendencies in deficit states. Finally, domestic rebalancing was characterized by what we call the paradox of internal adjustment in surplus countries. Voters' general support for domestic expansion translated into policies only in contexts in which bad domestic economic developments put the spotlight on the necessity of economic reforms. If voters cared enough, they pressured policymakers into overriding interest group gridlock, disregarding their own ordoliberal convictions, and to engage in meaningful adjustment policies. However, when the economic state of affairs was a low salient issue among voters, distributional conflicts between interest groups resulted in a political stalemate that allowed governments to pursue policies in line with ordoliberalism. This typically resulted in non-adjustment. Domestic politics thus led those countries, which could have contributed the most to stimulating European growth and reducing imbalances within the monetary union, to become the least-likely candidates for internal adjustment.

Appendix

Table A7.1 List of interview partners

Germany

Interview DE1	Dr. Klaus Günter Deutsch, Bundesverband der Deutschen Industrie, Head of Department Research, Industrial and Economic Policy
Interview DE2	Dr. Michael Stahl, Gesamtmetall, Head of Education and Economic Policy
Interview DE3	Eckhart Rotter, Verband der Automobilindustrie, Head of Department Press
Interview DE4	Dr. Peer-Robin Paulus, Die Familienunternehmer, Head of Politics and EconomicsDr. Daniel Mitrenga, Die Familienunternehmer, Head of Europe and Federal States
Interview DE5	Dr. Alexander Barthel, Zentralverband des Deutschen Handwerks, Head of Economic, Energy and Environmental Politics
Interview DE6	Dr. Reinhold Rickes, Deutscher Sparkassen- und Giroverband, Head of Economic Research
Interview DE7	Florian Moritz, Deutscher Gewerkschaftsbund, Head of European Economic Politics
Interview DE8	Dr. Dierk Hirschel, Vereinte Dienstleistungsgewerkschaft, Trade Union Secretary in the Department of Economic Policy
Interview DE9	Joachim Poß, Social Democratic Party of Germany, former Member of Parliament: Committees on Affairs of the European Union, Finance Committee
Interview DE10	Prof. Dr. Heribert Hirte, Christian Democratic Union of Germany, Member of Parliament: Committee for European Affairs, Finance Committee, Legal Affairs and Consumer Protection Committee; Professor at the University of Hamburg
Interview DE11	Dr. Ludger Schuknecht, Federal Ministry of Finance, Chief Economist and Head of the Directorate General Fiscal Policy and International Financial and Monetary Policy
Interview DE12	Felix Probst, Federal Ministry for Economic Affairs and the Environment, Ministerialrat
Interview DE13	Dr. Claus Michelsen, Deutsches Institut für Wirtschaftsforschung, Head of Forecasting and Economic Policy

Austria

Interview AT1	Dr. Christoph Schneider, Wirtschaftskammer Österreich, Head of Department for Economic Affairs
Interview AT2	Dr. Christian Helmstein, Industriellenvereinigung, Chief Economist
Interview AT3	Michael Ernegger, Verband Österreichischer Banken und Bankiers, Deputy Secretary General Retail Baning
Interview AT4	Dr. Markus Marterbauer, Arbeiterkammer Österreich, Head of Department for Economic Affairs and Statistics
Interview AT5	Karl Goldberg, Österreichische Verkehrs- und Dienstleistungsgewerkschaft, Department for Economic Affairs
Interview AT6	Kerstin Repolusk, Die Produktionsgewerkschaft, Department for Economic Policy
Interview AT7	Dr. Christoph Matznetter, Social Democratic Party of Austria, Member of Parliament: Committee for Finance and Budget Committee
Interview AT8	Dr. Christina Burger, Federal Ministry for Science, Research and Economic Affairs, Department for Economic Policy
Interview AT9	Harald Waiglein, Federal Ministry of Finance, Head of the Department for Economic Policy, Financial Markets and Customs

Netherlands

Interview NL1	Thomas Grosfeld, Confederation of Netherlands Industry and Employers, Department for Top Sector Policies
Interview NL2	Bart van Leeuwen, Nederlandse Vereniging van Banken, Head of Communication Department
Interview NL3	Sander van Golberdinge, Detailhandel Nederland, Director
Interview NL4	Irene Laureijs, Federatie Nederlandse Vakbeweging, Economic Policy Advisor
Interview NL5	Renske Leijten, Socialistische Partij Nederland, Member of Parliament: Committee for European Affairs, Budget Committee
Interview NL6	Focco Vijselaar, Federal Ministry for Economic Affairs, Director for Economic Policy, Chief Economist
Interview NL7	Michel Heijdra, Federal Ministry of Finance, Director Foreign Financial Affairs Directorate
Interview NL8	Niels Redeker, Federal Ministry of Finance, Head of the European Union Division

8
Conclusion

Why did the Eurozone crisis prove so difficult to resolve? Why was it resolved in a manner in which some countries bore a much larger share of the pain than other countries? Why did no country leave the Eurozone rather than implement unprecedented austerity? Who supported and who opposed the different policy options in the crisis domestically, and how did the distributive struggles among these groups shape crisis politics? Building on macro-level statistical data, original survey data from interest groups, and qualitative comparative case studies, this book has argued and shown that the answers to these questions revolve around distributive struggles about how the costs of the Eurozone crisis should be divided both among countries and among different socioeconomic groups within countries. Together with divergent but strongly held ideas about the "right way" to conduct economic policy and asymmetries in the distribution of power among actors, severe distributive concerns of important actors lie at the root of the difficulties to resolve the Eurozone crisis as well as the difficulties to substantially reform the Economic and Monetary Union (EMU).

Providing fresh insights into a topic such as the Eurozone crisis and the continuing problems of the European EMU, on which a rich literature of insightful research exists, is no easy task. Our approach has been to emphasize three aspects that have received scant attention in existing research: The importance of analyzing the Eurozone crisis in comparative perspective, the importance of examining the whole range of policy options, including the ones not chosen, and the importance of analyzing crisis politics not just in deficit-debtor, but also in surplus-creditor countries. Taken together, the emphasis on these three aspects has allowed us to generate a new perspective on the politics of the Eurozone crisis.

In this conclusion, we first discuss the insights that these three perspectives have yielded and summarize the book's main findings in the process. Because the bulk of our analyses have focused on domestic distributive struggles, we then turn to the question to what extent our approach is useful for understanding the distributive struggles on the European level as well. For this purpose, we examine how surplus and deficit states positioned themselves with regard to the core EMU-related issues and reforms that were discussed in the European Council during the Eurozone crisis (Wasserfallen et al. 2019). Our analysis shows that on policy issues related to questions of adjustment and financing, deficit and surplus countries aligned in opposing camps. Moreover, creditor-surplus countries managed to secure policy decisions in line with their preferences on almost all adjustment-related policy issues, which meant that deficit countries had to carry the bulk of the adjustment burden. In contrast, they showed more willingness to compromise on issues related to financing. We conclude our book with a discussion of the policy implications of our findings and an agenda for future research.

Three New Perspectives on the Eurozone Crisis

To generate new insights into the difficulties of resolving the Eurozone crisis, our book has analyzed crisis politics from three new perspectives. What insights has this approach generated?

What's So Special? Analyzing the Eurozone Crisis in a Comparative Perspective

The first consideration guiding the analyses in our book has been to take a *comparative perspective*. It is premised on the argument that both the economics and the politics of the Eurozone crisis have to be analyzed in a comparative manner in order to be fully understood. The Eurozone crisis was not a one-of-a-kind, *sui generis* event. Rather, it stands in a long line of financial crises shaking countries around the world that have also required balance-of-payment (BOP) adjustment. Analyzing the Eurozone crisis in a comparative perspective, both in theoretical and empirical terms, allowed us to draw on the rich literature on the political economy of past crises and debt and BOP crises more generally (Copelovitch et al. 2016). More importantly, it enabled us to explore in what respects the Eurozone crisis is similar to other crises, and in which respects the Eurozone crisis is unique.

To put the Eurozone crisis in comparative perspective, we constructed country-level vulnerability profiles for 142 episodes in which countries experienced balance-of-payments pressures between 1990 and 2014, including well-known crises such as the 1992 devaluation of the British pound, the 1994/5 Mexican Tequila Crisis, or the 2001/2 Argentine crisis. Based on this analysis, we were able to explore how the vulnerability profiles of Eurozone crisis countries compared to these other crisis countries. This analysis showed that with the exception of Cyprus, all Eurozone crisis countries concentrated in the "misery corner" of being highly vulnerable to both external and internal adjustment. This suggests that crisis resolution was not only bound to be extraordinarily costly for these countries, but also bound to be fraught with difficult choices between very bad options, a theme to which we return below. Our comparative analysis also revealed that in earlier sets of major crises, such as the 1992 European

Monetary System (EMS) crisis, the 1997 Asian financial crisis, and even the 2008/9 global financial crisis, crisis countries had exhibited less problematic vulnerability profiles. Turning to surplus countries, we repeated this exercise and constructed vulnerability profiles for 272 episodes in which countries exhibited sustained current account surpluses since 1995. As in our analysis of crisis countries, we once more found that the Eurozone crisis clustered mostly in the "misery corner," thus exhibiting a higher vulnerability to both external adjustment—in this case, Eurozone breakup—and internal adjustment of domestic economic policies than most other surplus countries.

Examining the Eurozone crisis in the context of other episodes characterized by balance-of-payments pressures (for the deficit countries) and sustained current account surpluses (for the surplus countries) thus allowed us to uncover just why the Eurozone crisis is often viewed as unique: What makes the Eurozone crisis distinct is that almost all Eurozone countries, both deficit and surplus countries, were located in the misery corner. None of the other major sets of crisis/surplus episodes we examined showed such a pattern. Although our analysis also showed that vulnerability profiles in the misery corner are not a unique characteristic of the Eurozone crisis, it does suggest that the Eurozone crisis is unusual, because crisis resolution thus had the potential to be extraordinarily costly for these countries. This, in turn, raised the stakes for the distributive struggles that ensued.

Examining the Road not Traveled: Policy Alternatives and Trade-Offs

The second feature of our approach has been to focus on the whole range of policy options, including the ones not chosen, and the trade-offs these policy options entail. This approach builds on the premise that policy preferences and policy choices can only be understood when three things are examined: (i) the small range of policies under close consideration, (ii) the policies that were chosen, and (iii) the alternatives that were not considered as viable options. This means taking seriously the whole range of—often bad—options. It also means that policy choices should not be considered in isolation, but rather in the context of the—often difficult—trade-offs they pose. Trade-offs are ubiquitous in policymaking. They are particularly difficult to resolve when the stakes are high and the potential costs of the different options are high, as is the case for countries or groups confronted with a vulnerability profile in the misery corner. Under such circumstances, the usual ways of generating support for unpopular reforms, such as combining them with more popular policies, adjusting policies in related areas, or compensating the losers of reforms (Häusermann et al. 2018), are not available. This makes such reforms politically contentious and hard to implement. Yet although trade-offs between bad options confront political actors with difficult decisions, they also create policy space and room for compromise that allow policymakers to implement policies that under other circumstances would have seemed impossible. Recognizing that the alternative options are even worse than the bad option chosen, therefore allows us to better understand policy choices that seem puzzling at first.

The whole range of policy options played an important role in our analyses, both in theoretical and in empirical terms. In theoretical terms, we explored preferences for the three possible crisis management strategies—external adjustment, internal adjustment, and financing, and how these preferences were shaped by the relative costs of the two main macroeconomic adjustment strategies available to policymakers in times of crisis, internal and external adjustment, encapsulated in the vulnerability profile. Empirically, we identified countries' vulnerabilities to external adjustment relative to their vulnerabilities to internal adjustment on the macro-level. In addition, based on original survey data from 716 interest groups in six Eurozone countries, we delved into a fine-grained analysis of interest groups' vulnerability profiles, their preferred crisis resolution strategies, as well as preferences of specific policies within each of these strategies. This allowed us to explore in detail how vulnerable domestic economic and social interest groups were to different crisis strategies, which types of policies they preferred, and how they assessed the difficult trade-offs that the crisis presented them with.

These analyses showed the importance of considering the alternatives: In deficit countries for example, interest groups were opposed to austerity policies, such as tax increases or spending cuts, and (to a lesser extent) to structural reform proposals. Nonetheless, they still preferred these internal adjustment policies to a crisis response that would have entailed a breakup of the Eurozone, an outcome toward which they displayed even more opposition. This choice became particularly clear when we explicitly pressed respondents to choose between these two bad options. Our analysis of crisis politics in deficit countries showed that at no point in time, not even in Greece, was there strong societal support for external adjustment. The willingness to accept unprecedented austerity is thus rooted in the fact that the alternative—Eurozone exit, possibly coupled with default—was widely viewed as even worse. It is also related to the fact that a majority of the groups strongly favored financing. The interplay of policies and the assessment of the different options against each other thus played an important role. The consensus that Eurozone exit was to be avoided at all costs did not mean, however, that crisis politics was a consensual matter. Rather, our analyses showed that different policy options were highly contested by different groups and that within the confines of room to maneuver left by the crisis, domestic politics was an important driver of who ultimately paid the highest cost of crisis resolution in deficit countries.

Our analysis of interest group preferences in surplus countries showed that although external adjustment was strongly opposed in surplus countries as well, there was much less opposition to internal adjustment in Austria, Germany, and the Netherlands than in Ireland, Greece, and Spain. The lack of internal adjustment thus appears puzzling. However, surplus country interest groups were heavily polarized about *how* internal adjustment should be achieved, and quite indifferent about financing. This mattered once we confronted interest groups with explicit trade-offs and forced them to choose between different options. Especially when confronted with bad options—packages containing those policies that each interest group disliked most—support for internal adjustment significantly decreased, whereas support for financing and the number of "don't know" answers went up. Faced with bad options, interest groups did not exhibit clear, broad-based preferences for any one strategy, let alone specific policies. At the same time, there was widespread skepticism of voters about generous financing, but no strong push on the part of voters for internal adjustment. This setting created room to maneuver for governments. Many surplus country policymakers such as German finance minister Wolfgang Schäuble were strongly wedded to ordoliberal ideas that made them firmly opposed to domestic expansion and wary of moral hazard. Governments therefore used this room to design crisis policies that mostly relied on piecemeal financing combined with high conditionality. That said, in instances such as in Austria, where interest groups began to push for expansionary policies, ordoliberal ideas become less dominant and governments were more willing to adjust domestic policies.

Overall, our analysis shows the importance of considering policy alternatives, actors' vulnerabilities to each of these (often bad) options, and the trade-offs they entail: The unusual trajectory of the Eurozone crisis becomes less puzzling if we consider that for the deficit-debtor countries, the alternatives to unprecedented austerity were Eurozone breakup and possibly default, an outcome that most actors opposed even more. Although this outcome was equally opposed by the surplus-creditor countries, the lack of strong support for specific internal adjustment policies, ordoliberal policymakers' opposition to such a strategy and the availability of a third alternative—financing conditional on adjustment in crisis countries—explains why the latter was implemented. Our analysis also showed that interest group preferences change depending on whether groups consider policies in isolation or in the context of trade-offs. This not only reinforces the insight from a recent wave of political economy research on the importance of trade-offs (e.g., Busemeyer and Garritzmann 2017; Emmenegger et al. 2018; Häusermann et al. 2018; Jacobs 2011), but also provides insights into how policymakers have agency in complex situations. Under these circumstances, governments are neither just the long arm of organized interests nor do they simply bow to electoral pressures, but they can skillfully shape the narratives and policies in a way that aligns with their own preferences.

Looking at Both Sides of the Coin: Crisis Politics in Both Deficit-Debtor and Surplus-Creditor Countries

The third guiding principle of our book has been to analyze crisis politics not just in deficit-debtor, but also in surplus-creditor countries. It is well known that surplus-creditor countries contribute to the buildup of large and persistent current account imbalances that often indicate trouble ahead (Obstfeld 2012) and often play an important role in the resolution of debt and balance-of-payments crises. Nonetheless, most existing research on financial crises focuses exclusively on crisis politics in deficit and debtor countries (Eichengreen 2003; Frieden 1991a; Haggard 2000; Haggard and Kaufman 1992; Nelson 1990; Pepinsky 2009; Walter 2013a). This is also true for the Eurozone crisis, where much more research has focused on crisis countries than surplus-creditor countries. This is surprising because surplus-creditor countries have been instrumental in shaping the European crisis-resolution framework (Redeker and Walter 2020). Nonetheless, this remains an underexplored issue. What is particularly missing is systematic research on how crisis politics in deficit-debtor and surplus-creditor countries are related and how they interact (Frieden and Walter 2017).

Our book has presented such a systematic analysis of the vulnerabilities, societal crisis resolution preferences, and crisis politics in both deficit-debtor and surplus-creditor countries in the Eurozone crisis. It has developed an encompassing and unified theoretical framework that suggests that the distributive struggles surrounding the politics of the Eurozone crisis in surplus and deficit countries are distinct, yet they also revolve around common themes and are intricately linked. Even though internal adjustment, external adjustment, and financing work in different directions in deficit and surplus countries, these are still the three principle policy strategies available to both sets of countries. Because each of these strategies has upsides and downsides, countries', interest groups', and voters' vulnerabilities to each of these strategies are likely to vary. And although these vulnerabilities take different forms, the relative costs of different strategies, and the trade-offs they entail, can be captured with a simple heuristic such as the vulnerability profile in both deficit and surplus countries. In both sets of countries, actors with a vulnerability profile in the "misery corner"—highly vulnerable to both internal and external adjustment—are confronted with the most difficult choices, and have incentives to support accepting financing from abroad (in deficit countries) or to provide such financing to crisis countries (in surplus countries).

Viewed in this way, the interdependencies between deficit-debtor and creditor-surplus countries fall into sharp focus. This allows us to better understand the domestic politics surrounding crisis politics in each set of countries, which in turn allows for a better understanding of the overall dynamics of Eurozone crisis politics and the interactions between both sets of actors. Our analyses showed, for example, that despite the similar set of choices and the deep interdependence between deficit and surplus countries, crisis politics played out differently in deficit and surplus countries. Although societal actors in surplus countries in principle viewed internal adjustment as more favorable than the alternative crisis strategies external adjustment and financing, this was not the main strategy implemented by governments. We show that this was because in most settings, there was no strong societal demand that pushed policymakers in this direction. Rather, interest groups were heavily divided as to how internal adjustment should be achieved, rebalancing was not a high salience topic among voters, and surplus country policymakers held strong ordoliberal beliefs that made them reluctant to pursue an expansionary macroeconomic strategy or restructure or even write-off debts. Instead, they opted for financing, coupled with strong conditionality for deficit states.

This, in turn, confronted the deficit states with a situation in which they were forced to carry most of the adjustment burden, in return for external financing that would allow them to stay in the Eurozone and avoid default. The choice set was thus much more constrained in crisis countries. They did not opt for internal adjustment coupled with financing because societal actors favored this strategy, but rather because it was viewed as the least bad among a series of bad options: Euro exit was strongly opposed by overwhelming majorities in deficit country societies. Yet this nonetheless meant that governments had to implement policies that under normal circumstances would have been unthinkable. Governments used what little room they had to design the policies within the confines of the possibilities that external creditors and domestic distributive struggles left them with. In most cases, this meant that business interests trumped the interests of workers and the poor, which is one reason why the Eurozone crisis has resulted in widespread political discontent among voters.

Our analysis thus complements existing work that has pointed to the structural diversity of the Eurozone as an important cause of the crisis and a major obstacle to its resolution (Armingeon and Baccaro 2012a; Armingeon and Cranmer 2017b; Hall 2012; Höpner and Lutter 2018; Johnston et al. 2014; Moravcsik 2012; Scharpf 2013; Streeck and Elsässer 2016). By analyzing the domestic preferences on and politics of Eurozone crisis management in both deficit and surplus countries, we have generated insights into how these structural constraints affected the interests of important societal and political actors, and how they, in turn, have shaped Eurozone crisis management.

The Politics of Bad Options in European Crisis Management

So far, our book has predominantly explored the domestic politics of Eurozone crisis management. Yet of course, the Eurozone crisis was shaped in important ways on the European (and international) level. Countries bargained over how the crisis should be resolved, how bailout programs should be designed, and what kind of institutional reforms should be implemented in order to better prepare the Eurozone against future crises. In this concluding chapter, we therefore return to the European level and examine to what extent Eurozone crisis politics, and the unequal distribution of the adjustment burden, is related to conflicts between surplus and deficit countries about how the burden of crisis resolution costs should be shared.

Research Design

For this purpose, we build on the "EMU Positions" dataset, a detailed dataset of negotiation positions on forty-seven Eurozone-related issues between 2010 and 2015 that were officially negotiated in the EU Council during the Eurozone crisis (Wasserfallen et al. 2019). It covers the initial negotiation positions of twenty-eight EU countries and all EU institutions for Eurozone-related negotiations in the EU Council, as well as the final bargaining outcome on each of these issues.[1] The dataset and related codebook provide detailed information on each of the issues under negotiation and codes countries' negotiation positions on a 0 to 100 scale, denoting the most extreme positions of each. It thus allows us to examine to what extent our argument that distributive struggles between deficit-debtor and surplus-creditor countries shaped Eurozone crisis politics is useful for understanding the distributive struggles on the European level as well.

We focus our analysis on the sixteen countries that were members of the Eurozone during the entire Eurozone crisis and their negotiation positions. Although some issues were decided by all EU member states, many of the issues predominantly affected Eurozone countries, which is why we limit our analysis to these countries.[2] We examined all issues in the dataset and classified them into three categories: The first category comprises policy issues related to how the burden of adjustment should be shared (six issues; for a list see Table 8.1), such as the treatment of current account surpluses and deficits in the macroeconomic imbalance procedure, but also questions about International Monetary Fund (IMF) involvement, as this is directly related to conditionality. A second category contains policy issues related to financing (fourteen issues; for a list see Table 8.2), such as the willingness to support bailouts but also more general questions about transnational redistribution. A final broad category comprises other policy issues (twenty-seven issues; for a list see Table A8.1 in the Appendix to this chapter),

---

[1] Constructing such a large-scale dataset necessarily requires making some difficult choices. For an evaluation of the merits and shortcomings of the dataset, see the discussion in Frieden and Walter (2019).
[2] The dataset therefore also contains considerably more "missings" for the negotiation positions of non-Eurozone EU countries.

Table 8.1 Eurozone country bargaining positions on policy issues regarding adjustment

Abbreviation	Description	N(out of 16)
EFSF2*	IMF involvement in EFSF programs	10
ESM3*	ESM conditionality	5
FC7	Purpose of the Fiscal Compact (stability vs. growth)	9
G3*	IMF involvement in the First Greek Program	16
SPA2*	Withholding of EU funds when member state breaches deficit limit	16
SPA5	Asymmetry in the treatment of current account deficits and surpluses in the macroeconomic imbalance procedure	10

Note: *Recoded so that lower values represent preferred surplus country position (adjustment predominantly in deficit countries) and higher values represent preferred deficit country position (adjustment burden shared equally across Eurozone member states). N refers to the number of countries for which information on the issue-specific bargaining position is available.

Table 8.2 Eurozone country bargaining positions on policy issues regarding financing

Abbreviation	Description	N (out of 16)
BU9	Single Resolution Fund fiscal backstop	12
EB1	Eurozone debt mutualization (Eurobonds)	14
EFSF1	Preparedness to issue loan guarantees	15
EFSF3	Enhancement of the EFSF's effective capacity	14
EFSF4	Allowing the EFSF to use additional instruments	11
ESM2	ESM size (effective lending capacity)	16
ESM4	Private sector involvement	16
ESM5	Number of support instruments available under the EFSF/ESM	16
ESM6	ESM financing	16
G1	Initial willingness to support Greece (First Program)	16
G4	Debt relief in the Second Greek Program	16
PR1	Short-term ambitions for the fiscal union	15
PR2	Potential redistribution within the fiscal union	15
TPA1	Redemption fund in two-pack	14

Note: N refers to the number of countries for which information on the issue-specific bargaining position is available.

which contains the majority of issues, such as institutional specifications, issues of timing of certain reforms, or issues such as a cap on bank bonuses that are unrelated to questions of macroeconomic adjustment and cross-national financing. Although some of these issues also have distributional consequences, we opted for a conservative approach and only coded those issues related to adjustment burden-sharing or financing that clearly fit in those categories.

We then made sure that all issues were coded in a way such that lower values denote a policy position more in line with creditor-surplus country interests and higher values a policy more in line with debtor-deficit countries and recoded issues where necessary. In a final step, we calculated the mean of each country's negotiation positions on all issues in the relevant category, to arrive at the country's average policy stance on issues related to adjustment and financing.

Eurozone Crisis Bargaining between Deficit-Debtor and Surplus-Creditor States

How did creditor-surplus and debtor-deficit states position themselves with regard to adjustment- and financing-related reforms that were discussed in the European Council during the Eurozone crisis? We begin with an analysis of policies related to how the burden of macroeconomic adjustment should be distributed among EMU members. One major issue in this category is the question of conditionality, because it forces program countries to accept often painful domestic reforms and macroeconomic adjustment in return for financial support. Conditionality is thus a means for creditor-surplus countries to shift the burden of adjustment onto debtor-deficit countries. But the category also contains issues such as whether fiscal policy should be geared more toward stability or growth, or whether large current account surpluses and deficits should be treated equally, or whether surpluses should be seen as less problematic than deficits.

To examine to what extent surplus and deficit countries varied in their policy preferences, Figure 8.1 shows the national negotiation positions based on countries' average current account position in the five years before the outbreak of the Eurozone crisis. Moreover, it lists the European Commission's (COM) and the European Parliament's (EP) average policy position, as well as the average outcome of the negotiation process (OUT). The figure shows that with the exception of Luxembourg, surplus countries indeed strongly favored policies that would push the bulk of the adjustment burden onto deficit countries. In contrast, most deficit countries favored an approach that would lead to more burden-sharing in terms of macroeconomic adjustment, an approach that was also supported by the European Parliament and the European Commission. Surprisingly, however, the outcome of these negotiations on average corresponds closely to the preferences of surplus countries: On all but one issue related to the question of adjustment, the final outcome scores a 0, that is, an outcome completely in line with surplus country interests. This results in an average value of 17 on a scale between 0 and 100, where 0 is the least and 100 is the most deficit-debtor-friendly policy. There was only one issue in which a deficit country-friendly outcome was decided, namely the decision not to withhold EU funds when a member state breaches the deficit limit (SPA2). It appears that in the context of complex,

254 THE POLITICS OF BAD OPTIONS

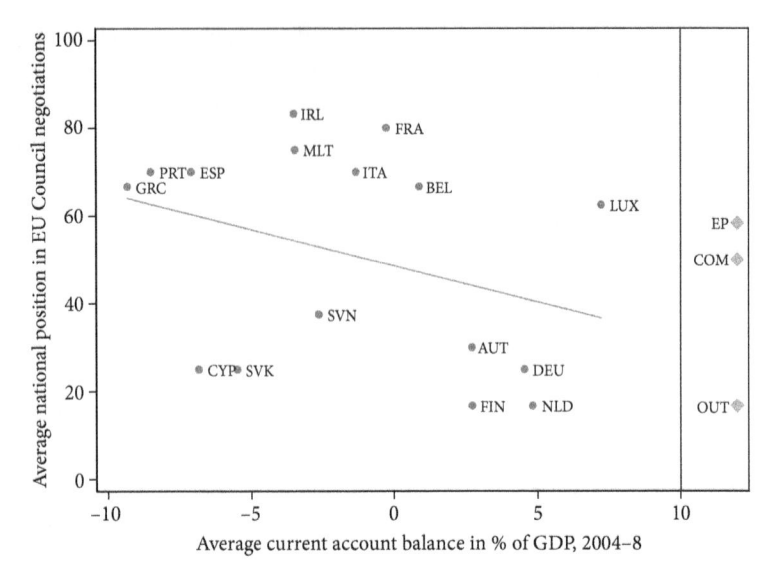

Figure 8.1 Negotiation positions of Eurozone countries on adjustment issues, by countries' average pre-crisis current account balance

Notes: COM = average preferred position European Commission, EP = average preferred position European Parliament, OUT = average policy decision (negotiated outcome).

multidimensional and multi-issue negotiations such as those in the Eurozone crisis, surplus countries managed to secure support for polices on almost all issues that allowed them to push the burden of adjustment predominantly onto deficit-debtor countries, whose bargaining power was weakened by market pressure and their financial difficulties (Finke and Bailer 2019).

We next turn to policies related to financing. Table 8.2 shows that these issues mostly concern the size of financial support packages during the Eurozone crisis, some questions about debt relief, and more general questions about redistribution within EMU and the EU, including, for example, the question of Eurobonds. These were highly salient questions, as the high number of recorded policy positions on each of these issues shows.

Figure 8.2 shows that national negotiation positions diverged even more strongly between debtor-deficit and creditor-surplus countries on issues related to financing. The figure shows that with the exception of Slovakia, all deficit states had strong preferences for generous financing schemes that would transfer financial funds from surplus to deficit states. This position was also largely supported by the European Commission and the European Parliament. Surplus countries, in contrast (and again with the exception of Luxembourg), were much more hesitant about these proposals. On average they supported policy proposals that implied much more restricted financing. Whereas the outcome of the negotiations strongly reflected the preferences of the surplus state, Figure 8.2 suggests that

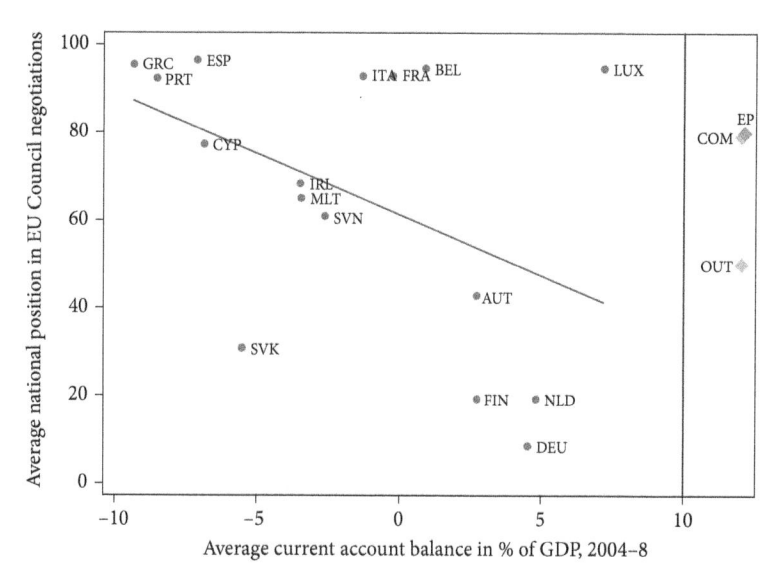

Figure 8.2 Negotiation positions of Eurozone countries on financing issues, by countries' average pre-crisis current account balance

Notes: COM = average preferred position European Commission, EP = average preferred position European Parliament, OUT = average policy decision (negotiated outcome).

the outcome of the negotiations on financing were more of a compromise. On the 0–100 EMUChoices-scale, the average outcome takes the value of 50, placing it exactly between the most favorable outcome (0) for creditor-surplus states and the most favorable outcome (100) for debtor-deficit states.

Overall, these analyses confirm that a core divide between Eurozone governments in all these negotiations ran between current-account surplus-running creditor states and debtor states with large current account deficits (see also Armingeon and Cranmer 2017b; Finke and Bailer 2019; Tarlea et al. 2019). On policy issues related to questions of adjustment and financing, deficit and surplus countries aligned in opposing camps. Ultimately, however, surplus countries, who were in a stronger bargaining position, managed to tilt the policy outcomes in their favor, especially with regard to adjustment. Given that Chapter 5 showed that the costs of both external and internal adjustment were very high for surplus states, it is not surprising that they attempted—and often succeeded—to push most of the adjustment burden onto deficit states in European level negotiations. However, surplus countries seem to have been more willing to compromise on issues related to financing, where the negotiation outcomes were much more balanced between the interests of surplus and debtor states. This is in line with the findings from our analysis of surplus country crisis politics in Chapters 6 and 7, which showed that financing was often seen as a politically expedient alternative to macroeconomic adjustment in surplus countries. Thus, although some studies find that Germany was willing to make considerable concessions in negotiations about Eurozone crisis management (Lundgren et al. 2019), this willingness did not extend to issues which concerned questions of adjustment. Here, surplus countries such as Germany successfully secured negotiation outcomes that pushed the burden of adjustment on deficit countries.

Policy Implications and Avenues for Future Research

Taken together, the findings of this book have a number of implications for policymaking. First, our analysis has shown that distributional conflicts facilitated a suboptimal crisis response. Many of the Eurozone's root problems persist (see e.g., Mody 2018), not least because a coordinated European response has been lacking or has occurred in a piecemeal fashion. The lack of cooperation has also led to an unequal burden sharing. Despite considerable international pressure, domestic distributional conflicts impeded internal adjustment in surplus countries and pushed the burden of adjustment largely onto deficit states. Similarly, domestic politics in surplus countries, especially the fact that international transfers remained very unpopular amongst surplus-country voters, contributed to harsh financing conditions for deficit countries. While strict budgetary targets and rapid timelines for refinancing may have served to appease skeptic voters in surplus countries, they also made adjustment in deficit states unnecessarily painful, produced deep-seated ill will amongst voters in crisis countries and left little space for fiscal compensation policies. These dynamics have proven to be harmful both economically and politically. This suggests that institutional reforms designed to encourage more burden sharing (especially in times of crisis) and to make financing decisions less susceptible to domestic political pressure might lead to more effective crisis management in the future. Examples include a strengthened macroeconomic imbalances procedure that supports more balanced forms of adjustment,[3] expanded competences of the European Stability Mechanism, or EU-wide automatic stabilizers.

A second policy implication of our analysis is that the changing landscape of organized interests in Europe is likely to have lasting effects on future distributional conflicts and macroeconomic imbalances in the Eurozone. Our study of crisis politics in deficit countries has shown that the political weakness of organized labor and social policy groups meant that business bore much lower adjustment costs than workers and ordinary citizens. At the same time, many adjustment measures taken in the course of the crisis further deteriorated the economic and political influence of trade unions, suggesting that the unequal

---

[3] During the negotiations that led to the current design of the Macroeconomic Imbalances Procedure, surplus countries insisted on an asymmetric treatment of the different current-account positions, in which deficits of more than 3% of GDP are characterized as unsustainable, whereas surpluses only get monitored if they are 6% of GDP or larger (Moschella 2014).

distribution of adjustment costs may be amplified in future crises. Similarly, a range of studies has shown that the decreasing bargaining power of labor in countries like Germany or the Netherlands has been one of the main drivers of low wage costs, high savings, and large capital exports from surplus countries (Klug et al. 2019; Redeker 2019). This suggests that measures designed to counter the trend of diminishing labor power might not only be effective in contributing to more burden sharing in the next crisis, but could also contribute to reducing the emergence of macroeconomic imbalances in the first place.

Third, the analyses in this book suggest that the macroeconomic imbalances in the Eurozone are less structural than often assumed. In recent years, a range of studies have emphasized that given the structural diversity of economic models in the Eurozone, the common currency has a built-in tendency to result in stark current-account imbalances and financial crises (Baccaro and Pontusson 2016; Höpner and Lutter 2014; Iversen et al. 2016; Mody 2018; Streeck 2015). Our findings show, however, that economic interest groups were not generally opposed to adjustment. For example, we find that resistance to internal adjustment in surplus countries was not rooted in a broadly shared interest in defending the export-oriented growth model, but in distributional conflicts about how to adjust. This suggests that the imbalances are not just structural, but also rooted in politics. However, this does not mean that they are easy to address. Arriving at a more balanced union will require difficult compromises and is likely to remain politically difficult. The main challenge for policymakers is thus the question of how to use their room for maneuver to reduce current-account imbalances. Nonetheless, the insight that this is a political possibility is good news for the Eurozone.

Finally, our book also suggests a number of fruitful avenues for future research. First, the book emphasizes the need to study the preferences of organized societal actors empirically. Many political economy approaches rest on micro-level assumptions about interest group preferences. However, our evidence from surveying more than 700 large economic interest groups in six European countries shows that economic policy preferences are shaped by complex trade-offs between a wide range of policy options. This makes them difficult to deduce on purely theoretical grounds. Our analyses show that studying interests empirically yields a number of counterintuitive results. For instance, a majority of interest groups in deficit countries preferred harsh internal adjustment over other crisis strategies or that most economic groups in surplus countries actually favored some policies that would boost domestic demand. These results can not only help inform future theories on preference formation amongst interest groups, but they also add to our understanding of the specific nature of domestic distributional conflicts in times of crisis. More generally, our study suggests that political economy research is likely to benefit from the insights of interest group research (e.g., Dür and Mateo 2013; Klüver 2013, 2018), and vice versa. Our book presents the results of a large data-collection effort on interest group vulnerabilities and policy preferences in six Eurozone economies. The data and replication packages for all analyses presented in the book, including the survey data from the 716 interest groups, are available for download and replication at the FORS data archive (https://forsbase.unil.ch/project/my-study-overview/16230/). These datasets will serve as an important and rich resource for all scholars interested in European politics, interest groups, and political economy. We hope that other researchers will use this data to further explore the micro-foundations of interest groups' economic policy preferences.

Second, our book points to the importance of analyzing how material interests and conflicts interact with public opinion and dominant ideas amongst political decision-makers. Often, the influence of interest groups, the pressure of the electorate, and the ideological orientation of political decision-makers are still treated as competing explanations for important political outcomes (Hacker and Pierson 2010; Jabko 2013; Matthijs 2016a; Schneider and Slantchev 2017; Thompson 2015). While focusing on one ontological perspective ensures a certain theoretical crispness, there is a lot to be learned from combining these different schools of thought and asking what matters when, instead of what matters most. Recent research has taken promising first steps into mapping the scope conditions of each perspective in greater detail (Culpepper 2011; Reinke 2014). Our findings contribute to this nascent literature, for example, by showing that the general economic climate matters a great deal for whether the politics surrounding economic reforms are dominated by interest group politics or voter preferences and electoral concerns. While our research focuses on debates about adjustment during severe balance-of-payment crises, this pattern is likely to hold for a multitude of economic reforms, ranging from the regulation of labor and product markets to fiscal policies and taxation.

Finally, our findings also provide new insights for studying the ways in which domestic conflicts translate into international arenas and how states can try to avoid domestic distributive conflicts by externalizing costs to other countries. This has particularly important implications for research on the political economy of balance-of-payment crises and global imbalances more generally (Broz, Duru, and Frieden 2016; Eichengreen 1992; Eichengreen and Frieden 2001; Kinderman 2008; Simmons 1997; Walter 2013a). So far, research on these issues has been characterized by a one-sided focus on the role of deficit states. However, our evidence from Germany, Austria, and the Netherlands suggests that distributional conflicts within surplus countries play a similarly crucial role in the build-up and maintenance of financial imbalances. Given that these conflicts made it difficult for surplus countries to rebalance even in a highly institutionalized setting such as the Eurozone crisis, in which both political and economic pressures were high, suggests that rebalancing in "normal times" is not an easily achievable policy goal. Understanding these conflicts and how they play into the stickiness of large current-account surpluses in more detail is an important avenue for future research aimed at a better understanding of the drivers of global financial imbalances.

Appendix

Table A8.1 Other Eurozone crisis policy issues

Abbreviation	Description
BU1	EU cap on bank bonuses (legal or shareholder-approved)
BU2	Capital buffers (centralization or exibility)
BU3	The scope of the Single Supervisory Mechanism (SSM) (all banks or some banks)
BU4	Double majority for the decisions of the European Banking Authority (EBA)
BU5	Institutional responsibility for the SSM at the ECB
BU6	SSM implementation deadlines
BU7	Single Resolution Mechanism (SRM) decision-making powers
ESM1	Changing EU treaties
ESM7	The role of supranational institutions in the ESM
FC1	Question whether all EU member should adopt the Fiscal Compact
FC2	Fiscal Compact adopted by the Treaty change
FC3	The legal form of the debt brake
FC4	The role of the European Court of Justice (ECJ) in the Fiscal Compact
FC5	The role of the European Commission (EC) in the Fiscal Compact
FC6	The participation of non-euro members at the Euro Summit
FC8	Tax policy coordination
FC9	Incorporation of the Fiscal Compact to EU Treaties
G2	First Greek Program Structure (ad hoc or systematic)
PR3	Political accountability
SPA1	The suspension of Council voting rights for SGP non-compliant government
SPA3	The blocking of SGP sanctions by reversed qualified majority
SPA4	Six-pack rules on "good" and "bad" debts
TPA2	Pre-approving budgets by the Commission
TPA3	Independent macroeconomic forecasts

Bibliography

Acharya, Viral, Itamar Drechsler, and Philipp Schnabl. 2014. "A Pyrrhic Victory? Bank Bailouts and Sovereign Credit Risk." *The Journal of Finance* 69(6): 2689-739.
Administration, Irish Institute of Public, ed. 2015. *Ireland: A Directory 2016*. Dublin.
Afonso, Alexandre, Sotirios Zartaloudis, and Yannis Papadopoulos. 2015. "How Party Linkages Shape Austerity Politics: Clientelism and Fiscal Adjustment in Greece and Portugal during the Eurozone Crisis." *Journal of European Public Policy* 22(3): 315-34.
Agénor, Pierre-Richard, Marcus Miller, David Vines, and Axel Weber. 2006. *The Asian Financial Crisis: Causes, Contagion and Consequences*. Cambridge University Press.
Aizenman, Joshua. 2007. "Large Hoarding of International Reserves and the Emerging Global Economic Architecture." *National Bureau of Economic Research Working Paper* 13277.
Aizenman, Joshua. 2015. "The Eurocrisis: Muddling through, or on the Way to a More Perfect Euro Union?" *Comparative Economic Studies* 57(2): 205-21. file:///Users/ray/Downloads/ces.2014.37.pdf.
Aizenman, Joshua, Mahir Binici, and Michael M. Hutchison. 2013. NBER Working Paper Series, *Credit Ratings and the Pricing of Sovereign Debt during the Euro Crisis*. Harvard University Press.
Aizenman, Joshua, Michael Hutchison, and Yothin Jinjarak. 2013. "What Is the Risk of European Sovereign Debt Defaults? Fiscal Space, CDS Spreads and Market Pricing of Risk." *Journal of International Money and Finance* 34: 37-59.
Aizenman, Joshua, Michael Hutchison, and James Lothian. 2013. "The European Sovereign Debt Crisis: Background and Perspectives, Overview of the Special Issue." *Journal of International Money and Finance* 34(Complete): 1-5.
Alesina, Alberto and Allan Drazen. 1991. "Why Are Stabilizations Delayed?" *American Economic Review* 81: 1170-88.
Alesina, Alberto, Carlo Favero, and Francesco Giavazzi. 2019. *Austerity: When It Works and When It Doesn't*. Princeton University Press.
Algieri, Bernardina and Thierry Bracke. 2011. "Patterns of Current Account Adjustment— Insights from Past Experience." *Open Economies Review* 22(3): 401-25.
Allen, Franklin, Elena Carletti, and Giancarlo Corsetti. 2011. *Life in the Eurozone with or without Sovereign Default?* FIC Press.
Alt, James, David Dreyer Lassen, and Joachim Wehner. 2014. "It Isn't Just about Greece: Domestic Politics, Transparency, and Fiscal Gimmickry in Europe." *British Journal of Political Science* 44: 707-16.
Altiparmakis, Argyrios and Jasmine Lorenzini. 2019. "Bailouts, Austerity and Protest: Representative Democracy and Policy-Making in Times of Austerity." In *Contestation during Times of Crisis*, ed. Hanspeter Kriesi and Silja Häusermann. Book manuscript.
Amiel, David and Paul-Adrien Hyppolite. 2016. "Is There an Easy Way Out? Redenomination Issues and Their Financial Consequences in Case of a Greek Exit from the Eurozone." In *A New Growth Model for the Greek Economy*, Springer, 115-39.
Amri, Puspa D. and Thomas Willett. 2017. "Policy Inconsistencies and the Political Economy of Currency Crises." *Journal of International Commerce, Economics and Policy* 8(1): 1750004.
Andreadis, Ioannis, Theodore Chadjipadelis, and Eftichia Teperoglou. 2016. *Hellenic Voter Study 2012*. https://www.openicpsr.org/openicpsr/project/100022/version/V6/view.

Andronikidou, Aikaterini and Iosif Kovras. 2012. "Cultures of Rioting and Anti-Systemic Politics in Southern Europe." *West European Politics* 35(4): 707–25.

Anduiza, Eva, Camilo Cristancho, and José M. Sabucedo. 2014. "Mobilization through Online Social Networks: The Political Protest of the Indignados in Spain." *Information Communication and Society* 17(6): 750–64.

Ardagna, Silvia and Francesco Caselli. 2014. "The Political Economy of the Greek Debt Crisis: A Tale of Two Bailouts." *American Economic Journal: Macroeconomics* 6(4): 291–323.

Armingeon, Klaus, and Lucio Baccaro. 2012a. "Political Economy of the Sovereign Debt Crisis: The Limits of Internal Devaluation." *Industrial Law Journal* 41(3): 254–75.

Armingeon, Klaus and Lucio Baccaro. 2012b. "The Sorrows of Young Euro: The Sovereign Debt Crisis of Ireland and Southern Europe." In *Coping with Crisis: Government Responses to the Great Recession*, pp. 162–97, ed. Nancy Bermeo and Jonas Pontusson. Russell Sage Foundation.

Armingeon, Klaus and Skyler Cranmer. 2017. "Position Taking in the Euro Crisis." *European Journal of Public Policy* 25(4): 546–66.

Armingeon, Klaus and Nathalie Giger. 2008. "Conditional Punishment: A Comparative Analysis of the Electoral Consequences of Welfare State Retrenchment in OECD Nations, 1980–2003." *West European Politics* 31(3): 558–80.

Armingeon, Klaus and Kai Guthmann. 2014. "Democracy in Crisis? The Declining Support for National Democracy in European Countries, 2007–2011." *European Journal of Political Research* 53(3): 423–42.

Armingeon, Klaus, Kai Guthmann, and David Weisstanner. 2016. "How the Euro Divides the Union: The Effect of Economic Adjustment on Support for Democracy in Europe." *Socio-Economic Review* 14(1): 1–26.

Åslund, A. 2012. "Why a Breakup of the Euro Area Must Be Avoided: Lessons from Previous Breakups." *Peterson Institute for International Economics Policy Brief 12–20* (August): 1–15.

Atoyan, Ruben, Jonathan Manning, and Jesmin Rahman. 2013. "Rebalancing: Evidence from Current Account Adjustment in Europe." *IMF Working Paper* 13(74).

Austria Presse Agentur (2011): "Österreicher lehnen EU-Rettungsschirm ab." https://www.diepresse.com/704181/osterreicher-lehnen-eu-rettungsschirm-ab (last accessed 05.05.2020).

Avdagic, S. 2010. "When Are Concerted Reforms Feasible? Explaining the Emergence of Social Pacts in Western Europe." *Comparative Political Studies* 43(5): 628–57. http://emedien.sub.uni-hamburg.de/han/WebofKnowledge/apps.webofknowledge.com/full_record.do?product=UA&search_mode=Refine&qid=5&SID=U1f8D5EkbAM32IgBbDo&page=1&doc=20.

Avram, Silvia, Francesco Figari, Chrysa Leventi, Horacio Levy, Jekaterina Navicke, Manos Matsaganis, Eva Militaru, Alari Paulus, Olga Rastrigina, et al. 2013. "The Distributional Effects of Fiscal Consolidation in Nine Countries." *Euromod Documento de trabajoNo* 2 (13): 34–41.

Baccaro, Lucio and Jonas Pontusson. 2016. "Rethinking Comparative Political Economy: The Growth Model Perspective." *Politics & Society* 44(2): 175–207.

Baccaro, Lucio and Lim Sang-Hoon. 2007. "Social Pacts as Coalitions of the Weak and Moderate: Ireland, Italy and South Korea in Comparative Perspective." *European Journal of Industrial Relations* 13(22): 27–46. file:///Users/ray/Downloads/European Journal of Industrial Relations-2007-Baccaro-27-46.pdf.

Baccaro, Lucio and Marco Simoni. 2008. "Policy Concertation in Europe: Understanding Government Choice." *Comparative Political Studies* 41(10): 1323–48. file:///Users/ray/Downloads/0010414008315861(1).pdf.

Baerg, Nicole Rae and Mark Hallerberg. 2016. "Explaining Instability in the Stability and Growth Pact: The Contribution of Member State Power and Euroskepticism to the Euro Crisis." *Comparative Political Studies* 49(7): 968–1009.

Bagnai, Alberto, Brigitte Granville, and Christian A Mongeau Ospina. 2017. "Withdrawal of Italy from the Euro Area: Stochastic Simulations of a Structural Macroeconometric Model." *Economic Modelling* 64: 524–38.

Baldwin, Richard and Francesco Giavazzi. 2015. *The Eurozone Crisis: A Consensus View of the Causes and a Few Possible Solutions*. CEPR Press.

Baldwin, Richard et al. 2015. "Rebooting the Eurozone: Step 1 – Agreeing a Crisis Narrative." *CEPR POLICY INSIGHT* 85: 1–15. http://cepr.org/sites/default/files/policy_insights/PolicyInsight85.pdf.

Bandau, Frank and Kathrin Dümig. 2015. "Verwaltung Des Deutschen 'Beschäftigungswunders' – Die Arbeitsmarktpolitik Der Schwarz-Gelben Koalition 2009-2013." In *Regieren Im Schatten Der Krise*, pp. 374–94, ed. Thomas Saalfeld and Reimut Zohlnhöfer. Springer.

Banerji, Angana et al. 2017. *Labor and Product Market Reforms in Advanced Economies: Fiscal Costs, Gains, and Support*. International Monetary Fund.

Bank of International Settlements. 2016. "Consolidated Banking Statistics." https://www.bis.org/statistics/consstats.htm.

Barro, Robert J. and David B. Gordon. 1983. "Rules, Discretion, and Reputation in a Positive Model of Monetary Policy." *Journal of Monetary Economics* 12: 101–21.

Barta, Zsófia. 2018. *In the Red: The Politics of Public Debt Accumulation in Developed Countries*. University of Michigan Press.

Bartels, Larry and Nancy Bermeo. 2013. *Mass Politics in Tough Times: Opinions, Votes and Protest in the Great Recession*. Oxford University Press.

Batini, N., L. Eyraud, L. Forni, and A. Weber. 2014. "Fiscal Multipliers: Size, Determinants, and Use in Macroeconomic Projections." International Monetary Fund, Technical Guidance Note, Washington.

Bauer, Simon and Nils Steiner. 2015. "Eurokrise, Economic Voting Und Der Erfolg Der Union Bei Der Bundestagswahl 2013. Positions- Und Performanzbasierte Sachfragenorientierungen Als Determinanten Der Wahlentscheidung." In *Wirtschaft, Krise Und Wahlverhalten*, ed. Heiko Giebler and Aiko Wagner, pp. 49–83. Nomos Verlagsgesellschaft.

Bauhr, Monika and Nicholas Charron. 2018. "Why Support International Redistribution? Corruption and Public Support for Aid in the Eurozone." *European Union Politics* 19(2): 233–54.

Baumgartner, Frank et al. 2009. "Does Money Buy Public Policy?" In *Lobbying and Policy Change: Who Wins, Who Loses, and Why*, pp. 190–215. University of Chicago Press.

Baumgartner, Josef and Serguei Kaniovski. 2015. "Steuerreform 2015/16 – Gesamtwirtschaftliche Wirkungen Bis 2019." *WIFO-Monatsberichte* 88(5): 399–416.

Bayoumi, Tamim and Barry Eichengreen. 1992. "Shocking Aspects of European Monetary Unification." *NBER Working Paper* No. 3949. http://www.nber.org/papers/w3949.

BDI. 2014. "Vertrauen Und Zuversicht Der Unternehmen Stärken – BDI-Präsident Ulrich Grillo Forderte Auf Dem Tag Der Deutschen Industrie Eine Investitionsoffensive."

Bechtel, Michael M., Jens Hainmueller, and Yotam Margalit. 2014. "Preferences for International Redistribution: The Divide over the Eurozone Bailouts." *American Journal of Political Science* 58(4): 835–56.

Bechtel, Michael M., Jens Hainmueller, and Yotam Margalit. 2017. "Policy Design and Domestic Support for International Bailouts." *European Journal of Political Research* 56(4): 864–86.

Becker, Gary. 1983. "A Theory of Competition among Pressure Groups for Political Influence." *The Quarterly Journal of Economics* 130(3): 371–402.
Bélanger, Éric and Bonnie M. Meguid. 2008. "Issue Salience, Issue Ownership, and Issue-Based Vote Choice." *Electoral Studies* 27(3): 477–91.
Bellucci, P., M. C. Lobo, and M. S. Lewis-Beck. 2012. "Economic Crisis and Elections: The European Periphery." *Electoral Studies* 31(3): 469–71.
Bentolila, Samuel, Juan J. Dolado, and Juan F. Jimeno. 2011. IZA Discussion Paper Series *Reforming an Insider-Outsider Labor Market: The Spanish Experience.* http://ftp.iza.org/dp6186.pdf.
Bentolila, Samuel, Juan J. Dolado, and Juan F. Jimeno. 2012. "Reforming an Insider-Outsider Labor Market: The Spanish Experience." *IZA Journal of European Labor Studies* 1(1): https://doi.org/10.1186/2193-9012-1-4.
Beramendi, Pablo and Daniel Stegmueller. 2016. "The Political Geography of the Euro Crisis." Unpublished working paper.
Bermeo, Nancy and Jonas Pontusson. 2012. "Coping with Crisis: Government Reactions to the Great Recession." *Review of International Political Economy* 20 (5): 1132–43.
Bernanke, Ben. S. 2015. "Germany's Trade Surplus Is a Problem." *Brookings Blog.*
Bernhard, William, J. Lawerence Broz, and William Roberts Clark. 2002. "The Political Economy of Monetary Institutions." *International Organization* 56(4): 693–723.
Bernhard, William and David Leblang. 2006. "Polls and Pounds: Public Opinion and Exchange Rate Behavior in Britain." *Quarterly Journal of Political Science* 1: 25–47.
Bernhard, William and David Leblang. 2016. "Sovereign Debt, Migration Pressure, and Government Survival." *Comparative Political Studies* 49(7): 907–38.
Bindseil, Ulrich and Philipp Johann König. 2012. "TARGET2 and the European Sovereign Debt Crisis." *Kredit und Kapital* 45(2): 135–74.
Bird, Graham and Thomas D. Willett. 2004. "IMF Conditionality, Implementation and the New Political Economy of Ownership." *Comparative Economic Studies* 46(3): 423–50.
Bird, Graham and Thomas D. Willett. 2008. "Why Do Governments Delay Devaluation? The Political Economy of Exchange-Rate Inertia." *World Economics* 9(4): 55–74.
Blanchard, Olivier, Christopher J. Erceg, and Jesper Lindé. 2017. "Jump-Starting the Euro-Area Recovery: Would a Rise in Core Fiscal Spending Help the Periphery?" *NBER Macroeconomics Annual* 31(1): 103–82.
Blomberg, Brock, Jeffry Frieden, and Ernesto Stein. 2005. "Sustaining Fixed Rates: The Political Economy of Currency Pegs in Latin America." *Journal of Applied Economics* VIII(2): 203–25.
Blustein, Paul. 2001. *The Chastening: Inside the Crisis That Rocked the Global Financial System and Humbled the IMF.* Public Affairs.
Blyth, Mark. 2002. *Great Transformations: Economic Ideas and Institutional Change in the Twentieth Century.* Cambridge University Press.
Blyth, Mark. 2013. *Austerity: The History of a Dangerous Idea.* Oxford University Press.
Boeri, Tito et al. 2001. "Would You like to Shrink the Welfare State? A Survey of European Citizens." *Economic Policy* 16(32): 9–50.
Bonatti, Luigi and Andrea Fracasso. 2013. "The German Model and the European Crisis." *JCMS: Journal of Common Market Studies* 51(6): 1023–39.
Börzel, Tanja and Thomas Risse. 2018. "From the Euro to the Schengen Crises: European Integration Theories, Politicization, and Identity Politics." *Journal of European Public Policy* 25(1): 83–108.
Bosco, Anna and Susannah Verney. 2012. "Electoral Epidemic: The Political Cost of Economic Crisis in Southern Europe, 2010-11." *South European Society and Politics* 17(2): 129–54.

Bosco, Anna and Susannah Verney. 2016. *Elections in Hard Times: Southern Europe 2010-11*. Routledge.
Boumans, Saskia and Maarten Keune. 2018. "Inclusive Growth Through Collective Bargaining in the Netherlands." *KU Leuven Working Paper* (June): 1-40.
Braun, Daniela and Markus Tausendpfund. 2014. "The Impact of the Euro Crisis on Citizens' Support for the European Union." *Journal of European Integration* 36(3): 231-45.
Brazys, Samuel and Aidan Regan. 2017. "The Politics of Capitalist Diversity in Europe: Explaining Ireland's Divergent Recovery from the Euro Crisis." *Perspectives on Politics* 15(2): 411-27. file:///Users/ray/Downloads/politics_of_ capitalist_diversity_in_europe_explaining_irelands_divergent_recovery_from_the_euro_ crisis(1).pdf.
Breen, Michael. 2012. "The International Politics of Ireland's EU/IMF Bailout." *Irish Studies in International Affairs* 23(1): 75-87.
Bremer, Björn and Reto Bürgisser. 2019. *Public Preferences towards Fiscal Policies: Survey Experiments on Budgetary Priorities and Trade-Offs*. Florence.
Bremer, Björn, Swen Hutter, and Hanspeter Kriesi. 2019. "Electoral Punishment and Protest Politics in Times of Crisis." In *Contestation during Times of Crisis*, ed. Hanspeter Kriesi and Silja Häusermann. Manuscript.
Brown, Brendan. 2012. *Euro Crash: The Exit Route from Monetary Failure in Europe*. Palgrave Macmillan.
Broz, J. Lawrence, Maya Duru, and Jeffry Frieden. 2016. "Policy Responses to Balance-of-Payments Crises: The Role of Elections." *Open Economies Review* 27(2): 204-27.
Broz, J. Lawrence and Jeffry Frieden. 2001. "The Political Economy of International Monetary Relations." *Annual Review of Political Science* 4: 317-43.
Brunnermeier, Markus K., Harold James, and Jean-Pierre Landau. 2016. *The Euro and the Battle of Ideas*. Princeton University Press.
Bulfone, Fabio and Alexandre Afonso. 2019. "Business Against Markets: Employer Resistance to Collective Bargaining Liberalisation During the Eurozone Crisis." *Comparative Political Studies*, https://doi.org/10.1177/0010414019879963.
Bulmer, Simon. 2014. "Germany and the Eurozone Crisis: Between Hegemony and Domestic Politics." *West European Politics* 37(6): 1244-63.
Bundesfinanzministerium. 2013. *Monatsbericht Des BMF - Dezember*. Berlin.
Burgoon, B. and F. Dekker. 2010. "Flexible Employment, Economic Insecurity and Social Policy Preferences in Europe." *Journal of European Social Policy* euro(2): 126-41.
Burstein, Paul. 2003. "The Impact of Public Opinion on Public Policy." *Political Research Quarterly* 56(1): 29-40.
Busemeyer, Marius R. and Julian L. Garritzmann. 2017. "Public Opinion on Policy and Budgetary Trade-Offs in European Welfare States: Evidence from a New Comparative Survey." *Journal of European Public Policy* 24(6): 871-89.
Busemeyer, Marius, Julian Garritzmann, and Erik Neimanns. 2020. *A Loud, but Noisy Signal? Public Opinion, Parties and Interest Groups in the Politics of Education Reform in Western Europe*. Oxford University Press.
Busemeyer, Marius, Achim Goerres, and Simon Weschle. 2009. "Attitudes towards Redistributive Spending in an Era of Demographic Ageing: The Rival Pressures from Age and Income in 14 OECD Countries." *Journal of European Social Policy* 19(3): 195-212.
Caballero, Ricardo J. and Arvind Krishnamurthy. 2009. "Global Imbalances and Financial Fragility." *Amercian Economic Review: Papers & Proceedings* 99(2): 584-8.

Calvo, Guillermo A. 1998. "Capital Flows and Capital-Market Crises: The Simple Economics of Sudden Stops." *Journal of Applied Economics* 1(1): 35–54.

Caraway, Teri L., Stephanie J. Rickard, and Mark S. Anner. 2012. "International Negotiations and Domestic Politics: The Case of IMF Labor Market Conditionality." *International Organization* 66(1): 27–61.

Cardarelli, Roberto, Selim Elekdag, and Ayhan Kose. 2009. "Capital Inflows: Macroeconomic Implications and Policy Responses." *IMF Working Paper* WP/09/40.

Carstensen, Martin B. and Vivien A. Schmidt. 2018. "Ideational Power and Pathways to Legitimation in the Euro Crisis." *Review of International Political Economy* 25(6): 753–78.

Cawley, Anthony. 2012. "Sharing the Pain or Shouldering the Burden?: News-Media Framing of the Public Sector and the Private Sector in Ireland during the Economic Crisis, 2008–2010." *Journalism Studies* 13(4): 600–15.

Cecchetti, Stephen G., Robert N. McCauley, and Patrick M. McGuire. 2012. "Interpreting TARGET2 Balances." *BIS Working Papers* (393).

Chang, Michele and Patrick Leblond. 2015. "All In: Market Expectations of Eurozone Integrity in the Sovereign Debt Crisis." *Review of International Political Economy* 22(3): 626–55.

Chin, Gregory T. 2010. "Remaking the Architecture: The Emerging Powers, Self-Insuring and Regional Insulation." *International Affairs* 86(3): 693–715.

Chinn, Menzie D., Barry Eichengreen, and Hiro Ito. 2014. "A Forensic Analysis of Global Imbalances." *Oxford Economic Papers* 66(2): 465–90.

Chiu, Eric and Thomas Willett. 2009. "The Interactions of Strength of Governments and Alternative Exchange Rate Regimes in Avoiding Currency Crises." *International Studies Quarterly* 53(4): 1001–25.

Chwieroth, Jeffrey M. 2009. *Capital Ideas: The IMF and the Rise of Financial Liberalization*. Princeton University Press.

Cioffi, John W. and Kenneth A. Dubin. 2016. "Commandeering Crisis: Partisan Labor Repression in Spain under the Guise of Economic Reform." *Politics and Society* 44(3): 423–53. file:///Users/ray/Downloads/cioffi_dubin.pdf.

CIS. 2011. *Opinión Pública y Política Fiscal: Estudio No. 2.910 (Julio 2011)*. Madrid.

Claessens, Stijn, Simon Evenett, and Bernard Hoekman. 2010. *Rebalancing the Global Economy: A Primer for Policymaking*. Centre for Economic Policy Research.

Claeys, Gregory, Zsolt Darvas, and Guntram B. Wolff. 2014. "Benefits and Drawbacks of European Unemployment Insurance." https://www.bruegel.org/wp-content/uploads/imported/publications/pb_2014_06_281114.pdf.

Clark, William Roberts and Mark Hallerberg. 2000. "Mobile Capital, Domestic Institutions, and Electorally Induced Monetary and Fiscal Policy." *American Political Science Review* 94(2): 323–46.

Cleeland Knight, Sarah. 2010. "Divested Interests: Globalization and the New Politics of Exchange Rates." *Business and Politics* 12(2): Article 3.

CNN. 2010. "Greek Workers Strike as Government Tightens Belt." *CNN Online*. http://edition.cnn.com/2010/WORLD/europe/02/10/greece.strikes/index.html.

Cohen, Benjamin J. 1993. "Beyond EMU: The Problem of Sustainability." *Economics & Politics* 5(2): 187–203.

Conefrey, Thomas and John FitzGerald. 2009. *Managing Housing Bubbles in Regional Economies under EMU: Ireland and Spain*. National Institute Economic Review, https://journals.sagepub.com/doi/abs/10.1177/0027950110364103

Cooper, Richard. 1971. "Currency Devaluation in Developing Countries." *Essays in International Finance* 86: 276–304.Copelovitch, Mark. 2010. *The International Monetary Fund in the Global Economy*. Cambridge University Press.

Copelovitch, Mark and Henrik Enderlein. 2016. *Kicking the Can Down the Road: The Euro Crisis and the Political Economy of Troika Bailouts*. University of Wisconsin Press.
Copelovitch, Mark, Jeffry Frieden, and Stefanie Walter. 2016. "The Political Economy of the Euro Crisis." *Comparative Political Studies* 49(7): 811–40.
Copelovitch, Mark and David Singer. 2020. *Banks on the Brink: Global Capital, Securities Markets, and the Political Roots of Financial Crises*. Cambridge University Press.
Copenhagen Economics. 2008. "Study on Reduced VAT Applied to Goods and Services in the Member States of the European Union," no. June: 103. http://ec.europa.eu/taxation_customs/resources/documents/taxation/vat/how_vat_works/rates/study_reduced_vat.pdf.
CORI Justice. 2008a. *Budget 2009: CORI Justice Analysis and Critique*. Dublin, IE.
CORI Justice. 2008b. *Submission to the Commission on Taxation: June 2008*. Dublin, IE.
Costa, Hermes Augusto. 2012. "From Europe as a Model to Europe as Austerity: The Impact of the Crisis on Portuguese Trade Unions." *Transfer: European Review of Labour and Research* 18(4): 397–410.
Cowen, Brian. 2008. "Speech by An Taoiseach, Mr Brian Cowen, TD (29.11.2008)." https://www.irishtimes.com/news/full-text-of-taoiseach-brian-cowen-s-speech-1.832374.
CPB. 2015. "Economy Most Urgent Problem According to Dutch Voters." *Centraal Planbureau Policy Brief*. https://www.cpb.nl/en/publications?author=89411&year=2015.
CPB. 2016. "Nederlandse Economie Stabiel." *Centraal Planbureau Policy Brief* 16(4): 733–43.
Crafts, N. 2014. "What Does the 1930s' Experience Tell Us about the Future of the Eurozone?" *Journal of Common Market Studies* 52(4): 713–27.
Cramme, Olaf and Sara Hobolt. 2014. *Democratic Politics in a European Union under Stress*. Oxford University Press.
Culpepper, Pepper. 2011. *Quiet Politics and Business Power: Corporate Control in Europe and Japan*. Cambridge University Press.
Culpepper, Pepper. 2014. "The Political Economy of Unmediated Democracy: Italian Austerity under Mario Monti." *West European Politics* 37(6): 1264–81.
Culpepper, Pepper and Aidan Regan. 2014. "Why Don't Governments Need Trade Unions Anymore? The Death of Social Pacts in Ireland and Italy." *Socio-Economic Review* 12(4): 723–45.
Culpepper, Pepper and Raphael Reinke. 2014. "Structural Power and Bank Bailouts in the United Kingdom and the United States." *Politics & Society* 42(4): 427–54.
Dahl, R. A. 1971. *Polyarchy: Participation and Opposition*. Yale University Press.
Daniele, Gianmarco and Benny Geys. 2015. "Public Support for European Fiscal Integration in Times of Crisis." *Journal of European Public Policy* 22(5): 650–70.
de Almeida, Luiza Antoun, and Vybhavi Balasundharam. 2018. *On the Impact of Structural Reforms on Output and Employment: Evidence from a Cross-Country Firm-Level Analysis*. International Monetary Fund.
De Barón, Íñigo. 2016. "Bank of Spain Says €26bn of Bailout Will Never Be Recovered." *El País*. https://english.elpais.com/elpais/2016/09/12/inenglish/1473674847_325160.html.
De Breadun, Deaglan. 2009. "Ictu Leader Rejects 'toxic' Plan to Cut Minimum Wage Level." *Irish Times*. https://www.irishtimes.com/news/ictu-leader-rejects-toxic-plan-to-cut-minimum-wage-level-1.704782.
De Grauwe, Paul. 2013a. "Design Failures in the Eurozone: Can They Be Fixed?" *LSE "Europe in Question" Discussion Paper Series* 57(February).
De Grauwe, Paul. 2013b. "The Political Economy of the Euro." *Annual Review of Political Science* 16: 153–70.
De Grauwe, Paul and Wim Moesen. 2009. "Common Euro Bonds: Necessary, Wise or to Be Avoided?" *Intereconomics* 44(3): 132–41.

de Guzmán, Sofía Pérez, Beltrán Roca, and Iban Diaz-Parra. 2016. "Political Exchange, Crisis of Representation and Trade Union Strategies in a Time of Austerity: Trade Unions and 15M in Spain." *Transfer* 22(4): 461–74.

De Hond, Maurice. 2011a. "De Nieuwste Ontwikkelingen Rondom de Schuldencrisis": 19–22.

De Hond, Maurice. 2011b. "Nieuw Haags Peil 15 Februari 2011." *www.peil.nl* (November).

De Hond, Maurice. 2012. "Hoe Verder Met Griekenland?"

De Hond, Maurice. 2015. "De Stemming van 28 Juni 2015": 28–30.

Degner, Hanno and Dirk Leuffen. 2016. "Keynes, Friedman, or Monnet? Explaining Parliamentary Voting Behaviour on Fiscal Aid for Euro Area Member States." *West European Politics* 39(6): 650–70: 1139–59.

del Rio Loira, Pablo and Menno Fenger. 2019. "Spanish Trade Unions against Labour Market Reforms: Strategic Choices and Outcomes." *Transfer: European Review of Labour and Research* OnlineFirst: 1–15.

Della Porta, Donatella. 2015. *Social Movements in Times of Austerity: Bringing Capitalism Back into Protest Analysis*. John Wiley & Sons.

Dellepiane-Avellaneda, Sebastian and Niamh Hardiman. 2015. "The Politics of Fiscal Efforts in Ireland and Spain: Market Credibility vs. Political Legitimacy." In *The Politics of Extreme Austerity: Greece in the Eurozone Crisis*, pp. 198–221, ed. Georgios Karyotis and Roman Gerodimos. Palgrave Macmillan.

DGB. 2013. "Gewerkschaftliche Forderungen Zur Re-Regulierung Des Arbeitsmarktes." *DGB-Pressekonferenz*.

Dhonte, Mr Pierre. 1997. *Conditionality as an Instrument of Borrower Credibility*. International Monetary Fund.

Die Presse. 2011. "Österreicher Lehnen EU-Rettungsschirm Ab." https://www.diepresse.com/704181/osterreicher-lehnen-eu-rettungsschirm-a.b

Dinas, Elias. 2010. "The Greek General Election of 2009: PASOK – The Third Generation." *West European Politics* 33(2): 389–98.

Dinas, Elias and Lamprini Rori. 2013. "The 2012 Greek Parliamentary Elections: Fear and Loathing in the Polls." *West European Politics* 36(1): 270–82.

Dinas, Elias, Ignacio Jurado, Nikitas Konstantinidis, and Stefanie Walter. 2015. "Tsipras Reaps Benefits of Brinkmanship Politics." *Peripheral Vision* (13 October 2015).

Dixit, Avinash and John Londregan. 1996. "The Determinants of Success of Special Interests in Redistributive Politics." *The Journal of Politics* 58(4): 1132–55.

Dolezal, Martin. 2014. "Five More Years in Opposition? The Austrian Greens in the 2013 Parliamentary Election." *Environmental Politics* 23(3): 525–30.

Dolezal, Martin and Eva Zeglovits. 2014. "Almost an Earthquake: The Austrian Parliamentary Election of 2013." *West European Politics* 37(3): 644–52.

Dolls, Mathias and Nils Wehrhöfer. 2018. "Attitudes towards Euro Area Reforms: Evidence from a Randomized Survey Experiment." CESifo Working Paper.

Dølvik, Jon Erik and Andrew Martin. 2014. *European Social Models from Crisis to Crisis: Employment and Inequality in the Era of Monetary Integration*. Oxford University Press.

Donnelly, Shawn. 2018. "Advocacy Coalitions and the Lack of Deposit Insurance in Banking Union." *Journal of Economic Policy Reform* 21(3): 210–23.

Donovan, Donal and Antoin E. Murphy. 2013. *The Fall of the Celtic Tiger: Ireland and the Euro Debt Crisis*. Oxford University Press.

Dooley, Michael, David Folkerts-Landau, and Peter Garber. 2004. "The Revived Bretton Woods System: Alive and Well." *International Journal of Finance & Economics* 9 (December): 307–13.

Dooley, Michael, David Folkerts-Landau, and Peter Garber. 2009. "Bretton Woods II Still Defines the International Monetary System." *Pacific Economic Review* 14(3): 297–311.
Downs, Anthony. 1957. "An Economic Theory of Political Action in a Democracy." *Journal of Political Economy* 65(2): 135–50.
Dowsett, Sonya and John Stonestreet. 2012. "Spain PM Pleads for Political, Fiscal Union in Europe." *Reuters Business News.*
Drazen, Allan. 2000. *Political Economy in Macroeconomics.* Princeton University Press.
Drazen, Allan. 2002. "Conditionality and Ownership in IMF Lending: A Political Economy Approach." *IMF Staff Papers* 49 (Special Issue): 36–67. http://papers.ssrn.com/sol3/papers.cfm?abstract_id=346620.
Dreher, Axel. 2009. 141 Public Choice, *IMF Conditionality: Theory and Evidence.* file:///Users/ray/Library/Application Support/Mendeley Desktop/Downloaded/Dreher - 2009 - IMF conditionality Theory and evidence.pdf.
Dreher, Axel and Roland Vaubel. 2004. "The Causes and Consequences of IMF Conditionality." *Emerging Markets Finance and Trade* 40(3): 26–54.
Duch, Raymond. 2007. "Comparative Studies of the Economy and the Vote." In *Encyclopedia of Comparative Politics,* ed. Charles Boix and Susan Stokes, pp. 805–44. Oxford University Press, 805–44.
Dullien, Sebastian. 2014. "The Macroeconomic Stabilisation Impact of a European Basic Unemployment Insurance Scheme." *Intereconomics* 4: 189–93.
Dullien, Sebastian and Ulrike Guérot. 2012. "The Long Shadow of Ordoliberalism: Germany's Approach to the Euro Crisis." European Council on Foreign Relations Policy Brief 22.
Dür, Andreas. 2019. "How Interest Groups Influence Public Opinion: Arguments Matter More than the Sources." *European Journal of Political Research* 58(2): 514–35.
Dür, Andreas and Dirk De Bièvre. 2007. "The Question of Interest Group Influence." *Journal of Public Policy* 27(1): 1–12.
Dür, Andreas and Gemma Mateo. 2010. "Irish Associations and Lobbying on EU Legislation: Resources, Access Points, and Strategies." *Irish Political Studies* 25(1): 107–22.
Dür, Andreas and Gemma Mateo. 2013. "Gaining Access or Going Public? Interest Group Strategies in Five European Countries." *European Journal of Political Research* 52(5): 660–86.
Dür, Andreas and Gemma Mateo. 2016. *Insiders versus Outsiders: Interest Group Politics in Multilevel Europe.* Oxford University Press.
Dustmann, Christian, Bernd Fitzenberger, Uta Schönberg, and Alexandra Spitz-Oener. 2014. "From Sick Man of Europe to Economic Superstar: Germany's Resurgent Economy." *Journal of Economic Perspectives* 28(1): 167–88.
Duval, Romain and Davide Furceri. 2018. "The Effects of Labor and Product Market Reforms: The Role of Macroeconomic Conditions and Policies." *IMF Economic Review* 66(1): 31–69.
Dyson, Kenneth. 2010. "Norman's Lament: The Greek and Euro Area Crisis in Historical Perspective." *New Political Economy* 15(4): 597–608.
Dyson, Kenneth. 2014. *States, Debt, and Power: 'Saints' and 'Sinners' in European History and Integration.* Oxford University Press.
Dyson, Kenneth. 2017. "Playing for High Stakes: The Eurozone Crisis." In Desmond Dinan and Kenneth Dyson, The European Union in Crisis, Macmillan Education.
EBRD. 2010. *Transition Report 2009.* London: European Bank for Reconstruction and Development.

ECB. 2012. "Technical Features of Outright Monetary Transactions." *ECB Press Release*.
Eckerstorfer, Paul and Doris Prammer. 2017. "Three Small Essays on Public Investment: Economic Rationales, the EU Fiscal Framework and Some Statistical Comparisons." *Monetary Policy & the Economy, Austrian Central Bank*: 32–47.
Ehlers, Fiona et al. 2015. "Schäuble's Push for Grexit Puts Merkel on Defensive." *Spiegel Online*.
Eichengreen, Barry. 1991. "Historical Research on International Lending and Debt." *Journal of Economic Perspectives* 5(2): 149–69.
Eichengreen, Barry. 1992. *Golden Fetters: The Gold Standard and the Great Depression, 1919-1939*. Oxford University Press.
Eichengreen, Barry. 1996. *Globalizing Capital: A History of the International Monetary System*. Princeton University Press.
Eichengreen, Barry. 2003. *Capital Flows and Crises*. MIT Press.
Eichengreen, Barry. 2010a. "Ireland's Rescue Package: Disaster for Ireland, Bad Omen for the Eurozone." *VoxEU. org*. https://voxeu.org/article/ireland-s-rescue-package-disaster-ireland-bad-omen-eurozone.
Eichengreen, Barry. 2010b. "The Breakup of the Euro Area." In *Europe and the Euro*, pp. 11–51. University of Chicago Press.
Eichengreen, Barry and Jeffry Frieden. 2001. *The Political Economy of European Monetary Unification*. Westview Press.
Eichengreen, Barry, Ricardo Hausmann, and Ugo Panizza. 2005. "The Pain of Original Sin." In *Other People's Money: Debt Denomination and Financial Instability in Emerging Market Economies*, ed. Barry Eichengreen and Ricardo Hausmann., pp. 13–47. University of Chicago Press.
Eichengreen, Barry, Naeun Jung, Stephen Moch, and Ashoka Mody. 2013. "The Eurozone Crisis: Phoenix Miracle or Lost Decade?" Journal of Macroeconomics 39(B): 288–308.
Eichengreen, Barry, Andrew Rose, and Charles Wyplosz. 1996. "Contagious Currency Crises: First Tests." *Scandinavian Journal of Economics* 98(4): 463–84.
Eichengreen, Barry and Peter Temin. 2010. "Fetters of Gold and Paper." *Oxford Review of Economic Policy* 26(3): 370–84.
Elekdag, Selim and Dirk Muir. 2014. "Das Public Kapital: How Much Would Higher German Public Investment Help Germany and the Euro Area?" *IMF Working Paper*, December 2.
Emmenegger, Patrick, Silja Häusermann, and Stefanie Walter. 2018. "National Sovereignty vs. International Cooperation: Policy Choices in Trade-Off Situations." *Swiss Political Science Review* 24(4): 400–22.
Enderlein, Henrik and Amy Verdun. 2009. "EMU's Teenage Challenge: What Have We Learned and Can We Predict from Political Science?" *Journal of European Public Policy* 16(4): 490–507.
Engel, Charles. 1993. "Real Exchange Rates and Relative Prices: An Empirical Investigation." *Journal of Monetary Economics* 32(1): 35–50.
Esaiasson, Peter and Christopher Wlezien. 2017. "Advances in the Study of Democratic Responsiveness: An Introduction." *Comparative Political Studies* 50(6): 699–710.
Estella, Antonio. 2015. "Potential Exit from the Eurozone: The Case of Spain." *Indiana Journal of Global Legal Studies* 22(2): 335–77.
Eurogroup. 2012. "Eurogroup Statement: 21.02.2012." https://www.esm.europa.eu/sites/default/files/2012-02-21_eurogroup_statement_bailout_for_greece.pdf.
European Commission. 2007. "Study on Reduced VAT Applied to Goods and Services in the Member States of the European Union." DG TAXUD 6530. http://ec.europa.eu/taxation_customs/sites/taxation/files/resources/documents/taxation/vat/how_vat_works/rates/study_reduced_vat.pdf.

European Commission. 2014. "Macroeconomic Imbalances Germany 2014." https://ec.europa.eu/economy_finance/publications/occasional_paper/2014/pdf/ocp174_en.pdf.
European Commission. 2015. "Macroeconomic Imbalances: Country Report Netherlands 2015." https://ec.europa.eu/economy_finance/publications/occasional_paper/2015/pdf/ocp221_en.pdf.
European Commission. 2016. "Country Reports 2016: The Netherlands."
European Commission. 2019a. "Standard Eurobarometer, No 64-84."
European Commission. 2019b. "Statutory Tax Rates in the European Economy Area."
Eurostat. 2019a. "General Government Gross Debt." https://ec.europa.eu/eurostat/web/products-datasets/-/teina230.
Eurostat. 2019b. "Monthly Minimum Wages - Bi-Annual Data." https://ec.europa.eu/eurostat/statistics-explained/index.php/Minimum_wage_statistics.
Evans, Adan. 2013. "The Threat of Geert Wilders Winning Snap Elections Is Likely to Be Enough to Force a Compromise on the Netherlands' 2013 Budget." *LSE - European Politics and Policy*: 1–3.
Featherstone, Kevin. 2011. "The JCMS Annual Lecture: The Greek Sovereign Debt Crisis and EMU: A Failing State in a Skewed Regime*." *JCMS: Journal of Common Market Studies* 49(2): 193–217.
Featherstone, Kevin. 2015. "External Conditionality and the Debt Crisis: The 'Troika'and Public Administration Reform in Greece." *Journal of European Public Policy* 22(3): 295–314.
Featherstone, Kevin and Dimitris Papadimitriou. 2008. *The Limits of Europeanization: Reform Capacity and Policy Conflict in Greece*. Springer.
Feenstra, Robert C., Robert Inklaar, and Marcel P. Timmer. 2015. "The Next Generation of the Penn World Table." *American Economic Review* 105(10): 3150–82.
Feld, L., E. Kohler, and D. Nientiedt. 2015. "Ordoliberalism, Pragmatism and the Eurozone Crisis: How the German Tradition Shaped Economic Policy in Europe". Freiburger Diskussionspapiere zur Ordnungsokonomik, No.15/04.
Fernandez, Raquel and Dani Rodrik. 1991. "Resistance to Reform: Status Quo Bias in the Presence of Individual-Specific Uncertainty." *American Economic Review* 81(5): 1146–55.
Fernández-Albertos, José, and Alexander Kuo. 2016. "Economic Hardship and Policy Preferences in the Eurozone Periphery Evidence from Spain." *Comparative Political Studies* 49(7): 874–906.
Fernández-Albertos, José, and Alexander Kuo. 2018. "The Structure of Business Preferences and Eurozone Crisis Policies." *Business and Politics* 20(2): 1–43.
Fernandez-Villaverde, Jesus, Luis Garciano, and Tano Santos. 2013. NBER Working Paper Series, "Political Credit Cycles: The Case of the Euro Zone."
Ferrara, Federico Maria, Jörg Haas, Andrew Peterson, and Thomas Sattler. 2018. "Exports vs. Investment: How Public Discourse Shapes Support for External Imbalances." *Investment: How Public Discourse Shapes Support for External Imbalances* (December 10, 2018).
Fetzer, Thiemo and Carlo Schwarz. 2019. "Tariffs and Politics: Evidence from Trump's Trade Wars." Center for European Reform Discussion Paper (DP13579).
Financial Times. 2016. "Spain Recoups Only a Fraction of Funds Pumped into Bank Bailouts." September 6. https://www.ft.com/content/6ca8fcb0-743b-11e6-b60a-de4532d5ea35.
Finke, Daniel and Stefanie Bailer. 2019. "Crisis Bargaining in the European Union: Formal Rules or Market Pressure?" *European Union Politics* 20(1): 109–33.
Flevotomou, Maria, Michael Haliassos, Christos Kotsogiannis, and Costas Meghir. 2017. "Tax and Welfare Reform in Greece." In *Beyond Austerity: Reforming the Greek Economy*, pp. 405–57, ed. Costas Meghir, Christopher A. Pissarides, Dimitri Vayanos, and Nikolaos Vettas. MIT Press.

FNV. 2016. "Loonontwikkeling En Arbeidsinkomensquote Notitie." *Notitie ten behoeve van het rondetafelgesprek met de commissie SZW.*
Forbes, Kristin J. and Michael W. Klein. 2015. "Pick Your Poison: The Choices and Consequences of Policy Responses to Crises." *IMF Economic Review* 63(1): 197–237.
Forschungsgruppe-Wahlen. 2016. "Politbarometer 2015 (Cumulated Data Set, Incl. Flash)." *GESIS Data Archive* ZA6700.
Foster, Chase and Jeffry Frieden. 2017. "Crisis of Trust: Socio-Economic Determinants of Europeans' Confidence in Government." *European Union Politics* 18(4): 511–35.
Frankel, Jeffrey and Andrew K. Rose. 1996. "Currency Crashes in Emerging Markets: An Empirical Treatment." *Journal of International Economics* 41: 351–66.
Frankel, Jeffrey and Shang-Jin Wei. 2004. *Managing Macroeconomic Crises: Policy Lessons.* NBER Working Paper No: 10907.
Frech, Elena, Thomas König, and Moritz Osnabrügge. 2015. "Öffentliche Unterstützung von Reformen Und Ihre Stabilität in Zeiten Der Eurokrise–Eine Experimentelle Untersuchung Der Wirksamkeit von Gegenargumenten." *ZPol Zeitschrift für Politikwissenschaft* 25(2): 219–45.
Freire, André, Marco Lisi, Ioannis Andreadis, and José Manuel Leite Viegas. 2014. "Political Representation in Bailed-out Southern Europe: Greece and Portugal Compared." *South European Society and Politics* 19(4): 413–33.
Frieden, Jeffry. 1991a. *Debt, Development, and Democracy.* Princeton University Press.
Frieden, Jeffry. 1991b. "Invested Interests: The Politics of National Economic Policies in a World of Global Finance." *International Organization* 45(4): 425–51.
Frieden, Jeffry. 2002. "Real Sources of European Currency Policy: Sectoral Interests and European Monetary Integration." *International Organization* 56(4): 831–60.
Frieden, Jeffry. 2015a. *Currency Politics. The Political Economy of Exchange Rate Policy.* Princeton University Press.
Frieden, Jeffry. 2015b. "The Political Economy of Adjustment and Rebalancing." *Journal of International Money and Finance* 52: 4–14.
Frieden, Jeffry and Stefanie Walter. 2017. "Understanding the Political Economy of the Eurozone Crisis." *Annual Review of Political Science* 20(1): 371–90. https://doi.org/10.1146/annurev-polisci-051215-023101.
Frieden, Jeffry and Stefanie Walter. 2019. "Analyzing Inter-State Negotiations in the Eurozone Crisis and Beyond." *European Union Politics* 20(1): 134–51.
Fuller, Gregory W. 2018. "Exporting Assets: EMU and the Financial Drivers of European Macroeconomic Imbalances." *New Political Economy* 23(2): 174–91.
Galindo, Arturo, Ugo Panizza, and Fabio Schiantarelli. 2003. "Debt Composition and Balance Sheet Effects of Currency Depreciation: A Summary of the Micro Evidence." *Emerging Markets Review* 4: 330–39.
Gallagher, Michael and Michael Marsh. 2011. *How Ireland Voted 2011: The Full Story of Ireland's Earthquake Election*, ed. Michael Gallagher and Michael Marsh. Palgrave Macmillan.
Gallego, Aina and Paul Marx. 2017. "Multi-Dimensional Preferences for Labour Market Reforms: A Conjoint Experiment." *Journal of European Public Policy* 24(7): 1027–47.
Ganghof, Steffen. 2006. "Tax Mixes and the Size of the Welfare State: Causal Mechanisms and Policy Implications." *Journal of European Social Policy* 16(4): 360–73.
Garicano, Luis. 2012. "Five Lessons from the Spanish Cajas Debacle for a New Euro-Wide Supervisor." In *Banking Union for Europe: Risks and Challenges*, pp. 79–86, ed. Thorsten Beck. Center for Economic Policy Research (CEPR).

Genovese, Federica, Gerald Schneider, and Pia Wassmann. 2016. "The Eurotower Strikes Back: Crises, Adjustments, and Europe's Austerity Protests." *Comparative Political Studies* 49(7): 939–67. http://cps.sagepub.com/content/49/7/939.abstract.
Georgiopoulos, George and Lefteris Papadimas. 2012. "Special Report: Greeks Rage against Pension Calamity." Reuters World News.
Ghosh, Atish R., Jonathan D. Ostry, and Mahvash S. Qureshi. 2013. "Fiscal Space and Sovereign Risk Pricing in a Currency Union." *Journal of International Money and Finance* 34: 131–63.
Gibson, Heather D., Stephen G. Hall, and George S. Tavlas. 2012. "The Greek Financial Crisis: Growing Imbalances and Sovereign Spreads." *Journal of International Money and Finance* 31(3): 498–516.
Gibson, Heather D., Theodore Palivos, and George S. Tavlas. 2014. "The Crisis in the Euro Area: An Analytic Overview." *Journal of Macroeconomics* 39: 233–39.
Giger, Nathalie and Heike Klüver. 2016. "Voting Against Your Constituents? How Lobbying Affects Representation." *American Journal of Political Science* 60(1): 190–205.
Gilens, Martin and Benjamin I. Page. 2014. "Testing Theories of American Politics: Elites, Interest Groups, and Average Citizens." Perspectives on Politics 42: 564–81.
Goerres, Achim and Stefanie Walter. 2016. "The Political Consequences of National Crisis Management: Micro-Level Evidence from German Voters during the 2008/9 Global Economic Crisis." *German Politics* 25(1): 131–53.
Gourchinas, Pierre Olivier, Philippe Martin, and Todd Messer. 2018. "The Economics of Sovereign Debt, Bailouts and the Eurozone." *Working Paper*.
Gourevitch, Peter. 1986. *Politics in Hard Times: Comparative Responses to International Economic Crises.* Cornell University Press.
Govan, Fiona. 2010. "General Strike in Spain to Protest against Austerity Measures." *The Telegraph.* https://www.telegraph.co.uk/travel/destinations/europe/spain/8032647/General-strike-in-Spain-to-protest-against-austerity-measures.html.
Grittersová, Jana. 2019. "The Politics of Bank Ownership and Currency Policies in Central and Eastern Europe." *Post-Soviet Affairs* 35(1): 1–24.
Groenendijk, Nico and Annika Jaansoo. 2015. "Public Finance Systems for Coping with the Crises: Lessons from the Three Baltic States." *Public finance and management* 15(3): 257.
Gros, Daniel and Dirk Schoenmaker. 2014. "E Uropean Deposit Insurance and Resolution in the Banking Union." *JCMS: Journal of Common Market Studies* 52(3): 529–46.
Grossman, Gene and Elhanan Helpman. 2001. *Special Interest Politics.* MIT Press.
Guiso, Luigi, Paola Sapienza, and Luigi Zingales. 2016. "Monnet's Error?" *Economic Policy* 31(86): 247–97.
Gutiérrez, Rodolfo. 2014. "Welfare Performance in Southern Europe: Employment Crisis and Poverty Risk." *South European Society and Politics* 19(3): 371–92.
Habit, Steffen. 2011. "Wir Brauchen Eine Europäische Ratingagentur." *Merkur*.
Hacker, Jacob S. and Paul Pierson. 2010. "Winner-Take-All Politics: Public Policy, Political Organization, and the Precipitous Rise of Top Incomes in the United States." *Politics & Society* 38(2): 152–204.
Hacker, Jacob S., Philipp Rehm, and Mark Schlesinger. 2013. "The Insecure American: Economic Experiences, Financial Worries, and Policy Attitudes." *Perspectives on Politics* 11(1): 23–49.
Haffert, Lukas. 2016. *Die Schwarze Null - Über Die Schattenseiten Ausgeglichener Haushalte.* Berlin: Suhrkamp.
Haffert, Lukas. 2018. "War Mobilization or War Destruction? The Unequal Rise of Progressive Taxation Revisited." *Review of International Organizations* 11: 59–82.

Haffert, Lukas, Nils Redeker, and Tobias Rommel. 2019. "Misremembering Weimar: Hyperinflation, the Great Depression, and German Collective Economic Memory." *Unpublished Working Paper*.

Haffert, Lukas and Daniel Schultz. 2019. "Consumption Taxation in the European Economic Community: Fostering the Common Market or Financing the Welfare State?" Manuscript.

Hagemann, Sara, Sara B. Hobolt, and Christopher Wratil. 2017. "Government Responsiveness in the European Union: Evidence from Council Voting." *Comparative Political Studies* 50(6): 850–76.

Haggard, Stephan. 1985. "The Politics of Adjustment: Lesson's from IMF's Extended Fund Facility." *International Organization* 39(3): 505–34. file:///Users/ray/Downloads/politics_of_adjustment_lessons_from_the_imfs_extended_fund_facility(1).pdf.

Haggard, Stephan. 2000. *The Political Economy of the Asian Financial Crisis*. Institute for International Economics.

Haggard, Stephan and Robert R. Kaufman. 1992. *The Politics of Economic Adjustment: International Constraints, Distributive Conflicts, and the State*. Princeton University Press.

Haggard, Stephan and Steven Benjamin Webb. 1994. *Voting for Reform: Democracy, Political Liberalization, and Economic Adjustment*. World Bank Publications.

Hall, Peter. 2012. "The Economics and Politics of the Euro Crisis." *German Politics* 21(4): 355–71.

Hall, Peter. 2014. "Varieties of Capitalism and the Euro Crisis." *West European Politics* 37 (6): 1223–43.

Hall, Peter. 2018. "Varieties of Capitalism in Light of the Euro Crisis." *Journal of European Public Policy* 25(1): 7–30. https://doi.org/10.1080/13501763.2017.1310278.

Hall, Peter and Robert J.Franzese. 1998. "Mixed Signals: Central Bank Independence, Coordinated Wage Bargaining, and European Monetary Union." *International Organization* 52(03): 505–35.

Hall, Peter and David Soskice. 2001. *Varieties of Capitalism*. New York.

Hall, Peter and Kathleen Thelen. 2009. "Institutional Change in Varieties of Capitalism." *Socio-Economic Review* 7: 7–34.

Halpin, Darren R. and Bert Fraussen. 2017. "Conceptualising the Policy Engagement of Interest Groups: Involvement, Access and Prominence." *European Journal of Political Research* 56(3): 723–32. file:///Users/ray/Downloads/HALPIN_et_al-2017-European_Journal_of_Political_Research.pdf.

Hamann, Kerstin, Alison Johnston, and John Kelly. 2013. "Unions against Governments: Explaining General Strikes in Western Europe, 1980-2006." *Comparative Political Studies* 46(9): 1030–57.

Hardiman, Niamh. 2017. "Tracking the State in a Liberal Economy: Empirical Indicators and Irish Experience." In *Reconfiguring European States in Crisis*, pp. 279–97, ed. Desmond King and Patrick Le Galès. Oxford University Press.

Hardiman, Niamh and Sebastian Dellepiane. 2012. *The New Politics of Austerity: Fiscal Responses to Crisis in Ireland and Spain*. Dublin.

Hardiman, Niamh and Aidan Regan. 2013. "The Politics of Austerity in Ireland." *Intereconomics* 48(1): 9–14.

Hassel, A. 2017. "No Way to Escape Imbalances in the Eurozone? Three Sources for Germany's Export Dependency: Industrial Relations, Social Insurance and Fiscal Federalism." *German Politics* 26(3): 350–79.

Hatzichronoglou, T. 1997. "Revision of the High-Technology Sector and Product Classification", *OECD Working Paper* No. 1997/02, OECD Publishing, Paris, https://doi.org/10.1787/050148678127.

Häusermann, Silja, Thomas Kurer, and Denise Traber. 2018. "The Politics of Trade-Offs: Studying the Dynamics of Welfare State Reform with Conjoint Experiments." *Comparative Political Studies*: https://doi.org/10.1177/0010414018797943.

Heinen, Nicolaus et al. 2015. "A Profile of Europe's Populist Parties." *Ann-Kristin Kreutzmann* 49(69): https://www.coursehero.com/file/p3582220/Authors-Nicolaus-Heinen-49-69-910-31713-nicolausheinendbcom-Ann-Kristin/.

Heins, Elke and Caroline de la Porte. 2015. "The Sovereign Debt Crisis, the EU and Welfare State Reform." *Comparative European Politics* 13(1): 1–7.

Helgadóttir, Oddný. 2016. "The Bocconi Boys Go to Brussels: Italian Economic Ideas, Professional Networks and European Austerity." *Journal of European Public Policy* 23(3): 392–409. file:///Users/ray/Downloads/The Bocconi boys go to Brussels Italian economic ideas professional networks and European austerity.pdf.

Helleiner, Eric. 2005. "A Fixation with Floating: The Politics of Canada's Exchange Rate Regime." *Canadian Journal of Political Science* 38(1): 23–44.

Hernández, Enrique and Hanspeter Kriesi. 2016. "The Electoral Consequences of the Financial and Economic Crisis in Europe." *European Journal of Political Research* 55(2): 203–24. file:///Users/ray/Downloads/HERN-NDEZ_et_al-2016-European_Journal_of_Political_Research.pdf.

Higgins, Matthew and Thomas Klitgaard. 2014. "The Balance of Payments Crisis in the Euro Area Periphery." *Current Issues in Economics and Finance* 20: https://papers.ssrn.com/sol3/papers.cfm?abstract_id=2477861.

Hobolt, Sara. 2015. "Public Attitudes towards the Euro Crisis." In *Democratic Politics in a European Union under Stress*, pp. 48–66, ed. Olaf Cramme and Sara Hobolt. Oxford University Press.

Hobolt, Sara and Patrick Leblond. 2013. "Economic Insecurity and Public Support for the Euro." In *Mass Politics in Tough Times: Opinions, Votes, and Protest in the Great Recession*, pp. 128–47, ed. Larry Bartels and Nancy Bermeo. Oxford University Press.

Hobolt, Sara and James Tilley. 2016. "Fleeing the Centre: The Rise of Challenger Parties in the Aftermath of the Euro Crisis." *West European Politics* 39(5): 971–91.

Hobolt, Sara and Catherine de Vries. 2016a. "Public Support for European Integration." *Annual Review of Political Science* 19: 413–32.

Hobolt, Sara and Catherine de Vries. 2016b. "Turning against the Union? The Impact of the Crisis on the Eurosceptic Vote in the 2014 European Parliament Elections." *Electoral Studies* 44: 504–14.

Hobolt, Sara and Christopher Wratil. 2015. "Public Opinion and the Crisis: The Dynamics of Support for the Euro." *Journal of European Public Policy* 22(2): 238–56.

Honaker, James, Gary King, and Matthew Blackwell. 2011. "Amelia II: A Program for Missing Data." *Journal of statistical software* 45(7): 1–47.

Honohan, Patrick and Brendan Walsh. 2002. "Catching up with the Leaders: The Irish Hare." *Brookings Papers on Economic Activity* (1): 1–77.

Hopkin, Jonathan. 2015. "The Troubled South: The Euro Crisis in Italy and Spain." In The Future of the Euro, pp. 161–84, ed. Mark Blyth and Matthias Matthijsuro. Oxford University Press.

Höpner, Martin and Mark Lutter. 2014. "One Currency and Many Modes of Wage Formation: Why the Eurozone is too Heterogeneous for the Euro." *MPIfG Discussion Paper* (14).

Höpner, Martin and Mark Lutter. 2018. "The Diversity of Wage Regimes: Why the Eurozone is too Heterogeneous for the Euro." *European Political Science Review* 10(1): 71–96.

Höpner, Martin and Alexander Spielau. 2018. "Better Than the Euro? The European Monetary System (1979–1998)." *New Political Economy* 23(2): 160–73.

Hospitality Ireland. 2016. "Abolish 9% VAT Rate For Hospitality and Tourism: ICTU." *Hospitality Ireland*.

Howarth, David and Lucia Quaglia. 2014. "The Steep Road to European Banking Union: Constructing the Single Resolution Mechanism." *Journal of Common Market Studies* 52 (S1): 125–40.

Howarth, David and Lucia Quaglia. 2015. "The Political Economy of the Euro Area's Sovereign Debt Crisis: Introduction to the Special Issue of the Review of International Political Economy." *Review of International Political Economy* 22(3): 457–84.

Howarth, David and Lucia Quaglia. 2018. "The Difficult Construction of a European Deposit Insurance Scheme: A Step Too Far in Banking Union?" *Journal of Economic Policy Reform* 21(3): 190–209.

Howarth, David and Charlotte Rommerskirchen. 2013. "A Panacea for All Times? The German Stability Culture as Strategic Political Resource." *West European Politics* 36(4): 750–70.

HRADF. 2019. "Founding Law, Mission and Vision." https://www.hradf.com/en/fund.

Hünnekes, Franziska, Moritz Schularick, and Christoph Trebesch. 2019. "Exportweltmeister: The Low Retuns on Germany's Capital Exports." *Kiel Working Paper* (2133).

ICTU. 2009. *Congress: 10 Point Plan for a Better Fairer Way*. Dublin.

ICTU. 2011. *A Better, Fairer Way: 2011 Pre-Budget Submission*. Dublin.

ICTU. 2013. *Pre-Budget Submission: Autumn 2013*. Dublin.

IEO. 2016. *The IMF and the Crises in Greece, Ireland, and Portugal*. Independent Evaluation Office of the International Monetary Fund. http://www.ieo-imf.org/ieo/pages/CompletedEvaluation267.aspx.

IEO of the IMF. 2016. *The IMF and the Crises in Greece, Ireland, and Portugal*. Washington DC.

Ilzetzki, E., C. M. Reinhart, and K. S. Rogoff. 2017. "The Country Chronologies to Exchange Rate Arrangements into the 21st Century: Will the Anchor Currency Hold?" NBER Working Paper No. w23135, National Bureau of Economic Research.

ILO. 2011. "Report on the High Level Mission to Greece (Athens 19–23 September 2011)." (September): https://www.ilo.org/global/standards/WCMS_170433/lang-en/index.htm.

IMF [International Monetary Fund]. 2011. "Germany: 2011 Article IV Consultation." *IMF Country Report* 11(168).

IMF [International Monetary Fund]. 2013a. *IMF Policy Paper: Fiscal Policy and Income Inequality*. Washington.

IMF [International Monetary Fund]. 2013b. "Ireland: Twelfth Review Under the Extended Arrangement and Proposal for Post-Program Monitoring." *IMF Staff Country Reports* 13 (366): 1.

IMF [International Monetary Fund]. 2014. "Euro Area Policies: Staff Report for the 2014 Article IV Consultation with Member Countries." *IMF Country Reports* 14(198).

IMF [International Monetary Fund]. 2015. "Germany: 2015 Article IV Consultation." *IMF Country Reports* 15(187): 1.

IMF [International Monetary Fund]. 2016a. "Balance of Payments Statistics: Current Account Balance."

IMF [International Monetary Fund]. 2016b. *IMF Country Report: Greece*. Washington D.C.

IMF [International Monetary Fund]. 2016c. "Kingdom of the Netherlands: 2015 Article IV Consultation." *IMF Country Report* 16(45).
IMF [International Monetary Fund]. 2017a. "External Sector Report." *IMF Policy Paper* (July): 55.
IMF [International Monetary Fund]. 2017b. "Kingdom of the Netherlands: 2016 Article IV Consultation." *IMF Country Report* 17(77).
IMF [International Monetary Fund]. 2018. "Kingdom of the Netherlands: 2018 Article IV Consultation." *IMF Country Report* 18(130).
Inacker, Michael. 2012. "BDI-Präsident Keitel Stützt Merkels Euro-Kurs." *Handelsblatt*.
Infratest-dimap. 2011. "ARD-DeutschlandTREND: September 2010." *GESIS Datenarchiv* ZA5555.
Infratest-dimap. 2016. "ARD-DeutschlandTrend 2015." *GESIS Datenarchiv* ZA6229.
Irish Department of Finance. 2007. "Budget 2008: Pre-Budget Submissions and Meetings": 1–38.
Irish Department of Finance. 2009. "Budget 2010: Pre-Budget Submissions and Meetings": 1–35.
Irish Department of Finance. 2010. "Budget 2011: Pre-Budget Submissions and Meetings": 1–22.
Irish Department of Finance. 2011. "Budget 2012: Pre-Budget Submissions and Meetings": 1–32.
Irish Department of Finance. 2012. "Budget 2013: Pre-Budget Submissions and Meetings": 1–35.
Irish Department of Finance. 2018. *Review of the 9% VAT Rate: Analysis of Economic and Sectoral Developments*. Dublin, IE.
Irish Examiner. 2009. "ICTU to Consider National Protest against Pension Levy." https://www.irishexaminer.com/breakingnews/ireland/ictu-to-consider-national-protest-against-pension-levy-398504.html.
Irish Examiner. 2011. "IBEC Welcomes Minimum-Wage Reduction." https://www.irishexaminer.com/breakingnews/business/ibec-welcomes-minimum-wage-reduction-489993.html?utm_source=link&utm_medium=click&utm_campaign=nextandprev.
Iversen, Torben and David Soskice. 2006. "Electoral Institutions and the Politics of Coalitions: Why Some Democracies Redistribute More than Others." *American Political Science Review* 100(2): 165–81.
Iversen, Torben and David Soskice. 2018. "A Structural-Institutional Explanation of the Eurozone Crisis." In *Welfare Democracies and Party Politics*, pp. 257–81, ed. Philip Manow, Bruno Palier, and Hanna Schwander. Oxford University Press.
Iversen, Torben, David Soskice, and David Hope. 2016. "The Eurozone and Political Economic Institutions." *Annual Review of Political Science* 19: 163–85.
Jabko, Nicolas. 2013. "The Political Appeal of Austerity." *Comparative European Politics* 11 (6): 705–12.
Jacobs, Alan. 2011. *Governing for the Long Term: Democracy and the Politics of Investment*. Cambridge University Press.
Johnston, Alison. 2016. *From Convergence to Crisis: Labor Markets and the Instability of the Euro*. Cornell University Press.
Johnston, Alison, Bob Hancké, and Suman Pant. 2014. "Comparative Institutional Advantage in the European Sovereign Debt Crisis." *Comparative Political Studies* 47 (13): 1771–800.
Jolliffe, Ian. 2011. "Principal Component Analysis." In *International Encyclopedia of Statistical Science*, pp. 1094–6. Springer.

Jones, Erik. 2015. "Getting the Story Right: How You Should Choose between Different Interpretations of the European Crisis (and Why You Should Care)." *Journal of European Integration* 37(7): 817–32.

Jones, Erik, Daniel Kelemen, and Sophie Meunier. 2016. "Failing Forward? The Euro Crisis and the Incomplete Nature of European Integration." *Comparative Political Studies* 49 (7): 1010–34.

Jorda, Oscar, Moritz Schularick, and Alan Taylor. 2010. "Financial Crises, Credit Booms, and External Imbalances: 140 Years of Lessons." *NBER Working Paper Series* 16567.

Jung, Matthias, Yvonne Schroth, and Andrea Wolf. 2013. "Politbarometer 2011 Cumulated Data Set, Incl. Flash." *GESIS Data Archive* ZA5633.

Jung, Matthias, Yvonne Schroth, and Andrea Wolf. 2014. "Politbarometer 2012 (Cumulated Data Set, Incl. Flash)." *GESIS Data Archive* ZA5641.

Jung, Matthias, Yvonne Schroth, and Andrea Wolf. 2015. "Politbarometer 2013 Cumulated Data Set, Incl. Flash." *GESIS Data Archive* ZA5677.

Jurado, Ignacio, Stefanie Walter, Nikitas Konstantinidis, and Elias Dinas. 2020. "Keeping the euro at any cost? Explaining attitudes toward the euro-austerity trade-off in Greece." *European Union Politics*: 1465116520928118. https://doi.org/10.1177/1465116520928118.

Kakoulidou, Theano, Panagiotis Konstantinou, and Thomas Moutos. 2018. *The Subminimum Wage Reform in Greece and the Labour-Labour Substitution Hypothesis*. Munich.

Kalla, Joshua L. and David E. Broockman. 2016. "Campaign Contributions Facilitate Access to Congressional Officials: A Randomized Field Experiment." *American Journal of Political Science* 60(3): 545–58.

Kaminsky, Graciela L. and Carmen M. Reinhart. 1999. "The Twin Crises: The Causes of Banking and Balance-of-Payments Problems." *The American Economic Review* 89(3): 473–500.

Kanthak, Leon and Dennis C. Spies. 2018. "Public Support for European Union Economic Policies." *European Union Politics* 19(1): 97–118.

Kaplanoglou, Georgia and Vassilis T. Rapanos. 2013. "Tax and Trust: The Fiscal Crisis in Greece." *South European Society and Politics* 18(3): 283–304.

Kato, Junko. 2003. *Regressive Taxation and the Welfare State: Path Dependence and Policy Diffusion*. Cambridge University Press.

Katsoulacos, Yannis, Christos Genakos, and George Houpis. 2017. "Product Market Regulation and Competitiveness: Toward a National Competition and Competitiveness Policy for Greece." In *Beyond Austerity: Reforming the Greek Economy*, pp. 139–77, ed. Costas Meghir, Christopher A. Pissarides, Dimitri Vayanos, and Nikolaos Vettas. MIT Press.

Kattel, Rainer and Ringa Raudla. 2013. "The Baltic Republics and the Crisis of 2008–2011." *Europe-Asia Studies* 65(3): 426–49.

Kaufmann, Hugo M. 1969. "A Debate over Germany's Revaluation 1961: A Chapter in Political Economy." *Weltwirtschaftliches Archiv* 103: 181–212.

Kawalec, S. and E. Pytlarczyk. 2013. "Controlled Dismantlement of the Eurozone: A Strategy to Save the European Union and the Single European Market." *German Economic Review* 14(1): 31–49.

Keller, Eileen. 2018. "Noisy Business Politics: Lobbying Strategies and Business Influence after the Financial Crisis." *Journal of European Public Policy* 25(3): 287–306.

Kenen, Peter B. 1969. "The Theory of Optimum Currency Areas: An Eclectic View." In *Monetary Problems of the International Economy*, pp. 41–60, ed. Robert Mundell and Alexander Swoboda. University of Chicago Press.

Kennedy, Paul. 2012. "From Unpopular Socialists to the Popular Party: The Spanish General Election of 2011." *West European Politics* 35(3): 673–81.
Kenny, Enda. 2012. "Speech by An Taoiseach, Mr Enda Kenny TD (02.2012)." https://merrionstreet.ie/en/News-Room/Speeches/speech-by-the-taoiseach-mr-enda-kenny-t-d-at-the-citizenship-ceremony-in-cathal-brugha-barracks.html.
Keohane, Robert. 1984. *After Hegemony: Cooperation and Discord in the World Political Economy*. Princeton University Press.
Van Kessel, Stijn. 2015. "Dutch Populism During the Crisis." In *Populism in the Shadow of the Great Recession*, pp. 109–24, ed. Hans-Peter Kriesi and Takis Pappas. ECPR Press.
Kim, Sung Eun and Yotam Margalit. 2016. "The Impact of Unions on Workers' Political Preferences." *American Journal of Political Science* 61(3): 728–43.
Kincaid, G. Russell. 2019. "The Euro Crisis: Its Unresolved Roots and Their Reform Implications." In *The Political Economy of Adjustment throughout and beyond the Eurozone Crisis*, pp. 17–37, ed. Michele Chang, Federico Steinberg, and Francisco Torres. Routledge.
Kinderman, Daniel. 2008. "The Political Economy of Sectoral Exchange Rate Preferences and Lobbying: Germany from 1960-2008, and Beyond." *Review of International Political Economy* 15(5): 851–80.
King, Gary, James Honaker, Anne Joseph, and Kenneth Scheve. 2001. "Analyzing Incomplete Political Science Data: An Alternative Algorithm for Multiple Imputation." *American Political Science Review* 95(1): 49–69.
Kinsella, Stephen. 2017. "Economic and Fiscal Policy." In *Austerity & Recovery in Ireland: Europe's Poster Child and the Great Recession*, pp. 40–61, ed. William K. Roche, Philip O'Connell, and Andrea Prothero. Oxford University Press.
Kleider, Hanna and Florian Stoeckel. 2018. "The Politics of International Redistribution: Explaining Public Support for Fiscal Transfers in the EU." *European Journal of Political Research* 58(1): 4–29.
Klug, Thorsten, Eric Mayer, and Tobias Schuler. 2019. "The Corporate Saving Glut and the Current Account in Germany Thorsten." *ifo Working Papers* (280).
Klüver, Heike. 2013. *Lobbying in the European Union: Interest Groups, Lobbying Coalitions, and Policy Change*. Oxford University Press.
Klüver, Heike. 2018. "Setting the Party Agenda: Interest Groups, Voters and Issue Attention." *British Journal of Political Science*: 1–22. doi:10.1017/S0007123418000078.
Kolk, H. van der, J. Tillie, P. van Erkel, M. van der Velden, and A. Damstra. 2012. "Dutch Parliamentary Election Study 2012 – DPES 2012. DANS." https://doi.org/10.17026/dans-x5h-akds.
Koller, Fabiana. 2018. "Public Opinion on Financial Risk Sharing Mechanisms in the Eurozone." ETH Zurich and University of Zurich.
Korte, Karl-Rudolf. 2013. *Die Bundestagswahl 2013: Analysen Der Wahl-, Parteien-, Kommunikations Und Regierungsforschung*. Springer.
Kraay, Aart. 2003. "Do High Interest Rates Defend Currencies during Speculative Attacks?" *Journal of International Economics* 59: 297–321.
Kranke, Matthias and Susanne Luetz. 2014. "The European Rescue of the Washington Consensus? IMF and EU Lending to Eastern European Countries." *Review of International Political Economy* 21(2): 310–38. file:///Users/ray/Downloads/The European rescue of the Washington Consensus EU and IMF lending to Central and Eastern European countries.pdf.
Kreile, Michael. 1977. *West Germany: The Dynamics of Expansion*. UZH Hauptbibliothek/Zentralbibliothek Zürich.

Kretsos, Lefteris. 2011. "Union Responses to the Rise of Precarious Youth Employment in Greece." *Industrial Relations Journal* 42(5): 453–72.

Kriesi, Hanspeter. 2012. "The Political Consequences of the Financial and Economic Crisis in Europe: Electoral Punishment and Popular Protest." *Swiss Political Science Review* 18(4): 518–22.

Kriesi, Hanspeter, Jasmine Lorenzini, Bruno Wuest, and Silja Häusermann, eds. 2019. *Contention in Times of Crisis*. Cambridge University Press.

Kriesi, Hanspeter and Takis S. Pappas. 2015. *European Populism in the Shadow of the Great Recession*. ECPR Press Colchester.

Kriesi, Hanspeter, Chendi Wang, Thomas Kurer, and Silja Häusermann. 2019. "Economic Grievances, Political Grievances and Protest." In *Contention in Times of Crisis*, pp. 1–35, ed. Hanspeter Kriesi, Jasmine Lorenzini, Bruno Wuest, and Silja Häusermann. Cambridge University Press.

Kritzinger, Sylvia, David Johann, Julian Aichholzer, Konstantin Glinitzer, Christian Glantschnigg, Patricia Oberluggauer, Kathrin Thomas, Markus Wagner, and Eva Zeglovits. 2016. "AUTNES Rolling-Cross-Section Panel Study 2013." *GESIS Data Archive* ZA5857.

Krugman, Paul. 2010. "Eating the Irish." *New York Times*. https://www.nytimes.com/2010/11/26/opinion/26krugman.html.

Krugman, Paul. 2015. "Opinion: Greece Over the Brink." *New York Times*. https://www.nytimes.com/2015/06/29/opinion/paul-krugman-greece-over-the-brink.html.

Kuhn, Theresa, Hector Solaz, and Erika J. van Elsas. 2017. "Practising What You Preach: How Cosmopolitanism Promotes Willingness to Redistribute across the European Union." *Journal of European Public Policy* 1763: 1–20.

Kurer, Thomas, Silja Häusermann, Bruno Wüest, and Matthias Enggist. 2018. "Economic Grievances and Political Protest." *European Journal of Political Research*: https://doi.org/10.1111/1475-6765.12311.

Kutter, Amelie. 2014. "A Catalytic Moment: The Greek Crisis in the German Financial Press." *Discourse and Society* 25(4): 446–66.

Lake, David A. 2009. "Open Economy Politics: A Critical Review." *Review of International Organizations* 4(3): 219–44.

Lall, Ranjit. 2016. "How Multiple Imputation Makes a Difference." *Political Analysis* 24(4): 414–33.

Lane, Philip R. 2012. "The European Sovereign Debt Crisis." *Journal of Economic Perspectives* 26(3): 49–67. Desktop/Downloaded/Lane - 2013 - The European Sovereign Debt Crisis.pdf.

Lane, Philip R. and Gian Maria Milesi-Ferretti. 2011. "The Cross-Country Incidence of the Global Crisis." *IMF Economic Review* 59(1): 77–110.

Leblang, David. 2002. "The Political Economy of Speculative Attacks in the Developing World." *International Studies Quarterly* 46(1): 69–92.

Leblang, David. 2003. "To Devalue or to Defend? The Political Economy of Exchange Rate Policy." *International Studies Quarterly* 47(4): 533–59.

Lehndorff, Steffen. 2012. *A Triumph of Failed Ideas European Models of Capitalism in the Crisis*. ETUI Brussels.

Leupold, Anna. 2016. "A Structural Approach to Politicisation in the Euro Crisis." *West European Politics* 39(1): 84–103.

Lewis-Beck, Michael S. and Mary Stegmaier. 2000. "Economic Determinants of Electoral Outcomes." *Annual Review of Political Science* 3: 183–219.

Lindblom, C. E. 1977. *Politics and Markets: The World's Political Economic Systems*. Basic Books.
Lorenzini, Jasmine and Sophia Hunger. 2019. "All Quiet on the Protest Scene? Repertoires of Contention and Protest Actors during the Great Recession." In *Contention in Times of Crisis*, ed. Hanspeter Kriesi, Jasmine Lorenzini, Bruno Wuest, and Silja Häusermann. Cambridge University Press.
Lundgren, Magnus et al. 2018. "Bargaining Success in the Reform of the Eurozone." *European Union Politics* 20(1): 65–88.
Lütz, Susanne and Sven Hilgers. 2018. "When Overlapping Organisations Play Two-Level Games: IMF-EU Interaction in Credit Lending to Latvia and Greece." *New Political Economy* 24(3): 299–312.
Lütz, Susanne, Sven Hilgers, and Sebastian Schneider. 2019a. "Accountants, Europeanists and Monetary Guardians: Bureaucratic Cultures and Conflicts in IMF-EU Lending Programs." *Review of International Political Economy* 26(6): 1187–210.
Lütz, Susanne, Sven Hilgers, and Sebastian Schneider. 2019b. "When the Numbers Don't Add up: Bureaucratis Culture and Conflicts in EU-IMF Relations." In *The Political Economy of Adjustment throughout and beyond the Eurozone Crisis*, pp. 38–57, ed. Michele Chang, Federico Steinberg, and Francisco Torres. Routledge.
Lyberaki, Antigone, Costas Meghir, and Daphne Nicolitsas. 2017. "Labor Market Regulation and Reform in Greece." In *Beyond Austerity: Reforming the Greek Economy*, pp. 211–50, ed. Costas Meghir, Christopher A. Pissarides, Dimitri Vayanos, and Nikolaos Vettas. MIT Press.
Lynch, Kathleen, Sara Cantillion, and Margaret Crean. 2017. "Inequality." In *Austerity & Recovery in Ireland: Europe's Poster Child and the Great Recession*, pp. 252–71, ed. William K. Roche, Philip J. O'Connell, and Andrea Prothero. Oxford University Press.
Lynn, Matthew. 2011. *Bust: Greece, the Euro, and the Sovereign Debt Crisis*. John Wiley & Sons.
Mabbett, Deborah. 2016. "The Minimum Wage in Germany: What Brought the State In?" *Journal of European Public Policy* 23(8): 1240–58.
Mabbett, Deborah and Waltraud Schelkle. 2015. "What Difference Does Euro Membership Make to Stabilization? The Political Economy of International Monetary Systems Revisited." *Review of International Political Economy* 22(3): 508–34.
Mcdermott, M. L. 2006. "Not for Members Only: Group Endorsements as Electoral Information Cues." *Political Research Quarterly* 59(2): 249–57.
MacInnes, Judy and Emma Pinedo. 2011. "Factbox: Policies of Spain's People's Party." Reuters World News. https://www.reuters.com/article/us-spain-election-policies/factbox-policies-of-spains-peoples-party-idUSTRE7AJ08F20111120.
McKinnon, Ronald I. 1963. "Optimum Currency Areas." *The American Economic Review* 53(4): 717–25.
McKinnon, Ronald and Huw Pill. 1999. "Exchange-Rate Regimes for Emerging Markets: Moral Hazard and International Overborrowing." *Oxford Review of Economic Policy* 15(3): 19–38.
McNamara, Kathleen. 1998. *The Currency of Ideas: Monetary Politics in the European Union*. Cornell University Press.
McNamara, Kathleen. 2015. "The Forgotten Problem of Embeddedness." In *The Future of the Euro*, pp. 21–43, ed. Matthias Matthijs and Mark Blyth. Oxford University Press.
Mahnkopf, Birgit. 2012. "The Euro Crisis: German Politics of Blame and Austerity – A Neoliberal Nightmare." *International Critical Thought* 2(4): 472–85.

Mallet, Victor. 2010. "Tough New Spanish Austerity Measures." *Financial Times*. https://www.ft.com/content/91ca42de-5d9e-11df-b4fc-00144feab49a.
Maltezou, Renee. 2011. "Greek Strike to Cause Public Sector Chaos." Reuters Business News. https://cn.reuters.com/article/greece-strike-idCNL5E7L43CV20111004.
Manasse, Paolo. 2014. "Privatisation and Debt: Lessons from Greece's Fiasco." *VoxEU.org*. https://voxeu.org/article/privatisation-and-debt-lessons-greece-s-fiasco.
Manger, Mark S. and Thomas Sattler. 2019. "The Origins of Persistent Current Account Imbalances in the Post-Bretton Woods Era." *Comparative Political Studies*: https://doi.org/10.1177/0010414019859031.
Mansbridge, Jane J. 1992. "A Deliberative Theory of Interest Representation." In *The Politics of Interests: Interest Groups Transformed*, pp. 32–57, ed. Mark P. Petracca. Westview Press.
Marchetti, Kathleen. 2015. "The Use of Surveys in Interest Group Research." *Interest Groups & Advocacy* 4: 1–11.
Markgraf, Jonas and Guillermo Rosas. 2019. "On Board with Banks: Do Banking Connections Help Politicians Win Elections?" *The Journal of Politics* 81(4): 1357–70.
Marsh, Michael and Kevin Cunningham. 2011. "A Positive Choice, or Anyone but Fianna Fáil?" In *How Ireland Voted 2011: The Full Story of Ireland's Earthquake Election*, pp. 172–204, ed. Michael Gallagher and Michael Marsh. Palgrave Macmillan.
Marsh, Michael, David M. Farrell, and Gail McElroy. 2017. "The INES 2011 Questionnaire." In *A Conservative Revolution? Electoral Change in Twenty-First Century Ireland*, pp. 223–52, ed. Michael Marsh, David M. Farrell, and Gail McElroy. Oxford University Press.
Martin, C. J. and D. Swank. 2012. *The Political Construction of Business Interests: Coordination, Growth, and Equality*. Cambridge University Press.
Martin, Cathie Jo and Kathleen Thelen. 2007. "The State and Coordinated Capitalism: Contributions of the Public Sector to Social Solidarity in Postindustrial Societies." *World Politics* 60(01): 1–36.
Martín, Irene and Ignacio Urquizu-Sancho. 2012. "The 2011 General Election in Spain: The Collapse of the Socialist Party." *South European Society and Politics* 17(2): 347–63.
Martin, Philippe and Thomas Philippon. 2017. "Inspecting the Mechanism: Leverage and the Great Recession in the Eurozone." *American Economic Review* 107(7): 1904–37.
Matsaganis, Manos. 2007. "Union Structures and Pension Outcomes in Greece." *British Journal of Industrial Relations* 45(3): 537–55.
Matsaganis, Manos. 2011. "The Welfare State and the Crisis: The Case of Greece." *Journal of European Social Policy* 21(5): 501–12.
Matsaganis, Manos and Chrysa Leventi. 2013. "The Distributional Impact of the Greek Crisis in 2010." *Fiscal Studies* 34(1): 83–108.
Matsaganis, Manos and Chrysa Leventi. 2014. "The Distributional Impact of Austerity and the Recession in Southern Europe." *South European Society and Politics* 19(3): 393–412.
Matsaganis, Manos, Chrysa Leventi, and Maria Flevotomou. 2012. "The Crisis and Tax Evasion in Greece: What Are the Distributional Implications?" In *CESifo Forum*, Institut für Wirtschaftsforschung (Ifo), 26.
Matsusaka, John G. 2010. "Popular Control of Public Policy: A Quantitative Approach." *Quarterly Journal of Political Science* 5(2): 133–67.
Matthijs, Matthias. 2016a. "Powerful Rules Governing the Euro: The Perverse Logic of German Ideas." *Journal of European Public Policy* 23(3): 375–91.

Matthijs, Matthias. 2016b. "The Euro's 'Winner-Take-All' Political Economy: Institutional Choices, Policy Drift, and Diverging Patterns of Inequality." *Politics & Society* 44(3): 393–422.
Matthijs, Matthias. 2016c. "The Three Faces of German Leadership." *Survival* 58(2): 135–54.
Matthijs, Matthias and Mark Blyth, eds. 2015. *The Future of the Euro*. Oxford University Press.
Matthijs, Matthias and Kathleen McNamara. 2015. "The Euro Crisis' Theory Effect: Northern Saints, Southern Sinners, and the Demise of the Eurobond." *Journal of European Integration* 37(2): 229–45.
Medina, Lucía. 2015. "From Recession to Long-Lasting Political Crisis?" *Working Papers, ICPS* (334): 1–24.
Mendoza, Ronald U. 2004. "International Reserve-Holding in the Developing World: Self Insurance in a Crisis-Prone Era?" *Emerging Markets Review* 5: 61–82.
Mény, Yves. 2014. "Managing the EU Crises: Another Way of Integration by Stealth?" *West European Politics* 37(6): 1336–53. http://dx.doi.org/10.1080/01402382.2014.929338.
Merler, Silvia. 2015. "Who's (Still) Exposed to Greece?" *Bruegel Blog*. https://www.bruegel.org/2015/02/whos-still-exposed-to-greece/.
Merler, Silvia and Jean Pisani-Ferry. 2012. "Sudden Stops in the Euro Area." *Review of Economics & Institutions/Economia, Societa e Istituzioni* 3(3). https://www.bruegel.org/2012/03/sudden-stops-in-the-euro-area-2/.
Meunier, Sophie. 2015. *A Tale of Two Ports: The Epic Story of Chinese Direct Investment in the Greek Port of Piraeus*. Princeton University Press.
Meyer, Norbert. 2011. "Noch Kein Klares Konzept Für Weg Aus Der Euro-Krise." *Neue Osnarbrücker Zeitung*.
Michaelides, Alexander. 2014. "Cyprus: From Boom to Bail-In." *Economic Policy* 29(80): 639–89.
Milesi-Ferretti, Gian-Maria and Cédric Tille. 2011. "The Great Retrenchment: International Capital Flows during the Global Financial Crisis." *Economic Policy* 26(66): 289–346.
Mitsopoulos, Michael and Theodore Pelagidis. 2015. "Give Greece a Chance." *Intereconomics* 50(2): 91–7.
Mody, Ashoka. 2014. "The Ghost of Deauville." *VoxEU. org*. https://voxeu.org/article/ghost-deauville.
Mody, Ashoka. 2018. *Eurotragedy: A Drama in Nine Acts*. Oxford University Press.
Molina, Oscar and Fausto Miguélez. 2014. "From Negotiation to Imposition: Social Dialogue in Times of Austerity in Spain." In *The Governance of Policy Reforms in Southern Europe and Ireland*, pp. 87–108, ed. Konstantinos Papadakis and Youcef Ghellab. International Labour Organization.
Monastiriotis, Vassilis et al. 2013. "Austerity Measures in Crisis Countries – Results and Impact on Mid-Term Development." *Intereconomics* 48(1): 4–32.
Moravcsik, Andrew. 2012. "Europe after the Crisis: How to Sustain a Common Currency." *Foreign Affairs* 91(3): 54–69.
Morlino, Leonardo and Mario Quaranta. 2016. "What Is the Impact of the Economic Crisis on Democracy? Evidence from Europe." *International Political Science Review* 37(5): 618–33.
Morrison, James Ashley. 2016. "Shocking Intellectual Austerity: The Role of Ideas in the Demise of the Gold Standard in Britain." *International Organization* 70(1): 175–207.

Moschella, Manuela. 2014. "Monitoring Macroeconomic Imbalances: Is EU Surveillance more Effective than IMF Surveillance?" *JCMS: Journal of Common Market Studies* 52 (6): 1273–89.

Moschella, Manuela. 2016. "Negotiating Greece: Layering, Insulation, and the Design of Adjustment Programs in the Eurozone." *Review of International Political Economy* 23(5): 799–824. https://doi.org/10.1080/09692290.2016.1224770.

Moschella, Manuela. 2017. "When Some Are More Equal than Others: National Parliaments and Intergovernmental Bailout Negotiations in the Eurozone." *Government and Opposition* 52(2): 239–65. https://www.cambridge.org/core/article/when-some-are-more-equal-than-others-national-parliaments-and-intergovernmental-bailout-negotiations-in-the-eurozone/2F92A63C5EB481EACBB7E131878BA50C.

Mosley, Layna. 2000. "Room to Move: International Financial Markets and National Welfare States." *International Organization* 54(4): 737–73.

Mosley, Layna. 2003. *Global Capital and National Governments*. Cambridge University Press.

Mundell, Robert. 1961. "A Theory of Optimum Currency Areas." *American Economic Review* 51(4): 657–64.

Mussa, Michael and Miguel Savastano. 1999. "The IMF Approach to Economic Stabilization." *NBER Macroeconomics Annual* 14(January): 79–128. file:///Users/ray/Library/Application Support/Mendeley Desktop/Downloaded/Mussa, Savastano - 2000 - The Approach to Economic Stabilization.pdf.

Neal, Larry and María Concepción García-Iglesias. 2013. "The Economy of Spain in the Euro-Zone before and after the Crisis of 2008." *Quarterly Review of Economics and Finance* 53(4): 336–44. http://dx.doi.org/10.1016/j.qref.2013.01.002.

Nelson, Joan Marie. 1990. *Economic Crisis and Policy Choice: The Politics of Adjustment in the Third World*. Princeton University Press.

Niedermayer, Oskar. 2013. "Europäische Integration Und Nationaler Parteienwettbewerb: Theoretische Überlegungen Und Empirische Befunde Am Beispiel Der Eurokrise Author(s): Oskar Niedermayer Source: Zeitschrift Für Staats- Und Europawissenschaften (ZSE)/Journal for Comparat." *Zeitschrift für Staats- und Europawissenschaften* 11(3): 413–34.

Nölke, Andreas. 2015. "Economic Causes of the Eurozone Crisis: The Analytical Contribution of Comparative Capitalism." *Socio-Economic Review* 2007(February): mwv031.

Nyberg, Peter. 2011. "Misjudging Risk: Causes of the Systemic Banking Crisis in Ireland." Report of The Commission of Investigation into the Banking Sector in Ireland. https://www.nuigalway.ie/media/housinglawrightsandpolicy/nationalpolicy/Nyberg-Report-Misjuding-Risk—Causes-of-the-Systemic-Banking-Crisis-in-Ireland.pdf.

Ó Cionnaith, Fiachra. 2014. "HSE Made Cuts of €2.7 Bn. during Recession." *Irish Examiner Online*. https://www.irishexaminer.com/ireland/hse-made-cuts-of-27bn-during-recession-263841.html.

O'Connor, Francis. 2017. "The Presence and Absence of Protest in Austerity Ireland." In *Late Neoliberalism and Its Discontents in the Economic Crisis*, pp. 65–98. Springer.

O'Malley, Eoin and R. Kenneth Carty. 2017. "A Conservative Revolution? The Disequlibrium in Irish Politics." In *A Conservative Revolution? Electoral Change in Twenty-First-Century Ireland*, pp. 208–22, ed. Michael Marsh, David M. Farrell, and Gail McElroy. Oxford University Press.

O'Rourke, Kevin H. and Alan M. Taylor. 2013. "Cross of Euros." *The Journal of Economic Perspectives* 27(3): 167–91.

Oatley, Thomas. 2011. "The Reductionist Gamble: Open Economy Politics in the Global Economy." *International Organization* 65(2): 311–41.
Obstfeld, Maurice. 2011. "The International Monetary System: Living with Asymmetry." *NBER Working Paper No. 17641* 33(10): 985–96.
Obstfeld, Maurice. 2012. "Financial Flows, Financial Crises, and Global Imbalances." *Journal of International Money and Finance* 31(3): 469–80.
Obstfeld, Maurice and Kenneth Rogoff. 1995. "The Mirage of Fixed Exchange Rates." *Journal of Economic Perspectives* 9(4): 73–96.
Obstfeld, Maurice and Kenneth S. Rogoff. 2009. *Global Imbalances and the Financial Crisis: Products of Common Causes*. CEPR Discussion Papers.
OECD. 1993a. *OECD Economic Survey: Denmark*. Paris: OECD Publishing.
OECD. 1993b. *OECD Economic Survey: Netherlands*. Paris: OECD Publishing.
OECD. 2012. "Social Spending during the Crisis." *Social expenditure (SOCX) dataupdate*: 1–8.
OECD. 2013. *Education Policy Outlook: Ireland*. Paris: OECD Publishing.
OECD. 2015a. *OECD Economic Survey: Austria*. Paris: OECD Publishing.
OECD. 2015b. *OECD Economic Survey: Austria*. Paris: OECD Publishing.
OECD. 2016a. *OECD Economic Survey: Euro Area*. Paris: OECD Publishing.
OECD. 2016b. *OECD Economic Survey: Finland*. Paris: OECD Publishing.
OECD. 2016c. "The OECD Tax Database." *OECD Tax Database*. Retrieved January 23, 2016 from http://www.oecd.org/tax/tax-policy/tax-database.htm.
OECD. 2019a. "Current Account Balance." *OECD Quarterly International Trade Statistics*.
OECD. 2019b. "Long-Term Interest Rates." *OECD: Main Economic Indicators*.
OGM. 2012. "Schilling Statt Euro?" https://www.ogm.at/wirtschaft/schilling-statt-euro/.
OGM. 2015. "ORF Bürgerforum Zum Thema Geld." https://www.ogm.at/wirtschaft/orf-buergerforum-zum-thema-geld/
Ojala, Markus and Timo Harjuniemi. 2016. "Mediating the German Ideology: Ordoliberal Framing in European Press Coverage of the Eurozone Crisis." *Journal of Contemporary European Studies* 24(3): 414–30.
ORF. 2012. "Arbeitnehmer: AK Gegen Höhere Sozialbeiträge." *Salzburg Österreichischer Rundfunk*.
Orriols, Lluis and Guillermo Cordero. 2016. "The Breakdown of the Spanish Two-Party System: The Upsurge of Podemos and Ciudadanos in the 2015 General Election." *South European Society and Politics* 21(4): 469–92.
Pagoulatos, George. 2019. "Greece after the Bailouts: Assessment of a Qualified Failure." In *The Political Economy of Adjustment throughout and beyond the Eurozone Crisis*, pp. 61–93, ed. Michele Chang, Federico Steinberg, and Francisco Torres. Routledge.
Panageas, Stavros and Platon Tinios. 2017. "Pension: Arresting a Race to the Bottom." In *Beyond Austerity: Reforming the Greek Economy*, pp. 459–516, ed. Costas Meghir, Christopher Pissarides, Dimitri Vayanos, and Nikolaos Vettas. MIT Press.
Papachristou, Harry. 2011. "Greece Faces Auditor Verdict, Fresh Aid at Stake." Reuters Business News. http://northwestprimetime.com/news/2011/sep/28/greece-faces-auditor-verdict-fresh-aid-at-stake/.
Papaconstantinou, George. 2016. *Game Over: The Insider Story of the Greek Crisis*. 1st edn. Athens: Papadopoulos Publishing.
Pappas, T. S. and E. O'Malley. 2014. "Civil Compliance and 'Political Luddism': Explaining Variance in Social Unrest During Crisis in Ireland and Greece." American Behavioral Scientist: http://abs.sagepub.com/content/early/2014/05/23/0002764214534663.abstract.

Paster, T. 2013. "Why Did Austrian Business Oppose Welfare Cuts? How the Organization of Interests Shapes Business Attitudes Toward Social Partnership." *Comparative Political Studies* 47(7): 966–92.

Peltzman, Sam. 1976. "Toward a More General Theory of Regulation." *The Journal of Law and Economics* 19(2): 211–40.

Pepinsky, Thomas. 2009. *Economic Crises and the Breakdown of Authoritarian Regimes: Indonesia and Malaysia in Comparative Perspective*. 1st edn. Cambridge University Press.

Pepinsky, Thomas. 2012. "The Global Economic Crisis and the Politics of Non-Transitions." *Government and Opposition* 47(2): 135–61.

Pérez, Claudi. 2014. "Spain Formally Exits Bank Bailout Program in Better Shape." *El País*. https://english.elpais.com/elpais/2014/01/22/inenglish/1390398651_636380.html.

Pérez, Sofía A. 2019. "A Europe of Creditor and Debtor States: Explaining the North/South Divide in the Eurozone." *West European Politics* 42(5): 989–1014. https://doi.org/10.1080/01402382.2019.1573403.

Perez, Sofia A. and Manos Matsaganis. 2018. "The Political Economy of Austerity in Southern Europe." *New Political Economy* 23(2): 192–207.

Peters, John. 2012. "Neoliberal Convergence in North America and Western Europe: Fiscal Austerity, Privatization, and Public Sector Reform." *Review of International Political Economy* 19(2): 208–35.

Petmesidou, Maria. 2013. "Is Social Protection in Greece at a Crossroads?" *European Societies* 15(4): 597–616.

Pew Research Center. 2015. "European Union: Topline Results." *Pew Research Survey Spring 2015*. https://www.pewresearch.org/global/wp-content/uploads/sites/2/2015/06/Pew-Research-Center-European-Union-TOPLINE-FOR-RELEASE-June-2-2015.pdf.

Pew Research Center. 2019. "Global Attitudes and Trends: Datasets." https://www.pewresearch.org/global/.

Picot, Georg and Arianna Tassinari. 2017. "All of One Kind? Labour Market Reforms under Austerity in Italy and Spain." *Socio-Economic Review* 15(2): 461–82.

Pierson, Paul. 1996. "The New Politics of the Welfare State." *World Politics* 48(2): 143–79.

Pirro, Andrea L. P. and Stijn van Kessel. 2017. "United in Opposition? The Populist Radical Right's EU-Pessimism in Times of Crisis." *Journal of European Integration* 39(4): 405–20.

Pisani-Ferry, Jean. 2012. *The Euro Crisis and the New Impossible Trinity*. Brussels: Bruegel Policy Contribution. http://www.econstor.eu/bitstream/10419/72121/1/683140442.pdf.

Pisani-Ferry, Jean, André Sapir, and Guntram B. Wolff. 2013. "EU-IMF Assistance to Euro-Area Countries : An Early Assessment." https://www.bruegel.org/2013/06/eu-imf-assistance-to-euro-area-countries-an-early-assessment/.

Pitsoulis, Athanassios and Sören C Schwuchow. 2016. "Holding out for a Better Deal: Brinkmanship in the Greek Bailout Negotiations." *European Journal of Political Economy* 48: 40–53.

Prasad, Eswar S. 2011. "Rebalancing Growth in Asia." *International Finance* 14(1): 27–66.

Pudschedl, Walter. 2013. "Austria's Regions Impacted by the Euro Crisis Weaker Economic Growth in 2012 – Hesitant Recovery in 2013." *Bank Austria Report* (April).

Putnam, Robert D. 1988. "Diplomacy and Domestic Politics: The Logic of Two-Level Games." *International Organization* 42(3): 427–60.

Quaglia, Lucia and Sebastián Royo. 2015. "Banks and the Political Economy of the Sovereign Debt Crisis in Italy and Spain." *Review of International Political Economy* 22(3): 485–507.

Raess D. and J. Pontusson. 2015. "The Politics of Fiscal Policy during Economic Downturns, 1981–2010", *European Journal of Political Research* 54(1): 1–22.
Rainsford, Sarah. 2011. "Spanish Government Reaches Deal to Raise Retirement Age." BBC News. https://www.bbc.co.uk/news/business-12305246.
Rathbun, Brian C., Kathleen E. Powers, and Therese Anders. 2018. "Moral Hazard: German Public Opinion on the Greek Debt Crisis." *Political Psychology*.
Rattinger, Hans et al. 2018. "Pre- and Post-Election Cross Section (Cumulation) (GLES 2013)." *GESIS Data Archive* ZA5702.
Redeker, Nils. 2019. "The Politics of Stashing Wealth – The Demise of Labor Power and the Global Rise of Corporate Savings." *CIS Working Paper* 101.
Redeker, Nils and Stefanie Walter. 2020. "We'd Rather Pay than Change. The Politics of German Non-Adjustment in the Eurozone Crisis." *Review of International Organizations*.
Regalia, Ida and Marino Regini. 2018. "Trade Unions and Employment Relations in Italy during the Economic Crisis." *South European Society and Politics* 23(1): 63–79. http://doi.org/10.1080/13608746.2018.1430608.
Regan, Aidan. 2012. "The Political Economy of Social Pacts in the EMU: Irish Liberal Market Corporatism in Crisis." *New Political Economy* 17(4): 465–91.
Regling, Klaus and Max Watson. 2010. "A Preliminary Report on the Sources of Ireland's Banking Crisis." Commission of Investigation into the Banking Sector in Ireland.
Reguly, Eric. 2019. "China's Piraeus Power Play: In Greece, a Port Project Offers Beijing Leverage over Europe." *The Globe and Mail*.
Reher, David Sven. 1998. "Family Ties in Western Europe: Persistent Contrasts." *Population and Development Review* 24(2): 203–34.
Reher, Stefanie. 2014. "The Effect of Congruence in Policy Priorities on Electoral Participation." *Electoral Studies* 36: 158–72.
Reinhart, Carmen and Kenneth Rogoff. 2010. *This Time Is Different: Eight Centuries of Financial Folly*. Princeton University Press.
Reinke, Raphael. 2014. "The Politics of Bank Bailouts." PhD thesis, European University Institute.
Reis, Ricardo. 2015. "Looking for a Success in the Euro Crisis Adjustment Programs: The Case of Portugal." *Brookings Papers on Economic Activity* 458: 433–58.
Reuters. 2010. "Greek Police, Rioters Clash." Reuters World News. https://www.reuters.com/article/us-greece-protest/greek-police-rioters-clash-idUSTRE65S4BO20100629.
Riain, Seán Ó. 2014. *The Rise and Fall of Ireland's Celtic Tiger: Liberalism, Boom and Bust*. Cambridge University Press.
Rixen, Thomas. 2015. "Hehre Ziele, Wenig Zählbares." In *Politik Im Schatten Der Krise: Eine Bilanz Der Regierung Merkel 2009–2013*, pp. 327–51, ed. Reimut Zohlnhöfer and Thomas Saalfeld. Springer Fachmedien Wiesbaden.
Rixen, Thomas. 2019. "Die Verwaltung Des Überschusses." In *Zwischen Stillstand, Politikwandel Und Krisenmanagement: Eine Bilanz Der Regierung Merkel 2013–2017*, pp. 345–72, ed. Reimut Zohlnhöfer and Thomas Saalfeld. Springer Fachmedien Wiesbaden.
Rocholl, Jorg and Axel Stahmer. 2016. "Where Did the Greek Bailout Money Go ?" *ESMT White Paper* (June): 24.
Rodrik, Dani. 1996. "Understanding Economic Policy Reform." *Journal of Economic Literature* 34(1): 9–41.
Rogowski, Ronald. 1989. *Commerce and Coalitions: How Trade Affects Domestic Political Alignments*. Princeton University Press.

Rose, Andrew Keenan. 2007. "Checking out: Exits from Currency Unions." *Journal of Financial Transformation* 19: 121-8.

Roth, Felix, Lars Jonung, and D. Nowak-Lehmann. 2016. "Crisis and Public Support for the Euro, 1990-2014." *JCMS: Journal of Common Market Studies* 54(4): 944-60.

Roubini, Nouriel and Jeffrey D. Sachs. 1989. "Political and Economic Determinants of Budget Deficits in the Industrial Democracies." *European Economic Review* 33(5): 903-33.

Royo, Sebastián. 2013. *Lessons from the Economic Crisis in Spain*. Palgrave Macmillan.

Royo, Sebastián and Federico Steinberg. 2019. "Using a Sectoral Bailout to Make Wide Reforms: The Case of Spain." In *The Political Economy of Adjustment throughout and beyond the Eurozone Crisis*, pp. 157-80, ed. Michele Chang, Federico Steinberg, and Francisco Torres. Routledge.

Rüdig, Wolfgang and Georgios Karyotis. 2014. "Who Protests in Greece? Mass Opposition to Austerity." *British Journal of Political Science* 44(3): 487-513.

Rueda, David. 2006. "Social Democracy and Active Labour-Market Policies: Insiders, Outsiders and the Politics of Employment." *British Journal of Political Science* 36(3): 385-406.

Rueda, David. 2014. "Dualization, Crisis and the Welfare State." *Socio-Economic Review* 12 (2): 381-407.

Rueda, David, Erik Wibbels, and Melina Altamirano. 2015. "The Origins of Dualism." In *The Politics of Advanced Capitalism*, pp. 89-111, ed. Pablo Beramendi, Silja Häusermann, Herbert Kitchelt, and Hanspeter Kriesi. Cambridge University Press.

Ryner, Magnus. 2015. "Europe's Ordoliberal Iron Cage: Critical Political Economy, the Euro Area Crisis and Its Management." *Journal of European Public Policy* 22(2): 275-94.

Sacchi, Stefano. 2015. "Conditionality by Other Means: EU Involvement in Italy's Structural Reforms in the Sovereign Debt Crisis." *Comparative European Politics* 13(1): 77-92.

Sadeh, Tal. 2018. "How Did the Euro Area Survive the Crisis?" *West European Politics*: 1-27. https://doi.org/10.1080/01402382.2018.1466478.

Sampedro, Víctor and Josep Lobera. 2014. "The Spanish 15-M Movement: A Consensual Dissent?" *Journal of Spanish Cultural Studies* 15: 61-80.

Sandbu, Martin. 2015. *Europe's Orphan: The Future of the Euro and the Politics of Debt*. Princeton University Press.

Sandbu, Martin. 2017. *Europe's Orphan: The Future of the Euro and the Politics of Debt*. Princeton University Press.

Sanz de Miguel, Pablo. 2011. "Government Approves Law Proposing Urgent Labour Market Reform." Eurofound. https://www.eurofound.europa.eu/publications/article/2010/government-approves-law-proposing-urgent-labour-market-reform.

Sapir, André, Guntram B. Wolff, Carlos de Sousa, and Alessio Terzi. 2014. The Troika and *Financial Assistance in the Euro Area: Successes and Failures*: Study on the Request of the European Parliament's Economic and Monetary Affairs Committee. European Parliament.

Sattler, Thomas and Jörg Haas. 2018. "The Societal Sources of International Economic Imbalances: Individual Attitudes, Public Discourse and the Current Account in Australia and Germany."

Sattler, Thomas and Stefanie Walter. 2009. "Globalization and Government Short-Term Room to Maneuver in Economic Policy: An Empirical Analysis of Reactions to Currency Crises." *World Political Science Review* 5(1): 464-90. http://www.degruyter.com/view/j/wpsr.2009.5.1/wpsr.2009.5.1.1073/wpsr.2009.5.1.1073.xml.

Sattler, Thomas, and Stefanie Walter. 2010. "Monetary Credibility vs. Voter Approval: Political Institutions and Exchange-Rate Stabilization during Crises." *Economics and Politics* 22(3): 392–418.

Schäfer, David. 2016. "A Banking Union of Ideas? The Impact of Ordoliberalism and the Vicious Circle on the EU Banking Union." *Journal of Common Market Studies* 54(4): 961–80.

Scharpf, Fritz. 2013. "Monetary Union, Fiscal Crisis and the Disabling of Democratic Accountability." In *Politics in the Age of Austerity*, pp. 108–42, ed. Armin Schäfer and Wolfgang Streeck. Polity Press.

Schelkle, Waltraud. 2013. "Fiscal Integration by Default." In Beyond the Regulatory Polity? The European Integration of Core State Powers, pp. 1–28, ed. Philipp Genschel and Markus Jachtenfuchs. Oxford University Press.

Schelkle, Waltraud. 2017. *The Political Economy of Monetary Solidarity: Understanding the Euro Experiment*. Oxford University Press.

Schimmelfennig, Frank. 2014. "European Integration in the Euro Crisis: The Limits of Postfunctionalism." *Journal of European Integration*: https://doi.org/10.1080/07036337.2014.886399.

Schimmelfennig, Frank. 2015. "Liberal Intergovernmentalism and the Euro Area Crisis." *Journal of European Public Policy* 22(2): 177–95.

Schimmelfennig, Frank. 2018. "European Integration (Theory) in Times of Crisis: A Comparison of the Euro and Schengen Crises." *Journal of European Public Policy* 25 (7): 969–89.

Schirm, Stefan A. 2018. "Societal Foundations of Governmental Preference Formation inthe Eurozone Crisis." *European Politics and Society* 19(1): 63–78.

Schmitter, P. C. and Wolfgang Streeck. 1991. "Organized Interests and the Europe of 1992." In *The European Union*, ed. B. F. Nelson and A. C. G. Stubb. Palgrave.

Schneider, Christina. 2018. *The Responsive Union: National Elections and European Governance*. Cambridge University Press.

Schneider, Christina and Branislav Slantchev. 2018. "The Domestic Politics of International Cooperation: Germany and the European Debt Crisis." *International Organization* 72 (1): 1–31.

Schneider, Christoph. 2013. "WKÖ Austria – Business Perspective and Policy Recommendations." https://www.eib.org/attachments/general/events/20170320_presentation_christoph_schneider.pdf.

Schwander, Hanna and Silja Hausermann. 2013. "Who Is in and Who Is out? A Risk-Based Conceptualization of Insiders and Outsiders." *Journal of European Social Policy* 23(3): 248–69.

Seabrooke, Leonard and Duncan Wigan. 2017. "The Governance of Global Wealth Chains." *Review of International Political Economy* 24(1): 1–29.

Simmons, Beth. 1994. *Who Adjusts? Domestic Sources of Foreign Economic Policy During the Interwar Years*. Princeton University Press.

Simpson, Kathryn. 2019. "European Union Crises and Irish Public Opinion: Continuity and Change in Patterns of Support." *Irish Political Studies* 34(4): 507–29.

Singer, Matthew and Francois Gélineau. 2012. "Heterogeneous Economic Voting: Evidence from Latin America 1995–2005." Paper presented at MPSA Annual Conference 2012, Chicago.

Skreta, Vasiliki. 2017. "Privatizations: Auction and Market Design during Crisis." In *Beyond Austerity: Reforming the Greek Economy*, pp. 179–210, ed. Costas Meghir, Christopher A. Pissarides, Dimitri Vayanos, and Nikolaos Vettas. MIT Press.

Smith, Helena. 2015. "Greece Crisis: Yanis Varoufakis Admits 'contingency Plan' for Euro Exit." *Guardian Online.* https://www.theguardian.com/business/2015/jul/27/greece-crisis-yanis-varoufakis-admits-contingency-plan-for-euro-exit.
Social Justice Ireland. 2009a. "Majority Want Fair Budget – Would Increase Tax Rather than Cut Welfare or Services: Budget 2010." *SJI Budget Reports.*
Social Justice Ireland. 2009b. "Unfair, Unjust Budget Fails the Vulnerable, Damages the Economy: 2010 Budget." *SJI Budget Reports.*
Social Justice Ireland. 2010. "Unjust Choices Rob the Poor, Protect Gamblers, Damage the Economy Budget 2011." *SJI Budget Reports.*
Social Justice Ireland. 2011. "Social Justice Ireland Meets with Oireachtas Committee on Finance." *SJI Budget Reports.*
Soroka, Stuart. 2006. "Good News and Bad News: Asymmetric Responses to Economic Information." *Journal of Politics* 68(2): 372–85.
Stallings, Barbara. 1992. "International Influence on Economic Policy: Debt, Stabilization and Structural Reform." In *The Politics of Economic Adjustment*, pp. 41–88, ed. Stephan Haggard and Robert R. Kaufman. . Princeton University Press.
Statistics Netherlands (CBS) (2018). "Supply- and use, input-output and sector accounts", Den Haag. https://www.cbs.nl/en-gb/custom/2019/29/supply-and-use-input-output-and-sector-accounts.
Statistik Austria (2018). "INPUT-OUTPUT-TABELLEinklusive Aufkommens- und Verwendungstabelle," Vienna. http://www.zbw.eu/econis-archiv/handle/11159/883.
Statistisches Bundesamt (2018). "Input-Output-Tabelle (Revision 2014) – Inländische Produktion (Herstellungspreise): Deutschland," Berlin. https://www-genesis.destatis.de/genesis/online?operation=abruftabelleBearbeiten&levelindex=1&levelid=1586169401858&auswahloperation=abruftabelleAuspraegungAuswaehlen&auswahlverzeichnis=ordnungsstruktur&auswahlziel=werteabruf&code=81511-0003&auswahltext=&werteabruf=starten#astructure.
Steenbergen, Marco, Erica Edwards, and Catherine de Vries. 2007. "Who's Cueing Whom?: Mass-Elite Linkages and the Future of European Integration." *European Union Politics* 8 (1): 13–35. https://doi.org/10.1177/1465116507073284.
Stein, Ernesto and Jorge Streb. 2004. "Elections and the Timing of Devaluations." *Journal of International Economics* 63(1): 119–45.
Steinberg, David. 2015. *Demanding Devaluation: Exchange Rate Politics in the Developing World.* Cornell University Press.
Steinberg, David. 2017. "Interest Group Pressures and Currency Crises: Argentina in Comparative Perspective." *Comparative Politics* 50(1): 61–82.
Steinberg, David and Stefanie Walter. 2013. "The Political Economy of Exchange Rates." In *Handbook of Safeguarding Global Financial Stability: Political, Social, Cultural, and Economic Theories and Models*, pp. 27–36, ed. Gerard Caprio. Elsevier.
Steinberg, Federico and Mattias Vermeiren. 2015. "Germany's Institutional Power and the EMU Regime after the Crisis: Towards a Germanized Euro Area?" *JCMS: Journal of Common Market Studies* 54(2): 388–407.
Steinbrecher, Markus. 2014. "Wirtschaftliche Entwicklung und Eurokrise." In *Zwischen Fragmentierung und Konzentration: Die Bundestagswahl 2013*, pp. 225–38, ed. Rüdiger Schmitt-Beck et al. Nomos Verlagsgesellschaft mbH & Co. KG.
Stigler, George J. 1971. "The Theory of Economic Regulation." *The Bell Journal of Economics and Management Science* 2(1): 3–21.
Stiglitz, Joseph. 2015. "Joseph Stiglitz: How I Would Vote in the Greek Referendum." *Guardian Online.* https://www.theguardian.com/business/2015/jun/29/joseph-stiglitz-how-i-would-vote-in-the-greek-referendum.

Stimson, James A., Michael B. MacKuen, and Robert S. Erikson. 1995. "Dynamic Representation." *American Political Science Review* 89(3): 543-65.
Stockhammer, Engelbert. 2016. "Neoliberal Growth Models, Monetary Union and the Euro Crisis: A Post-Keynesian Perspective." *New Political Economy* 21(4): 365-79.
Stoeckel, Florian and Theresa Kuhn. 2018. "Mobilizing Citizens for Costly Policies: The Conditional Effect of Party Cues on Support for International Bailouts in the European Union." *JCMS: Journal of Common Market Studies* 56(2): 446-61.
Stone, Randall. 2008. "The Scope of IMF Conditionality." *International Organization* 62: 589-620.
Streeck, Wolfgang. 2015. "Why the Euro Divides Europe." *New Left Review* 26(95): 5-26.
Streeck, Wolfgang and Lea Elsässer. 2016. "Monetary Disunion: The Domestic Politics of Euroland." *Journal of European Public Policy* 23(1): 1-24.
Streeck, Wolfgang and Armin Schäfer. 2013. *Politics in the Age of Austerity*. John Wiley & Sons.
Streeck, Wolfgang and Kathleen Thelen. 2005. *Beyond Continuity: Institutional Change in Advanced Political Economies*. Oxford University Press.
Sturzenegger, Federico and Mariano Tommasi. 1998. *The Political Economy of Reform*. MIT Press.
Suiter, Jane and David M. Farrell. 2011. "The Parties' Manifestos." In *How Ireland Voted 2011: The Full Story of Ireland's Earthquake Election*, pp. 29-46, ed. Michael Gallagher and Michael Marsh. Palgrave Macmillan.
Sweeney, Paul. 2008. *Ireland's Economic Success: Reasons and Lessons*. Dublin, IE: New Island.
Tarlea, Silvana et al. 2019. "Explaining Governmental Preferences on Economic and Monetary Union Reform." https://www.researchgate.net/publication/330253208_Explaining_governmental_preferences_on_Economic_and_Monetary_Union_Reform.
The Irish Times. 2012. "ICTU to Stage National Debt Protests." https://www.irishtimes.com/news/ictu-to-stage-national-debt-protests-1.754219.
Thompson, Helen. 2015. "Germany and the Euro-Zone Crisis: The European Reformation of the German Banking Crisis and the Future of the Euro." *New Political Economy* 20(6): 851-70. https://doi.org/10.1080/13563467.2015.1041476.
Thompson, Helen. 2016. "Enduring Capital Flow Constraints and the 2007-2008 Financial and Euro Zone Crises." *The British Journal of Politics and International Relations* 18(1): 216-33.
Tinios, Platon. 2015. "'Off-the-Shelf Reforms' and Their Blind Spots: Pensions in Post-Memorandum Greece." In *The Politics of Extreme Austerity: Greece in the Eurozone Crisis*, pp. 91-105, ed. Georgios Karyotis and Roman Gerodimos. Palgrave Macmillan,.
Trichet, Jean-Claude. 2010a. *Letter of the ECB President to the Irish Minister for Finance on the Large Provision of Liquidity by the Eurosystem and the Central Bank of Ireland to Irish Banks (15.10.2010)*. Frankfurt am Main, DE.
Trichet, Jean-Claude. 2010b. *Letter of the ECB President to the Irish Minister for Finance on the Large Provision of Liquidity by the Eurosystem and the Central Bank of Ireland to Irish Banks and the Need for Ireland to Agree to an Adjustment Programme (19.11.2010)*. Frankfurt am Main, DE.
Tsatsanis, Emmanouil and Eftichia Teperoglou. 2016. "Realignment under Stress: The July 2015 Referendum and the September Parliamentary Election in Greece." *South European Society and Politics* 21(4): 427-50.
Tsebelis, George. 2016. "Lessons from the Greek Crisis." *Journal of European Public Policy* 23(1): 25-41.

Usherwood, Simon and Nick Startin. 2013. "Euroscepticism as a Persistent Phenomenon." *JCMS: Journal of Common Market Studies* 51(1): 1–16.

Van der Meer, Tom, Henk Van der Kolk, and Roderik Rekker. 2017. *Aanhoudend Wisselvallig: Nationaal Kiezersonderzoek 2017*. SKON.

Vasilopoulou, Sofia. 2018. "The Party Politics of Euroscepticism in Times of Crisis: The Case of Greece." *Politics* 38(3): 311–26.

Vasilopoulou, Sofia and Daphne Halikiopoulou. 2013. "In the Shadow of Grexit: The Greek Election of 17 June 2012." *South European Society and Politics* 18(4): 523–42.

Vasilopoulou, Sofia, Daphne Halikiopoulou, and Theofanis Exadaktylos. 2014. "Greece in Crisis: Austerity, Populism and the Politics of Blame." *JCMS: Journal of Common Market Studies* 52(2): 388–402. http://dx.doi.org/10.1111/jcms.12093.

Viehoff, Juri. 2018. "Eurozone Justice." *Journal of Political Philosophy* 26(3): 388–414.

VNO-NCW. 2014. "Europese Prioriteiten van VNO-NCW En MKB-Nederland."

VNO-NCW. 2016. "POSITIONPAPER VNO-NCW / MKB-NEDERLAND Ten Behoeve van Het Rondetafelgesprek in de Tweede Kamer over de Loonontwikkeling En Arbeidsinkomensquote." *Notitie ten behoeve van het rondetafelgesprek met de commissie SZW.*

Vogiatzoglou, Markos. 2017. "Cyprus' Explosion: Financial Crisis and Anti-Austerity Mobilization." In *Late Neoliberalism and Its Discontents in the Economic Crisis*, pp. 243–59. Springer.

Vreeland, James Raymond. 1999. "The IMF: Lender of Last Resort or Scapegoat?" https://www.researchgate.net/publication/2637479_The_IMF_Lender_of_Last_Resort_or_Scapegoat.De Vries, Catherine. 2018. *Euroscepticism and the Future of European Integration*. Oxford University Press.

Wagstyl, Stefan. 2015. "Schäuble Eyes an Opportunity in Greece's Crisis." *Financial Times* July 5. https://www.ft.com/content/d69ceb4c-22ff-11e5-bd83-71cb60e8f08c.

Wall Street Journal. 2013. "IMF Document Excerpts: Disagreements Revealed." https://blogs.wsj.com/economics/2013/10/07/imf-document-excerpts-disagreements-revealed/.

Walter, Stefanie. 2008. "A New Approach for Determining Exchange-Rate Level Preferences." *International Organization* 62(3): 405–38.

Walter, Stefanie. 2009. "The Limits and Rewards of Political Opportunism: How Electoral Timing Affects the Outcome of Currency Crises." *European Journal of Political Research* 48(3): 367–96.

Walter, Stefanie. 2013a. *Financial Crises and the Politics of Macroeconomic Adjustments*. Cambridge University Press.

Walter, Stefanie. 2013b. "Verteilungskonflikte in Der Eurokrise Und Die Politische Handlungsfähigkeit von Demokratien." In *Die Versprechen Der Demokratie*, pp. 77–88, ed. Hubertus Buchstein. Nomos.

Walter, Stefanie. 2016. "Crisis Politics in Europe: Why Austerity Is Easier to Implement in Some Countries than in Others." *Comparative Political Studies* 49(7): 841–73.

Walter, Stefanie, Elias Dinas, Ignacio Jurado, and Nikitas Konstantinidis. 2018. "Noncooperation by Popular Vote: Expectations, Foreign Intervention, and the Vote in the 2015 Greek Bailout Referendum." *International Organization* 72(4): 969–94.

Walter, Stefanie and Thomas Willett. 2012. "Delaying the Inevitable: A Political Economy Model of Currency Defenses and Capitulation." *Review of International Political Economy* 19(1): 114–39.

Wasserfallen, Fabio and Thomas Lehner. 2018. "Political Conflict in the Reform of the Eurozone." https://emuchoices.eu/2018/12/12/thomas-lehner-and-fabio-wasserfallen-2018-political-conflict-in-the-reform-of-the-eurozone-emu-choices-working-paper/.

Wasserfallen, Fabio, Dirk Leuffen, Zdenek Kudrna, and Hanno Degner. 2019. "Analysing European Union Decision-Making during the Eurozone Crisis with New Data." *European Union Politics* 20(1): 3–23.

Watts, Martin, Timothy Sharpe, and James Juniper. 2014. "Reformation or Exodus: Assessing the Future of the Euro." *The Economic and Labour Relations Review* 25(3): 465–83.

Webb, Michael C. 1991. "International Economic Structures, Government Interests, and International Coordination of Macroeconomic Adjustment Policies." *International Organization* 45(3): 309–42.

Wendler, Frank. 2014. "End of Consensus? The European Leadership Discourse of the Second Merkel Government during the Eurozone Crisis and Its Contestation in Debates of the Bundestag (2009–13)." *German Politics* 23(4): 446–59.

Whelan, C. T. and B. Maitre. 2014. "The Great Recession and the Changing Distribution of Economic Vulnerability by Social Class: The Irish Case." *Journal of European Social Policy* 24(5): 470–85.

Whelan, Karl. 2014. "Ireland's Economic Crisis: The Good, the Bad and the Ugly." *Journal of Macroeconomics* 39: 424–40. file:///Users/ray/Downloads/1-s2.0-S0164070413001304-main.pdf.

Wihlborg, Clas, Thomas Willett, and Nan Zhang. 2010. "The Euro Debt Crisis: It Isn't Just Fiscal." *World Economics* 11(4): 51–77.

Willett, Thomas D. 1998. "The Credibility and Discipline Effects of Exchange Rates as Nominal Anchors: The Need to Distinguish Temporary from Permanent Pegs." *The World Economy* 21(6): 803–26.

Willett, Thomas D. 2007. "Why the Middle Is Unstable: The Political Economy of Exchange Rate Regimes and Currency Crises." *The World Economy* 30(5): 709–32.

Willett, Thomas D. and Eric M. P. Chiu. 2012. "Power Relationships and the Political Economy of Global Imbalances." *Global Economic Review* 41(4): 341–60.

Willett, Thomas D., Ekniti Nitithanprapas, Isriya Nitithanprapas, and Sunil Rongala. 2005. "The Asian Crises Reexamined." *Asian Economic Papers* 3(3): 32–87.

Willis, Andrew. 2010. "Zapatero Defends the Euro Zone." Bloomberg.com.

Winnett, Robert and Bruno Waterfield. 2010. "British Banks Have £140 Billion Exposure to Ireland's Economic Crisis." *The Telegraph*. https://www.telegraph.co.uk/news/worldnews/europe/ireland/8141618/British-banks-have-140-billion-exposure-to-Irelands-economic-crisis.html.

Wlezien, Christopher and Stuart N. Soroka. 2012. "Political Institutions and the Opinion-Policy Link." *West European Politics* 35(6): 1407–32.

Wölfl, Anita and Juan S Mora-sanguinetti. 2011. "Reforming the Labour Market in Spain." *OECD Economics Department Working Papers No. 845, OECD Publishing* (845): 1–33.

Woll, Cornelia. 2007. "Leading the Dance? Power and Political Resources of Business Lobbyists." *Journal of Public Policy* 27(1): 57–78. https://www.cambridge.org/core/article/leading-the-dance-power-and-political-resources-of-business-lobbyists/598E8D8D542D80550DD02550E1C263B0.

Wonka, Arndt. 2016. "The Party Politics of the Euro Crisis in the German Bundestag: Frames, Positions and Salience." *West European Politics* 39(1): 125–44.

Woodruff, David M. 2005. "Boom, Gloom, Doom: Balance Sheets, Monetary Fragmentation, and the Politics of Financial Crisis in Argentina and Russia." *Politics & Society* 33(1): 3–45.

Woodruff, David M. 2016. "Governing by Panic: The Politics of the Eurozone Crisis." *Politics & Society* 44(1): 81–116.

World Bank. 2016a. "GDP (Constant LCU)."
World Bank. 2016b. "Unemployment, Total (% of Total Labor Force)."
Yan, Ho-don. 2007. "Does Capital Mobility Finance or Cause a Current Account Imbalance?" *The Quarterly Review of Economics and Finance* 47: 1–25.
Young, Brigitte. 2014. "German Ordoliberalism as Agenda Setter for the Euro Crisis: Myth Trumps Reality." *Journal of Contemporary European Studies* 22(3): 276–87.
Zapatero, José Luis Rodríguez. 2013. *El Dilema: 600 Dís de Vertigo*. Planeta.
Zettelmeyer, Jeromin. 2018. "Managing Deep Debt Crises in the Euro Area: Towards a Feasible Regime." *Global Policy* 9: 70–9.
Zettelmeyer, Jeromin, Christoph Trebesch, and Mitu Gulati. 2013. "The Greek Debt Restructuring: An Autopsy." *Economic Policy* 28(75): 513–63.
Zettelmeyer, Jeromin, Christoph Trebesch, Mitu Gulati, et al. 2013. "The Greek Restructuring: An Autopsy." *Economic Policy* 28(75): 515–65.
Zimmermann, Hubert. 2014. "A Grand Coalition for the Euro: The Second Merkel Cabinet, the Euro Crisis and the Elections of 2013." *German Politics* 23(4): 322–36.
Zohlnhöfer, Reimut and Thomas Saalfeld. 2017. *Zwischen Stillstand, Politikwandel Und Krisenmanagement - Eine Bilanz Der Re*. Springer.

Index

For the benefit of digital users, indexed terms that span two pages (e.g., 52–53) may, on occasion, appear on only one of those pages.

Adjustment
  cost 14–16, 66
  external, see *external adjustment*
  internal, see *internal adjustment*
  strategies 4, 17–18, 153 see also *Crisis resolution strategies*
  burden sharing 17–18, 252–5
Alternative for Germany (AfD) 225
Argentina 42–3, 62
Argument 22–7, 36–43, 71–2, 74–6, 250
Asian Financial Crisis 22, 35, 55–7, 154, 160
Austerity 19–20
  consequences 11–12, 15, 66
  in the Eurozone 14, 33, 66, 69–70
  see also *internal adjustment*
Austria 152–3, 167
  external adjustment politics 223–4
  financing politics 225–9
  internal adjustment politics 234–7
Austrian People's Party (ÖVP) 235–7

Bailouts 8–10, 153
  Sovereign 50–9, 88–90, see also *financing*
    Ireland 113–14, 120–2
    Spain 124, 130–2
    Greece 133–4, 143–7
  Banking sector
    Ireland 112–13
    Spain 123
    Greece 145–6
Balance of payments 1–2, 5
  adjustment 12–13, 17–22, 36–7
  crisis 34–5
  history 151–2
  rebalancing 1–2, 17–20
Banking union 10, 21
Banks
  In deficit-debtor countries 16, 112–13, 123–4, 130–1, 145–6
  in creditor-surplus countries 8–10, 152–3
Bargaining power 12–13, 13 n.11
Burden sharing 2–3, 12–18, 254–5

Choice set 17–22, 251
Christian Democratic Union (CDU) 231–3
Comparative Capitalism 154–5
Competitiveness 37–8, 154–5, 161
Conditionality 20, 37, 44–5, 53, 69, 75–6, 88, 95, 153, 227–8, 254
Coordinated market economies 174
Creditor country 2, 18 n.13
  banks 8–9
Crisis
  comparative analyses 33–65, 150–71, 246
  episodes 43–5, 62
  negotiations 10–11, 31
  politics 12–13, 25–6, 29–31
  resolution costs 12–17, 45–50
  resolution strategies 17–22, 74–6
Currency union 158–9
  break-up scenarios 81–3
Current account
  adjustment 1–2, 36–7, 72
  deficit 1–2, 36–7, 67, 74, 90
  imbalance 4–5, 36–7, 75–6
  rebalancing 1–2, 12–13, 37
  surplus 2

Debtor country 1–2, 18 n.13
Debt
  accumulation 5–6
  crisis 151
  costs 150–1, 159, 163
  default see *sovereign debt default*
  external 38–9, 45–6
  haircut 8–9
  relation to balance of payments 1–2, 18 n.13, 36–43
  relief 13, 62
Deficit country 5, 18 n.13
  bargaining positions 254–7
  distributive effects 14–16
  external adjustment 18–21, 38–9, 45–7, 49, 71–2, 81–3
  interest groups 25–6, 29, 66–7, 69–70, 248
  preferences external adjustment 80–3

Deficit country (*cont.*)
    preferences financing 80–1, 88–90
    preferences internal adjustment 80–1, 83–8
    relative adjustment preferences 96–102
    internal adjustment 17–18, 21, 39–41, 46, 48–50, 72–4, 83–8
    international pressure 69
    politics 11–12, 16, 26, 30
    preferences 10–11, 23–5
    vulnerabilities 27, 45–50
Deleveraging 8–9
Demand elasticity 192
Denmark 54, 170
Deregulation 73, 84–8
Dijsselbloem, Jerome 227–8
Distributive conflicts 3–4, 12–13, 22–7
    Domestic level 22, 62, 66, 155
    European-level 10–11, 251–7
Distributive consequences 12–17
    Domestic level 16–17
    European-level 13–16

Emergency Liquidity Assistance (ELA) 13, 113–14, 120–1, 178
EMU > see *European Monetary Union*
Estonia 34–5, 42, 57–8
EU Council negotiations 251–7
Euro
    Support for 11–12
Euro crisis > see *Eurozone crisis*
Eurobonds 11–12, 228
European Central Bank (ECB) 11, 69
    see also *Emergency Liquidity Assistance, Outright Monetary Transactions* and *Securities Market Programme*
European Commission 69, 254–6
European Financial Stability Facility (EFSF) 10
European integration 11
European Parliament 254–6
European politics 10–11, 31, 251–7
European Monetary System (EMS) 151–2
    Crisis 53–5, 153, 170–1
European Monetary Union (EMU)
    Dissolution 11–12, 14–16, 20–1, 34–5
    Future of 12
    Institutions 6
    Problems 5–7, 11
    Reform 31, 251–7
European Stability Mechanism (ESM) 10
Euroskepticism 11–12, 214–15
Eurozone crisis 4–12
    Causes 5–7
    Compared to other crises 33–65, 150–71, 246–7
    Consequences 11–12, 14–16

Narratives 9–10, 24–5
Politics 13, 20–1, 152–3, 168, 251–7
Strategies 17–22, see *adjustment strategies*
Trajectory 7–11
Exchange rate 158–9
    Market pressure 43–5, 161
    Pass-through 158
    Regime 46–7, 158–9, 163
    Stability 72
External adjustment 17–19
    in the Eurozone 20–1
    in deficit countries see *Deficit country external adjustment*
    in surplus countries see *Surplus country external adjustment*
Export
    Industry 154–5, 172–3
    Dependence see *Trade dependence*

Faymann, Werner 228
Fianna Fail 109–10, 112–13, 117–22
Financial markets 7, 11
Financial regulation 6
Financing 20, 153, 156–7, 255–6
    In the Eurozone 21
    In deficit countries 75–6, 80–1, 88–90
    In surplus countries see *Surplus country financing*
    Policy proposals 89, 252–3
Fine Gael 109–10, 119–22
Finland 54–5, 168–9
Fiscal compact 10
Fiscal policy
    coordination 6
    reform 15
Fiscal stimulus 159 see also *Surplus country - internal adjustment*
Foreign assets 151, 158, 162
Freedom Party of Austria (FPÖ) 225, 227–8

Germany 53, 151, 167, 170–1
    External adjustment politics 223–4
    Financing politics 225–9
    Internal adjustment politics 229–34
Global Financial Crisis of 2008/2009 57–9, 168
Greece 8–9, 11, 33, 51–4, 56, 58–62, 152–3
    Country vulnerability profile
    Adjustment politics and policies
        Financing 133–4, 143–7
        Internal adjustment 133–5, 137–43
        External adjustment 135–7, 145
Grexit 98, 133, 135–7, 146, 187, 210–11, 224–5
Growth Models 154–5, 172–3

INDEX

Ideas 24–5, 154, 220, 249
Inflation 153–4, 163
Interest groups 25–6, 39–40, 164
  in deficit countries, see *Deficit country interest groups*
  in surplus countries, see *Surplus country interest groups*
  surveys 77–9, 181
  vulnerability profiles 28–9, 90–6, 175–9
Internal adjustment 19–20
  In the Eurozone 21
  In deficit countries, see *Deficit country internal adjustment*
  In surplus countries, see *Surplus Country Internal Adjustment*
International Monetary Fund 37, 69, 96–7, 153, 252–3
Ireland 33, 52, 54, 59–61
  External adjustment politics 114–15
  Financing politics 113–14, 120–2
  Internal adjustment politics 112, 115–20
Italy 35, 42, 51–4, 56, 58, 60, 62

Japan 151–2, 154–5

Latin American Debt Crisis 22

Merkel, Angela 34–5, 150, 226–8
Minimum wage 187–8, 212–13, 233–4
Misery corner 24–5, 200
  In deficit states 50–62, 74–7, 89, 91–3, 100, 103
  In surplus countries 157, 168
Moral hazard 227–8

Negotiations
  Bargaining power 12–13, 13 n.11
  On EMU reform 31, 251–7
  Negotiation positions 254–7
Netherlands 150–1, 167, 170
  External adjustment politics 223–4
  Financing politics 225–9
  Internal adjustment politics 237–40
New Democracy (ND) 109–10, 133, 140–2
No bailout commitment 5–6
Norway 169

Ordoliberalism 69, 154, 172–3, 232–3
Organized interests 257–8
Outright Monetary Transactions (OMT) 11, 88–90

Panhellenic Socialist Movement (PASOK) 109–10, 133–4, 137–44
Party for Freedom (PVV) 225

People's Party of Spain (PP) 109–10, 124–6, 128–31
Policy Options 17–22, 247–50
Policy salience see *Salience*
Portugal 33, 42, 51–4, 56, 58–62
Price Stability
  see *Inflation*
Principal Component Analysis 45–50, 164–7
Private Sector Involvement (PSI) 133–4, 144–6
Privatization 73, 84–8, 111–12, 115–16, 124, 128–9, 142–3
Public Investment
  in deficit countries 72–3, 84–6
  in surplus countries 153, 189, 212–13, 232
Public Opinion, see *Surplus country voters*
Puzzle 1–3, 22–3, 245

Rajoy, Mariano 69–70, 109–10, 126, 131
Research Questions 3, 245
Rutte, Mark 226

Savings 154, 158, 163–4
Salience 219–20, 223–4, 230–1, 234–5, 238–9
  Interest group policy salience 195–7
Schäuble, Wolfgang 135, 224–5
Schwarze Null 167
Securities Market Programme (SMP) 144
Social Democratic Party of Germany (SPD) 227–8
Socialist Worker's Party of Spain (PSOE) 109–10, 124, 126–31
Sovereign debt 16
  default 7, 17, 72, 75, 88–90, 95, 105–6, 152–3
  Exposure 8–9
  restructuring 34–5, 43
Spain 33, 35, 42, 51–4, 56, 58–62
  External adjustment politics 125–6
  Financing politics 124, 130–2
  Internal adjustment politics 123–4, 126–30
Stability and Growth Pact 10
Statutory tax rates 14
Surplus country 5, 18 n.13, 151
  Banks 8–9, 190
  Bargaining positions 254–7
  Crisis experience 8–10, 150–1
  Case selection 179–80, 221–2
  Distributive effects 17
  External adjustment 18–21, 152–3, 158, 169–70, 223–5
  Financing 225–9
  Interest groups 25–6, 29, 174–5, 218–19, 249
    Preferences external adjustment 185–7
    Preferences financing 190
    Preferences internal adjustment 190
  Internal adjustment 17–18, 21, 153–5, 229–41

Surplus country (*cont.*)
  Policymakers 9–10
  Politics 26, 30–1
  Preferences 10–11, 23–5
  Voters 9–10, 218
    Preferences external adjustment 209–12
    Preferences internal adjustment 212–14
    Preferences financing 214–16
  Outside the Eurozone 151, 169–70
  Vulnerabilities 27–8
Sweden 54–5, 169
Switzerland 169
SYRIZA 109–10, 134, 136–7, 140–1, 146

TARGET balance 44, 152–3, 227
Trade-offs 13, 23–5, 32, 247–50
  in deficit countries 41–3, 74–6, 96–9
  in surplus countries 155–6, 161, 197–200
Trade openness 159, 164
Trade dependence 192

Troika 7–8, 167–8
Trump, Donald 151–2
Tsipras, Alexis 146, 224–5

United States 151–2

Varoufakis, Yanis 136–7
Vested interests 16, 25–6
Voters 25–6
Vulnerability
  to macroeconomic adjustment 22–3
Vulnerability profile 23–6
  National 27–8, 41–60, 153, 155–8, 165–6
    Measurement 45–50, 161–4
    Over time 59–61
  Interest groups 28–9, 90–6
  Policy specific 176–8, 200–4

Zapatero, José Luis Rodríguez 109–10, 125–6, 131